D1188204

THE AUTOBIOGRAPHY OF
William Plomer

William Plomer

THE AUTOBIOGRAPHY OF
William Plomer

With a Postscript by
SIMON NOWELL-SMITH

TAPLINGER PUBLISHING COMPANY
NEW YORK

FIRST PUBLISHED IN THE UNITED STATES IN 1976 BY
TAPLINGER PUBLISHING CO., INC., NEW YORK, NEW YORK
COPYRIGHT © 1975 THE EXECUTORS OF THE ESTATE OF WILLIAM
PLOMER
POSTSCRIPT COPYRIGHT © 1975 BY SIMON NOWELL-SMITH

Thanks are due to Mr J. C. Longhurst for permission to quote from
a letter contributed by him to the *Spectator* in 1957.

LIBRARY OF CONGRESS CATALOG CARD NUMBER 75-10548
ISBN 0-8008-0543-7

PRINTED IN GREAT BRITAIN

Contents

CONTENTS

Illustrations

Preface

In 1943 I produced an autobiographical book, *Double Lives*, and in 1958 a sequel to it, *At Home*. In the hope of making a better book I have left out parts of both, have altered and added to them, and have made them into one.

I have happened to look at many books of reminiscence which have never been printed. Why not? Because the writers wrongly took it for granted that what had seemed exciting or amusing or important to them would seem the same to other people. I have tried to avoid their mistake and not to write as if the world revolved round my navel.

I have not wanted to try and magnify myself, or justify myself, or make an exhibition of myself, or turn myself inside out. To have lived through nearly three-quarters of this century has not made for monotony, and I hope that is one thing I have avoided in trying to relate myself, without undue name-dropping, to my background and various environments, to a variety of other people, and to different aspects of the social, literary, and political life of my time.

W.P.

Note

When William Plomer died, on 21 September 1973, he had accomplished more than half his task. *Double Lives* he had cut, altered and rewritten so heavily as to make it almost another book. *At Home*, written so much later, required much less attention, and the three chapters he had completed are little altered except for some omissions. As his literary executor I decided, in consultation with his publishers, that the book should be published as he left it, with the first twenty-four chapters revised and the last fifteen as they appeared in *At Home*. Simon Nowell-Smith has kindly contributed a postscript describing the final years of his old friend's life.

RUPERT HART-DAVIS

1

Forebears

It has been common in recent years for people to speak of searching for their own identity. A glance at their own passports is not enough for them. They have found themselves transplanted or uprooted or unsettled, uncertain where they belong, or whether they belong or can attach themselves anywhere, or whether they are wanted or necessary, or can look forward with any hope or confidence at all. Some of them, by learning about their origins, might understand their strengths and weaknesses better, and so adapt themselves better to circumstances. A background of poverty, hardship, and insecurity might at least teach one what to try and avoid; a background of health, wealth, and happiness can, with education, give one a sense of obligation to one's progenitors and of responsibility to one's contemporaries.

I wish when young I had asked my older relations a great many more questions about the past. Too many fascinating facts perish with old people because nobody has bothered to write them down or, in these days, to record them. But I did from an early age feel curious about variations of character and behaviour. If this curiosity was mainly about persons I knew, it was no less strong about my own forebears.

Perhaps one reason for this was that both my parents, as I shall explain, were uprooted from the environment into which they had been born, and their lives became nomadic and often isolated. Like those nomadic Arabs who are given to commemorating their ancestors in song and story because they would otherwise feel rootless, they attached a perhaps undue significance to their origins. Innately class-conscious, they became set in their sense of their origins, using it unconsciously as a defence against the indifference of others and against their own rootlessness, insecurity, and deprivations. No doubt they influenced me, but I suppose I am now old enough to have discovered my own identity and to be free of any false or inflated pride in my heredity.

The name Plomer is obviously an occupational name, like Butcher or Baker. Originally le Plomer or le Plumer, it is said to have signified either a plumber, or worker in lead, or a *plumier*, or worker with feathers. Since there is no verb 'to plome', the spelling of the name seems corrupt. Pronounced to rhyme with Rumour, one can plume oneself on having a light touch rather than a leaden one.

One of my great-aunts married a Bruce, and in 1847 his father-in-law published a Plomer genealogy. 'The remote antiquity of the family of Plomer, or Plumer,' he wrote, 'precludes all accuracy of the development of its origin.' Isn't that true of every family on earth? He gave Burke as his authority for saying of the Plomers that 'traditionally they derive from a noble Saxon Knight, who lived in the time of King Alfred'. Ought that to make one feel happier? What was more, the Plomers

have long been seated in Hertfordshire, where they ranked with the most distinguished gentry of that county; so far back as the year 1361 Peter le Plomer, a person of considerable note, and great opulence, was M.P. for St Albans, and Robert Plomer was sheriff of the county in 1495.

I would rather know what Peter and Robert did in their spare time, or what they looked like, or what their friends said about them; but there they are, without glory or disgrace or the faintest savour of reality, mere names and dates.

In Radwell church, in Hertfordshire, can be seen the effigy, kneeling and wearing armour, of Sir William Plomer, who had been knighted by James I in 1616 and died in 1625. In the chancel is an alabaster monument to his wife Mary and their children. She has a ruff round her neck and a short, coif-like mantle over her head. Her left hand rests on an hour-glass, which stands upon a pedestal, and beside it lies an infant in swaddling clothes. This infant was the death of her: it was her eleventh child, and when she gave birth to it, in 1605, she was only thirty. Below her, in high relief, are carved the kneeling figures of six sons, the three elder ones in long cloaks; over a double prayer-desk they face their four kneeling sisters. On a tablet of black marble is poor Mary's epitaph, which has sometimes found its way into anthologies of such things:

> See Virtue's Jewel, Beauty's Flower,
> Cropt off in an untimely hour,
> Religion, Meekness, Faithful Love
> To Parents, Husband, God above:
> So that the stone itself doth weep
> To think of her which it doth keep;
> Weep thou, whoe'er this stone may see,
> Unless more hard than stone thou be.

Not a word, of course, about excessive child-bearing. Her husband married again and added four more children to his quiverful. His eldest son became sheriff of the county.

In the eighteenth century we come across a parson or two. One of them, John Plomer, was headmaster of Rugby from 1731, when the number of boys was low, until 1759, when it was lower still. Another John, whose son was sheriff of Northamptonshire, took the name and arms of Clarke in addition to his own, and sired the family of Clarke of Welton Place in that county. I am more closely concerned with William Plomer, born in 1725, the son of a country parson in Buckinghamshire, who went to London to make his fortune and made it, ending up as what would now be called a millionaire. I have heard that his career suggested or that he served as a model for Hogarth's Industrious Apprentice, but I don't know if this can be true. What I have never been told is how he made his money. His offspring seem to have taken its existence for granted. He became Lord Mayor of London and also president of the Honourable Artillery Company. His wife Susannah, presumably tired of the opulence of a City man's wife, went in her old age to live in a log cabin in Epping Forest. There exists a print of her, sitting before this leafy hermitage, which was humorously known as Lady Plomer's Palace. She looks as placid as a Chinese sage, seated on a bench before her door, while comfortable smoke rises from her chimney, where perhaps a kettle was ready to provide her with a nice cup of tea.

Her son William was a sheriff of London, a Whig, and for seven years in Napoleonic times a colonel of militia. Her grandson, another William, was a deputy lieutenant for Edinburgh, where he had settled after marrying in 1819 a Scottish lady, Catherine Wilhelmina Pagan. This interesting surname does not signify heathendom: it derives from *paganus*, a countryman. She came of an 'opulent' Glasgow mercantile family of, I have been told, Huguenot origin.

Of this marriage the third and youngest son was my grandfather. He was born in 1829 and christened Alfred, perhaps because of that mythical 'noble Saxon Knight' who was supposed to be a contemporary of King Alfred, or perhaps simply because Saxon names were coming into fashion.

I remember him well, and his deep voice, which I believe had an eighteenth-century tone and tempo. As a small child I thought him kindly but rather grand. Like very many youngest sons with no special ability he had been, as my father put it, shoved into the army. After active service in India he returned to England in 1860, married, and took his wife back with him to India, where his three eldest children were born. He continued his career in the Bombay Staff Corps until 1880, when he retired, after thirty-five years' service, on full pay, with the rank of colonel and a frizzy black beard like a Sikh's. It will do his memory no injustice to say that he was steady, not brilliant, and certainly not imaginative. Physically strong and of a naturally placid temper, it pleased him at times to play popular songs of the period on the flute. His politics were Conservative, his manners those of a gentleman, and his opinions and social standards rigidly those of his class, profession and time. It seems to me that the greatest distinction of his military career was not in pursuing, with Outram, the Persian army (goodness knows why) or in helping to capture Gwalior, but in having had his life saved during the Indian Mutiny by his Muslim butler, Osman. I have written a poem which tells how the photograph of this handsome, dark-skinned young man was very properly inserted among the palefaces in a Victorian album of our family photographs. I cannot forget that Osman made my existence possible.

Alfred Plomer had married the orphaned only child of Francis Bush, a doctor at Frome in Somerset. This reminds me of a character in one of Charlotte Yonge's novels, Lady Leonora Langdale, who questioned a young girl about her friends. Hearing who they were, Lady Leonora said, 'Physician's daughters; Oh!' Into that disparaging 'Oh!' is compressed the whole formidable weight of Victorian class-consciousness. Today it seems incomprehensible to look down upon doctors in general for social reasons, and I believe Dr Bush may have been a more valuable member of society than many a Lady Leonora.

His end was dramatic. One morning in September 1843 he was present in Frome at a meeting of the Board of Guardians, when, according to the *Bath Chronicle*, 'a discussion ensued respecting the dietary'. In fact there was a mean proposal to reduce the already too small rations of the paupers in the workhouse, and this put him into such a violent rage that 'while in the act of turning to address a person standing behind him, he staggered and fell a corpse at his feet'. Francis Bush's death was attributed to 'the visitation of GOD' and to 'an affection of the heart', not to an inflammable temper or a social conscience.

The obituary notice calls him candid, independent, and urbane, 'while in private life he was universally beloved, and by the poor looked up to as their general advocate'. As soon as they heard of his death all the shopkeepers in Frome put up their shutters.

He left behind him his wife, Laura Matilda, who died four years later, and their only surviving child, Helen Lucretia. Only twelve, she was adopted by a relation, Admiral Edgell, and is believed to have been too much allowed to have her own way.

The image of my grandmother reflected in the memories of her children was not a lovable one. Their attitude was not at all like that of an old Sussex woman who said of another woman whom she had not liked: 'But there, I'll give 'er 'er due, she 'ad 'er good faults as well as 'er bad ones.' I should like to give her her due, but have little means of doing it.

She first emerges in the family legend in a fit of uncontrolled and perhaps uncontrollable temper. Her father had dropped dead in a rage of philanthropy; I have never heard that any of his daughter's rages were philanthropic. Was this unstable tendency hereditary? If so, what were the physical and psychological reasons for it? My father, though a man with affectionate impulses, had the same characteristic. I remember him saying complacently, after some violent scene he had made about some trivial matter, 'Of course I'm quick-tempered, like my mother.' He spoke as if drawing attention to an interesting trait.

'What you mean,' said my own long-suffering and quiet-voiced mother, 'is that you have no self-control; you get into violent rages about nothing, and other people have to endure it, God knows why.'

Much later in life I came to understand why. It was because my father's rages did him good. He was a chronic asthmatic and they induced a beneficent flow of adrenalin which melted tension away. 'Other passions may be bad for asthmatics,' wrote the author of *A Lawyer's Notebook*, 'but anger is excellent.'

After a display of frenzied anger, so unreasonable that it seemed (and in my view was) insane, my father sometimes behaved as blandly as if nothing had happened. He was too self-centred and unimaginative to perceive that his wife and whichever of his children was present were exhausted by nervous strain, and resentful as well. Evidently some states of tension in him, as in his mother and his mother's father, could only be relieved by a brain-storm.

What I have heard and read of English life in the Victorian age has made me regard it as inexhaustibly strange; it was extreme in its delights and horrors. No doubt Trollope, for example, was far more aware of its strangeness and its crudities than he felt able to show himself in his novels. I wonder what he would have made of my grandmother.

In Somerset of the Trollopian time she became engaged to a socially suitable young man whom we will call Maitland, tall, fair, and virile, with curly golden hair and a beard to match. They seemed much in love. Maitland used to take her out riding, but one morning he arrived at the admiral's door leading a horse which, for some unknown reason, she had previously told him she did not wish to ride. After an outburst of incomprehensible fury she snatched off her engagement ring, threw it down, and ground it under her heel. That was the end of the engagement—but not, as will appear, the last of Maitland.

I don't know whether she accepted the proposal of Alfred Plomer on the rebound, nor do I know how much trouble that stolid, patient, reliable being had with her temperament during the forty years and more of their marriage. I do know that she had what used to be called 'a good figure' and that she could make herself very agreeable. 'She was thought a most entertaining person,' an old relation once said, 'but self-willed.'

Why had she been given the uncommon name of Lucretia? While she sails off to India with her soldier husband, that question shall be my excuse for some account of an interesting man from whom she was descended, Martin Folkes. Léautaud once remarked that a man who has done nothing with his life makes the most of the little he has done: equally, if one's family tree is hung with a fruitage of country clergymen, trustworthy colonels, and solid City or country worthies and their ladies, with a sprinkling of drop-outs and deviants, one makes the most of a forebear of more originality. Not at all an ancestor-worshipper, I can't resist a character.

2

'The Godfather of all Monkeys'

Martin Folkes, a Norfolk man, was born in 1690, the son of a barrister. His mother was one of the three daughters of Sir William Hovell of Hillington Hall, near King's Lynn, and her sister Etheldreda was married to the Archbishop of Canterbury, William Wake, an eminent medieval scholar. At the age of nine, Martin was handed over to a tutor who had been a professor of Hebrew. They worked together for seven years and the tutor then described his pupil as 'a choice youth of a penetrating genius, and master of the beauties of the best Roman and Greek writers'. At sixteen he was ready for Cambridge and when only twenty-three was elected a Fellow of the Royal Society. That was in the year 1714.

In the same year he did a most extraordinary thing: he married an actress. This must have had an electrifying effect upon his family and friends and the London gossips. Only since the Restoration had women begun to appear professionally on the English stage, and neither social convention nor puritanical tradition was anything like flexible enough to admit the possibility of a gentleman marrying an actress.

Her name was Lucretia Bradshaw. For seven years she had been seen constantly at the Haymarket Theatre and at Drury Lane, as Ophelia, Desdemona, Portia, and Anne Boleyn, in *The Duchess of Malfi*, *The Beaux' Stratagem* and *The Country Wife*, and was regarded as one of the best actresses of her time. Folkes is said to have taken her off the stage 'for her exemplary and prudent conduct'. No doubt there was something more than prudence to attract him.

Four years later Jonathan Richardson painted him in a velvet coat and an open-necked shirt, looking at the world with large,

interested eyes. In 1722 Newton appointed him vice-president of
the Royal Society, and he is said to have been 'indefatigable in
observing the secret operations and astonishing objects of Nature'.
When little more than a boy he had been elected to the Society of
Antiquaries, and his curiosity being supported by ample means he
had become a great collector of books, prints, drawings, gems,
pictures, coins, and odds and ends of scientific interest. Trendy
intellectuals were at that time attracted by Druidism, and he had a
scale model of Stonehenge made in mahogany. One of his friends,
William Stukeley, nicknamed 'The Arch-Druid', was full of
fanciful notions: the Druids, he said, doted on foxgloves because
the shape of the flower was like the purple mitres they used to
wear for their ceremonial. It seems plain that whatever bonnets
the Druids wore, they cannot have had more bees in them than
Stukeley had in his.

Like Folkes, this engaging crackpot was an enthusiastic poly-
math. As an undergraduate at Cambridge he used to steal dogs and
dissect them, he became a physician, and a Fellow of both the
Royal Society and the Society of Antiquaries. One of his old
friends described him as a mixture of 'simplicity, drollery,
absurdity, ingenuity, superstition, and antiquarianism', and called
him 'conceited and fanciful'.

In 1726 Stukeley confided to his diary that Folkes was his 'good
friend' and had given him useful introductions. Folkes's uncle,
Archbishop Wake, encouraged Stukeley to enter the Church, and
he was ordained: a few years later he wrote a book to prove that
Jehovah and Bacchus were the same, a theory which certainly
makes the former seem more companionable.

Amusement was caused a few years ago by an American lady
who claimed to have discovered that Emily Brontë had a lover
called Louis Parensell. This unlikely name was found to be a mis-
reading of two words in manuscript, namely, Love's Farewell.
Without knowing it, the lady was emulating Stukeley. Having
found a battered coin of the Roman Emperor Carausius with a
defaced inscription, FORTUNA AUGUSTA, he chose to read it as
ORIUNA AUGUSTA, and rushed to the exciting conclusion that

Oriuna must be the name of the wife of Carausius. As somebody remarked, he 'made a new personage start up in history'. 'That we have no history of this lady', Stukeley wrote, 'is not to be wondered at.' He lost no time in inventing one. Oriuna, he explained, was of a martial disposition, 'signalised herself in battle', and obtained a victory. He based this upon the fact that the bust of the supposed Oriuna on the coin was surrounded by a laurel wreath. Her name, he explained, was Gaulish, an 'equivalent to what we now call Lucia'. In fact the whole story was equivalent to what we now call poppycock. No wonder that when Gibbon came to write about Carausius he said of Stukeley in a footnote, 'I have used his materials and rejected most of his fanciful conjectures.' I shall have more to say about Stukeley presently.

By his wife Lucretia, Folkes had three children, Martin, Dorothy, and Lucretia. In 1733 he took the whole family on a tour of Italy lasting more than two years. They came home by sea from Leghorn, and after his return he composed papers on ancient coins, on Trajan's Column, and on sculpture. But all was not well: his wife Lucretia had developed a religious mania and had to be put away in an asylum at Chelsea.

Folkes was consulted by learned men about mathematical, optical, numismatical, or antiquarian matters; for instance by Theobald, the editor of Shakespeare, and Dr Smith, the Plumian Professor of Mathematics at Cambridge. In 1739 he was in Paris, 'conversing with the learned men who do honour to that city ... by whom he was received with all the testimonies of reciprocal regard', and was elected a member of the Académie des Sciences. In 1741 he became President of the Royal Society in succession to Sir Hans Sloane. A little later he was awarded honorary degrees at both Oxford and Cambridge, and also became President of the Society of Antiquaries.

I am unqualified to judge, but it looks as though the Royal Society often concerned itself in those days with rather small matters. Folkes made experiments with a fresh-water polypus, he read papers on weights and measures, on coins and maps and glass, and on some old bones and stones he had seen in Italy. But on

8 March 1749 something happened to rattle the tranquillity in which the Society pursued enlightenment: London was shaken by a slight earth-tremor. It was called 'The Earthquake', and the observations elicited from the Fellows of the Royal Society by this trivial vibration seem deliciously solemn.

Folkes's house was in the handsome and recently built Queen Square, which was then open to the fields in the north, where, to quote Fanny Burney, there was 'a beautiful prospect of the hills ever verdant of Hampstead and Highgate, at that time in un-obstructed view'.

> At very nearly half an hour after 5 this morning, being then in bed, but perfectly awake (wrote Folkes), I felt a very strong shake, or rather 3 or 4 successive shakes of an earthquake, as I immediately took them to be. I judge the whole phae-nomenon to have lasted about 3 or at most 4 seconds of time ... I instantly jumped out of bed, to see if there was any damage done; and going to my Chamber-door, I met my daughter running in a fright from her room, who said she was wak'd with such a *shock*, that she thought her room had been falling; two menservants also, who lay in the garret, and whom I had called to, answer'd me whilst I was talking to my daughter, that they were both wakened by the shock, and that they felt, as they both expressed it, such a motion, as they had sometimes known given to a child in a cradle ...
>
> I sent a servant out about 7 o'clock, and he met a country-man who was bringing a load of hay from beyond Highgate, and who was on the other side of the town when the shock happened; *he* did not, he said, feel it, as he was driving his waggon; but the people he saw in the town of Highgate were all greatly surprised, saying they had had their houses very much shock'd, and that the chairs in some were thrown about in their rooms.
>
> The chamber I lie in is up two pair of stairs forwards, and my bed stands north-west and south-east. I took particular

notice, that there was neither cart nor coach going by, but that everything was entirely quiet at the time.

And what of the other Fellows?

'When I came down to my Study on the first floor,' wrote Mr Birch of Norfolk Street, off the Strand, 'I found a book thrown down from an upper shelf ... I have since been told by a gentleman, who resided many years in the West Indies, that this last shock was more violent than any he felt there, except one at Carthagena, in which a city, about 200 leagues distant from thence, was swallow'd up at that instant ... Another gentleman describ'd to me the sensation, upon being awakened by the motion, to be like that of falling into a fit.'

'Some milkwomen,' wrote Mr Baker, another Fellow, 'felt it very strongly as they were milking their cows near Maribone.' And Mr Clare, F.R.S., was walking near Kensington Gravel-Pits, near what is now Notting Hill Gate, though why he was walking there at 5 o'clock in the morning science does not relate. In his report he wrote: 'I am not certain the building near me moved; but I fancied it did. My feet I am sure felt great emotion.'

Scientific precision was evidently the forte of Mr Russel, of Bloomsbury. He wrote that he had two China figures placed on a cabinet, 'with their faces fronting the west, which were, by the several shocks, turned about facing the north-east, which I took to be nearly one-third of the circumference of a circle'.

As for Mr Mortimer, the Secretary of the Society, he was 'credibly informed of a Pannel of Wainscot in the City being wrenched out of the Groove, and not returning into it again.'

What would they all have thought and said about a real earth-quake? Or of London in the second world war, when half the City was 'wrenched out of the Groove'?

Folkes had to face a far worse shock than the earthquake. His only son, Martin, a most promising young man, who had been sent to finish his education in France, was thrown from a horse and killed.

Folkes is said to have been a regular frequenter of Slaughter's

Coffee House, a resort of Garrick, Fielding, Roubillac and Hogarth. He bequeathed his portrait (1741) by Hogarth to the Royal Society, a fresh, lively picture and no doubt a speaking likeness. The eyes are as bright as ever, and he extends an expressive hand, as if explaining how an earthquake makes you feel as if you are being rocked in a cradle. There is by now a fullness about the face and a portliness of body, which suggest no disinclination for the habit in his day of eating and drinking too much.

It is an attractive face and seems to justify various contemporary opinions of him. He was described as 'a man of great modesty, affability, and integrity', and somebody wrote that

> the generosity of his temper was no less remarkable than the civility and vivacity of his conversation. His love of a studious and contemplative life, amidst a circle of friends of the same disposition, disinclined him to the business and hurry of a public one; and his only ambition was to distinguish himself by his zeal and activity for the promotion of science and literature.

One can get an oblique view of him through the diary of Stukeley – oblique, because Stukeley is fanciful and inaccurate and because he allowed his friendship with Folkes to be, in the end, poisoned by disapproval and, perhaps, envy.

Stukeley had been appointed rector of St George-the-Martyr in Queen Square, near Folkes's house. The living was in the gift of a friend of Folkes, the Duke of Montagu, and it may well have been Folkes who brought Stukeley to his notice. *The Dictionary of National Biography* says the Duke was a man of some talent, but with much of the buffoon about him. That was evidently the opinion of the Duke's mother-in-law, who was none other than the formidable Sarah, Duchess of Marlborough.

> All my son-in-law's talents (she wrote) lie in things natural to boys of fifteen, and he is about two-and-fifty. To get people into his gardens and wet them with squirts, to invite people to

his country house and put things in their beds to make them itch, and twenty other such pretty fancies.

The Duke of Montagu died in 1749, and in his diary Stukeley wrote:

Mr Martin Folkes and I walked by 5 a clock in the morning to the Castle, Kentish-town, to pay our last respects to the illustrious remains of the Duke of Montagu. Soon after 6 the herse came by, on which I threw some honey-suckle flowers I had got out of the hedges.

It was Folkes who obtained for Roubillac the commission to carve the monument for the Duke.

A year later Stukeley wrote in his diary that one Sunday the Duke of Richmond and Martin Folkes, instead of going to church ('a matter unfashionable with great folks'), went to view the Duke of Argyll's garden by Hounslow Heath. 'Both caught cold; it had nearly proved fatal to Mr Folkes.' Which was uppermost in Stukeley—the professed Christian, the offended Sabbatarian, or the old friend, perhaps a little envious of Folkes's grand acquaintances? Ah well, it seems that too many dukes spoiled the cloth.

They continued on good terms. In 1751 Stukeley invited Folkes to a party in Kentish Town, where he lived. It was a party for learned men. The guests were entertained with flints, bones, shells, petrifactions, incrustations, 'a Roman cup and saucer', an orrery, a clock, and a bust of Julius Caesar carved by Stukeley himself in a material called clunch.

'After this dry entertainment,' says Stukeley with endearing playfulness, 'we broached a barrel—of fossils from the Isle of Portland. Lastly, to render it a complete rout, I produced a pack of cards made in Richard II's time, and showed the British bridle dug up in Silbury Hill.'

He made large claims for the bridle, thought it 'probably the greatest antiquity in the world' and 'the strongest proof in the world that the Britons came from the east'.

Soon after this party Folkes had a stroke. For three years he was paralysed, and he died in June 1754. Stukeley at once sat down and wrote a note in his diary—a disagreeable note, I think, to write about an old friend.

This morn about 4 [so it reads] dyed Martin Folkes of a repeated paralytic stroke. He had just finished his new house adjoining his own in a most elegant manner, though altogether incapable of having the least enjoyment from it. He has remained for this 3 or 4 year a most miserable object of dereliction from that Deity, which he supposed took no account of our actions and had not provided for our immortal part.

The religious grievance against Folkes may have been genuine, but it seems to have been mixed with and intensified by other resentments, and he allowed himself to write inexactly and, it seems, to gloat over his old friend's misfortunes.

Among his papers, after his own death some years later, was found an unkind account of Folkes, seen through the distorting glass of embitterment. Although inaccurate and not to his credit it gives a view of Folkes which could never be got from formal obituary tributes. He wrote that Folkes, while still a minor (which he was not), had married 'Mrs Bracegirdle off the stage', and that Folkes's mother 'grieved at it so much that she threw herself out of a window and broke her arm'. If you happen to live in the reign of Queen Anne, and your sister Etheldreda is the wife of the Archbishop of Canterbury, and your only son, who is not yet of age, actually marries, without consulting anybody, an *actress*— that is to say, a low, designing, shameless creature, and almost certainly a strumpet—and you begin to worry about what Etheldreda and the Archbishop will say, and how your son has irrevocably ruined himself—why then, you must just as well go and jump out of the window, preferably on the ground floor.

Whether this defenestration occurred, I don't know, but I do know that Lucretia Bradshaw was not Mrs Bracegirdle.

Stukeley goes on, 'His only son broke his neck off a horse back, at Paris,' and out comes tumbling a torrent of grievances against Folkes:

> Quarrelling with Sir Hans Sloane about the Presidentship of the Royal Society, he went to Rome with his wife and daughters, dog, cat, parrot, and monkey. There his wife grew religiously mad. He went to Venice and got a dangerous hurt upon his leg. Losing his teeth, he speaks so as not to be understood. He constantly refuses all papers that treat of longitude. He chuses the Council and Officers [of the Royal Society] out of his junta of Sycophants that meet him every night at Rawthmill's coffee house, or that dine with him on Thursdays at the Mitre, Fleet Street. He has a great deal of learning, philosophy, astronomy; but knows nothing of natural history.

Now we come to the main accusation:

> In matters of religion an errant infidel and loud scoffer. Professes himself a godfather to all monkeys, believes nothing of a future state, of the scriptures, or revelation. He perverted the Dukes of Montagu and Richmond, Lord Pembroke, and very many more of the nobility, who had an opinion of his understanding; and this has done an infinite prejudice to religion in general, made the nobility throw off the mask, and openly deride and discountenance even the appearance of religion, which has brought us into that deplorable situation we are now in, with thieves, and murderers, perjury, forgery, etc. He thinks there is no difference between us and animals, but what is owing to the different structure of our brain, as between man and man.

Surely this was an advanced opinion at that time: can it be that if

Folkes had been less the learned and omnivorous dilettante and had elaborated on paper his views about men and monkeys, he might have seemed a precursor of Darwin?

The allusion to Lord Pembroke reminds me that at Wilton is Roubillac's bust of Folkes: it gives the impression of a powerful intellect and of physical decline. There are also portraits of him by Vanderbank, Hudson, and Gibson, and two portrait-medals, one of them struck in Rome.

He was survived by unbalanced Lucretia, to whom he left an annuity for life, and by his two daughters. To the younger daughter, Lucretia, he left his plate, his great library, his fine collection of coins, and his vast gatherings of curious and beautiful things of scientific or antiquarian interest. Two years later she married and sold the whole lot: the sale lasted fifty-six days, of which the selling of the books took forty-one. Two years after that she died.

3

'Is My Papa Black?'

My grandmother, named after Martin Folkes's wife, felt that it was creditable to derive from so remarkable a man. So did my father, who had little curiosity about the past. 'At least,' he remarked, 'we can say that *somebody* in our family had some brains.' I guess that he had heard his mother utter those very words.

My uncles, William and Durham, and my aunt, Laura, were all born in India, two of them at Poona, that byword for the limitations of the Anglo-Indian. For the sake of their health my grandfather brought his wife and children home to England, took a house for them in Stanhope Street, Lancaster Gate, and returned to India. In Stanhope Street, in the year of the Franco-Prussian war, my father was born. He was christened Charles Campbell, the latter name after a great-uncle, Sir Donald Campbell, 16th Captain of Dunstaffnage, a baronet, and—oh, what a Victorian designation!—Governor of Prince Edward Island.

One summer morning, in the Isle of Wight, a man in his thirties, dressed in black and wearing black cotton gloves, was strolling along the sands. A clergyman and a don, he liked to dress little girls up as gypsies or shepherdesses and then photograph them. ('I'm very fond of children,' he once said, 'except boys.') His attention was caught by a pretty little girl with a pink complexion, bright eyes, fair ringlets, and a red skirt which stuck out stiffly round her (so she told me about sixty years later) 'like a penwiper'. It was my Aunt Laura. She was digging in the sand, and her governess, some way off, was sitting gossiping with a crony and eating cherries out of a bag.

'Good morning,' said the stranger in black.

The little girl drew herself up.

'Mamma says I'm not to speak to *anybody* on the beach.'

The stranger was not to be rebuffed.

'Ah,' he said, 'then it's quite all right. You see, I'm not *anybody*, I'm *somebody*.'

True: he was Lewis Carroll.

His next step was to call on the little girl's mother, but he was not cordially received. My grandmother thought there was something fishy about a grown-up man who picked up strange little girls on beaches, and she may have resented interest being shown in her daughter rather than herself. The little Laura received an inscribed copy of *Alice in Wonderland* from its author, and that was the end of her relationship with Lewis Carroll.

The prettier and more lively Laura grew, the less her mother cared for her. According to my father, his mother frankly disliked all her children except Durham, who could do no wrong. They were brought up to obey many rules. My father was the most highly strung of the children, pale, with silky black hair and startled brown eyes. He had a great need for the give-and-take of affection of a demonstrative kind, but this was never provided by his mother. He respected his father, whom he always remembered as just and kind, though firm. His sister was good to him and did her best to make up for the want of maternal love – which nothing can ever really make up for.

When Charles was still small his mother told him one day that his father was coming home from India and would arrive late that very night, after he himself had gone to sleep. She came to say good night to him before going down to dinner, and in solemn innocence he asked her, 'Is my Papa black?' This became a family joke.

His innocent look appealed to an old apple-woman who knew him by sight. One day she offered him an orange and asked for a kiss in return. Just as he was about to oblige her, his mother prevented him, no doubt from a reasonable fear of infection. In any case the caste system in Bayswater in the 1870s was no less rigid than in the India she had left, and the apple-woman was clearly an untouchable. At the same time she may have resented the display of affection. She forbade him ever to speak to the old woman again or to go near her, and this struck him as bitterly unjust. The reproof went deep: this was one of those incidents of childhood which mark a man for life, and it is not surprising that he developed a tendency to try and escape from his surroundings.

One afternoon his mother, while entertaining a female friend to tea, glanced out of the window and was astonished to see a growing and excited crowd staring up at the house. Thinking a chimney must be on fire she rang the bell to find out; presently the agitated butler informed her that Master Charles had somehow got through the bars of the nursery window and was at large on the very narrow parapet at the top of the house.

A little later, when he was attending a day school in Albion Street, Charles and another little boy decided to run away. His friend had tenpence, Charles had half a crown and three pennies, so off they went into the great world. They got as far as Richmond Park, where they lay down in the bracken and fell asleep. Emerging at evening, they were questioned by a policeman and promptly returned to their homes in a hansom cab. For this his father beat him.

I believe my grandmother managed her house well. She had come from the country, where it was not thought that because a gentlewoman could afford to do nothing it was therefore proper. She knew about cooking and sewing, and used to make both soap and pomatum. Pomatum! What made all those female ringlets glisten, those heavy chignons and plastered-down coiffures? What was used to oil and scent the dangling tresses of hippy-headed dandies, their floating whiskers and well-combed, vigorous beards? If not macassar oil, pomatum. Nothing in the Victorian time is more bizarre than its recipes:

POMATUM. Take 25 lbs. of hog's-lard, 8 lbs. of mutton suet, 6 oz. of oil of bergamot, 4 oz. of essence of lemons, $\frac{1}{2}$ oz. of oil of lavender, and $\frac{1}{4}$ oz. of oil of rosemary ...

Or did my grandmother ever make this?:

OPIATE, ANTI-TUBERCULAR. Spermaceti, crabs' eyes, and sulphur, of each 2 drachms, conserve of roses ½ oz., pepper and mushroom 2 drachms, honey sufficient to make an electuary ...

Or this homely remedy? ('Just go round to the apothecary's, my dear, and order a pound or two of that useful cannabis, to be charged to my account ... '):

INDIAN HEMP, EXTRACT OF. Boil the resinous tops of the Indian hemp plant ... in spirits of wine ... then distil off the spirits ... This is a dangerous medicine, stimulant in small doses of a grain or two, and sedative in doses of from 10 to 20 grains ...

My grandmother was no doubt able to give some impression of being a conventional wife and mother, but she dressed with style, loved worldly pleasures and entertaining, and was by prudes considered 'fast'. She was in the habit of smoking cigarettes, and considerable excitement was caused when she was seen, in what was known as respectable society and some time before 1870, not only smoking, but sitting on a table and *swinging her legs*.

One day, when she was taking her children for a walk in the park, there occurred one of those ominous coincidental encounters more commonly devised by romantic novelists than by destiny. Charles ran on ahead, climbed a railing, could not get down, and burst into tears. A handsome, well-dressed man, who happened to be passing, kindly lifted him down and was consoling him when Mrs Plomer approached. She was about to thank him when he took off his hat, bowed, and smiled, and she was startled to recognise Maitland, her former fiancé.

He was still unmarried, his old feeling for her instantly revived, and he became a constant visitor at Stanhope Street and elsewhere. I am inclined to suppose that in my grandfather's absence he became her lover. When my grandfather returned to England, Maitland was constantly received as a friend of the family. I do not know whether my grandfather was trusting and unsuspecting, or a *mari complaisant*, but I can imagine that there may have been in my grandmother some resemblance to Hedda Gabler, attached for convenience' sake to a worthy man, and aware of her power over another, a bewitching one. The children detested Maitland, seeing him clearly, perhaps because of some chance adult revelation, as a usurper both of their father's pre-eminence and of the affection due to themselves from their mother. When Maitland was staying with the family at a house my grandfather had taken in the Lake District, they demonstrated their feelings by emptying into his top hat quantities of salt, pepper and mustard. They were found out, of course, and punished.

Having retired from the Indian Army, my grandfather bought a house in Chesterfield Street, Mayfair. When Disraeli was dying a few yards away, in Curzon Street, Charles was sent out every morning after breakfast by his father to read the latest bulletin outside the invalid's house. One morning he had the satisfaction of rushing back and crying, 'Dizzy's dead! Dizzy's dead!' The news was received by my grandfather with the gravity becoming to a diehard Conservative, now convinced that the country's progress towards 'the dogs' would be greatly accelerated. The colonel regarded liberals and radicals as synonymous and as having designs on the pockets, property, and privileges of those who had inherited wealth and position, and he had a belief that a kind of divine right to these things was innate in their possessors. Although the youngest son he had inherited a comfortable fortune, but unwisely and unluckily tried, rather later, to increase it by speculation. He lost £25,000 'in one day', my father told me. I suppose that would be the equivalent today of £100,000. The money would at any time have been convenient to his descendants.

At the age of nine my father was sent to the United Services College at Westward Ho!, the school about which Kipling wrote *Stalky and Co.*, which I have no wish to read. He was fairly contented there, and the boys used to brew quantities of sloe gin, which made them so exalted that they were often late for call-over; but he suffered from a painful eczema on the legs, and it was suddenly decided that he should be sent instead to a small school in France; this was ostensibly for his health's sake, but he believed that his mother wished him out of her way; although the school was no further off than Guînes, in the Pas-de-Calais, he was not allowed to return home for the holidays.

The eczema got worse, and the schoolmaster thought the boy should return home. The ravages of the disease made such an impression on my grandmother that she wept, so she was not heartless about him after all. It was the only time, my father said, that he saw her in tears. She nursed him carefully and took him to an eminent dermatologist, who sent him to Bath to take the waters externally and internally.

He attended Bath College, a local public school now extinct, and was housed with one Willan, an assistant master. The head-master was a sadist, and when he attacked Charles's hands with a cane (which he used with a skilful technique in order to break the skin) the gloating expression on his face was too much for the boy, who flew at him and kicked him hard on the shins. When Willan set up on his own as a crammer, Charles stayed with him and was well treated.

When the boy was nearly fourteen his eczema had almost healed, but the dermatologist said it would leave him either tubercular or asthmatic: he was right, my father suffered greatly from asthma all his life. This is a good illustration of a saying of Hardy's, that 'a physician cannot cure a disease, but he can change its mode of expression'.

Two incidents at Sherborne, my father's fifth school, seem to belong to the world of *Tom Brown's Schooldays*, which I do not intend to read. It was the custom there to toss new boys in a blanket, and at the beginning of his second term he distinguished himself by helping to toss a boy so vigorously that the little victim went through the ceiling — a feat for which Charles was given an imposition involving five hundred lines of Virgil. More chivalrous

2

was his attack in the fives court on a bully whose pleasure in torturing a small boy Charles had interrupted. Fighting was generally punished, but not in this case, although it was advertised by four black eyes. The bully, with two other boys, was shortly afterwards expelled for homosexual activities.

Holidays in Chesterfield Street were not greatly to be looked forward to. Much younger than his brothers, he was generally at a loose end. He was sometimes sent on an errand, perhaps to the Army and Navy Stores, and about once a week he was allowed to go to the Aquarium, where he saw Blondin walk the tightrope and a lady called Zoe shot out of a cannon, or to the Egyptian Hall to see conjurors, or the St George's Hall, which offered minstrels or Corney Grain. Often he was turned out into the streets by himself 'for exercise', and the pale, dark-eyed boy in a top hat, Eton suit, and patent-leather shoes was several times accosted by strange men who wanted him to have tea with them or go to their rooms. One of these admirers, a rich Australian, was so *épris* that he used to lie in wait for the lad and even called on my grand-parents and offered to 'adopt' him. It suggests innocence or trustfulness on my grandfather's part that he allowed his youngest son, whom he was quite fond of, to be exposed to the dubious adventures and predatory loiterers in the streets of mid-Victorian London.

Returning as a rule to Chesterfield Street in time for tea in the drawing-room, Charles, though naturally restless and active, was expected to sit quietly reading Dickens, Thackeray, or Scott until it was time to dress for dinner, and was sometimes offered a bribe of sixpence if he would lie quite still on the hearth-rug for half an hour. I must say I should have wanted more than that for having to pretend to read *Ivanhoe*. His mother would return from driving in the park or from paying calls in her yellow-wheeled brougham and the heavy bourgeois evening *en famille* began to close in. The meal was heavy, in the fashion of the time, the dining-room sultry with crimson hangings, the proceedings stately, with the old mayoral and shrieval plate gleaming and silver livery-buttons winking as the men-servants moved about in the lamplight. As for the knives, their handles were made of the horns of some rare antelope of which my grandfather had shot specimens in some Asian wilderness. Afterwards in the drawing-room boredom took command of all but my grandfather. That placid man was content, or appeared so, with the latest three-volume novel from Mudie's or a game of bezique or piquet. My grandmother found the needlework with which she often occupied herself a poor substitute for the 'fast' society she preferred. This was not a cultured, not a musical, not a merry household, and the children were sent early to bed.

4

Rebellious Daughter

My grandfather's sister, Catherine, had married George Browne, a farmer in Lincolnshire. She was his second wife, the first having been a Miss Allenby of Cadwell, of the family that produced Edmund Allenby, the eminent soldier. Uncle George and Aunt Kitty lived at Maidenwell House, near Louth, in a self-contained and patriarchal style. The days were punctuated, as in most well-regulated Victorian families, by family prayers morning and evening, which were attended by the servants.

This reminds me that there was in the neighbourhood a dictatorial old lady who thought, reasonably enough, that illegitimate births were made more likely by propinquity. She therefore obliged her maid-servants to sleep in the attics and her men-servants in the basement. After evening prayers she dismissed them all with a formula which used to astonish visitors not accustomed to it.

'Now then!' she would cry, clapping her hands. 'Skirts up! Trousers down! And a good night to you all!'

At Maidenwell the farm bailiff, the shepherd, the carpenter, the coachman, and the gardeners all enjoyed the use of rent-free cottages, but each was expected to lodge one of the farm-hands. For this he received a small subsidy, in addition to his wages and allowances of milk, ham, bacon, corn, and other produce of the farm. They were expected, unless ill, to attend church on Sundays; if they were ill, they were cared for. When Uncle George eventually died, in 1901, he had a splendid country funeral, the coffin being conveyed on a cutt[1] drawn by four well-matched

[1] Two pairs of wheels with a long pole between, used as a timber cart (Webster's Dictionary).

farm horses. The six bearers were all farm servants, who between them had served him for 104 years, and among the vast swarm of mourners were the widow of the carpenter, who had spent all his seventy years on the estate, and Grant the coachman who had been with him for thirty-nine. Continuity was the thing at Maidenwell.

In terms of poetry this is the world of Charles Turner, the parson at Grasby, not far away, who read his poems in 'deep organ tones' with a stronger Lincolnshire accent than that of Tennyson, who was his younger brother. It is a yet utterly un-mechanised world of master and servant, of horse-drawn lives ruled by plodding drudgery through the seasons, and by a sense of community and rootedness. Charles Turner, rebuilding the church at Grasby, wrote the Pre Raphaelite line: 'Through vacant quatrefoils the hodman sings.' The poetry is in the piety, a tender, Anglican, Victorian parish piety, and in what he called the 'old ruralities', the sound in a wayside barn of 'the slip-shouldered flail', 'the low of oxen on the rainy wind', and those moments of now irrecoverable peace:

> The moonrise seems to burn a golden oil
> To light a world of plenty, while it shows
> The woodland, listening in its dark repose.

My grandmother would not go and stay with her sister-in-law, because, she alleged, she had once at Maidenwell found ducks' feathers in her bath-water: probably the real reason was that she found it too countrified and dull. Aunt Kitty, who used to wear blue spectacles and once while watching a thunderstorm com-plained that the lightning was blue, may well have been short of worldly up-to-dateness. In fact she and Uncle George were benevolent and hospitable, liked nothing better than a houseful of nephews and nieces, and once a year drove with all their guests into Louth to attend the hunt ball.

My father remembered an afternoon drive with Uncle George in a conveyance known as the 'minibus'. It was shaped like a matchbox standing on end, there was a seat on the roof for the coachman and a door at the back opening to admit one person to a single seat on either side, where they sat facing each other. Sometimes, peering out at the grey rain drenching the wolds, when the drive was just a drive with no definite objective, Uncle George would murmur resignedly, 'My dear, this is a wild-goose chase.'

Grant the coachman, a genial soul, was occasionally called in, when the house was full, to help wait at table. Wearing white cotton gloves with loose flaps at the ends of the fingers (since he could never get them properly on to his weather-worn hands) and sweating freely, he made a most friendly though not a polished butler. Once, when a new local female grandee was being entertained to dinner at Maidenwell for the first time he handed her a jelly on a large dish. Just as she was about to help herself the jelly began to slither dangerously towards the edge, and in a hearty voice, as he righted the dish, he called out 'Whoa, mare!'

One spring day Charles was sitting on a haystack with two lively nieces of Uncle George's, Edythe and Hilda Waite-Browne. He was teasing them, and they shoved him over the edge. One might say he fell for Edythe. While he was still a schoolboy his two elder brothers had both gone into the army. William, the eldest, served in various wars, and was proficient in his profession. Chosen out of three hundred candidates for the antique-sounding post at Sandhurst of Instructor of Fortifications, he was, in 1900, sent by the War Office to Queensland, where he became commandant of the military forces—'the youngest officer ever placed in such a trust in Australasia'. A local paper described him as 'over the middle height, with quick, elastic, alert step, of good features' and 'distinctly muscular, though not of an aggressive type'. He was said to possess 'the rare quality of attracting all open minds brought in contact with him'. 'To those endeavouring to advance, his sympathetic hand and kindly counsel are ever available, but upon the malingerer and wrong-doer he descends as a veritable Avatar.' My Uncle Avatar had a literary bent when young, but I believe the only book he wrote was a manual of infantry training—of which the Library of Congress in Washington once asked me, to my surprise, if I was the author. I think of him as one of those rare people to whom happiness comes later rather than earlier.

Of my Uncle Durham I have already spoken as my grandmother's favourite child. My father looked up admiringly to this handsome brother as a delicate boy will to a strong one. At Cheltenham, at Sandhurst, and in the army Durham excelled at ball games; he swam, shot, played polo, and pursued or was pursued by the opposite sex. He was always in debt, and his mother would sometimes secretly sell a piece of jewellery to keep him in pocket. In her eyes he could do no wrong.

After leaving Cheltenham he went to 'Jimmy's', a London crammer well known in those days, to prepare for Sandhurst. Once, when his parents were away and the servants at Chesterfield Street were on board wages, he and a friend entertained to dinner there a couple of chorus girls. The party went with a swing, but by a curious mischance my grandfather had suddenly decided to come up from the country for the night. The colonel's ears, as he put his latchkey into the front door, were greeted by sounds of unaccountable revelry. When he opened the door of the dining-room they diminished abruptly.

'I'm afraid,' he said quietly, with a bow, 'that I haven't the pleasure of these ladies' acquaintance. No doubt they've come to the wrong house – by mistake.'

He then withdrew, and Tamlin the butler hastily shepherded them out of the house. My grandfather explained to Durham that it was not 'the thing' to foul one's own nest.

Does anybody ever speak of 'The Thing' in these days? It was a great fetish of that age, and its uncountable unwritten rules made it a tyrant. Lady Ottoline Morrell was of my father's generation, and when her half-brother succeeded to the dukedom of Portland and she, still a child, was taken to live at Welbeck, the process began of making her conform to what she later called the 'unimaginative arrogance' of doing 'The Thing'. Starved (she wrote) in the intellect and the senses, she rebelled.

My Aunt Laura was eight years older than my father, and all

through her life was kind and protective towards him. She had great natural vivacity, and a quick wit, and needed them. She was sent to a school for the daughters of officers and returned without pleasure to Chesterfield Street for the holidays, since she had to face being snubbed, ignored, humiliated, and ordered about by her mother. Mutual animosity between a mother and daughter may arise from some resemblance between the two characters, and may arouse a feeling of rivalry. One can hardly call it un-natural, because we are all liable to dislike those whom we most resemble, even if only in one particular trait. And so many miseries have been caused by over-fond and possessive mothers and by too conscientious filial piety on the part of daughters, that disharmony can turn out to be a blessing in horrible disguise.

Laura was sent to be 'finished' in Dresden, which may have been a relief, but a photograph taken of her there shows a shadow of tension over her charming young face. When she returned home, she was lonely. She found herself often relegated to the company of the servants, who were fond of her and sorry for her, while her mother pointedly made much of two girls of her own age, daughters of another Anglo-Indian family, and took them out for drives or to parties or the theatre.

For Laura 'The Thing' was clearly defined. What was expected of her was to marry as soon as possible a man with money, of at least her own but preferably of a grander social status. This obligation was dinned into her unceasingly. Being pretty and sprightly, an only daughter and evidently not without fortune, she was still very young when prospective suitors began to appear. Since they received every encouragement from her mother, Laura delighted in turning them down. This led to disagreeable scenes.

When, unexpectedly, she saw her chance of escape and happi-ness she resolved to take it. Her mother sometimes allowed her to go and stay in other people's houses, being glad to get the obstinate girl out of her sight and hoping she might fall in with some eligible *parti*. In some country house-party she met a tall and distinguished-looking young man and they were at once attracted to each other.

His name was Emslie Horniman, and he was the only son of a Liberal Member of Parliament. Originally Quakers, the Hornimans were rich tea-merchants, and were a most enlightened family, and patrons of learning and the arts. It was Emslie's father who gave London the remarkable Horniman Museum, the whole conception of which was brilliant and in advance of its time, and his sister Annie was to become famous for her friendship with Yeats and for subsidising the Abbey Theatre and enabling it to present plays no commercial theatre would have put on. She was the first person to finance a play by Bernard Shaw for public performance. The late St John Ervine wrote that the Irish were ungrateful to her, and he was annoyed when, in accounts of the Abbey Theatre, she was made to seem far less important than 'the Widow Gregory who never gave a farthing to it'. Annie Horniman was interested in the occult and in astrology, she wore bloomers and an ornamental silver dragon which she used to say was a likeness of herself, was a chain-smoker, rode a man's bicycle, and was said to have crossed the Alps alone from Italy to Munich. The entire repertory-theatre movement arose from her devotion and patronage, and late in life she was made a Companion of Honour.

Emslie Horniman had been educated privately, and was a highly cultivated young man with an enquiring mind and a knowledge of the fine arts. He proposed to Laura and was accepted. The fact that she had engaged herself to a young man whom her parents had never seen would have been enough to set her mother against the match. She was ordered to put the matter out of her head at once and hold no further communication with the young man. Her intention showed a total disregard for 'The Thing'. What were the objections? The Hornimans were 'in trade'. All fortunes presumably originate in trade, war, politics, or plunder, and in any case my grandfather owed his own private means to a fortune made by his great-grandfather in the eighteenth century. She was told that enquiry had shown that the young man was 'an atheist and a radical', and no doubt he was also hated as an aesthete. That he was handsome, amiable and intellectual, the only son of a rich

2*

man, and in love with Laura, were facts to be brushed aside. It can only be said that the forces of convention, narrow prejudice, and philistinism must have ossified the common sense and humane feelings of my grandparents during their life in the cantonments of Poona. These forces were now open threats to young happiness and freedom of choice.

The conflict of wills was intense. My grandmother was determined to show her power over her daughter and to defeat Laura's purpose; but Laura was not one of those drooping, docile Victorian daughters. To tell her not to speak of the young man or give him any further thought — let alone see him or communicate with him — made her determine to do the opposite. As stolen fruit her love must have been the sweeter, and who can now count the wrongs the poor girl had to avenge? Once, coming home from school, she had found that her mother, invading the privacy of her room, had made a clean sweep of her treasures and girlish bric-à-brac.

Though by now almost grown up, Laura was actually imprisoned in her room until she should 'come to her senses' — but they were exactly what she had come to. Her first wish was to write to her lover. But how? She had no writing materials, so she persuaded the housemaid who brought meals to her to get her some, but the maid was too afraid of my grandmother to provide a stamp or to be willing to post the letter when it was written; and in that opulent house Laura had not a single penny to buy a stamp with. How to get one? Besides determination, a pink complexion, and bright eyes, she had one asset which seemed to her instantly marketable — a magnificent head of fair hair, so long that she could stand on it. Such a posture was useless; it was scissors that were needed. She accordingly cut from the middle of her scalp — from which its absence could be easily disguised — a great switch of hair like a horse's tail, coiled it up in a wrapping, and contrived to escape from the house for long enough to sell the trophy to the nearest Mayfair *posticheur,* to visit a post office and buy stamps, to post her letter — then to get back to her room undetected.

There were more battles to come, appeals to reason, duty, and a non-existent affection. The colonel sided with his wife in the direct threat: 'If you marry this man, we shall no longer look upon you as our daughter. You will be disgracing yourself, and we shall never wish to see you again. You will be to us exactly as if you were dead.'

When at last it was obvious to the stubborn pair that nothing would deflect the girl, they gave in, I suppose with a bad grace, and allowed her to be married from her own home. The wedding was at the then fashionable church of St George's, Hanover Square, but at Chesterfield Street afterwards, when Laura was about to drive away for ever with her 'radical' aesthete, the presence of the constant Maitland was too much for her. She spoke to her mother in terms of an uncompromising plainness, uttered a malediction to Maitland, and then drove off with a new name to a new life and, for the next half-century or so, health, wealth, and much happiness.

Some years later, Laura and her husband, going one evening to a play, were a little late and took their seats in the stalls when the theatre was already darkened. In the interval, when the lights went up, she looked about her. So did the bediamonded matron next to her. Their eyes met. It was her mother. They did not speak, but sat out the evening cheek by jowl yet as separate as strangers.

They met once more. Early in the present century, when Laura was the happy mother of three children, her mother, old and disintegrating, sought a reconciliation: she wrote and asked Laura to come and see her. Laura made no move to do so, but one afternoon, after some weeks, she was trying on a new green velvet dress and admiring herself in the glass, and suddenly decided to go and see her mother. Two sentences of the conversation have been recorded.

'I wonder what your children think of me,' said the old woman, who was in bed.

'My children?' cried Laura, full of radiant vitality and catching sight of her reflection and that of the green velvet dress in a glass. 'My children! Why, they don't even know that you exist!'

5
Wander-Years

As Laura had been more of a mother to Charles than his mother had been, he kept affectionately in touch with her throughout her life. But what was he now to do with his own life? He told his father he wished to follow his two brothers into the army. No, said the colonel, he would do better to go into trade! One of my grandfather's own brothers had done very well with a sheep station in Australia, so the wool trade was seen as being just 'The Thing': Charles should learn it thoroughly. He was taken from school, apprenticed to a firm of wool merchants in Bradford, lodged with a suitable clergyman, and given a small allowance.

Always of a sociable inclination, Charles took to playing cards and billiards, fishing and shooting with the sons of rich manu-facturers, and what with the high standard of living of the gilded youth of Yorkshire, and a romance with a gamekeeper's daughter (he was, I am glad to say, generous to those he loved), his modest allowance was scarcely adequate, so he got a little, really very little, out of his depth. This slight imprudence changed the course of his life.

He went to his father and laid the facts before him. The colonel listened in silence but was evidently much displeased. He told his son that he had been 'most dishonourable' to get into debt, that he would talk matters over with his mother, and would let him know what they decided. It is not known what share my grandmother had in the decision, but again there was a sentence of banishment, this time to a remoter region than the Pas-de-Calais.

My grandfather said he would pay Charles's debts, but he was to go to South Africa. It was 'the coming country' and one with great prospects, it was said, in the matter of wool: besides, the climate was good for asthma. Convention had again triumphed: the lightly erring youngest son was to be packed off to 'the Colonies', to sink or swim. So at the age of nineteen, with a letter of credit for a hundred pounds and a letter of introduction to Cecil Rhodes, my father sailed for Capetown. Before he left he told Edythe Waite-Browne he would marry nobody but her and would come back to her as soon as he was in a position to marry.

Capetown in those days was still picturesquely exotic. A little dazed by the brilliance and strangeness of his surroundings, Charles presented his letter to the empire-building tycoon. Still in his thirties, Rhodes was in the full flush of success. He had obtained the charter for his company, which, with a capital of a million pounds, and the Dukes of Fife and Abercorn on the board, was to open up a vast *Lebensraum* for the white man in the African interior; and he was about to become Prime Minister at the Cape. In his high, squeaky voice Rhodes fired off numerous questions, staring hard at Charles. Then he carried him off to lunch with two of his political friends, ignored him during the meal, and having made him feel very young and green suggested that he should join the Cape Mounted Rifles, a regiment of police consisting largely of more or less 'pukka sahibs'.

Charles was in two minds what to do. To reduce them to one he went to the castle to see an old friend of his father's, General Sir William Cameron, then acting governor. Cameron received him kindly and was curious to know why he had come to the Cape, thinking perhaps to smell out a misdemeanour. Charles said, truthfully enough, that he suffered from asthma and his father thought South Africa would do it good, besides being 'the coming country'. Cameron, as an old soldier, thought enlistment in the Cape Mounted Rifles would provide 'a splendid oppor-tunity' for Charles to get to know the country: he could always pursue the wool trade, or whatever he fancied, later on.

My father joined the regiment at its headquarters in King-williamstown, and the young asthmatic went through riding-school, took many a fall, and before long was able to do all the tricks, to ride with a carbine at full gallop, brandish a sword, and jump without stirrups. It was a strenuous life; he stuck it for a year, then, on the advice of the medical officer, bought himself out.

Now the wander-years began in earnest. He was swindled by a partner with whom he had opened a café at Port Elizabeth. Then a hotel-keeper asked him to help in organising a banquet. It was to be offered to the governor, Sir Henry Loch, at the township of Molteno, away up in the mountainous hinterland, to mark the opening of the extension of the railway to Bethulie, on the Orange River. Charles agreed to take charge of the proceedings, the waiters, food, drinks, cutlery, crockery, linen, flowers, ice — and the bunting.

All went well with this typically nineteenth-century occasion. On the appointed day a train, much beflagged, drew into Molteno amid cheering spectators. The governor emerged, received local worthies, made a suitable speech, and was then escorted to the banquet. Charles was taken aback to find that the governor wasn't the governor, Sir Henry Loch, after all, but the acting governor, Sir William Cameron. The banquet went with a swing, there were more speeches, and His Excellency at last rose to depart. Charles was pleased to have escaped notice when an aide-de-camp arrived and told him that Sir William wished to see him, and was waiting in his saloon coach.

'What the devil does this mean?' Sir William demanded — a little ungraciously, since my father had organised the successful banquet. 'What would your father think of this?'

Charles gave his reasons for appearing in the role of maître d'hotel, not realising that he hadn't been doing 'The Thing'.

'Then why on earth didn't you write to me, if you were in need of help? Or to Mr Rhodes? There are certain things a gentleman doesn't do, and what you've been doing is one of them. I will advance you twenty-five pounds to help you, and I'll write and get it back from your father.'

A kind act, but the young man was surprised that he had

committed a social gaffe so far from being 'The Thing' that no less a person than the representative of the Queen had felt it necessary to reprimand him for it. My father was never a man who would have thought useful work of any kind beneath his dignity, particularly if it had to do with food. In later life he often pleased his family with dishes of his own cooking.

He now took to the land, managed a sheep-farm near Queenstown, acquired a delightful Basuto pony, planted nearly a quarter of a million eucalyptus and pine trees, then trotted off on a tour of the Winterberg and Tafelberg, making his way by sorting wool-clips. Then he turned tutor. Then he went off with an Afrikaner, Barend van der Linde, constructing fences. Then he became the manager of a native trading-station at Driver's Drift, near Lady Frere.

This he much enjoyed. He liked and admired the Africans, who were of the Xhosa tribe, but one day a young show-off offended him. Charles ordered him out, but he would not budge. Then, perhaps feeling difficulty in breathing because of his asthma, he flew into one of those hereditary sudden rages, seized the nearest thing handy, which happened to be a hatchet, and rushed at the man, intending no doubt to frighten rather than attack him. The Xhosa, whose name was Ulangene, naturally thought he was about to be murdered and in self-defence struck Charles on the head with his knobkerrie and knocked him out.

The next morning Charles went to discuss the matter with the local chief. They had a formal interview. The chief ruled that he had been wrong to lose his temper and take up a hatchet. Ulangene, he said, was also wrong; he had behaved rudely in the first place; and had no right to assault a white man. He ordered Ulangene to be flogged there and then with a strip of untanned ox-hide, no light punishment.

Neither young man bore the other any ill-will. My father was sorry to have got Ulangene into trouble, Ulangene admitted that he had been in the wrong at first, and they became good friends. When Ulangene, who was a splendid swimmer, later distinguished himself by saving a post-cart, containing mailbags and drawn by mules, from being washed away in a flooded river, Charles took great trouble to get him an official grant of a sum of money as a reward.

Charles showed no sign of settling down. After a holiday in Queenstown he had spent all his money. This time he set out on foot, with a billy-can and a bundle on a stick like Dick Whittington, for a place on the Zwart Kei river where a bridge was being built. He was taken on as storeman and clerk, but as soon as he had saved money thought he would like to return to trading with Africans. He engaged himself as assistant to an old man near Queenstown and served him so well that his employer grew fond of him. But the old man had a daughter who kept house for him, a crabbed virgin with white eyelashes, lustreless eyes of an indeterminate colour set in a dead-white face, and sandy hair like veld-grass after a hot summer. She invariably dressed in black merino, in perpetual mourning for her mother, long dead. She never smiled or showed any emotion except for fleeting moments when talking to her father. Charles was privately warned that she was insanely jealous of his influence with the old man, and finding her presence too sinister to be endurable, he went on his way.

What a strange wandering life! He was as free as could be, and apparently showed no application to his purpose of marrying. The sun shone, he was his own master, life was one long adventure. The country was infested with fortune-hunters, headed by Rhodes, and the Kimberley diamond-field was a special attraction. Travelling partly by rail, partly on foot, he made off in that direction.

One day, feeling tired, he made his way to a lonely farmhouse he had seen in the distance. He was offered a characteristic welcome and hospitality by the farmer, a Boer of the poorer class. The house, or shack, was built of dried mud and roofed with corrugated iron. The interior was divided in the middle by a calico curtain. On one side of it was an enormous bed, on the other a rough table and some chairs and benches. This simple dwelling was lived in by the farmer, his wife, three sons, and five daughters, the eldest child being nearly grown up, the youngest still at the breast.

At sunset the whole family gathered round the table. The farmer, whose name was Scheepers, read a chapter from a large Bible and offered up a long prayer for his family, himself, and the work of his hands; then a coloured girl brought in a cauldron of stewed mutton, a dish of stamped boiled maize and another of sweet potatoes, the meal being completed by a large loaf and copious draughts of sour milk. At bedtime the table was pushed back and a large mattress was spread on the ground and covered with goatskins.

'You can sleep there with the children,' said Scheepers politely, 'but I shall put one of the boys between you and my eldest girl.'

He and his wife retired to their vast bed, accompanied by the youngest members of their brood, and Charles tumbled in with the older boys and girls—and the fleas. In the morning, after breakfast and prayers, being a person of regular habits and wishing to observe the local *convenances*, he approached his host, who was smoking an early pipe in the fresh morning air, and asked the whereabouts of the sanitary arrangements.

'Ah,' said Scheepers in his homely Afrikaans, and he took his pipe out of his mouth and with a wide and sweeping gesture waved it towards a magnificent panorama of mountains and pastures, 'it is *all* my land. Shit wherever you like.'

After this memorable experience of primitive good manners, Charles, who had sixty pounds in hand and drifted along, enjoying the sun and his by now much improved health, found himself not at Kimberley but at the little dorp of Aliwal North, a clean town with clear rivulets running at the sides of its streets. Here he came across a lonely young Englishman, who had come there for his health but was dying of consumption, and tried to ease his last days with kind companionship. One night, after Charles had been reading to him, the young man had a fearsome haemorrhage. Charles washed him, dressed him in a clean night-shirt, and gave him some brandy and milk. For a few days he seemed better and was able to sit out on the shady verandah, but then he died

calmly one night in Charles's arms. Charles had grown fond of
him, was much affected by his death, and felt he could not stay in
the town, but as he left it he wondered if he was wise to leave such
a peaceful haven for places he knew nothing of and in search of he
knew not what.

6

The Only Comfortable Time

In the train to Kimberley a fellow-passenger warned him that he would there be robbed of anything he had, and as a newcomer he would be in danger of being used unknowingly as a go-between for the conveyance of illicitly bought diamonds. The stranger told him of a young man who had been asked at a Kimberley hotel if he would mind taking a note and a parcel to a house about a hundred yards away. He agreed, and when he delivered the note was asked to sit down and wait for an answer. The house was instantly rushed by detectives, he and the householder were arrested, and the parcel was opened and found to contain seven diamonds. Protesting his innocence, the young man was convicted as an accessory to illicit diamond-buying and sent to a convict settlement for five years.

The stranger told Charles he had no hope of getting work in Kimberley unless he was personally known to one of the 'big diamond men', and suggested that he should join the Bechuanaland Border Police, so my father made his way to Mafeking and enlisted in this mounted corps. Before long he was involved in what was to become a notorious fiasco. In later life he showed less than an understanding of politics; I should say that he was politically unconscious. As a young man, brought up to do what he was told and whatever was regarded as 'The Thing', he would have been politically docile.

It was 1895, and the air was full of rumours that the British, exasperated by the unfairness of Kruger, were going to take up arms and force the Transvaal Republic to make concessions to them. The Bechuanaland Border Police were paraded and informed that the British in Johannesburg had asked Dr Jameson for armed assistance 'to protect the women and children' in case of more trouble. The Bechuanaland Police were to join forces with Jameson at Malmani, just inside the Transvaal.

'I can't order you to go', said their colonel, 'but I hope you're all willing to go.'

The men cheered, and soon moved off, themselves cheered by such of the local inhabitants as were of British extraction. It did not occur to Charles, nor perhaps to any of the others, that there was anything questionable about the adventure into which they had been manœuvred, ostensibly as volunteers, by an appeal to their patriotism—'the savage superstition of patriotism', as Tolstoi had defined it some time before this. This was not an assemblage of Tolstoians. These were empty-headed, adventurous young pawns of rapacious adventurers like Rhodes. Their column joined Jameson's small force of mounted police from Mashonaland, led by boyish young Guards officers not lacking in courage but in military experience.

Skirmishing ended in surrender, which Jameson notified by borrowing a woman's apron to use as a white flag. After a parley, terms of surrender were arranged, the invaders were disarmed, and they rode off between armed guards to Krugersdorp, where they were jeered at by women and children. They then rode on in the direction of Pretoria, their guards jubilantly firing off their rifles, singing their national anthem, the *Volkslied*, and assuring the prisoners that they would all be shot on arrival, but they were too tired, hungry, thirsty, and despondent to care, and many dozed in the saddle.

At Pretoria they were interned in the grandstand on the racecourse, and after a few days were told they were to be sent to England, by way of Natal, to stand trial for entering a friendly state with arms, intending to commit a breach of the peace. They travelled in open trucks to Volksrust, the border town between the Transvaal Republic and the British colony of Natal, and there they filed before the local commander-in-chief of the British forces, a General Cox. Charles, on being asked his name and giving it, received a quizzical and amused look from the general. Some months later his eldest brother, William, told him he had had a letter from his friend General Cox, saying, 'I have just signed for your scallywag brother and sent him home with the other filibusters.' A filibuster, yes, but Charles could only in a playful way have been called a scallywag.

When the men arrived in England they were told they were free: Jameson and the officers with him would be tried, but no action would be taken against the rank and file. They arrived on a Sunday, and Charles, in dirty flannel trousers, his battle-stained tunic, and a grey cap, was pursued by news-hounds, to whom he would not talk. Early the next norning he drove off to the family tailor in Conduit Street to get some clothes. In these, as soon as they were ready, he went to lunch with his father at the United Services Club.

'What on earth do you think *you're* doing,' said the colonel, 'playing at soldiers! But by God, my boy, I'm proud of you!' and Charles was fondly introduced to some old military buffers and club cronies of the colonel, including Lord Napier of Magdala.

Such was the temper of the time that the men were lionised as heroes. A rowdy evening at the Pavilion with other repatriated filibusters ended for Charles with a seductive invitation by a more or less *grande cocotte* to her house in Sloane Street. She was the mistress of a successful barrister, temporarily absent in Scotland, and the idea of an adventure with one of the popular heroes of the moment quite took possession of her. Her opening remark had been, 'You must be one of those delicious men who have been making Oom Paul dance.' Could fatuity go further? He also enjoyed some cosy suppers with Mabel Love, a successful and pretty musical-comedy actress of the day.

Charles now proposed himself for a visit to the mother of Edythe Waite-Browne at Southwell in Nottinghamshire. The little town was all agog at the prospect of a visit from a Jameson Raider and was with some difficulty restrained from providing a civic welcome, complete with band. He was very pleasantly

received, but having no money or position or immediate prospects
felt he had no right to try and tie Edythe to a formal engagement,
but he made plain his unchanging hope and intention to marry
her. For the present he was still a mounted policeman from
Bechuanaland, and in that capacity was shortly recalled to
Africa.

Rhodes's *Lebensraum* was now the scene of 'native trouble', and
Charles, as a mere pawn in the game of imperialism, found
himself attached to the so-called 'relief force' under Colonel
Plumer (later Field-Marshal Lord Plumer, and no relation). He
had as his companion one of those romantic young Afrikaners
with whom from time to time he was associated. This one, called
Willy Buissine, came from the Cape. 'The only man,' Charles was
later heard to say, 'who could stand a bottle between his feet and
flick it away with the lash of a forty-foot wagon whip.' News of
this freakish and useless skill evoked the only possible comment:
'Oh.'

Part of the process of 'relieving' the white settlers in Matabele-
land was to push on with building the railway from Mafeking to
Bulawayo, to bring them supplies, and it was with the transport
of supplies that Charles was concerned. Out beyond the advancing
railway he was able to shoot a variety of game, and at his camp on
the Mahalapswe river had the pleasure of entertaining Prince
Alexander of Teck and F. C. Selous, the celebrated hunter. By
the time he reached Bulawayo the so-called Matabele rebellion
was over, but he received a medal for his services all the same. I
don't think he ever paused to wonder whether the proceedings
had been just.

Drifting as usual, he drifted out of the mounted police and on
to the staff of a Pretoria newspaper, the *Press*. He lodged with a
Mr and Mrs Preller. Preller was an official at the High Court, and
his wife, when a small girl, had come from the Cape with the
Voortrekkers in 1836. Mrs Preller told Charles she never thought
she could like a *rooinek* (= red neck, i.e. Englishman) but, she
said, he was 'like another son' to her. Possibly she was like a mother
to him: he needed one.

Mrs Preller was so pleased with him that she took him to call on the President of the Republic, Paul Kruger himself, and Kruger took a liking to him too. The editor of the *Press* encouraged Charles's visits to the Presidency and urged him to gather snippets of political gossip. With engaging candour Charles used to tell the President that he had been asked to find out what the Volksraad or Kruger himself were going to do about such and such a matter. Sometimes Kruger would reply, 'I cannot say', and sometimes 'Tell your editor to wait and see', but sometimes he spoke plainly and the news went round the world.

Charles thought that Kruger's religion was deep and genuine, and that he guided his whole life by the Bible, often choosing for quotation some passage which agreed with intentions he had already formed. It was now Oom Paul who made the 'delicious' man dance. The old man had a curious habit of pinching Charles's leg when his attention was diverted, and then roaring with laughter at the young man's surprised or pained outcry.

Charles had become secretary of the local swimming club. He had been 'taught' to swim as a small boy by his father's having thrown him out of a boat into the sea. He was a swimmer born and made, and his asthma never affected him in the water. He now persuaded the President to attend the club sports. A strip of red baize was laid down at one end of the swimming bath, with an armchair in the middle for the top-hatted and frock-coated old father of his people, and other chairs for members of his Cabinet: he was attended by Generals Burger and Joubert and by Dr Leyds, the State Secretary. Charles did a high dive and then swam round the bath under water, picking up as he went twenty-four plates, which he gracefully deposited in a pile at the President's feet.

'*Machtig!*' said Kruger. '*De Kerel swimmt net als een visch!*' ('Good God! The fellow swims just like a fish.')

Charles was ready for his next trick. He was tied up in a sack, and shoved off the top of the high-diving platform into the water. He had a knife in his hand, ripped open the bag, rose to the surface, and saluted the President, who could not think how it was done and had to have it explained to him. He then laughed loudly, saying *'Maar dit es slim!'* ('Very cunning!')

Hearing that his brother Durham, now captain and adjutant of his regiment, had arrived at the Cape from Jamaica, Charles made the long journey to see him. He drove up to the Royal Hotel in Capetown in a hansom cab, and there was Durham on the verandah among his brother-officers. As Charles got out of the cab, Durham, unfamiliar with the picturesque fashions for males in the far-off Transvaal, called out, 'My God, where did you get that hat?'

When the South African War broke out there was a great exodus of English people to the coast. Charles did not quite know what to do. He had good Afrikaner friends, he knew their language, their ways, and their kindliness, and among his acquaintances were Botha and Smuts. He was not in the least interested either in fighting against 'the Boers' or in fighting with them. Besides, he had engaged in a business venture which was developing nicely. Louis Botha offered him a permit to remain in Pretoria if he so wished, but no doubt he felt that he would be in an impossible position: he decided that he had better depart. Botha wrung his hand and wished him good luck.

He travelled south in a cattle-truck with a boy of fifteen who had been entrusted to his care, and they saw the Bethulie bridge over the Orange River blown up behind them. Still only in his twenties, Charles had taken a great fancy to the boy, and they spent some idyllic weeks together on the Buffalo river near East London, swimming, fishing and idling. But his departure from Pretoria meant good-bye to coffee with the President in the sun on the stoep, good-bye to the dusty, wide and peaceful roads of the capital, the bicycle rides and picnics, the high dives and the friendly Afrikaner girls, good-bye to the weeping and motherly Mrs Preller, good-bye to the abandoned Edison Bell phonograph, good-bye to the old Transvaal, good-bye to the nineteenth century ...

The end of one century and the beginning of another make an absurdly arbitrary division. The last years of the nineteenth were full of forebodings of the twentieth; many beliefs and habits customary in the nineteenth were still unchanged in 1914; but the disgraceful and inept South African War seems clearly to mark the fatal puncturing of imperialist complacency and the beginning of effective resistance to it. As a non-thinker, with no inclination for analysis and no far-sightedness to look ahead, Charles was not likely to be weighing the past against the future, but even he may have had moments of looking back over his decade of sunlit drifting and of knowing that nothing quite like it would ever happen again.

If he had been a thinker he might have had a sudden insight like Samuel Butler, who wrote in 1890:

> At any rate, so far as I can see, the present is about the only comfortable time for a man to live in, that either ever has been or will be. The past was too slow, and the future will be much too fast.

Or he might have concluded with Bertrand Russell that the eighteenth and nineteenth centuries were a brief interlude in the normal savagery of man, who was about to revert to that condition. Or he might have known what Renan meant, when he sank into a comfortable armchair, murmuring, 'Qu'il est bon de vivre en une époque de décadence!'

Wherever his future lay, it would not be on the banks of the Buffalo river. For some unknown reason he decided to go to England, but when he got there this did not seem to his father at all 'The Thing'.

'What on earth have you come for?' said the astonished colonel. 'Aren't we fighting for you? It's your duty to go back at once and help.' That phrase 'fighting for you' suggests that he now regarded his youngest son as a naturalised South African.

So back Charles went, without any conscientious objection to doing what he was told was his duty, and was appointed an inspector of transport. This at least meant that he need not shoot at men who were defending their independence. Now that transport is almost universally mechanised it seems marvellously antiquated to have set off, as he now did, from Burghersdorp to Aliwal North with a train of thirty wagons, each drawn by six-teen oxen. It was like some picture of the Great Trek, but these wagons were loaded with military supplies for the mismanaging General Gatacre. After this there were long escorted convoys, sometimes of a hundred and twenty wagons, across the Orange Free State. Charles did well but had occasional trouble with ignorant but peremptory generals, among them Hector Macdonald.

One day scouts ahead of the long column of wagons were fired upon and killed by snipers hidden in a farmhouse displaying a white flag. Macdonald turned every living being out of the farm, old women and two babies included, and had the house burnt to the ground, leaving these people with nothing but the clothes they stood in. 'It was a pitiable sight,' said Charles, 'but war is no discriminator of persons. The lives of our scouts were taken by treachery and were of equal value with the lives of Dutch-men.'

A thousand head of cattle had now to be taken by Charles from Bethlehem, in the Orange Free State, to Johannesburg. This convoy was attacked twice, with a loss of seven men and twenty-three oxen. Charles had with him a Captain Luscombe, a regular soldier who was in charge of the escort. Being asked impertinently one day by some of his fellow-officers who the devil was the fellow in civilian clothes with whom he was riding, Luscombe said crushingly, 'Oh, only the brother of the man at Sandhurst who taught you blighters the little soldiering you know.' This was an allusion to his brother William's position on the staff at Sandhurst before the war.

Having handed over his vast herd of oxen at Johannesburg and having brought them so far so well, Charles went on to Pretoria, now in English hands, and was handed a telegram from the commanding officer of his brother Durham. It is headed *Z.A. Republiek* but stamped *Army Telegraphs, 13.ix.00*:

Captain Plomer buried Nooitgedacht. All his things except

carbine and pony sent 8th Brigade depot Maritzburg. Wire instructions about horse, etc.

So perished from a Boer bullet a healthy, hearty, unthinking male, leaving 'horse, etc.' It was a blow from which Helen Plomer never recovered.

Charles now obtained his release from military service and left for England. His reason this time was not obscure. He had turned thirty, and it was marriage he had in mind. He made straight for Southwell.

7

Cathedral Town

The venerable John Henry Browne, archdeacon of Ely and rector of Cotgrave in Nottinghamshire, was certainly venerable in appearance. His figure was tall and erect, his brow calm and lofty; his features, though not aggressive, were as commanding as they were regular; he had a long upper lip which would have suited a judge; his mouth suggested self-control, laudable prejudice, and scholarly precision; and beneath his chin a pair of snowy bands hung like an accent over his flowing black gown. He was sometimes known as 'the Archduke'. This may have been because of his stately bearing or because by some of his descendants it was believed – and by others primly denied – that he was the natural son of a local peer, with whose family he was certainly on terms of close friendship. His learning and piety were conspicuous, and he might have made an impressive bishop, but at a time when the Tractarian movement was hatching he had already become a hard-shelled Evangelical. He was addicted to public controversy over peculiar dogmas like justification by faith, and I doubt if his printed writing would make thrilling reading. His archdiaconal 'charges' were praised in their time as models of their kind, but perhaps such things are no longer printed, read, or even composed.

The Archduke made a respectable marriage and fathered five sons and three daughters. His sons never went to school; he himself prepared three of them for Cambridge, where one became a second wrangler. Two of them went into the Church and were presented to country livings in the gift of the nobleman with whom their father was associated; two of them farmed land which he owned. One of these was George Browne of Maiden-well, the other was Edward, who lived at Cotgrave, and chose to call himself Waite-Browne. One of his nieces, whose father's names were Samuel Benjamin, said jokingly, 'I think I had better call myself Miss Benjamin-Browne.'

Edward Waite-Browne farmed his land well, lived in some style, and had the reputation, like so many Victorian sportsmen, of being the best shot in the county. In appearance he was rather a Dundreary, with heavy eyelids that gave him a look of languor, but he had a playful streak, and one of his daughters was astonished to see him, in middle age, tickling one of his usually dignified clergyman brothers, who was helplessly struggling on a sofa and kicking like a mule. He married twice, his second wife being his cousin, Edith Alethea Franklyn, by whom he had five children. Of the three who survived, one was my mother.

Edith Waite-Browne was the youngest daughter of George Franklyn, Conservative M.P. for Poole for a good many years in the mid-century, who once said in an election address that he 'would advocate in the widest sense education to all classes'. Warden and Master of the Guild of Merchant Venturers, he came on his father's side from a family of rich Bristol tobacco merchants ('Franklyn's Fine Shag, Good to the End' one used to see advertised in the west country), and on his mother's from a pleasant and prolific county family, the Wards of Ogbourne St Andrew in Wiltshire, whose sole claim to fame was, I believe, that in the seventeenth century they had simultaneously given Ossory a bishop and the University of Dublin a vice-chancellor.

George Franklyn had married, in 1825, Mary Arden, the seventeenth and last child of the Rev. John Henry Arden of Longcroft Hall in Staffordshire: when her eldest brother was a major of dragoons she was still in long clothes.

Shakespeare's mother's name was Mary Arden, and when he was born her surname had greater distinction than his. To produce such a son, must she not have been one of the half-dozen most remarkable women who ever lived? It is natural to wonder whether it was she who made him so conscious of the implications of rank, authority, and power. Her family was ancient enough to have regarded William the Conqueror as a parvenu. Experts regard the Ardens as one of only three English families able to prove their descent from pre-Conquest days; they counted among their ancestors King Athelstan, the half-mythical Guy of Warwick, and Alwyne, who was Earl of Warwick before the Conquest. Domesday Book showed his son in possession of forty-nine manors.

Their long tradition and lineage made the Ardens, it seems, inclined to regard those who had risen later to power and possessions as upstarts. For example, five hundred years later, Edward Arden, sheriff of the county, offended Leicester, Queen Elizabeth's favourite, by his independence. He was a faithful Catholic and when, later, his unbalanced son-in-law openly declared that he meant to kill the Queen, Edward with others was also arrested, tried, sentenced, and beheaded in the Tower.

It is not unusual for ancient families to develop peculiarities. With some of the Ardens this took the form of an indifference to the outside world which turned, if not to agoraphobia, at least to a tendency to hide themselves away from all but their intimates and servants. Centuries of comparative isolation, an inherited sense of sempiternal social status, and economic self-sufficiency perhaps had a cumulative effect. I was told when young of two Arden sisters who had all their ground-floor windows permanently shuttered, although their house stood in its own small park, because they thought they might be spied upon by strangers. Later I knew someone who went to call on an Arden and found him 'not at home', but on departing caught sight of a pair of big blue eyes peering out of the shrubbery. For such elusiveness there may have been more than one reason: visitors can be unwanted.

Having sixteen brothers and sisters, the Mary Arden who in 1825 married George Franklyn and became my great-grand-mother hardly grew up an isolationist. Besides, her mother, known as Madam Arden, had been sociable as well as fecund. As a young woman she used to hold on to a bed-post while two maids tugged at her stay-laces to give her a waist like a wasp. And it was remembered how, when going to a ball, her hair was dressed so high and so elaborately that she had to sit on the floor of the carriage to avoid disarranging it.

Mary Arden's daughter, Edith Franklyn, was quick-witted, warm-hearted, and had a lively mind, enlarged by reading and by travels abroad in various countries, including Hungary, a country her father particularly liked and where he had friends. Edward Waite-Browne died at no great age, and Edith found herself a widow, comfortably off but not rich. She chose to remain in Nottinghamshire, and settled at Southwell, in a roomy white Georgian house, to bring up her family.

Her two eldest sons, Guy and Harold, had died young; one had been called after Guy of Warwick, the other after King Harold. 'After all,' she was heard to say, 'on my mother's side we go back to the Heptarchy.' The survivors were Edythe, with this fancy archaic spelling; Hilda, whose other name was Alys, a quaint form of Alice; and Franklyn. The fashion for medieval or Anglo-Saxon names had gained momentum with Romantic revivalism. It had found a homely expression in the linguistic purism advocated by the poet William Barnes.

That learned and delightful man plumped for plain English, though whether he always penned it is a moot point: for example, of the degrees of comparison he observed that 'these pitch-marks offmark sundry things by their sundry suchnesses'. Barnes wanted us to call democracy *folkdom* and botany *wortlore*, a depilatory a *hairbane*, a concert a *gleemote*, an appendix a *hank-matter*, a butler a *winethane*, a perambulator a *push-wainling*, and a globule a *ballkin*. It is true that Mrs Waite-Browne did not boggle at benaming her afterkin after her forekin, but I never heard that she was ready to join Barnes, whose poetry she admired, in these Nordic daydreams of markworthy word-moulding.

In a small cathedral-town a hundred years ago society was rigidly graded, but the boundaries between castes were slowly, here and there, becoming blurred. At Longcroft, in Madam Arden's time, early in the last century (I was surprised to hear when young), the family doctor, when sent for, was expected to go round to the back door like any other tradesman. My grand-mother would not have expected this, but if she had occasion to write to her doctor, she wrote in the third person. My mother, until at least 1914, used the third person when writing to trades-people, but grew out of the habit.

Life in Southwell was mostly placid, at least on the surface. Gossip was one of its mainstays, and often had to do with the niceties of social status. Readers of the memoirs of minor royalties in the nineteenth century cannot fail to notice that in the stiffly regulated and stylised world they inhabited, the slightest deviation from routine was seized upon as a relief. Their sense of humour, lightly tinged with *Schadenfreude*, fed greedily upon trifling acci-dents, slight and unwitting breaches of ritual behaviour, or actions for which there appeared no precedent. Any real display of individuality created amazement, and an elopement or a suicide shook them like a cataclysm. Every mannerism of every clergy-man who set foot in the Minster was noticed and discussed, and at Easthorpe Lodge, where the Waite-Brownes lived, mimicked. There was for instance a canon who, while preaching, removed his false teeth, held them at arm's length, gave them a long and quizzical look, and then popped them into place again. And when on fine days a bishop's widow, herself the daughter of an earl, was seen seated, peacefully knitting, on her husband's grave, this habit was much discussed; by some it was thought to show with too much emphasis that in death she and her husband were not divided.

The precise relations between curates and spinsters, the gau-cheries of the former, the obsessions of the latter, were carefully followed. Indiscreet remarks travelled faster than they had been uttered, and if social relations were sometimes *en délicatesse*, sometimes *en froideur*, everybody knew why, or pretty soon invented a reason. Amorous advances, matrimonial prospects, conjugal irregularities, testamentary hopes or disappointments, the shortcomings or quaint sayings of servants or children, the absurd pretensions to gentility of successful tradespeople, other people's new clothes, the arrivals of strangers or visitors, unusual

Martin Folkes, P.R.S. (bust by Roubillac, at Wilton)

Charles and Edythe Plomer

sermons, clerical or family intrigues—such were the main interests of this community, and they were canvassed in an idiom nowhere more exactly caught than in the novels of Firbank.

Religion in Southwell meant more than assiduous church-going. It involved a strong sense of duty on the part of the well-to-do towards the 'deserving' poor. To be 'deserving' they had to be civil and conceal their delinquencies. If money was freely subscribed for the hoped-for conversion of the heathen in hot and distant countries, material comforts were often willingly provided for the locals who lacked them, unless of course they were judged to drink too much. Nor was culture absent. Among the clergy were men of literary culture and taste, including a kinsman of John Donne, and educated Southwell had a lively consciousness of its associations with Byron. My grandmother had been on terms of friendship with Elizabeth Pigot, one of Byron's earliest female friends, and so had heard recollections of him at first hand.

I have the impression that my grandmother was a little aloof, not through haughtiness, but by nature: not for nothing was she half an Arden. She had a household to order and children to bring up; she liked being alone with them, or simply alone; and although still a youngish woman she had settled down, in the fashion of the time, to widowhood. If others were observant, she missed nothing. Others might have a sense of the ridiculous; hers was intense. Others did some reading, she was well read; others had travelled, she had lived abroad in countries they knew little of. She did not give herself airs, but was conscious of what she might have called her position, and lived quietly, comfortably, and apparently contentedly, with apparently contented servants, and was as fond of her children as they were of her.

8

Kindred and Affinity

Mrs Waite-Browne did not send her daughters to school; they were taught by French and English governesses. They also had drawing lessons, dancing lessons, and music lessons, but no domestic science; I doubt if they could have boiled a kettle, still less an egg. If they wanted to buy anything they told their mother, and if she approved she ordered it and had it put down to her account. They accordingly had little idea of the value of money and knew nothing about business of any kind. Nor were they given the least rudiments of sex education. I have learned from other women of their generation that until their wedding nights they had only vague or fanciful ideas about what to expect.

Edythe and Hilda grew up in a society which nursed the illusion that its advantages and beliefs were secure and would continue indefinitely. Their religion had taught them that they had duties as well as advantages. Their conscientiousness and feminine capacity for self-sacrifice had been fortified by the Evangelical heritage, but had not in the least weakened their cheerfulness and high spirits; they had the good, easy, considerate manners that come from an instinctive knowledge of complex canons of behaviour; and in moments of crisis a sense of authority not only prompted their own actions but could make them give orders to others with perfect firmness.

Their lives had not been divided between going to church, teasing their governesses, and sharing jokes with their mother. As children at Cotgrave they had been taught to ride; as girls at Southwell they had been among the first to take to bicycles, and had been thought 'fast' for doing so. Edythe wielded a resourceful racquet at tennis, and made many a curate run like a hare after a maliciously placed ball.

Having reached an age of some discretion, Edythe and her brother Franklyn were allowed to go off on a visit to France. In the Waite-Browne family, as in many others, it was customary to speak French before the servants when anything was being discussed which was thought unsuitable for them to hear. This habit, also prevalent among the upper class in Russia, seems a breach of good manners, because a loyal servant might suppose himself or herself to be the topic of conversation and so feel ill at ease, or in any case not trusted. The brother and sister had the habit of quick and critical observation and of describing or discussing people candidly. Having crossed the Channel they suddenly discovered that they were still talking French so that those near them should not understand. Had their French accent been like that usually achieved by the English they would have been as safe as if they had been talking Choctaw, but they had been properly taught, so quickly switched to English.

Mrs Waite-Browne, contented with her comfortable, reclusive life at Southwell and having when young seen something of the *beau monde* in London and abroad, made little effort to let it be seen by her daughters, nor did she trouble to present them, as she had been presented, at Court. But they did go and stay with relations in London during the season and got carried off to Henley or Ranelagh or dances or garden parties, managing so well to retain their fresh country complexions that one of their aunts suspected them of make-up, not then 'The Thing'. 'My dear,' she untruthfully told an acquaintance, 'they keep *pink stuff* in a saucer on their dressing tables.'

Another aunt, Agatha, had married Charles James Augustus Rumbold, a genial soul with a house in Sussex Square at Brighton, where Edythe used to go and stay with them. She rightly thought them eccentric. Uncle Charles had a grand piano in his bedroom, Aunt Agatha wore her clothes until they were in rags, to which she fastened impressive diamond ornaments, and the beautiful drawing-room was shrouded in dust-sheets and never used. The

Brighton air agreed very well with Uncle Charles and quickened the blood of a nabob which ran in his veins. With Edythe facing him, he would drive along the front in an open carriage, trolling at the top of his voice and with gusto some operatic aria or a popular song of the moment, to the amusement of passers-by. 'Won't you take a cup of cawfee, my dear creature?' was a remembered saying of his, and he left behind him an aura of benevolence. His nephew told me that Uncle Charles used secretly to go and buy chickens and wine and take them himself to people he thought poor and ill. He started a campaign for 'kneelers for charwomen'; he hated to see them kneeling on cold stone to scrub steps. He supplied or got the municipality to supply spectacles for the old road-menders who endangered their sight when knapping flints. A Dickensian character, a sort of Cheeryble, whose soft-heartedness obliged his wife to watch his extravagances.

In Victorian times there was often a very strong sense of kinship and a cult of kinship. See, for example, that name-dropping autobiographer, Augustus Hare. A great many people carried in their heads a detailed who's-who not only of their antecedents and near relations but of their distant collaterals and connexions. In all classes, from the aristocracy to the peasantry, a whole group of families would tend to intermarry and overlap. This point may be illustrated by the following bewildering paragraph, drawn from records of the families of Plomer, Browne, Arden, Franklyn, Ward, Blackden, and Allenby.

Edythe Waite-Browne's father and mother were second cousins. Her father's sister married one of his wife's brothers. Another sister married her first cousin. So did one of his nephews. Two of his nieces married two brothers, themselves the children of first cousins. The son of one of these unions married his first cousin, and their daughter married my brother, who was her third cousin. Edythe Waite-Browne's stepsister married the nephew of her aunt by marriage, and one of my great-uncles married the aunt of his sister-in-law's brother's wife, whose nephew later married that brother's first cousin twice removed — but enough!

It seems that this semi-incestuous intermarriage and inbreeding (for which there is a notable precedent in the Ptolemy family) was largely the work of that old matchmaker, propinquity. So it was too among villagers and slum-dwellers, who were often interrelated in such a way as to defy elucidation, flout the law, and make mincemeat of the tables of kindred and affinity: also, people were far less mobile in those days. Among the 'respectable' classes it may have been a symptom of solidarity in a world already threatened and increasingly controlled by near-fortunes deriving from the industrial revolution still in progress, and by the increasing numbers, prosperity, and influence of the smaller urban bourgeoisie.

At Easthorpe Lodge there was a lively awareness of this inter-mingling of families, and with it a perhaps undue respect for class distinctions. Its occupants spoke quite naturally of persons of their own class marrying 'well' or 'beneath' themselves, but never of marrying 'above' them, so probably that was hardly considered possible. If these inter-related families had a respect, possibly excessive, for people's origins and manners — so long as these conformed with their own — one cannot blame birds of a feather for flocking together. They belonged to a stratum which regarded itself, with some reason, as 'the backbone of England', since it had produced innumerable men and women, dutiful, able, and admirable in many walks of life.

A formal society aims at producing types, but individuality will out. Mrs Waite-Browne, outwardly conventional enough, was strongly individual, with a marked indifference to public opinion. Among her three children her aesthetic sense came out strongest in her son Franklyn, who had linguistic gifts as well as a talent for painting: in his old age he taught Russian to a Spaniard. He went through the routine of preparatory school, Repton and Cam-bridge, and emerged with an ironical wit and no signs of ambition: a double strain of Arden blood was unlikely to animate the sort of person who thinks in terms of 'getting on'. He did not belong to that large majority whom Sydney Smith called the Sheep-walkers, 'those who never deviate from the beaten track, who think as their fathers have thought since the Flood, who start from a new idea as they would from guilt.' His sister Edythe paid the price and enjoyed the advantages of being more tuned up and more imaginative than the large majority. Her character was formed, but she had developed no strong bent, and apparently saw Charles Plomer as a deliverer.

Mrs Waite-Browne had expected her children to marry 'well', and although she was quite fond of Charles she did not show any strong craving to see him married to her elder daughter. He was decently bred and seemed kind-hearted but had no 'position', no money, and no apparent prospects, and had led an odd roving life in 'the Colonies', which she thought, quite rightly, physically and socially unsuitable for Edythe; but she was not going to thwart them if they thought they were going to be happy.

Edythe and Charles had known each other since childhood; her Uncle George had married his Aunt Kitty; he had obviously set his heart on marrying Edythe and had been constant in his attach-ment to her. It is easy to understand his wish to carry off with him to his strange new world a living representative of his familiar old world, and one who might compensate him for the want of loving kindness in his childhood. As for Edythe, she had refused other offers of marriage, I suppose out of loyalty to Charles. She was a young woman of spirit—of more spirit than physical toughness—and marriage to him offered a complete escape from the caged routine of life in a small cathedral town. No doubt Africa seemed to offer adventure and the possibility of happiness, though she can have known nothing about it except what he had told her. Did nobody warn her of her rashness?

9

Tropical Outpost

Charles Plomer and Edythe Waite-Browne were married in London in June 1901. The old colonel was delighted with the marriage, having feared that Charles might take to himself some uncouth colonial girl. He apologised for only giving his son five hundred pounds as a wedding present: it would have been more, he said, if he had been luckier with his investments.

The wedding was conducted by a cousin of Edythe's, Edmund Franklyn, who was chaplain at the Savoy Chapel. Some glossy magazine reported that it was a very quiet wedding, owing to a family bereavement — the death, in fact, of Uncle George at Maidenwell. Edythe wore 'her travelling gown of pale fawn voile with a bolero and smart collar of Brussels lace', and a hat with pink and red roses. She was attended by her sister Hilda in 'white net muslin over turquoise silk', topped with 'a black picture-hat'.

After a honeymoon at Brighton they sailed for Africa, accompanied by a large quantity of furniture, some of it wedding presents. Nobody seems to have reminded Charles that there was still a war on, and when they arrived at the Cape they were told that the railway line to Pretoria had been cut in many places by guerrillas, and that they would have a better chance of reaching their destination by way of Natal. Delayed by storms, they had a rough sea-passage to Durban. General William Franklyn, a cousin who was 'something in the War Office' and later military secretary to Kitchener, had given them an official letter asking that they should be allowed through to Pretoria as soon as possible, but as the journey had no military usefulness it was not yet

71

permitted. They thought it would be prudent to move from the best hotel to a boarding-house. Here, at their first meal, a young man sat down opposite Edythe, removed the yellow kid gloves he was wearing, and began cleaning his nails with a penknife. If this was a specimen of colonial manners, she thought, they were quite distant from civilisation.

Durban was crowded with refugees from the Transvaal and the Orange Free State, many of whom were as anxious as Charles to return there and had more to return to. He was jobless, and had to think about money. His furniture, on which he was having to pay, as weeks went by, exorbitant wartime charges for storage, was, for want of warehouse room, lying in the open covered with tarpaulins. He was assured that there would be no hope of getting it to Pretoria until the war was over, so he and Edythe decided to sell it, were sad to part with it, and got little for it. Then Edythe, bravely trying to adapt herself to her new surroundings and prospects, was suddenly taken ill and removed to a nursing home for an operation. She always remembered gratefully how the doctor considerately sent his carriage to take her out for drives when she began to convalesce. He was a Dr Campbell, who had lately become the father of the poet-to-be Roy Campbell.

Her husband now received the long-delayed permission to travel to Pretoria. As soon as the train had passed Ladysmith new graves were to be seen at each station, and the journey hardly had the charm of a prolonged honeymoon. Along the line bloated, decomposing carcasses of horses and cattle, stinking and glittering and seething with flies and maggots under the burning sun, were varied by wrecks of trains, twisted rails, and war debris, and by fortified blockhouses festooned with barbed wire and still guarded by sweating, scarlet-faced tommies whose khaki uniforms, intended to blend with the biscuit-coloured landscape vibrating round them in the heat, contrasted with the blue distances.

When the train came to a stop, by day the air was loud with cicadas trilling like burglar-alarms, but at sunset there was an uncanny silence. A hot puff of wind would rustle the dry leaves of

a few eucalyptus trees near the line, and voices on a lonely platform were magnified by the stillness of the surrounding emptiness
of darkening veld and rocky hills which had been in the news but
had no history. The grassy plains which not very long before had
been alive with immense herds of antelopes and with bigger game
were now colonised, at great intervals, with clusters of whitewashed wooden crosses, far above which the stars, improbably
brilliant and numerous, flashed their perpetual indifference.

At Pretoria the newly arrived couple managed to find and
furnish a house. The war had become a process of 'mopping up'
guerrilla bands here and there, and plans were already being made
to administer the conquered country. Charles obtained a minor
post in the Treasury, and Edythe taught herself to run a house
under strange conditions and a war economy. Englishwomen in
Pretoria just then were a rarity, and she was sought after by officers
of the garrison, who included relations and acquaintances. She
entertained them as well as she could, and all seemed to be going
well when she was knocked flat by a combination of malaria,
dysentery, and peritonitis. It nearly killed her, and the doctor told
Charles that if he wished her to live she must return to England.
Hardly fit to travel, off she went with a special pass, in a train
preceded by an armoured train. A gallant captain handed her his
field-glasses from time to time so that she might watch incidents
of guerrilla warfare, but that was not her idea of enjoyment. So
far South Africa had offered her war, heat, dust, ill-health,
domestic difficulties and crises, and anxieties about the present and
the future.

Without his wife, Charles had to wind up the household she
had struggled to establish. With the expenses of doctors and
nurses and her passage to England, and with food still at exorbitant prices, the small capital on which he had married had almost
melted away. But his knowledge of the country made him em-
ployable. A friend of his brother William had just been appointed
resident magistrate of the Zoutpansberg district of the northern
Transvaal. He now applied for Charles's services as local secretary
of the Repatriation Commission. This had been set up to restore

3*

Afrikaner prisoners of war to their farms, and to allow them such material aid as would enable them to resume their way of life.

The job was perfect for him: it made him free to wander again. He spent six months touring the region in a Cape cart drawn by six mules, checking the often grossly exaggerated claims put in by the freed prisoners. This gave him a detailed knowledge of a vast tract of country in many parts of which no white man had ever before set foot; he enjoyed some excellent shooting; and when his task was done received special commendation for his thoroughness. But he had a grievance. While the English administration, as he put it years later, 'were pouring out thousands upon thousands of pounds to the Dutch as a reward for fighting against England', he was given no compensation for the loss of some property in Pretoria which had been looted, in the presence of reliable witnesses, by English soldiers.

As a reward for his useful work with the Repatriation Commission he was offered, and accepted, a post at Pietersburg in the Department of Native Affairs. As a married man, he needed a steady job, and I suppose the news was received with some relief at Southwell.

Pietersburg, called after General Piet Joubert of Majuba fame, was then a small pioneer village: it is now a town of some importance. In those days it was the terminus of the railway; now it has an airfield. It was no health resort, and the salaries of civil servants were augmented by a 'fever allowance'. There was for the time being a British garrison, which seems to have had little to do. There were dances and dinners, picnics and tennis tournaments, gymkhanas and polo, puns and practical jokes, charades and drawing-room ballads. Charles obtained and did up a small house. Like all the others it had a roof of corrugated iron, which intensified the heat. There were no electric fans or refrigerators.

Early in 1903 he was rejoined by Edythe, who can hardly have been enraptured by the prospect of returning to South Africa. Alternating garrison gaieties with the struggle of running an ill-equipped house with amiable but untrained African servants, who were ignorant of the white man's needs and habits, so much more elaborate than their own, in due course she found herself pregnant.

So it was in 1903 (when men were just at last beginning to fly, though in contraptions more like birdcages than birds) that I was brought into the world. My entry was not well managed. Pietersburg was an out-of-the-way birthplace, and its amenities did not then include the deftest of obstetricians. Much went wrong. My father was told it was unlikely that either mother or child would survive, but our vitality had been underestimated. It is true that the child, yelling blue murder for months on end, suffered in turn, or simultaneously, from many of the disorders of infancy. Maternal care and perhaps its own obstinacy kept it going, but before it was a year old medical opinion said it was urgent that the noisy malarial brat should be taken away to England to rally its meagre forces. So for the second time my mother set out on the long journey by rail to the Cape and the 6000-mile sea voyage.

It would have been understandable if my father had said to himself that if only he had married some hardy, leathery, local girl these recurrent complications, separations, and expenses need never have happened. He had interesting and responsible work to do. This included the delimiting of land to be set aside as native reserves, and involved much travelling and consultation with the Africans themselves. They had already learnt that subjection to the white man had to be paid for in taxes — two pounds a head as poll tax, two pounds for each extra wife, ten shillings for a dog, and so on. The taxes were payable in gold to the district commissioners, and once a month my father went out to collect the proceeds. He travelled in a mule-cart escorted by mounted police, and sometimes carried as much as £40,000 in sovereigns, which in those days was a lot of money. At one time three highwaymen were known to be planning a hold-up and an escape with the loot over the border to Portuguese East Africa, but they were forestalled.

In June 1905 my mother returned with me to Pietersburg. We were much improved, and it was no doubt expected that life would now go along smoothly enough. Not at all; my father was now prostrated by malaria to such an extent that he was granted six months' leave on full pay. This time the whole family left for England. On my grandmother's daisied lawn at Southwell and on the sands at Scarborough we drank the English air until it was time to go back. We had become habitual migrants: before I was two my mileage had exceeded that of the circumference of the earth.

Back once more in the Transvaal my father and Gideon Murray (later Lord Elibank), as itinerant magistrates and tax-gatherers, used to traverse an immense area between the Dwars and Limpopo rivers, travelling in a covered wagon drawn by eighteen donkeys and accompanied by eighteen mounted policemen, twelve black and six white. When the day's work was over, they used to amuse themselves by shooting bush-buck or water-buck, guinea-fowl or Namaqualand partridges, to feed this large party.

In remote places they came across some remarkable white men living independent of their own kind, of apartheid, and sometimes of the law. An able-bodied seaman, who had deserted from one of Her Majesty's ships at the Cape in the 1860s, had taken a wife locally and worked his way northwards, trading and hunting, and at last acquired a large tract of land. Now, forty years later, he derived a comfortable income in the form of rents paid by African tenants for land where their forefathers had ranged freely before the coming of the white man. They were at least luckier than some of their North American Indian contemporaries.

Then there was another Englishman, whom we will call Fitzgilbert because I have forgotten his name, and who had, as they used to say, 'gone native'. His brother was at this time in command of a 'crack' regiment in England, but he himself had been living in the wilds with a black mistress. By her he had had two sons, who were happily named Very Nice and Very Good, and he was evidently very fond of them.

Although he was living in the first decade of the present century he had never seen a bicycle, a telephone, or a sewing machine, or felt any need for such things. His manners were polished, but he was not the sort of exile from civilisation who couldn't eat in the evening without wearing a dinner jacket. His usual dress was pyjamas, a handsome Japanese silk kimono, and a pith helmet. He was hospitable, and whenever my father and Gideon Murray turned up he had to be restrained from having an ox slaughtered in their honour.

'It was pathetic,' said my father, 'to see how pleased Fitzgilbert was to be able to talk to someone of his own race and class and in his own tongue.'

Perhaps their visits and their romantic tales of bicycles and telephones unsettled him. Three years later he suddenly left for England, where he married a widow and settled in Devonshire, where he may or may not have found her and the climate very nice and very good. Before leaving the Transvaal he had a legal document drawn up and deposited with the nearest magistrate. This was a deed of gift to his ex-mistress of his land, huts, livestock (including 300 head of fine cattle), and chattels, besides a provision for the education at a mission school of Very Nice Fitzgilbert and Very Good Fitzgilbert.

Mission stations were among my father's stopping-places, and at that of Waldezia he and Murray used, while taking tea on the verandah with the missionary and his wife, to put down their cups or thin bread-and-butter and take shots at crocodiles in the Levubu river a hundred feet below. Here and there they called at trading stations, usually known as 'Kaffir stores', like the ones where my father had worked briefly in his wandering days. One was kept by a duke's nephew, another by the son of a Lord Chief Justice of England, another by two educated homosexual Greeks, another by a family with a well-known English name who could not speak a word of English and were reputed to descend from a survivor of the loss of the *Birkenhead*. All these people were too scattered and isolated to constitute a society, but they were a social phenomenon of the place and time, and it seems a pity that there was no novelist about to give it an imaginative form.

Other characters included a pushing little man, a good linguist, who managed to get himself appointed to a local magistracy. In order to establish his authority he summoned the local African chiefs to an *indaba*, or council, and announced that he wished to be

known as 'The Great Lion'. Africans are very good at giving
white men nicknames. They generally have an acute sense of
character, and from this time they always alluded to the man as
'The Little Calf'. (My father, because of his restless energy, was
called 'Quick-as-Lightning'.)

Then there was a very nineteenth-century oddity called Bill
Eagle. He was a half-bred American Indian whose one ambition
was to shoot a lion. When he did succeed in shooting one he only
wounded it, and in a rage it clawed him off his horse by the thigh.
On the ground he thrust his hand into its jaws and seized and
twisted its tongue. The lion shook him as a dog shakes a rat, but
he did not let go, and the lion, nearly choked, suddenly got free
and bolted into the bush. Bill Eagle was too badly mauled to
recover, and it fell to my father to read the burial service over
him.

My father was now appointed to act as resident magistrate at
Louis Trichardt, an outlandish and unhealthy spot at the foot of
the Zoutpansberg mountains, well inside the tropics and highly
malarial. By this time my brother John had enlarged the family.
He had been born at Pietersburg in 1907, and in spite of the attentions of a bibulous midwife he burst into the world with all the
thrusting health and cheerfulness I had lacked. It was thought that
he might take after 'poor Uncle Durham, who was killed in the
war'.

It is strange that my father should have arranged to take his
wife and two young children with him to such a place. A civil
servant goes where he is told, and naturally wants his family with
him. He was not yet forty, very active and enterprising, and his
roving, open-air life had greatly improved his health, but I doubt
if he allowed for the hazards. I cannot think that my mother was
enthusiastic, but her sense of loyalty would have persuaded her
that her place was with her husband.

Louis Trichardt was about eighty miles from Pietersburg.
There was no railway, and there were no made-up roads. This was
before the age of the automobile, and the only way to get there
was by trundling ox-wagon through the blazing wilderness, like

voortrekkers. I was nearly four, and can remember something of the journey, which seemed unending.

Louis Trichardt took its name from the commandant of a number of burghers, alleged to have been tiresome, lazy, or importunate men banished by Kruger to found a settlement there. At the time of our arrival the so-called township consisted mostly of a few derelict or ruined houses. Most of the inhabitants had been scattered or eliminated by malaria or by the Magato and South African wars. The surrounding district was romantic in a Rider Haggardish way. Diamonds and emeralds, copper and gold were to be found, and although game, with the destructive advance of the white man, was getting scarcer, there were still, besides lions, not a few giraffes and hippopotami, besides wilde-beeste, eland, sable, and tsesebe. In the mountains, not easily accessible, was a wonderful lake with weird surroundings and no apparent outlet. It was covered with wild-fowl of many kinds. They were seldom disturbed, because it was shunned by the Africans, who believed it bewitched. It was said to have been formerly the scene of human sacrifices.

African life was not yet completely spoiled. At times there were spectacular primitive dances *en masse*, carried out with great vigour and sexual posturing, to the vibrant music of drums and giant xylophones. 'Can the white people dance like mine?' a local chief asked of a visiting white official. He received an evasive reply, with an allusion to splendid balls given in the palace of the Great White Queen, whom he was perhaps left imagining in the performance, almost nude, of a frantic and provocative *pas seul* in the presence of her loyal and enthusiastic subjects.

The only dwelling available for my father and his family was primitive and barely habitable. It consisted of three rooms with walls of *pisé de terre*, faced and roofed with corrugated iron. The floors were of stamped clay. There was some sort of wood-burn-ing stove, no bathroom, no water laid on, and an earth-closet at a distance which gave shelter to spiders, hornets and lizards. The previous occupant had fenced off an acre or so from the open veld and had tried to make some sort of a garden, for which the land was well suited, as the soil was fertile and a stream flowed through it. He had planted a few cypresses and indigenous trees, and there was a flourishing banana grove.

Autobiographers who enlarge at length upon their trivial recollections of infancy are to be shunned like lakes bewitched, but the first episode or vision of a man's surroundings to stick in his memory is often a strong clue to his future character. This was true of my father, my mother, and myself. (Skip the next page or two, reader, if you are allergic to this sort of thing.)

My father's first memory was of a fit of rage. He was playing when very small with his brother Durham in Kensington Gardens, near the water-garden at Lancaster Gate. Durham picked up a bottle that was lying on the grass, threw it at him, and hit him on the nose—whereupon Charles flew at him in a blind fury but somehow caught a front tooth on a button of Durham's coat, and the tooth was wrenched from its socket.

My mother's first memory was of Cotgrave. No more than four or five years old, she was at luncheon with her governess. Her parents being away from home, the footman who was waiting on them had not troubled to wear his livery. The child instantly noticed this and ordered him to go and put it on. There spoke the being who believed all her life long in custom and ceremony—in which alone, according to Yeats, are innocence and beauty born.

As for me, my first memory of any significance is of a brilliant spring morning at Louis Trichardt. It had rained in the night, but now the sky was cloudless and the world of a celestial freshness and fragrance, exhaled by the sparkling green veld and wafted in the air. I strayed out of the garden, and standing on the bank of the stream suddenly saw on the opposite bank, perhaps twelve feet away, two large birds, a kind of wild duck perhaps. One was resting on the ground; the other stood beside it. Their plumage gleamed like many-coloured enamel in the sun against a background of reeds, their eyes glinted like jewels, and they showed no sign of alarm, but watched me as I watched them. My feeling was partly one of delighted discovery, like that of an ornithologist discovering a new species, partly of pure delight, both heightened into a kind of ecstasy, as of mutual understanding and joy, as if the birds and I knew that we were part of the same life and that life was splendid.

After this there came a rush of sensuous experience of a growing and a shining world which could be touched and heard and smelt and tasted as well as seen – the forms and textures of plants, the rasping leaves of the Cape gooseberry; the clear yellow flowers and hairy swollen pods of a nameless shrub; the long white thorns like steel nails that stuck out everywhere from the thorn trees; the intense perfumes of the small aromatic flowers of the veld; the metallic dinning of the cicadas at midday and the cool colloquies of doves in the afternoon. Then there were insects – the multitudes of flying ants that came fluttering and flickering out after rain, shedding their talc-like wings, which they left thickly littered upon the moist earth; the flexible, hard-shelled, varnished millipedes which curled up when touched; the striped hornets; the tarantulas that waited, motionless as ornaments, on a white-washed wall.

At night one could hear lions roaring far off, or the nearer howling of jackals, more sad and wonderful than frightening, or the loud choruses of frogs never tired of congratulating the full moon on its brilliance and always using the same formula:

FIRST FROG: *Le roi*
SECOND FROG: *est allé.*
THIRD FROG: *Et où? et où?*
ALL: *A Cognac, à Cognac, à Cognac*

When the veld, in a very dry season, caught fire one night, the flames roared and crackled all round the house, mounting higher and higher in raging arabesques, while our servants tried to fend them off with branches: then suddenly a man on horseback, who had come to see if we were all right, burst magically through the curtains of flame.

At night, almost every night, could be heard the far-off singing of Africans, monotonous, melancholy, strangely stirring. With the touch of warm brown skins I was already familiar. Maud Dgami was my first and faithful African nursemaid, and I remember the house-boys, their gentle and easy movements, their white teeth and their clean loose clothes smelling of soap and cotton, the pink palms of their hands, their horny feet; and how once, when the bridge over the stream had been swept away after a cloud-burst, they helped my father to mend it. I see him now, with the turbulent muddy water swirling round his white thighs and their dark brown thighs, and their naked arms lifting great stones into place, all under a blue-black sky, while on the bank flowering pinks were shaking in the rain-fresh wind.

My laughing brother John, now more than a year old, continued as healthy as I had been ailing and querulous. He was too good to last. My father was far away on a tax-collecting journey when a message reached him that John was dangerously ill. Riding night and day for thirty-six hours, he arrived to find my mother and a doctor (who had also been summoned from a great distance) exhausted with a long struggle to save the life of John, who was in the throes of diphtheria and malarial fever.

He made my mother lie down while he watched by the child's bed. I lay by her side. I listened to her weeping as I watched through the open window the light of a full moon glittering on the flowing stream. Just before dawn my father saw the child grow restless, and roused the doctor, who decided that the only hope was to attempt a tracheotomy. My mother held the child in her arms while the doctor cut its throat, but John was dead before he even had time to insert a tube.

Louis Trichardt could not provide so common a necessity as a coffin, and old packing-cases had to be knocked together to make one. It was lined with cheap velveteen bought from the local store kept by an Indian. Nor was there a cemetery. A plot of ground had once been surveyed for the purpose but never enclosed. My parents later had John's grave consecrated and put up a memorial stone of white marble, on which lizards used to sun themselves.

To go on living in that place cannot have been easy for my mother. The child's death caused her (as she told me long after) to question for the first time the benevolence, if not the existence, of the God in whom she had been taught to believe, and to whom she had prayed, and taught me to pray, every day.

Fearing some equally sudden threat to the lives of his wife and surviving child, my father sent them 'home'. It was my third voyage to England. After we had gone he was very ill with a tropical disease, and was advised to follow us, being granted six months' leave for the purpose. For us that was the last of Louis Trichardt, but our double lives, divided between England and Africa, had a long way to go.

10

Edwardian Interlude

By the time we reached England, Helen Plomer, my father's mother, was dead. Her last years had not been happy. Her favourite child was dead, she had estranged herself from her only daughter, and was anyway a woman who could not easily bear to grow old. Had she any old friend, besides her husband, to complain to? I don't know.

After her death the colonel had moved to a flat in Kensington. Nearly everybody we knew lived in a house; the idea of living in a flat seemed strangely modern and independent. On fine afternoons he might have been seen walking along Kensington Gore, in a top hat and a black, beaver-lined coat with an astrakhan collar, on his daily constitutional to the United Services Club. To his old friends he complained about symptoms of national decline, particularly Lloyd George. To my father he apologised, because (he reminded him) having been in the past ill-advised about his investments he would not be able to leave his two surviving sons anything like so well off as he had hoped.

Taken to lunch with him one day I insisted afterwards, against my mother's advice, on tasting black coffee with brandy in it. I promptly spat it out again, much to the amusement of the old man. He regarded me as his 'only' grandchild, never having seen the children of my Aunt Laura, whom he had disowned. Did he ever regret this? I don't know. Without his knowledge, my father was on affectionate brotherly terms with her and had also brought about a reconciliation between her and their brother William, who had for a time followed his father's example of complete aloofness.

84

My grandfather insisted that Charles should consult Sir Patrick Manson, the authority on tropical medicine. Manson, after treating him successfully, said he must on no account return to a fever district, and wrote accordingly to the Native Affairs Department in Pretoria. They obligingly posted him to Johannesburg. Even so, my grandfather said, it would be best to leave me in England.

From London we went to stay with my mother's mother, who had left Southwell for Buxton. Between her and me there was an instinctive understanding. I thought her wise and charming and was always anxious to please her. Winter in bleak Buxton toned my father up, and in the spring we went to stay at Longcroft Hall in Staffordshire, the ancient home of the Ardens, which had now passed to my cousin Alwyne Franklyn, who had been a military attaché or observer with Kuropatkin in the Russo-Japanese War. The house was architecturally unremarkable, but had atmosphere. It had formerly been surrounded by a moat, but this was filled up in the eighteenth century after one of Madam Arden's sons had been drowned in it. Even without the moat, the place seemed like a quiet and remote island, a breeding-place for isolationists – but the doctor no longer went to the back door.

For some unknown reason we went on to Matlock Bath, where I slept in a heavily curtained four-poster in a dark bedroom which must have been unaltered since the middle of the eighteenth century. I was enchanted with the petrifying wells full of strange encrusted objects – vases and walking sticks, busts and birds' nests – and rode enthusiastically on a switchback railway in charge of my governess, splendidly named Miss de Montmorency. I had doubts about her sex, because the often-uttered formula 'Miss de Montmorency' reached my ear as 'Mr Montmorency'.

My mother's sister, my Aunt Hilda, had married a schoolmaster, Telford Hayman, the son of a clergyman and the grandson of Dr Brewer, compiler of the *Dictionary of Phrase and Fable*. He kept a successful preparatory school at Spondon House, near Derby. I was left with him and my aunt when my parents returned to Africa, and was happy there. Spondon, now I believe highly industrialised, was then a quiet country village. As I was only five I was too young to join in lessons and games with the other boys, and so found myself in one of those anomalous, marginal situations which have recurred all through my life.

My early impressions of life and landscape may have been especially vivid because the land was strange to my blood; I was coming to consciousness in a world unfamiliar to it. England was just as vivid because it was in the marrow of my bones. My senses recognised what touched them, as a mirror recognises a face. 'You must have the bird in your heart,' said John Burroughs, 'before you can find it in the bush.'

The shapes of trees in Locks Park, the smell of ferns and ground-ivy near the hermit's cave in Dale Abbey, the cave itself, were as real and fresh as food or drink. I dreamily gazed at the summer skies, with their light clouds continually changing shape; through heavily curtained windows I looked out at the fog and the snow, and at those who plodded through them for a living; at lawns netted over with dew and daisies; at borders sumptuous with carmine peonies. I wandered between low hedges of sun-warmed, wholesome-smelling box and under lofty thickets of ripple-fruited yews, inside which were caves of darkness, full of dead twigs furred and powdered with black dust. I noticed the first snowdrops, the frail filigree of skeleton leaves, the ivy on the wall. I loved the richness of early summer, ditches full of mares' tails and ragged robins, the meadows waving with rusty sorrel and silky fescue, quaking grass and corn-rattle, and I touched the rosy heads of clover and the hard-faced, faintly fetid moon-daisies. On autumn mornings, after a blustery night, yellow leaves had been pressed so flat on the asphalt pavements that they seemed to have been painted on them, and varnished horse-chestnuts lay thick on the ground, waiting to be picked up.

How good the food tasted — the cup of milk, the bread and butter, apple dumplings, the savoury sausages and pork-pies of Derbyshire. As for children's parties, in the Midlands in Edwardian days they were lavish with whipped cream, and black cakes separated from white icing by thick bands of marzipan, and trifles full of cherries, almonds, and angelica, and ruby and emerald jellies, and elaborate decorations and fancy dresses. Under the hoarse, incandescent gas-mantles the young girls used to wear dresses of *broderie anglaise* with wide, coloured sashes tied in a big bow at the back, and neat dancing-slippers, and together with the boys in sailor suits (I wore one myself) gazed spellbound at the conjuror or the Punch and Judy show provided for the occasion.

I am grateful to my aunt for having taught me to collect, name, press, and mount wild flowers, which helped to make me observant and fostered a love of knowledge and a love of order. Like most children I enjoyed drawing and painting, but had no taste for mechanical things and had already taken against cricket, which seemed to make an irksome appeal to duty and gave me no pleasure. By some of its addicts, it seemed to me later, it had been inflated from a rustic game into 'the done Thing' and even into a kind of mystic-patriotic cult bound up with notions of English racial superiority. My Uncle Telford was a devotee. He supported his trousers round the waist with a silk scarf in the M.C.C. colours and evidently thought the game important in a boy's education. We were not drawn to one another. He did not understand me and I think I underestimated him. In later life I heard him spoken of with admiration as a teacher of exceptional ability.

In the hall at Spondon House lay an embellishment not uncommon in those days, the skin of a polar bear dressed and mounted on scarlet baize with scalloped edges, to serve as a rug. The head had been realistically preserved, with glass eyes which seemed to express some fixed idea, and open jaws showing a fine set of fangs protruding from dry scarlet gums. One summer's morning I was lying on my back in the pleasant white fur, with my head resting on the back of the polar bear's head, when my aunt, who happened to be passing and was carrying a large armful of flowers from the garden to be arranged in vases, stopped to talk to me. She asked me if I knew what I wanted to be when I grew up. A little earlier it was thought that I wanted to be an engine-driver, but now, without the least hesitation, I said, 'Yes, I'm going to be an artist.'

My aunt recoiled as if stung by some harmful insect, and cast her eyes up dramatically with a look of horror.

'Good heavens! I hope *not*!'

I was much puzzled. I had apparently said something outrageous; but what, I thought, could be better than to be an artist? Perhaps I was thinking of my Uncle Franklyn, who painted. Perhaps my aunt was thinking of him too. She was fond of her only brother, but almost certainly thought that his unworldly, unambitious way of life was too 'Bohemian' and ineffectual, and that one such person in a family was enough. My Uncle Telford, whatever his virtues, was the opposite of an aesthete, and she had perhaps been influenced by her husband's hearty, cricketing attitude to life, which was prevalent, particularly among schoolmasters, in the heyday of Edwardian philistinism and in a most conventional environment.

When I said I wanted to be an artist I evidently knew my own mind. I had already entered upon the artist's double life. Taken to church or to watch a cricket-match I did not conform. One Sunday, while a hymn was being sung in church, my aunt noticed that although I was singing lustily I was not singing the words of the hymn. She told me long afterwards that, on stooping to listen, she had discovered that I was singing an improvisation of my own 'all about the flowers'.

The church was always full and in the tedious intervals between the hymns I used to study the members of the congregation, their looks, their mannerisms, and their clothes. As it was only a few years after the death of Queen Victoria old women who had more or less modelled themselves upon her would still wear small black bonnets, ornamented with black lace and jet beads and perhaps with a small bunch of artificial violets, or sometimes having wide black ribbons tied in a bow or dangling over the neat, severe buns into which their steely hair had been moulded. Over their shoulders they would wear a short cape, encrusted with black braid, or bugles, or jet, and this already outmoded style gave them the look of ancient survivors devoted to past customs. Younger women might have artificial cherries or marguerites or decorative fur or feathers in their hats, and the younger men tended to wear very high, stiffly starched collars, which were overlapped by the lobes of their ears.

My first visit to a theatre—a production of Maeterlinck's *Blue Bird*—spirited me away into a vivid dream-world which seemed to embody truths concealed by the realities of everyday life: it seemed more important and more beautiful than cricket or arithmetic. In everyday life I began to perceive social and political distinctions. It became quite clear that the world was largely populated by beings called the lower or working classes and that they were a race apart. In towns they lived in long rows of small houses joined together, in the country in cottages sometimes joined in pairs, sometimes separate. Driving into Derby, one saw that while some of their dwellings had tiny gardens in front, with cinder paths, others had none. When they were not 'the poorest of the poor' living in slums, they seemed to take care of appearances. Doorsteps were kept scrubbed and whitened, lace curtains hung formally in parlour windows, and under the June sun little girls, in shady hats and pinafores, and little boys in caps, celluloid collars, made-up bow ties, shoddy Norfolk jackets and knicker-bockers, black stockings and heavy, laced-up boots, would rush hopefully over melting asphalt, in a strong smell from the gas-works, past a traction engine with polished brass fittings, past a brewer's dray drawn by gigantic, hairy-hoofed cart-horses, also with shining brass ornaments, to buy at some little shop pink and white sweets with mottoes printed on them, or bottles of tepid, gassy mineral waters with glass marbles imprisoned in their necks. One stared in silent curiosity at 'the working classes', aware of their difference.

The difference was noticeable at election time. One had been born, evidently, a little Conservative (just as one had been born, or at least christened, in the Church of England). Accordingly a rosette of blue ribbon was pinned to one's jersey or sailor blouse, but in the streets there were rowdies with much larger, bright yellow rosettes which showed that they had been born little

Radicals, and probably Dissenters as well. One of them rushed at me, tore off my blue rosette, and threw it in the road.

'Yahoo!' said Miss Daisy Day, in whose care I was, and she led me away from further molestation.

The sight of a drunken labourer, from whom one was told to look away, was interesting. What could be the matter with such a big, strong man? What made him move so unsteadily, uttering words which were unfamiliar but evidently coarse. Was he unhappy? Or was he lurching in some wonderful world of his own? One never saw 'gentlemen' in such a state and had not yet learnt that they ever entered it. Another labourer, displaying in an alleyway what is not usually displayed in public in this chilly climate, was evidently drawing attention to another level of experience, which one knew to be important but was evidently unmentionable. To be told to look away merely excited one's curiosity.

Although we always spoke of Darby and Spoondon, the working people always pronounced Derby and Spondon as they are spelt. When I asked why, I was told that they didn't know any better, but that didn't explain why each place should have two names. I fancied that there were two Derbys and two Spondons within the boundaries of each. It was not a bad guess: I had never heard then of 'the two nations' but I had grasped the doubleness of English life.

Working people generally seemed merry and civil, but this impression was chiefly gained from servants, a gardener, a big benevolent cook, lively errand boys, homely countrywomen, and especially housemaids—some buxom wench who was always blushing or giggling, wore a silver brooch lettered *Mabel* or *Mizpah*, and on her afternoon out did her fair hair in a bang and perched on top of it a huge hat as light as a soufflé and trimmed with calico roses. If, romping with Mabel, one pinched her bottom, she would only laugh and say, 'Oh, aren't you artful!' In what was called 'one's own class' one never heard the word 'artful' at all.

The solitary labourer, the rosy maid, the playful dogs in the street—all these had something to do with the business of sex (another word one never heard), which somehow seemed nearer the surface in the working class, who accordingly began to figure in the fantasies which came into my mind before I fell asleep.

While life for me had been unfolding every hour, with the popular tune of *Yip-i-addy-i-ay* being sung, hummed, or whistled continually, my mother, far away in Johannesburg, where my father was now posted, was expecting another baby. In view of previous misfortunes, they agreed that she had better have it in England. Besides, she wanted to see me.

In her absence her mother had died. So had the colonel, her father-in-law. She and her contemporaries were no longer 'the younger generation', and their children belonged to the twentieth century, however much they were trained to accept without questioning the beliefs, habits, and delusions of the nineteenth.

After her arrival at Spondon (and the process of 'coming home' to England always gave her a new lease of life) my mother asked me one day what the time was. I looked across the room at her travelling clock and could see neither figures nor hands. It was discovered with alarm and resentment that ignorance had allowed me to read in a bright light while in bed with the measles, and this had left me myopic. This circumstance strongly affected the course of my life and dashed my mother's unaccountable hope that I might go, by way of Osborne, into the Navy—a hope which meant nothing to me.

In the spring of 1911 we left Spondon for a house called Lowicks, near Frensham Ponds, which had been lent to my mother by her sister-in-law. In sticking to her choice of a husband my Aunt Laura had married a man of taste and hospitality, who had had two remarkable houses built for him by Voysey. This now famous architect, as Sir Nikolaus Pevsner has said, had 'ventured on a new style of an original and highly stimulating nature, before Art Nouveau had begun,' a style full of freshness and *joie de vivre*. The first of Uncle Emslie's houses was Garden Corner, next to the old Physic Garden on the Chelsea Embankment, and from time to time during the first thirty years or so of my life I much enjoyed staying there. With its light, unstained oak panelling and fittings, and its plain, soft carpeting everywhere, it seemed the setting for a new kind of life, and far away from all those conventional Victorian interiors one had seen, with their mahogany furniture, heavy chimney-pieces, plethora of pictures and ornaments, oppressive crimson wall-papers, and suffocating curtains and table-cloths. One's spirits rose as one went up in the neat electric lift; one wanted to sing, and sang, in the bathroom with its bluey-green tiles and those marvellous wall-papers, with their motifs of trees and birds, which made Henri van de Velde say to Pevsner, 'It was as if Spring had come all of a sudden.' There were lofty fireplaces ornamented with a wide expanse of plain gold mosaic, and in the drawing-room (which overlooked the Embankment, then a quiet promenade, and the Whistleresque moods of the river and Battersea Park) there was a row of softly coloured flower paintings let into a high dado of dove-grey slate. In every room could be found writing-paper die-stamped in black or green mannered lettering to match that on the front door and in the lift.

Lowicks was equally beguiling, and seemed even more idio-syncratic, partly because everything was very high or very low. The roof came down steeply, almost to the ground; the casement windows were wide and low, the window seats very low; but the latches on the doors were so high that to open them one had to make the gesture of someone proposing a toast to the architect. High-backed chairs, like those at Chelsea, were pierced with heart-shaped openings, and on high shelves near the ceiling stood vases of crafty green pottery filled with peacocks' feathers in defiance of the superstition that they shouldn't be brought indoors. Coal scuttles, hot-water cans, and electroliers were made of beaten or hammered brass or copper. The house, so fresh and modern in design, was perfectly comfortable, light and warm.

The spring sunshine lit up the honeycomb on the breakfast table, the dining-room was redolent with coffee and narcissus, and through the small-paned windows could be seen yews trimmed in the shape of peacocks. If we went, as we often did, beyond the garden, we found ourselves in a sun-warmed world of pine trees and heather, with dry, sandy paths, and sedgy ponds.

There were no trippers or traffic or litter, and it was so quiet that one could hear the crackle of the wings of the various dragonflies which haunted the region. My aunt and her husband were probably abroad, doing what was then daring and new, motoring in their Rolls with their capable chauffeur, Ashby, in countries like Bosnia or Morocco, over unmade roads and stopping at fleabitten village hostelries.

In the height of the summer my mother and I moved, for some unknown reason, to Bexhill to await her confinement. The summer of 1911 was excessively hot, and the sun, blazing upon striped awnings and the slightly Mauresque buildings on the sea front, made them seem almost foreign. Decidedly exotic was the presence of the Maharajah of Cooch Behar, whose courtiers went about in splendid costume, in silks and jewels and turbans adorned with aigrettes. I knew it was 'rude to stare', but as I made my way to the beach with a shrimping net I heard somebody say, 'Bexhill is getting more like the Arabian Nights every day.' Presently the Maharajah died, and members of his suite were seen sticking cut carnations into the flower beds in their small front garden and then gravely and ceremoniously dancing round them. Many a nose must have been flattened against the windows of the adjacent Chatsworths, Miramars and Fernleas as their occupants jockeyed for position to get an eyeful of so unusual a scene. The death of the potentate is commemorated by a monument on the sea front.

11

Upstart City

In August my brother was born, and as soon as my mother was strong enough to travel, we returned, with an English nanny, to Africa. That meant to Johannesburg, to a small house my father had taken near Joubert Park. What had been happening to him? He was now in a different branch of the Department of Native Affairs, and was concerned solely with Africans employed in the gold mines or in domestic or other service in the city. At this period Johannesburg (to quote the brilliant Lewis Mariano Nesbitt, who left in *Gold Fever* a memorable account of it) was 'an ultra-modern city on the American plan, where every vice had its panders, and every kind of licentious orgy is perennial'. Standing more than five thousand feet above sea-level in a limpid, sun-baked, rarefied atmosphere, the city, only twenty-five years old, had been conjured out of the waving grass by greed for gold. Seen from a distance it differed from others by the prevalence of whitish mounds, which seemed to have risen among the very streets. Composed of quartz dust impregnated with cyanide of potassium, these small mountains, the excreta of gold-grubbing, gave the urban landscape unusual perspectives. Beneath them man-made shafts extended for three or four miles vertically into the earth, and in these mines, a single one of which might employ ten thousand men, a large population, mainly black, toiled hard and sometimes dangerously for gold.

The black men had come to the Rand not because they wanted to but because they had to earn money to pay their taxes and could not earn it at home. This economic pressure, or exploitation, would now, I suppose, be called 'colonialism'. This propagandist word had not then been invented: the process of developing, or milking, 'new' countries was still called colonisation. Sensible men knew that, like other human activities, including Christianity and Socialism, colonising sometimes led to horrible abuses but need not necessarily or entirely be an evil thing. Mid-Victorians, like my father, who had been brought up to be obedient and to think and do what they were told, and who were not of a questioning or analytic turn of mind, took it for granted that colonisation was on the whole a good thing, which, properly managed, brought the supposed benefits of civilisation to the colonised as well as undoubted profits to European entrepreneurs and prestige to European empire-builders.

His attitude to the blacks would now, I suppose, be called paternalist. I can think of stronger terms of abuse. He did not think it was wrong for Africans to have to come to Johannesburg and be obliged to further an industrial revolution, though he knew the hardships and deprivations they suffered. He did think it right that, being there, they should be as well looked after as possible. In the civil service he was regarded accordingly as a negrophilist, unfit for any really important post.

Arriving from all parts of southern Africa to seek work, the unskilled black migrants of many tribes came as strangers, uneducated and bewildered, to the white man's new, urban, industrial world. Just as we, here in England, whether white or black, have to be enrolled as ratepayers, voters, and taxpayers, conscribed into the system of social security, national insurance, and education, and sometimes into the armed forces, so these immigrant blacks, who were no stranger to tribal compulsions, now had, first of all, to be submitted to a bureaucratic system of registration.

On arrival they were obliged by law to report to a 'pass office', where each new arrival was medically examined and vaccinated, and had his fingerprints taken. He was then provided with an identity card, called a pass, recording his name and tribe and the name of his local chief, together with particulars of his new employment. This document was handed to his employer, and he was given a duplicate, renewable every month at a cost to him of one shilling. When his contract expired his pass was signed by his employer, who gave particulars of his character for the benefit of any prospective employer.

There were pass offices in every part of the widely scattered city, and there was a large central office. There my father, at the head of a regiment of white and black clerks, interpreters, and police, supervised the administration of this system. At this office were kept the records of registration and tax-gathering. Attached to it were a court of law, in which breakers of contracts and other minor offenders were tried, and a large compound for feeding and housing new arrivals until they found or were provided with jobs. There was also a complaints office which my father thought most important. To this office employed Africans had the right to bring their troubles, and where complications had arisen, efforts were made to settle them amicably in order not to overburden the courts. Many of the complaints were frivolous or trivial. Some involved accusations of theft, the non-payment of wages, or assault. Some were sexual complaints, either against the employer or members of his family, or against fellow-workers. It was by no means unknown for an African man-servant (or 'house-boy') to complain that when his white employer was away in the daytime his employer's wife had been making excessive demands on his virility. In later days repressive racial laws must have dried up the occurrence of such complaints and discouraged the frolics which had given rise to them.

The pass system came to be regarded as a kind of slavery and much hated by Africans, not least because failure to produce a pass on demand led more and more as the years passed to their being bullied, victimised, and penalised by hectoring and vindictive policemen. In any case the obligation to carry a pass was imposed by white men and may well have seemed to be the stigma of a serf: but it is difficult to see how so large and fluctuating a migrant population could have been controlled or provided for without some such system. At least no African, I believe, ever thought my father a slave-driver or indifferent to social justice or to what may

William Plomer with his
father and nurse, 1903

Louis Trichardt

Growing Up

be called human rights. He thought it his duty to protect Africans from being wronged or to try and put their wrongs right. When, a few years later, he left Johannesburg for another task at the Cape, twenty of his African staff offered him a testimonial of 'deep regret' at losing him. He treasured this document until the end of his life. They said they had felt 'not only protected but under a kind hand, which dealt leniently with our ignorant people and listened kindly to the wants of all who came within your reach'. I wince a little at the use of the word 'ignorant', which seems to suggest a feeling of superiority on the part of those who were literate to those who were not, but it is good to know that my father's hand was lenient and he was a kind listener to the wants of all. His maternal grandfather, Dr Bush, would have been pleased. There may have been moments when instances of injustice to 'ignorant people' brought on attacks of asthma, from which my father may have liberated himself by a violent rage, but at least none of his rages was lethal.

Although Johannesburg had only had a quarter of a century in which to become the second largest city in Africa, after Cairo, it had all the material amenities of contemporary life—at least for those who could afford them. From the social life of my parents the miners and their 'licentious orgies' were remote. They went to theatres or drove to visit friends in the country, they went to the races, played golf, tennis and bridge, entertained and were entertained by their friends. Left to themselves, they would not inevitably and perhaps not often have made the same sorts of friends. When two persons of fairly marked individuality and a limited common experience choose to marry, a divergence in the choice of society is liable to occur.

My father, having gone out young to Africa and having lived a free and easy life, unambitious and without dependents, had mixed on equal terms with the 'ordinary' people of the country. He had a real affection for the Afrikaners, from *bywoner* to President, and had received much kindness from them. In spite of his liability to use terms like 'not a gentleman, of course' or 'not quite of our class', he rather preferred in general, I think, simple and

4

unpretentious people, and was often quite tolerant of blatantly 'common' ones. So he led a double social life. He would not have departed from the accepted canons of decent social behaviour, but was less fastidious than my mother.

While he had been wandering over the veld for more than ten years she had still been living at Southwell; he had wandered in a wide and casual world, she had remained in a narrow, sheltered, ritualistic one. Her standards of character and behaviour were like a creed; one could not imagine her adapting herself to lower standards of, say, honesty, considerateness, and cleanness. This did not always make her life in South Africa easier. Colonial South Africans born and bred, particularly the women, sometimes felt animosity towards those whom they called 'home-born', by which they meant born and bred in England. Since the home-born had often had advantages of breeding, money, or education, which might have given them an air of easy assurance, they naturally provoked at times a feeling of inferiority in the colonial-born. Also the English, though proud of their empire, had been known to speak disparagingly of some of those who had done much to make it. But when colonials, as naturally sometimes happened, were uncouth and displayed bumptiousness or spite, the English were naturally not lost in admiration; they might defend themselves, perhaps unconsciously, in an aura of superiority. Then the colonials might call them, not unreasonably, stuck-up. This social maladjustment was very often resolved by good-heartedness, adaptability, and tolerance on both sides, but when the home-born made it clear that they lived only for the day when they could go back where they came from, the colonials could not expect to do anything but cheer.

My father would not have minded settling in Africa for good or bringing up his children there, as he might have done if he had married a tougher kind of woman, but my mother was too deeply attached to her native country ever to think of South Africa as 'home'. As a good and loyal wife she had from the first tried to adapt herself to her new surroundings, and she had never shirked difficulty or danger. At Pietersburg some of the local women, when she tried to be nice to them, thought she might be condescending to them. When, in one or two instances, she found them uncivil or untrustworthy, she did not choose them as intimates, so they no doubt thought her stand-offish. She could not help being better dressed, less self-conscious, and quieter-voiced, and they could not forgive her and her sister Hilda (who had once been there on a visit) for winning both the singles and the doubles in the local tennis-tournament.

I have seen the same sort of conflict between Afrikaners and immigrants from the Netherlands. Such a conflict, no doubt discernible in any colony or 'new' country, was probably intensified in South Africa by the fact that the local whites, though lacking all the important attributes of an aristocracy, were the masters of a vast African population five times their own number and virtually serfs. How galling for the whites to be reminded by the presence among them of persons fresh from Europe that they were not universally recognised as the lords of creation! And how infuriating when the 'home-born' tended to treat Africans as human beings!

In 1911 the streets of Johannesburg were orchestrated with the clanging, hissing, and whining sounds of trams, with the clop-clop of horses' hooves, and occasionally with the crack of a forty-foot wagon-whip. The older residential parts of the town, such as Doornfontein, near which we lived, already had atmosphere. Quick-growing cypress, mimosa, and eucalyptus groves were already tall and shady; they lent an air of age and mystery to villas and small mansions built in the Nineties by newly rich German Jews, Scotch engineers, speculators in real estate, successful doctors, or tarts. Often rather German in style, with bizarre turrets of hot red or mustard-yellow brick and with ornamental verandahs trimmed with cast-iron lace and muffled with flowering creepers and grenadilla vines, they already had the glamour of outmoded mannerism (like twenty-year-old fashion magazines) and even a touch of secretive melancholy: even then they looked to me like settings for hidden dramas of family life.

In these surroundings, so adaptable is a child, I felt no less at home than I had in English gardens or drawing-rooms, or in the streets of London. I listened with excitement to the big hailstones drumming on the corrugated-iron roofs in summer thunderstorms, when flashes of lightning, like vast magnesium-flares, made the livid landscape jump. As at Louis Trichardt, swarms of flying ants came out on moist evenings, and the last rays of the sun, as the dark-blue thunder-clouds rumbled away with fainter echoes, picked out the yellow fruit of the dark-leaved loquat trees and the bunches of pink, beadlike fruit on the feathery-leaved pepper trees, while a light steam rose from the fresh-smelling earth. Indoors our Zulu house-boys moved about bare-footed, dressed in loose white blouses and shorts piped with scarlet—active, patient, warm-hearted, warm-blooded beings, handsomely made, and perfect in their goodness to this child. But it was time for this child to go to school.

The city was spreading rapidly, not only along the gold-bearing Rand itself but out on to the surrounding hills, valleys and tracts of veld. Pleasant suburban houses in ample, well-planted grounds were, like the houses in the inner suburbs, also already screened by hedges and by pine-trees and jacarandas. On the brow of a hill, on what were then the outskirts of the town, stood St John's College, which had been founded in the Nineties by fathers of the Community of the Resurrection, from Mirfield in Yorkshire. They had an admirable purpose—to radiate, in the words of the school motto, *lux, vita, caritas* on the Transvaal high veld by means of education. In a sense *lux* and *vita* were already omnipresent there, but no doubt they were thought also to be needed in a theological sense: for *caritas* there is always room. The fathers had brought with them, evidently, their High Church principles and their reverence for the memory of Bishop Gore, and one's eye was often caught by some representation of the school badge: beneath the words *Collegium S. Johannis* an eagle, bearing in his beak a scroll inscribed *Quem diligebat*, was scotching with his claw a snake which had twined itself round a chalice.

The site of the school had been grandly chosen and it had been nobly and simply designed, and built of rough-hewn local stone, with spacious cloisters, terraces, and quadrangles. Facing the school were the playing-fields of red earth, with outcrops of soft shale and planted round with pine-trees and macrocarpa hedges; behind it was an uninhabited valley, beyond which rose a wild hill of considerable size scattered with big quartzy rocks and known as the Kopje.

The fathers were mostly excellent creatures, late-Victorian Englishmen from Oxford and Cambridge, dedicated to a somewhat austere Anglo-Catholicism. Neither cranks nor fanatics — though one had a fierce, ascetic look like a half-starved bird of prey — they were mostly more like large good boys than schoolmasters. Their cassocks and birettas lent them an air of distinction. As soon as we were dressed of a morning we assembled in the chapel and sang, as plainsong, the simple hymn

> Now that the daylight fills the sky
> We lift our hearts to God on high,

which, more than fifty years later, and in its Latin version, *Jam lucis orto sidere*, was going to renew itself in an unforeseeable context of special importance to me. After the brief early service we ran like stags, headed by an athletic, long-legged Resurrection father in a flapping cassock, across the main playing-field and back to our breakfast, which always began with maize-meal porridge.

It was not at all a bad beginning to the day, and in that almost perfect climate, so light and warm and dry, our days were good. Not being addicted to cricket and football, I spent many a long afternoon wandering with schoolfellows on the rocky, solitary Kopje, which had many enchantments. The South African War at the turn of the century had been over before we were born. It seemed to us very remote, but near one or two small ruined forts one could pick up cartridge-cases left over from it. On the farther side was a cave which sometimes contained the ashes of recent fires and other signs of life: it was said to be used by some of those African gangsters known as *amalaita*, and this made it agreeably sinister. Lizards and conies lived among the soft feathery red grasses, wild montbretias and red-hot pokers; there were wild fruits, *stamvrugte*, to be gathered from low bushes, and the strange flavour of their pink flesh to a young palate was unsurpassed. I have always found that a special quickening of one of the senses, particularly those of taste and smell, acts instantly in me like a stimulant drug and produces a feeling of quickened vitality.

Here and there stood taller flowering shrubs, their sweet, rank fragrance drawn out by the heat of the sun and radiating from them where they stood over their shadows, which were like pools of Indian ink. We did not have to go any great distance to find corner shops kept by Greeks, who sold fruit, sweets, ices, and cold drinks. On their walls hung crude coloured prints of national heroes, the reigning King of the Hellenes, Lord Byron, or stirring episodes from the war of independence less than a century before. Like my mother, I suppose, they were patriotic exiles, always a little aloof at heart from their African environment.

When night fell, the whole sky seemed to throb and crepitate with brilliant stars, among which one instinctively picked out the Southern Cross, as one would the Great Bear in England; and until it was time for prep we collected glow-worms on the rocky slope below the school or were playful in other pleasant ways.

It was the custom at St John's to produce every year a play of Shakespeare's. The Resurrection father who directed it always seemed to know and love the play and to be an experienced producer. When the play was ready it was repeated several times, twice in the great gymnasium before an audience of parents and friends, and once at a distant hospital called the Lazaretto, to which we drove in brakes and from which we came back by moonlight, singing in chorus.

At the age of about nine I had the interesting experience of appearing in *Macbeth* as Lady Macduff's son, who is taunted with being an 'egg'. I had very good notices for my performance in *A Midsummer Night's Dream*—as Titania. How would Lucretia Bradshaw have judged it? That this part should be played by a bright and nimble boy was in the Shakespearean tradition. I felt light-footed and ethereal in a robe of white crêpe-de-chine and spangles, but there was an anxious quarter of an hour on the second night when this garment, which I had hitched up for the purpose, suddenly came unhitched while I was making water shortly before the curtain rose. Fortunately it was in the winter and there was a portable stove behind the scenes, so it was possible to dry out quickly the evidence of what might have suggested unladylike, unfairylike, and far from regal incontinence.

The successive deaths of my grandparents had left my parents much better off, so they moved to another and larger house nearer St John's, and I became a day-boy. It had a large garden, and a little gallantry of my father's was to go out very early in the morning, cut the most perfect rose he could see, and offer it to my mother with the dew on it. They were fond of entertaining, and on their table were now to be seen the colonel's knives and forks with deer-horn handles, his three silver owls with red eyes to contain three different kinds of pepper, and sundry family plate, including a big-bellied soup tureen which had belonged to Sir William Plomer, the eighteenth-century Lord Mayor. I too entertained my friends, finding it pleasant to know people of various origins. Among my schoolfellows some were Afrikaners, some were Jewish, French, and Italian, and there was a burly, gentle German who was touchingly protective towards me, possibly as a result of playing Bottom to my Titania. I think he would have pleased Walt Whitman.

There were holidays, with visits to Pretoria, to old friends on farms, or to Vereeniging to row on the Vaal river. Once a year there was a grand family holiday at the Cape. We stayed at St James's, on the shores of False Bay. There my father gently and skilfully taught me to swim, and impressed me with his own fish-like agility under the clear water. At Simonstown one year Admiral Bush, a distant relation of my father's, was in command of the Cape station: he invited us to Admiralty House, pleasingly built in 1814, and showed us over his flagship. There were visits to Cape Point and picnics among sparkling granite boulders, with

Venus'-ear shells lying here and there on the beach like abandoned dishes of violet nacre. Among the sandy dunes of Fish Hoek, then 'underdeveloped', or at Muizenberg, watching or joining the surf-bathers, the smell of the sea was primevally strong and salty.

In 1913 a revolutionary strike broke out in Johannesburg. Nesbitt left a dramatic eye-witness account of it. The rioters were charged by cavalry and fired upon by troops with machine-guns: General Smuts was at this time Minister of Mines, of the Interior, and of Defence. After scenes of courage, panic, and slaughter my father took me to see the the smoking ruins of a newspaper office in the middle of the city. There were heaps of debris in the street, and people were standing about, staring vacantly at the rubble as if waiting for it to reassemble itself, just as one saw them staring after air raids in London thirty years later. Only a year or two after this, when news came of the sinking of the *Lusitania*, there were anti-German riots, with looting and arson; and in 1922 came another and graver revolutionary strike.

Early in 1914 my parents' thoughts, my mother's in particular, were turning to England. I was now ten, and it was thought high time for me to go to an English preparatory school. Reviewing their finances, they came to the conclusion that there was no reason why my father should not retire from the South African civil service. He was still only in his early forties, but they believed that with careful management they could live independently and tolerably well on the Continent. It would be cheaper than England, where I could be sent to school. Various places were considered – Dieppe, perhaps, St Malo, or Scheveningen. Before taking any decisive step, they prudently decided to reconnoitre, and my father, instead of resigning, applied for six months' leave.

In fact their income was smaller than it might have been. They had grown up and were still living in a time when the quiet-living middling gentry gave little thought to money. They were accustomed to receiving, as regularly as if by clockwork, the dividends on their capital – South American railway shares, or whatever they were – and thought only how they were to be spent. It was a complacent world my grandparents had lived in, and complacency, like other sins, is visited upon the children, unto at least the third and fourth generations. My parents had a streak of unworldliness, and were incapable of making money or making it breed. Perhaps, too, they were really living beyond their means. All those voyages backwards and forwards to England, that standard of living, the prospective education, so well-intentioned, of the children — perhaps these were extravagances.

We returned to England in two batches, I forget why. My mother and still infant brother went first, my father and I followed a month later. In the ship he let me run free, and I enjoyed myself. The ship's carpenter decided that I was to be a Red Indian at the children's fancy-dress party, so he made me a tomahawk, obtained a magnificent pair of albatross wings as a head-dress, and stained me all over with red ochre. A peculiar interest was taken in me by a young steward, but my father knew nothing about it.

It was exciting to see the peak of Teneriffe at dawn. It was exciting, as we approached Liverpool, to see gliding calmly in after us from the Atlantic on a sunny May morning, the *Lusitania*, unconscious of her doom.

12
Beechmont and Burford

My parents were in no great hurry to decide where to settle on the Continent, so we did a round of visits to relations and a motor tour. The next thing was to find a school for me. From private recommendations and from glowing prospectuses supplied by a firm of scholastic agents they narrowed down their list of schools to two or three, and considerately took me with them to see what I was being let in for. One school to which I took a fancy they had some objection to; and elsewhere, after glimpses of sodden playing-fields, draughty gymnasiums, sharp-faced pedagogues and their over-eager wives, I felt low-spirited.

The choice fell on Beechmont. My mother rightly thought it was healthy to live on a hilltop, my father considered the headmaster properly qualified; but my father was no judge of character, and the three years I spent there I regard as a term of imprisonment, relieved fortunately by agreeable holidays.

An early Victorian country house which had been much and rather imposingly enlarged, Beechmont stood, and probably still stands, on the North Downs near Knole. It was approached by a long Gothic nave of very tall and blackish monkey-puzzles, and stood in a good many acres of fields and woods. Near the house there were wide lawns and fine trees—cedars, wellingtonias, and copper beeches—and vast thickets of rhododendrons. There were wide views over the Weald. It was settled that I was to become an inmate of this pleasance at the beginning of the autumn term.

This was 1914. During the summer it became clear that something was brewing, and my parents put off their search for a dwelling-place on the Continent. In July, in perfect summer weather, we were staying at a perfectly delightful house. This was Burford Priory in Oxfordshire, which my Uncle Emslie Horniman had bought not long before. This handsome Elizabethan place had at one time been allowed to fall into disrepair; it still had a ruined wing, and an arcade led from the house to an uncommon late-Renaissance chapel, also in disrepair. Uncle Emslie rebuilt the wing but did not restore the chapel; he was some kind of agnostic. The walled gardens were splendid, and a great silent wood, full of moths and ground-ivy, sloped down to the Windrush and its banks aromatic with water-mint.

After breakfast on that morning early in August after war had been declared, *The Times* was much in demand. We were sitting out in the sun in the flagged courtyard, where a profusion of Alpine strawberry plants grew between the paving-stones. Was it possible that the atmosphere of warmth and peace and hope and infinite leisure was not as eternal as it seemed? It was.

My Uncle William, who was present that morning, looking rather grave and distinguished, and wearing a bow tie with white spots, was soon in France, no longer a retired colonel, but on active service. My father offered his services to the War Office, where it was thought that his knowledge both of French and Afrikaans, which is akin to Flemish, might make him useful as an interpreter or liaison officer. Presently he was ordered to France, but it was suddenly discovered that he was a member of the South African civil service, so he was told to report to the High Commissioner, who said he must go back at once to South Africa, where his services were needed. After seeing me settled at Beechmont, my mother followed him, taking my infant brother with her.

Bellyaching about Beechmont is not going to entertain anybody, but as I spent the greater part of three years there, I beg to be allowed to air my grievances. The headmaster of a preparatory school, in those days if not in these, was in a position of extraordinary independence. A man of ungenerous character, exercising absolute power over a herd of young boys in an isolated country house, was a tyrant bound to make their lives unpleasant. The

Reverend Clement William Louis Bode was such a man. An elderly Etonian, he was the son of another preparatory school-master, also a clergyman, and the very man whom Norman Douglas described in *Looking Back* as 'a pious hog'. Bode's mid-Victorian notion of education was to inure his charges to the drabbest form of Anglicanism, to give them a sound training in the classics, and to make them proficient cricketers. A false quantity or a missed catch were to him, it seemed, sins equal to theft, emotional spontaneity, 'impurity', a taste for any of the fine arts, or any other of a long catalogue of deviations from an unlovable, impossible norm. I never saw him smile or laugh, and cannot forget his self-righteousness, meanness, and coldness. Apart from cricket, he allowed little or nothing for a boy's natural bents or gifts and did his best to repress them. I feel only obliged to him for his real faculty for teaching the classics and for awakening appreciation of the use of words in the poetry of Virgil and Horace.

The pleasantest memories of the place are of those rare occasions when the prison-like routine was varied by outdoor activities other than cricket, hockey, or football — such as haymaking in the summer, or, in the hard winter of 1916–17, skating on a pond in the Weald every afternoon for a fortnight, and the exhilaration of tobogganing on the snow-muffled slopes of Knole Park in a tingling, frosty silence.

Every boy is a mass of physical, mental and emotional potentialities. Organised games, puritanical discipline, and an attempt to impose uniformity do not combine to provide a fruitful, humane, or enjoyable kind of education. Take, for example, the matter of religion. At St John's the religious instinct was given full play. A boy could enjoy and practise and believe in the Mirfield kind of religion without becoming mawkish or goody-goody. At Beechmont religion was repulsively boring, colourless, and hypocritical, poisoning some boys with superfluous feelings of sin and guilt. At St John's the Kopje was a paradise of which the boys had the freedom; at Beechmont the lovely environs of the house were permanently out of bounds.

To put harmless and delightful places a few yards away under a taboo for no good reason was to invite all but priggish and timorous boys to enter them. Just as in an adult community, the multiplication of petty rules and regulations brought them and their propagators into contempt with spirited boys (who set out to defy them), and tended to turn the rest into ciphers by persuading them that obedience was a virtue in itself. A harsh and narrow government provokes conspiracy and resistance: we livelier boys therefore conspired to break bounds, and sexual and other taboos, to smoke, and so on. No appeal, apart from that of Euclid and the team spirit, was made to our reasoning powers or sense of personal responsibility. Conformity meant dullness, nonconformity meant impositions, beatings, petty persecution, being held up to sarcastic ridicule, or at worst expulsion. Obviously nonconformity was the more attractive, since it had the spice of danger.

Perhaps the most symptomatic of our conspiracies was excited by the troubles and the Easter Rebellion in Ireland: we were as much stirred by these in 1916 as many young men were, twenty years later, by events in Spain. None of us was Irish, none of us wished to injure our country, but the Sinn Fein movement and the fate of Sir Roger Casement excited our sympathy. It was the idea of adventurous upsurgence against a repressive authority (associated in our minds with the odious Bode, with Kipling, cricket, sabbatarianism, gimcrack patriotism, and all that bag of tricks) which prompted us to form fanciful plots, send coded messages in invisible ink, plan sabotage, and so on, though nothing came of all this outwardly. Inwardly some of us had had a lasting subversiveness inculcated in us: self-respect had made it necessary.

It was disgraceful that no scope was given to our creative faculties. There was, it is true, a carpenter's shop. There was also a dancing class, at which, directed by a desperately animated Miss Nepean, we galumphed without conviction in the polka or the barn dance, but with some enjoyment in the Lancers or Sir Roger. Amateurish tendencies towards acting, gardening, modelling, botanising, bug-hunting, bird-watching, chemistry, astronomy, mechanics, writing, calligraphy, drawing, or music were given no encouragement or scope at all. Bode evidently considered that such deviant activities would unfit boys for adult life: the proper preparations for that were the composition of Latin verse, practice in wicket-keeping, and the study of Hebrew mythology. There was no valid reason why boys should not have been taught, let us say, the elements of gardening and cooking, and the functioning of the body from which each of us was inseparable.

Even if, when young, Bode had read *Horae Subsecivae*, a book then conspicuous, he would have scorned Dr John Brown's advocacy of 'education through the senses'. In boys, said Dr Brown, 'cultivate observation, energy, handicraft, ingenuity, outness ... How,' he asked, 'are the brains to be strengthened, the sense quickened, the genius awakened, the affections raised – the whole man turned to the best account?' Among his prescriptions were the personal pursuit of natural history, field botany, geology, and zoology.

Give the young, fresh unforgetting eye exercise and free scope upon the infinite diversity and combination of natural colours, forms, substances, surfaces, weights, and size – everything, in a word, that will educate their eye or ear, their touch, taste, and smell, their sense of muscular resistance ... and, above all, try and get hold of their affections, and make them put their hearts into their work.

Affections to be got hold of, and the idea of 'the whole man', were either unknown to Bode, or feared or ignored or punished by him; Dr Brown was full of unregarded ancient wisdom and a century at least ahead of his time.

The war atmosphere was increasingly obtrusive. On still days at Beechmont, when we were bent over Xenophon or quadratic equations, the windows would be rattled by a sudden crescendo of the interminable thunder of the guns in Flanders, and a wandering breeze would stir the war-map on the wall, where little flags on pins marked the graph of the Western Front, and, to the east, the progress of what the foolish newspapers wishfully called 'the Russian steam-roller'. At one moment we might be listening in the chapel to the Sermon on the Mount; at another we might be watching bayonet practice in a park, where overgrown errand-boys in khaki were being taught by a sergeant to stab sacks filled with straw and daubed with a rough likeness of the Kaiser. Could both be right?

Ours too, it seemed, when we were old enough and if the war went on long enough, to 'do and die', but we were not really convinced that the way men were dying in France was *dulce et decorum*. Vague feelings of resentment arose, even in a young breast, against those who, in comfort and security, expressed themselves on the rightness and justice of this war and even of all wars. So did feelings of pity for its victims, when at times during the holidays one visited wounded or mutilated soldiers in hospital or helped to serve unwounded ones in canteens. In a mist of steam from tea-urns they stretched out their clumsy innocent hands for Woodbine cigarettes, while their thick coarse uniforms, soaked with the sweat of route-marches, gave off a rank, sour, khaki odour.

During the holidays the war often seemed to be in another world. At a country house in Lincolnshire, not far from Maiden-well, one might almost have been living in the eighteenth century, all was so peaceful. The primroses came out in the Long Walk; the keeper added a jay and a stoat to his 'larder', where the out-lines of tiny skulls, as delicate as eggshells, showed through rotting or withered tissue; the engravings of Hogarth's *Marriage à la Mode* over the staircase became slightly more foxed with damp; new issues of *Punch* and *Country Life* appeared promptly on a table in the hall. At a commuter's house in Sevenoaks or a widow's seaside villa in Devonshire there was a cosy domesticity.

The Christmas of 1915 I spent with my Aunt Hilda. What had once been Spondon House School had twice moved, first to Deal, then, because of the war, to Kenfield Hall, near Canterbury, a beautiful Queen Anne house. In the grounds was a pinctum, where the conifers let fall, not without risk to those who walked beneath them, a variety of surprising objects, resembling hand-grenades, Negro carvings, or wooden rissoles. A fellow-guest was a relation who had been my father's best man at his wedding. A permanent civil servant in London, he appeared dressed very much 'for the moors' in the shaggiest of tweeds and attracted some attention by his assumed rusticity. Some years later he retired and bought a house in the country, where he was said to act to perfection the part of a Victorian squire, greeting the yokels with kindly condescension and acknowledging salutes which it had not always occurred to them to give. The great-nephew of a duke, he was evidently trying to revert to genteel feudalism on the land at a time when that form of life was on its last legs: such is the power of heredity. This is, I think, the only instance I have to give in these pages of a really determined attempt by one of the stranded gentry to revert to the lost world from which they derived. It was as if some dinosaur, having been domesticated and taught to pull its weight between the shafts of a vehicle, should return to its ancestral swamp and jungle, only to find the one drained and the other cleared.

Bob Synge, the only close friend I made at Beechmont, lived in Radnorshire, and there I went to stay with him and his family one summer, and fell in love at first sight with what, thirty years later and as a result of some diligence on my part, began to be known as 'the Kilvert country'. At that time it was less than forty years since Kilvert's death, and there must have been a good many people about who remembered him: but his diary was still un-discovered and there was no special reason for 'dropping' his name.

Bob's father had the memorable name of Captain William Makepeace Thackeray Synge. To reach his house one travelled by the now extinct but then charmingly intimate railway which ran from the then pleasantly sleepy Hereford, through quiet and sleepier Hay, along the Wye towards Brecon. The garden at Cwmbach sloped to the fields, and the fields to the Wye, beyond which the Black Mountains rose and varied in the ever-varying light: it was as good as an African landscape but infinitely softer. Away up on the wild moors we wandered, lay in the bracken, or bathed naked in some icy pool, breaking the silence and the reflection of a mountain ash, or explored dingles loud with the isolated sounds of water descending an irregular stairway of rocks in cascades, rapids, runnels, and gushes, fanning as it fell the cool green plumes of ferns. Bob died soon after he had gone to a public school, and I have never returned to Cwmbach.

As I spent every summer during the war at Burford, I got to know it well. Like Ditchling, or Broadway, it tended to attract persons interested in the arts. An ancient cottage harboured an obscure poetess with a fringe like Katherine Mansfield's and a string of beads like black cherries. In one of the handsome seventeenth-century burgesses' houses lived an academic painter with ample private means. One day my Aunt Laura introduced me to the famous publisher John Lane, whose name I knew, though I did not then know of his close association with literary celebrities of the Nineties: nor did I then know that because of his susceptibility to women he had been nicknamed Petticoat Lane. Occasionally my aunt would delegate me to show some much-laddered bluestocking the house and its treasures, to which I had become an informed guide, and then I would take her round the garden, where she would contrast strongly with one of the strapping lady-gardeners shoving a barrow-load of dung, to the accompaniment of derisive-sounding cat-calls from the peacocks.

A deep false peace had settled over Burford and the Cotswolds like a warm miasma, and the silence quickened one's awareness of the past. I read all I could of local history and that of the Priory in particular, and it became populous with the dead. When I went up alone to bed, and the moon shone in upon the waxed oak staircase, or when in the night-time I wandered alone in the dark, my imagination was so attuned to the past that it sometimes seemed more actual than the present. In April 1697 the corpse of a murdered man had been discovered in these grounds. The lady of the house, left a widow by John Lenthall (son of the Speaker of the Long Parliament), had married her cousin, the Earl of

Abercorn. The murdered man was a trustee of her sons by her first marriage, and gossip held that he had quarelled with Lord Abercorn over some matter concerning the Lenthall boys. Lord Abercorn was tried for the murder, but acquitted. In the owl-haunted twilight I seemed to see the crime enacted: it took shape in my mind like a memorable scene in a play.

There was not much entertaining, but sometimes interesting men came to stay — Sir Michael Sadler, whose beautiful manners made me feel not just a boy, but a person; Sir Walter Raleigh, who, to get down to my level, lifted a huge stone ball off one of the garden terraces and playfully invited me to join him in using it as a football; and Sir Hamo Thornycroft the sculptor, whom Aunt Laura teased by making him do some topiary work. Sir Hamo was the uncle of Siegfried Sassoon, unforgettably engaged just then in the horror of trench warfare.

Uncle Emslie spent much time in his study, planning the preservation or restoration of the architectural beauties of the town, of which, as of its ancient grammar school, he was a benefactor. The beautiful old houses and hidden corners of Burford, the carved stone doorways and windows untouched since the Middle Ages, deeply engaged his sensibility and his sense of social responsibility. He had sat on the London County Council, and in Parliament as a Liberal member for Chelsea, and, like his father and his sister, he used his money largely for the public benefit. Tall, mild, and kindly, he had travelled much and had an enquiring and well-stored mind. The *New Statesman*, to which he had been one of the original subscribers, was a paper I had never seen anywhere else or even heard of. The way it was printed and the way it was written, without peevishness, bigotry or conceit, took me into a world of ideas half a century ahead of Beechmontism.

And what would the odious Bode have thought if he had picked up, as I did, a copy of Havelock Ellis's *Psychology of Sex* from a table in the drawing-room? Stimulating reading for a boy, it provided startling information about the private behaviour of many adults, and showed how this behaviour embodied the secret fantasies of children. There were still stupid adults capable of asking one if one had read *Ivanhoe* or *Westward Ho!*, not knowing that one was already being geared to the permissive future. Since those days Liberals have often been sneered at, but if they did not always realise how far removed their way of life, their even temper, and their enlightenment were from the loathsome struggles and ugly passions of most of mankind, they believed in the possibilities of happiness and intelligence. I believe Uncle Emslie would have revered, as I do, that diamond saying of W. R. Lethaby's: 'The task of civilization lies in adding to what may be loved.'

Thirty years earlier, in the winter of 1885–6, Uncle Emslie had been a fellow-student with Vincent van Gogh at the Académie des Beaux Arts at Antwerp. That was a difficult time in Van Gogh's life, and he was under-nourished, over-working, and *farouche*. He looked and dressed like a peasant (said Uncle Emslie, who later noted down his recollections for me) and 'gave the idea of red earth' with his short hair, wiry red beard, and sabots. His eyes were 'green-blue' and his face very lined. He used to crouch over his drawing-board making strange faces and noises, was 'subject to violent passion', and seldom spoke. Why did he not speak? It is perfectly clear in his letter of January 1886 to his brother Theo. 'Although I keep going there, it is often almost unbearable, that nagging of the people at the academy.' They nagged at him because he went his own way, and could not obey their insistence that he should *'faire d'abord un contour'*. 'I wanted at least twenty-five times to say, "*Votre contour est un truc, etc.,*" but I have not thought it worth while to quarrel. Yet though I do not say anything, I irritate them, and they me.' And here is my uncle's clear view of the conflict:

He worked very rapidly in charcoal, looking steadfastly at the plaster cast of an antique figure and then at a great pace making a strong black drawing of, say, a landscape with peasant figures in a storm. The visiting master used to be very annoyed, but I think recognized his talent. We thought him mad and were in awe of him—his work was so strange that in those days, when even Whistler was hardly accepted, few conceived that a new school was already in being.

And none conceived—how could anybody?—that this great exemplar of the singlemindedness of the artist, the Protestant artist, was writing those letters which, as John Russell has said, 'display a profound, unceasing, constructive and deeply intelligent concern for other human beings, and for the future of humanity', and are 'one of the great books of all time'. But of course that book was not open to his contemporaries: it was still being written.

13

Eastbourne and Rugby

In 1917 it was decided that my mother should return to England to see to my transition from Beechmont to Rugby. Bringing my small brother with her, she had a tense and roundabout voyage, menaced by U-boats and by the German raider *Moewe*, which was at large and was in fact sighted.

She chose to settle at Eastbourne. Feeling unequal to wartime housekeeping, she took rooms in a boarding-house near Devonshire Park. Its inmates were just one sample of all the depressed or displaced men and women of the middle classes, ageing or old, who have eked out more or less barren and lonely existences in lodgings all over England ever since the great nineteenth-century illusion of peace, plenty, and progress began to crumble.

The only inmate under forty was a thin schoolmaster with locomotor ataxia who was said to be unmercifully baited by his pupils. There were two nondescript spinsters, neither young nor old, living perhaps on small allowances or private incomes. They were not on speaking terms, and communicated with one another by leaving notes, which one supposed to be haughty or cool, under an embroidered 'runner' on the top of the piano in the drawing-room. In that room there were little occasional tables covered with footling bibelots, and on one of them lay two small books bound in floppy mauve suede, magic books — Keats's Odes and FitzGerald's *Rubaiyat* — much of which I soon knew by heart.

I cannot think of the house without thinking of a rich stew which appeared in the dining-room at regular intervals. It would have been good, even very good, except that it had a haunting, peculiar flavour and a strong aroma which seemed to fill the house. One sometimes heard a murmur, 'What *does* she put in it?' The answer was discovered. Round the house was a dense hedge of bays; the cook had been told that a bay leaf or two could be helpful in cooking; her motto was evidently the more the merrier; she must have thrown handfuls of bay leaves into her casserole; and nobody had the heart to correct her, or perhaps the courage.

Among those who consumed this dish was a kind, ancient and plain old maid who wanted to be wanted, but her well-meant visits to wounded soldiers in hospital were not a success. When they saw her they pretended to be asleep and snored loudly like naughty boys, a ruse which did not deceive but saddened her.

Sadder still was an elderly, retired captain of Marines, wretched in his dignity and solitude. Almost blind, he would sit in the window, half veiled in shabby lace curtains, reading the newspaper through a large magnifying-glass held up to his eye, and grunting, as well he might, at what he read. Sometimes he could be seen in profile by the window, gazing over the flavoursome bay-hedge at what can only have been the murky blur of the middle distance. It was said that on retiring from the Marines he had taken a lump sum in lieu of a pension and had squandered it, leaving himself penniless, and now grudgingly maintained by two sisters, who paid for his board and lodging and allowed him exactly sixpence a week as pocket money. This wretched solitary never complained, had good manners, and kept himself clean and tidy. My mother treated him with unobtrusive consideration, listening with as much attention to what he had to say as if he were a diplomatist of distinction. It was almost too much to bear when he spent his weekly income on sweets for my brother, who, though still only a child, sensitively tried to dodge acceptance of this sacrifice.

I was not wholly immured in this house of no prospects, and became an addict of the South Downs, then free from cars, trippers and litter, and not yet ploughed up. Under a canopy of ecstatically singing larks, great flocks of Southdown sheep peacefully browsed over miles of springy turf inlaid with thyme and

milkwort, cowslips and devil's-bit scabious, and on the skyline a
shepherd, not 'of military age', could sometimes be seen apparently
posing for a statue by Hamo Thornycroft. Down in the valley
near East Dean, now all built over, I saw a plough being drawn by
oxen.

Not far from us was Blackwater Road (its name derived from
the river in County Cork) and there lived two Blackden connexions of my mother's. An aged brother and sister known as
Uncle Walter and Aunt Ada, they lived very snugly and had
never done a stroke of work in their lives. Aunt Ada, a gentle old
thing, once offered me a copy of *Punch* and then said gravely,
'But perhaps you would rather not be seen carrying it on a
Sunday?' She sat in a room like a museum, with pictures almost
from floor to ceiling, and a profusion of little treasures, souvenirs
and ornaments. There tea was served with elaborate ritual by
notably well-nourished servants. She had snowy white hair like
swansdown, which her maid washed every morning; and she
would not accept money from her bank unless it was new; even
the new coins had to be scrubbed by a servant with a nailbrush, in
hot water to which washing soda had been added, before she
would touch them. 'They've always led such a sheltered life,' my
mother said. 'They really don't know in the least what life out in
the world is like.'

Their sheltered life was led within earshot of the perennial
cannonade in the Channel. Throughout my life I have been
astonished by the different life-styles, as they are called now, being
pursued at any given moment. And how strange it is to think that
it was at Eastbourne, by his special wish, that the ashes of Engels
were cast into the sea. It can never have been quite the same after
that.

By the time I went to Rugby in 1917 the war was no longer
being regarded so lightly as in the fatuous ditties sometimes heard
in its earlier stages:

> Hats off to Tommy Atkins
> Taking his chance,

On duty with the Blankshires
Somewhere in France,

or,

Three cheers for little Belgium
So small and yet so true.

The longer and longer casualty lists, raids by Zeppelins, the success of German submarine warfare, and shortages of food left not even 'sheltered lives' immune.

Because of conscription, schoolmasters were often dotards, freaks, or nincompoops, but not at Rugby. Dr David, later Bishop of Liverpool, was the headmaster and also my house-master. A tall, dark man with a rugged face, he differed greatly from the blander type of ecclesiastic. I was grateful to him for treating me as an individual and not just as one of six hundred Rugbeians. From his own shelves he lent me books by Turgenev, and when my school life began to be affected by special circumstances he gave them careful and sympathetic consideration.

Then there was Mr Brigstocke, who taught French by shock tactics. His handsome head, with a wing of grey hair brushed back on either side, was full of ideas, and there was intelligence, and perhaps a touch of cynicism, in every line of his face. He seemed full of vitality and up-to-date knowledge. In my first term, insignificant and bewildered, I was amazed to receive from him an invitation to a tea-party, to celebrate my birthday. He had asked three or four of the brightest of my contemporaries to meet me and we used afterwards to meet at his house from time to time. He encouraged us to think, and to prepare and read papers on subjects that interested us. Two of us were outstanding. One was Robert Birley, later headmaster of Eton, and later still a noble protector of voiceless Africans. The other was Darsie Gillie, who, after his death in 1972, was described in *The Times* as 'a champion of the downtrodden and oppressed' who practised what he preached.

I soon got used to the routine and the system of taboos, official and unofficial, which governed the life of the school: by comparison with Beechmont they allowed a dizzy freedom. I wonder if there is still a system of fagging. A prefect would bawl for a fag, all the new boys would scuttle down passages or stairs to answer the call, and the last to arrive would be given some task or errand. This seemed to me so silly that I didn't bother to leave my study. Only energetic when interested, I might have answered a fag-call by a boy I wished to please, and should then have taken care to arrive last.

Games were obligatory, but I took no notice of them. I had already spent a good part of several years in keeping balls out of goals or away from wickets, or propelling them towards those structures. Why waste more time in such ways? Darwin, who in his youth had a passion for 'sport', in the form of shooting, put on record his discovery that the pleasures of observing and reasoning were much higher. I already used my eyes; efforts at reasoning were to be made later.

If I did not play games, I did a good deal of running and was also involved in the Officers Training Corps. As a preparation for human sacrifice in the trenches it was taken seriously. I was soundish in wind and limb, except for progressive myopia, but food was inadequate and I was outgrowing my strength. It was decreed that we were to have an extra half-hour in bed in the mornings to help to make up for the shortage of food, but malnutrition, puberty, and too much book-work by artificial light began to tell on me. Every time I saw the oculist in Harley Street he found my sight growing weaker. Dr David accordingly allowed me to give up some of my form-work and to resign from the Corps.

I got a bicycle and went out, not always alone, into the countryside. It would never be so quiet again, but its placidness was not free from melancholy and tension. The cancer of war was in everybody, but the quietness of Newbold-on-Avon or Hillmorton or Dunchurch or Ashby St Ledgers or Stoneleigh in the summer days of 1918 seemed enchanted. A sense of the past made one seem a revenant, not a sightseer. When the wind suddenly caught the willows of a water-meadow in a silver net, tugging them sideways against a stormy background, rustling the plumage of ivy in a ruin, and shifting the fragrance of may or meadow-sweet or water-mint, or when a shaft of sunlight slanted upon some memorial urn or tomb in a silent, musty church, surrounding with its radiance the kneeling alabaster children of some Jacobean squire, all rendered headless by Puritan zeal — was this 1818? Or 1718?

The landscape might suggest Constable or Cotman, but incongruities did occur: the telegraph wires did not cease to hum; on my way to the fields I might have to pass through the industrial squalor of New Bilton and might later catch sight, in the blue distance, of the smoking chimneys of Coventry; and sometimes on the high roads appeared a long procession of army lorries, like migrating monsters.

In a lane I met a German prisoner driving a farm-cart, somebody's blue-eyed boy, 'And his teeth made for laughing round an apple.' With him I exchanged a few words of classroom German: a human contact which for a moment made the war a half-forgotten nightmare.

On Sundays, in Butterfield's great, stripy Rugby Chapel, a portrait plaque of Rupert Brooke, that cult-poet, had already been set up beside a fitting Victorian one of Matthew Arnold. I doubt if there has since been added to them any memorial of a far greater poet than Brooke, one who happened also to have been schooled at Rugby — Arthur Waley. We were encouraged, in school, to appreciate the poetry of Tennyson; out of school those of us who were so inclined read the latest volume of *Georgian Poetry*, still no doubt too daring and uncanonical for the classroom. 'The Lake School', Roy Campbell remarked a few years later, 'trickled gradually away until it ended in the Marsh School,' but I must say I enjoyed decorating my study with a rhyme-sheet from the Poetry Bookshop of a poem by de la Mare decorated by Lovat Fraser. When, in the school library, I routed out a little edition of *The Marriage of Heaven and Hell*, it was a door into a new world.

Presently other doors opened. The oculist was unwilling for me to go on doing book-work, so it was pointless to stay at school. Dr David wrote me a kind and encouraging letter, suggesting that I might be able to do something good in life which would not fit in with an ordinary career. The oculist recommended an outdoor life, at least until my short sight ceased to be progressive, so my mother sent me to a farm in Berkshire, between Lambourne and Newbury. The farmer's wife was a reader of Swinburne. I was not of much use, though I worked hard at threshing time, and one frosty morning might have been seen driving two recalcitrant heifers all the way back to Boxford from Newbury market. We did not see a single car. Those were the days.

Shy and gawky, I was not much at ease with the locals. There was a dear old farm-hand I used sometimes to work with, but I could at first scarcely understand a word of his broad local speech. Radio had not begun to make users of dialect self-conscious about it. When there was a shoot I used to go sometimes with the guns and sometimes with the beaters. This ambivalence introduced me to a gamekeeper of about thirty, somehow spared from the trenches, who treated me not like 'a young gentleman' but like what I was, a lonely boy, and whom I remember with gratitude.

Suddenly the war came to an end, and on Armistice Day the Kaiser was burnt in effigy in the streets of Newbury. My mother decided that it was time to go back to Africa. She had felt the strain of taking decisions by herself, and was not pleased to have been so long separated from my father, though the years had taught her that she had less in common with him than she may have supposed when she married him. I was not whisked away like a piece of luggage. Treating me as a more reasoning being than I had yet become, she explained to me the arguments for and against my going with her, and then gave me the choice. As any enterprising boy would have done I chose Africa.

'After all,' she said, 'if your eyes settle down in two or three years' time, there's no reason why you shouldn't come back and go to Oxford, or do whatever you want to do.'

14

A Passage to Africa

When my father had returned to South Africa in 1914 he was
commissioned with the rank of captain in the South African
forces, and put on to help with the enrolment and transport of
large numbers of African drivers and carriers for the campaign
against the Germans in East Africa. He attached great importance
to the status and welfare of every individual, and chose to keep
full records of the enlisted men. This was not done in East Africa,
where the men were no doubt regarded as expendable. Many
were lost there, and never heard of again. Many others, returning
to Durban in the last stages of dysentery and fever, died at sea,
into which not only their bodies but their identity discs were
dropped. My father tried to make some amends to these obscure
victims of the war by seeking out evidence of their deaths, so that
their next-of-kin might be notified and payment made allowances
of money owing to them. This solicitude, this trouble taken over
not merely expendable but expended black nobodies, confirmed
the official view of my father as a conscientious civil servant, but
a cranky and tiresome negrophilist.

In the middle of the war my father, who had been refused active
service either in South-West or East Africa, made another
attempt to be sent to France. The War Office in Whitehall had
asked the South African Government to recruit and equip a labour
corps of Africans for service as stevedores at ports and rail-heads
in France. He had much to do with the raising of this corps and
managed to obtain permission to go with it to Europe, but was
told at the last moment that it was essential, because of his experience, to remain in South Africa as its records officer. Possibly

it was thought that if he went to France with the corps he might over-stimulate the self-esteem of its members. He established his office near Capetown, and was kept busy there until the end of the war, when he awaited the return of his wife and children.

To an observant boy the voyage out, after the drabnesses of England in wartime, was as good as a play. The ship was crowded, mainly with people who had been waiting for the end of the war to return to their homes, families, or vested interests in South Africa. As happens in ships and in prisons, they quickly revealed mutual attractions, antipathies, or indifference. It was a society constituted by chance and existing briefly in isolation and idleness, and individuals were brought into clear focus, like moths under a magnifying-glass.

Usually seated together on deck were two semi-millionaires from the Rand. Slightly too well dressed, they stuck together, talking, one supposed, much about money and a little about politics. 'The knights,' said somebody, 'are so exclusive' – an observation which might have annoyed one of them: he was a baronet of very recent creation.

Two of the female passengers, if one chose to compare them, afforded a striking contrast and symbolised two different kinds of society. One was Lady Buxton, the Governor-General's wife, whose quiet dignity, easy simplicity of manner, and good humour tinged with sadness were not merely charming but fitting to one who presides but does not struggle. One felt she had taken on, without fuss or a grain of self-importance, what may sometimes have been the uncongenial share of her husband's fraction of authority in a still vast and powerful empire – a perfect embodiment of what is meant, in the best sense, by a ruling class, its best sense being that of responsibility.

The other was a Johannesburg Jewess, who was travelling with her husband.

'Almost the only woman on this boat,' said my mother, 'who dresses with any style, but it's a style too splendid for the boat.'

The lady was in her forties, tallish, quite handsome, with a shapely body skilfully corseted, and a collection of smart new clothes which she meant to try out long before rejoining her circle in Johannesburg. In an evening dress of Venetian-red lace, with stockings and high-heeled satin shoes to match, she would appear on deck alone after dinner, her big eyes gleaming under heavily darkened lids. Then, with a too carefully manicured hand weighted with two or three conspicuous diamonds, she would raise a more than ordinarily long cigarette-holder to a mouth made up to match her dress.

Everybody stared at her and made remarks about her, but hardly anybody seemed to talk to her, and her husband, obese and taciturn, was generally in the smoking-room with a cigar. There was something distressing in her decorated solitude. Her restless glances made it seem that her clothes and jewels had not given her confidence. Her very vitality seemed to make her ill at ease, as if she didn't quite know what to do with it. She seemed worldly, but for the moment at least, without a world of her own. It was as if she enjoyed what are called the good things of life but was waiting for the best things. By over-stressing her appearance she became a figure of drama, and in her mobile eyes the torments, past and future, of her race seemed to be glinting darkly.

My mother did not like people to feel uncomfortable, and wanted to talk to her, all the more because we have always been a pro-Semite family; but she would have hated to appear to be taking any initiative out of anything like idle curiosity or a sentiment akin to pity, and she kept waiting for a suitable opportunity to fall casually into conversation, and kept being thwarted by circumstances until quite late in the voyage.

The usual shipboard pairings-off occurred, quickening as we neared the Equator, and mostly tending to cool as we drew nearer to the ties and separations waiting just beyond the horizon. All this was vivid to a schoolboy escaping from murky wartime winters in England: so were our ports of call.

One day Ascension Island sprang from the sea like an old coloured print, with its rufous rocky foreground, a few white buildings, on one of which a magenta bougainvillaea had spread like a stain, and the Green Mountain towering in the background. I had been sharing a cabin with a landowner from St Helena. When we got there he was met by his own carriage and invited us to drive with him on a conducted tour of the interior, so off we drove through Jamestown, in the wake of Lady Buxton and the local Governor. St Helena was not at all the horrid rock which history books had led one to imagine. There were flowers and pretty people everywhere. Wisps of tropical mist ran past like long scarves of grey chiffon in mysterious levitation. The sun came out on groups of peasants working without haste and without rest in a steeply sloping field of sisal. On the winding upland roads donkeys trotted past with loads of melons or brushwood on their backs, and by the roadside young girls offered for sale necklaces of dyed Job's-tears. At Longwood the tepid Atlantic breeze blew through Napoleon's empty rooms with their austere remains of decorations in the Empire style, like faint echoes of Malmaison, and through the windows one could see rows of blue agapanthus lilies wagging and nodding like the heads of people in a crowd. A smell of wood-smoke from a hut in a ravine, flowering creepers, flying mists, and steamy fragrance—a lovely place of exile, but not for a self-made militarist emperor. The whole ambience was still of the early nineteenth century.

When the ship docked at Capetown, in the enormous warmth and radiance of a perfect afternoon, we looked down and saw my father standing alone on the quay to meet us. He looked slender and sunburnt in an elegant lightweight uniform of bleached khaki. I suppose I ought to have felt some lively emotion, but he seemed almost a stranger. I had seen little of him in my life, and the last four and a half years in war-darkened England were something he had neither lived through nor was capable of imagining. I had very few memories, thoughts, or jokes to share with him, and the rare remembered happy moments of companionship with him were eclipsed by memories of his senseless angers, grievances, and prejudices. I knew he 'meant well' towards me, but the sight of him gave me no sense of homecoming. He

was a man with a craving for the affection he had missed in childhood, but not, apparently, for the affection of his sons.

There is an understanding poem by Cowper against the sending
of boys away to boarding schools. To a father he says it is no good
complaining of 'filial frankness lost':

> Thou well deserv'st an alienated son ...
> Add too, that thus estranged, thou canst obtain
> By no kind arts his confidence again.

But my father had never really had my confidence.

In London I had been very ill with the Spanish influenza, but
he was more interested in telling us how he had not had it himself, and of its ravages in Capetown. At its height, he said, the
main street, Adderley Street, had been empty at noon, except for
a wagon laden with uncoffined corpses. The coloured people had
died in thousands and many had been buried in common graves.
I don't think he ever asked a single question about my life in
England, or my feelings.

He had been living for some time at the International Hotel, and
we joined him there. It was a long, low building on an elevated
site and had a long, wide, shady verandah behind scarlet-flowering
hibiscus hedges. The food was better and more abundant than we
had seen for a long time, and I found the physical pleasure of being
at the Cape intense. Drunk with warmth, like a bee in spring, I
wandered the streets or in the resinous stony pinewoods on the
slopes of Table Mountain, or under the heavy-shadowed oaks
planted in the seventeenth century by Simon van der Stel, or into
the gallery of minor Dutch masters – clean, cool pictures of a
domesticated civilisation.

Sociable, my father had a taste for good living, old furniture,
fine china, and gardens, but none for literature or painting. If he
did nothing, at this or any time, to encourage my preferences, it
was because they didn't interest him. And there was soon a head-
on collision over a triviality. One day at lunch there were some

magnificent grapes for dessert. I took some, and noticing that they looked a little dusty washed them in a finger-bowl before eating them. My father surprised me by making a scene. He was white with rage, and, as always when he was emotionally tense, one could see the whites of his eyes showing demonically all round the iris. I think the objection was that my niceness was out of place in one who had his way to make in the world. After all, I wasn't on my way to join the long-disbanded Cape Mounted Rifles, where such finicky behaviour might have been not at all 'The Thing'. I replied, with what must have been a maddening air of condescension, that I wasn't going to eat dirty grapes to please him or anybody else. I then took a few more, which I also washed, with what must have been infuriating deliberateness, before eating them. By nature too docile, I had always had a core of independence, which was now very gradually, too gradually, beginning to harden.

We visited or entertained some of his hospitable friends – the cultivated woman with a collection of eighteenth-century fans, and a bishop, to lunch, the rich couple with a house in the old Dutch colonial style, the English colonel with a fruit farm. Presently we moved out to the remembered salty air and white sands (as Kipling observed) of Muizenberg, and then, before returning up-country, to the delicious town of Ceres. Lost on an inland plateau at the end of a branch railway, it was famous for its variety of heaths and proteas.

To arrive in Johannesburg, in the thin bright air of the high veld, five thousand feet above sea level, was exhilarating. It was especially so in 1919, if one was young: the world was supposed to have been changed for the better by the war, and bright hopes floated about like cheap balloons. Peace had not yet freed my father: though now out of uniform, he was to be occupied for many months more in tidying up the affairs of the African labourers who had returned or failed to return from France. After so many nomadic years he would have liked a settled home among cherished possessions, but my mother was not physically strong enough to run a house. We therefore went to live in a

5

comfortable and well-run boarding house in the well-to-do
residential quarter called Parktown.

It was thought that I must go back to school. I was only just
fifteen, and my father superstitiously believed that unless one
passed examinations and gained degrees or certificates one would
have no future. I went back to St John's, as a day-boy. Although I
had been happy there before, I had been so conditioned by my
years in England that I returned almost as a stranger.

'Look who's here,' I heard one boy say to another on the very
first day, 'the Emperor of China.'

I hid my hands in opposite sleeves and made a grave and
courtly bow, as if to confirm my identity.

Not only the trees but the buildings had grown. There was a
handsome new chapel, a swimming bath, and two sides of a new
quadrangle, with cloisters: the place had quite lost the pioneering,
Early Christian air which had formerly given it such a character of
its own. Father A. was now the headmaster; before long he was to
startle everybody by forsaking the celibate Community of the
Resurrection for the connubial bed. Father B. had returned from
France, where he had been a chaplain to the forces, with a wound
and a decoration, and looked more like an eagle than ever.
Father C. had become a bishop. Father D. had vanished. And
Father E., with his skimpy, reddish, Apostolic beard, was still
shambling about in cassock and biretta, a football in one hand and
a bunch of keys in the other, still smiling and nodding gently and
resignedly at me because I wouldn't play games.

Pink and white cosmos still waved below the terrace; on windy
days red dust-devils still raced across the grassless playing-fields;
a play of Shakespeare's was still produced every year—but
somehow the spell was broken. Houses were being built on the
Kopje, so why climb it? I felt no incentive to work, I was not in
harmony with my surroundings, there was nobody to direct my
mind, the future was indistinct. I fooled about, idled and dreamed,
head and heart were hungry, I was driven in upon myself.

In the holidays I pursued culture by choice and society under
parental pressure. Society meant mostly tennis and dancing,

though I was not predestined to be either a tennis-player or a dancing man. For the first time I got used to the company of girls and young women – the dumb *ingénue*, the jolly tomboy, the clinging goose, the sinewy sports-girl, the prim prig, the maternally inspired social climber fresh from a Swiss finishing-school, the calculating teaser, the nubile monkey. One's attention was directed, as an awful warning, to a nymphomaniac. She was in her thirties and married to a most respectable husband. Women told each other that no man was safe alone with her, 'even for a moment'. Men confirmed this, and made jokes about it. To me she looked predatory. Lean and supple as a cat, she dressed very well but very plainly, often in well-cut tweeds, as it were *en chasseuse*. Her dark hair, done in a modest and even severe style, set off an always colourless face, and in its 'interesting pallor' her restless dark eyes, not large, glittered observantly. It was the mouth that chiefly caught one's attention, the thin, unappeasable lips of a monomaniac. And were there no nice, ordinary girls? Oh, yes. Aren't there always? And there was an intellectual, a finely bred Jewess with a delicate profile like an ancient Egyptian queen and a quiet voice and manner.

I did not take much to most of those whom I partnered on the tennis court or steered round the dance floor – nor they, I dare say, to me. 'William is so critical,' somebody said to my mother. I was. A displaced adolescent in a state of physical and emotional excitement, I found the consumer society in which I moved wanting in charm; it seemed mostly boring and second-rate. Nobody was making anything except money or plans to make more money. Most people climbed and pushed in pursuit of illusory gains or prestige. And for many of the women their chief happiness, or ambition, was to receive invitations to entertainments given by the Governor-General, at this time royal, Prince Arthur of Connaught.

Imagine him standing, dutiful but surely bored, to receive his guests at a dance. His consort stands at his side. Her golden hair is bobbed, and this is thought almost outrageously modern and daring. Her face is unmarked by thought. And a great many very large diamonds scintillate, with every movement, on her head, in her ears, round her neck, on her corsage, wrists, and fingers. Some of them no doubt came out of the African earth above which they now give out an incessant display of coloured prismatic sparks. Royal liveries of scarlet flit or linger in the background, and among the dressed-up guests approaching to be announced and received an anxious debate can be heard on the theme, 'does one or does one not remove one's gloves before shaking the proffered hand of Royalty?' This scene is the crowning ornament of a materialistic city, beneath which at this very moment white men and black are incessantly grubbing for gold.

Since, fortunately, all societies are mixed, even Johannesburg had its saints and simpletons, its persons of taste and creative solitaries. There were at least three connoisseurs of painting, all Jews. One possessed a Courbet; another several Matisses (he was later to open an imposing gallery in Mayfair, later still to take his own life); the third was himself a painter of talent. This was Edward Wolfe. Slight in stature, with a Byzantine face under a heavy black fringe, and gifted with a lively zest for life, he made his own world and lived in it. He had worked with Roger Fry at the Omega Workshop, and was later associated with the London Group. He was as good a friend to me as a nomad who brings one dates and water in a desert. His work and his talk and the vivid environment which, like a bower-bird, he had created for himself, refreshed my eyes and spirit and easily lured me away from the tennis parties and coming-out dances. At one time he went to live in a vacant barrack of a compound on a gold mine, the machinery of which thundered in the background as he showed me his drawings. These had caught in flowing lines the shapely sadness and exiled vigour of naked black miners.

Sweating and shut in underground, the African miners loved when above the surface to dress themselves in gaudy finery, and would wander about playing mouth-organs or zithers; or, wrapped in cherry-coloured blankets they would sit smoking or singing mournfully in the sun. On Sunday mornings they were allowed to indulge in their tribal dances, and nothing could be more splendid than the strength, freedom, and precision of their movements and the barbaric music of the drums and xylophones which accompanied them. But a deep underlying melancholy pervaded the proceedings, and I was gradually becoming aware of the reasons for it. They had been well put by Nesbitt, in the book I have already mentioned, *Gold Fever:*

> The natives, whose own social and economic systems have been trampled under foot by the invaders, are debarred from any real participation in the benefits of that civilisation to the introduction of which those invaders point as the justification for their acts. While the natives are kept down by the legal imposition of inferior status, and by the denial of their right to undertake and be paid for skilled work, they can never taste the fruit of Western progress. At the mines they are, in fact, kept herded like cattle in compounds, from which it is extremely difficult for any of them to go out, even for a few hours. They are kept in close confinement, overworked, underpaid, and denied even such rights as are indispensable for the maintenance of their dignity as human beings. As for progress, that is quite out of the question for the native. His deprivation of all chance of profiting by it is ensured by the administration of laws made by those who are devoted to progress, for themselves.

I had not at this time come across any such clear expression of these facts, but I was beginning to see, to feel, and to think.

I had much to learn, much to read. I was not starved for books. The landscape painter Enslin du Plessis — humorous, independent, sensitive, and hospitable today, just as he was then — lent me Proust: there were not many people in South Africa in 1920 who had even heard of Proust. Somebody else lent me *Ulysses*. To read these books then, at the age of sixteen, was to be carried away and to return to earth with an immensely enriched perception of the nature of life and the possibilities of language. There was an excellent municipal library, which enabled me to read a great variety of books, and some of the best new prose and verse, including the writings of D. H. Lawrence. What freshness, life, and clarity, what a revolutionary newness of vision he brought, however fanciful his doctrines, to replace the increasing staleness, thinness, triviality, and flippancy of the English novel of his time!

In a turmoil of imaginative and sensory experience I would hide myself in the eucalyptus forest known as the Sachsenwald, and in that dry, balsamic air would compose immature verses. I used to draw. And I would practise physical culture—muscle control, and so on—with a professional who made my growing body more resilient and better able to enjoy the mere acts of breathing and walking in the electric air under the clear sky. And when we went down to the Natal coast for holidays, and a tepid wind blew in from the Indian Ocean and rustled the stiff leaves of the sugar-cane, and walking through an orange grove one encountered a thin Indian girl dressed in a magenta sari, with big humid eyes and garnet studs in her nostrils, this different world seemed to invite one on to others more remote and exotic. I was hungry for life, ready to voyage beyond the commonplace.

Not that the Natal coast was all glamour. When the wind blew from the direction of Park Rynie, it brought with it the effluvia of a whaling station, compared with which burning rubber smells as good as mignonette; and an acquaintance who went for a swim rose from under the water unexpectedly wrapped in a clinging pelisse of decomposing blubber. And we were a little disturbed, when staying at a simple hotel in what was then an idyllic solitude, by the private life of its owner. At dead of night he chased his wife round the garden, firing a revolver as he ran, and only desisting when she took refuge in a place made not for drama but convenience. However, the Plomer family did not come under fire, and breakfast the next morning was as usual punctual and appetising.

Sometimes my father would ask me if I had made up my mind what I wanted to do in life. There are times when an adolescent feels he could do almost anything, when the whole of life seems to boil in his veins, but the workings of destiny, temperament, and genes must limit his scope. My father, if chance had allowed, might have made good as a regular soldier, an upholder not so much of 'colonialism' but of what might be called 'colonelism', which seemed to come naturally to his family. Or he might have succeeded as a professional swimmer, or a wool merchant, or a collector of antiques, or, if he had become the 'adopted son' of that rich Australian, as goodness knows what.

My mother once said that if she could have her life over again she would be an actress. She had religious feeling and energy enough to have made a good wife for a parson, but perhaps not enough tolerance. Her good sense, tact, and dignity would have made her an excellent wife for a diplomatist. As things were, she tried to make the best of the marriage and of the disadvantages to which she had vowed herself.

As for me, I have managed to earn a living as a farmer, a shop-keeper, and a schoolmaster. If I had been strongly encouraged when young in my talent for drawing, or if I had grown up in a world where painting was an important interest, I might have made it my life's work. At sixteen, I remember, I put it to myself that I must renounce either writing or painting: it was to write that I felt most impelled. Looking back, I count the influence of my mother as the chief part of my education. It was she who chiefly sharpened my curiosity, my sense of character, my powers of seeing, enjoying, and discriminating, my beliefs and my scepticism, and my consciousness of the fate of the larger and more vulnerable part of mankind, unprotected by money or power.

My father and mother, never rich, had stuck to their joint resolve to give both their sons, at whatever sacrifice, the best sort of education they could. They now most generously offered me the chance of preparing myself for Oxford, as I should have done if I had stayed at Rugby. I refused the offer, which was attractive, for several reasons. First, I did not wish to strain their resources. Next, it was uncertain whether my eyesight was yet stabilised. Then, I fancied some more erratic course.

Oxford might have given me a better education, the chance of working out ideas among my coevals instead of by myself, the chance of making lifelong friends (though I made others else-where), and the chance to take some part, however slight, in the English life of my time, among my own compatriots. I see also the narrowing effects it might have had: it might have made me more of a prig and pedant than I am. Isolation, remoteness, self-reliance, and frugality were to be my tutors. It never occurred to any of us that I might enter a local university, I suppose because in the world from which my parents came the word 'university' was a synonym only for Oxford or Cambridge.

One more visit to the oculist directed me to the great open spaces rather than to books, at least for the time being. My parents began discussing with me how this could best be done.

15

In the Stormberg

In the year 1820 there had been an organised immigration of odds and ends into South Africa from the United Kingdom. A century later a body was founded, with the title of The 1820 Memorial Settlers' Association, to attract a new influx of white settlers, of what its founders would have called 'a desirable type', into the Union. The real pioneering days were over, railways had been built, the land taken up, and the Africans thoroughly exploited. Gone were the days when younger sons were 'kicked out to the Colonies' with a letter of introduction, a hundred pounds, and a sense of adventure. If the new settlers were to settle and not become a burden on the country it was judged essential that each should have a capital of at least two or three thousand pounds.

The plan was that each settler should be expertly advised by the Association as to what kind of farming to take up, and should then be placed on a suitable farm for two or three years to learn the rudiments. During this period he would make himself useful to his hosts in exchange for his keep and tuition, and when qualified to set up on his own would be again advised by the Association on the choice and purchase of land and other cognate matters.

The scheme was well thought out, and was often advertised in *The Times* and elsewhere. The aftermath of the First World War had left many youngish English people at a loose end, and the prospect of peddling vacuum cleaners or running chicken farms did not appeal to the more enterprising. South Africa once more appeared to many a 'coming country', among them retired soldiers or civil servants from India and other parts of the Empire

—not least because of its attractive climate and cheap African labour.

I suppose the founders of the scheme, whoever they were, had political motives. They may have thought it would do something to counterbalance the growth of Afrikaner nationalism. It was now twenty years since the end of the South African War, and naturally enough the Afrikaners were doing all they could to gain control of what they regarded as their own country. In the civil service a good deal was heard at this time about retrenchment—a polite word for getting rid of Englishmen and replacing them with Afrikaners. My father felt sure that his turn would come before long. In the meantime it seemed to him and my mother that the Settlers' Scheme could provide a niche for me, at least until my eyes were all right. It seemed sensible to agree.

'There's no reason,' they said, 'why you shouldn't write or do whatever you want to do later on.'

There would be no difficulty about my candidature, as I was a 'desirable type'—that is to say, I was not some hunted and penniless Lithuanian Jew, or a talented mulatto, and had no convictions for selling illicit liquor to the blacks. If I decided to set up as a farmer on my own, my parents were still likely to be able to launch me with something better than a mortgage. So I became an 1820 Memorial Settler, in my own interest, not in that of any fantasy like a 'White South Africa'.

I said I should like to train as a fruit farmer, growing grapes and peaches at the Cape, or pawpaws and oranges in the Transvaal, but allowed myself to be persuaded, by arguments I have now forgotten, against this intention. My father was convinced, and I allowed him to convince me, that the eastern part of the Cape Province would be a suitable region for me. He cherished his memories of his own early years in those parts, and perhaps he hoped to re-live that part of his life, by proxy, in the life of his son.

A farm was chosen, my boxes were packed, and in the middle of the winter of 1921, that is to say in June, at the age of seventeen, I found myself bound for far-off Molteno—the little dorp where my father had been reproved, some thirty years earlier, by Sir William Cameron for breaking the laws of caste by organising an official banquet.

No banquet awaited me, but an extremely cold and sparsely furnished bedroom in the small hotel. I had to wait a couple of days for my farmer to come in from the country and fetch me, and was most kindly entertained by an old English clergyman and his wife, whose ideas, manners, and tastes had been formed round about 1870.

Molteno itself was like a Middle Western scene a little later in the century. It was a one-horse town, with its main street, railway station, and police station, a few shops with chickens pecking about on the threshold, a Dutch Reformed church, a Wesleyan Methodist chapel and, much smaller, an Anglican church. The streets were few, wide, dusty, and drowsy. An occasional ox-wagon creaked past. Everybody knew everybody else's business, and small scandals took on large proportions. Europe seemed a conception as remote as heaven or hell; and the cats, asleep on window-sills or hearth-rugs, looked as tranquil and detached as images of Buddha. In due course a buggy appeared at the door, my luggage was strapped on behind, and off I drove in an icy wind, seated beside my unknown farmer, Fred Pope by name, to an unknown new life as a farmer's boy.

A 'Memorial Settler' was neither precisely a guest nor an employee of the farmer under whose roof he was living, so good sense and goodwill were needed on both sides. An idle or frivolous apprentice-settler wouldn't be worth his keep. One too young or docile might be exploited or harshly treated by the farmer. I heard of one young man so oppressed by loneliness and unkindness that he hanged himself in a barn. I was lucky. I tried to make myself useful and was treated always with friendly consideration, although I may have seemed a strange specimen from the outside world.

As we drove out of Molteno in the direction of Dordrecht we found ourselves on a third-rate road, in places no more than a stony track, devoid of traffic, and with wide treeless prairies or occasional cultivated lands on either side, backed by the bare rocky mountains of the Stormberg, then turning blue and violet as the westering wintry light gave way to advancing shadow. Once or twice in the course of our fourteen-mile drive I caught sight of some distant clump of trees and the walls of a farmhouse, and at last, as the light was beginning to fail, we came to a great amphi-theatre of flat lands enclosed by mountains. At the foot of one of these stood our destination. The farm bore the Brontëesque name of Marsh Moor, which was appropriate enough to its wild character.

As one turned off the road there was a short approach to the house. On the right were flat arable lands, and on the left kraals, or enclosures, with stone walls about five feet high, some roomy stone sheep-sheds, a barn, a wagon-house, and other farm build-ings. Behind the kraals was a row of circular, thatched huts where the African labourers and their families lived, and behind the huts a plantation of conifers. The farmhouse itself was a cottage of one storey, with a thatched roof, no stoep or veranda, and a central living-room, out of which doors led to three bedrooms, a kitchen, and a small unkempt garden, where in the summer lilies and parsnips jockeyed for position. Beyond the house was a dam overhung by one enormous willow, and beyond the dam loomed the rocky spur of a mountain. The farm had first, I think, been won from the wilderness by the occupant's father, whose fore-bears were from Dorset. It was of a couple of thousand acres, half flat and half mountainous, and supported a great many sheep and some cattle.

Soon after I arrived there was a blizzard and a heavy fall of snow (the Stormberg is more than five thousand feet above sea level, and so cold that maize, for example, cannot be successfully grown there). It was the lambing season, and I at once began to learn the arts of midwifery among the ewes and the curious variations among them of the maternal instinct. Many an evening have I spent in stone sheds by lantern light, obliging a reluctant udder to accept the blind mouth of an unwanted lamb, or dressing a live lamb in the skin of a dead one in order to persuade the bereaved

ewe to bring up the changeling as her own offspring. These were
exercises in patience.

Persons unfamiliar with the ways of sheep think of them as
merely silly and timid and as being all alike. The widow of
Thomas Hardy once told me that her husband, leaning with her
on a gate in Dorset, drew her attention to what every shepherd
knows—that the sheep in a flock all have different faces. Among
sheep there are as many variations of character as among horses,
cats, or dogs. Like human beings they are capable of affection,
cunning, and wilfulness. 'The rage of the sheep' does not seem a
contemptuous phrase when one has seen a man charged and
knocked out by a full-grown Merino ram with great voluted
horns, testicles like a bull's and the light of battle in its eyes.

After the snow had thawed I was sent one morning on horse-
back to an outpost of the farm to count a flock of some thousand-
odd sheep grazing on a mountain in charge of a shrewd and
wizened old Xhosa shepherd. The usual medium of communication thereabouts between masters and servants was Afrikaans, of
which I then knew very little. I had never counted sheep in my
life, even imaginary ones as a soporific, so the proceedings were
liable to more than one technical hitch. The great flock was
driven, according to custom, towards a fence, from which I stood
at a distance and perched on a rock, and was then chivied past by
the shepherd. Sometimes they ran past in ones or two, sometimes
in crowded dozens; sometimes, having run past, they felt mis-
givings and bolted or straggled back again in twos or threes or
disorderly bunches; so it was no wonder that I, never a ready
reckoner, had to count them three times and arrived at three
different totals; but practice made me perfect.

Merino sheep are bred chiefly for their wool, of which they
carry a surprising quantity. It is beautiful in density, texture, and
length, and pearly or creamy in its lustre, which can be seen only
when it is shorn or when the surface of the growing fleece is
parted with the fingers. At shearing-time, when the tawny
mountain-sides were softened into summer green, we worked,
glistening with sweat and the natural oil in the wool, from

daylight to dark, the muscular African shearers looking like heroic bronzes in their gleaming nakedness as they bent over the task and then gathered up the heavy white fleeces and shook them out flat on the sorting-table. There I sorted them, packed them up, and sewed up the bales, learning the poetry of manual labour involving skill, rhythm, and exhilaration.

My chief joy at Marsh Moor was health. The dry, temperate climate, the superb and sunny mountain air, the long days out of doors, the brilliant cloudless nights, the sweet sleep and wholesome food, youth, freedom from anxiety — these were great things. It was a nineteenth-century way of living: there was no motor-car, no radio, and no telephone. Life was simple. We rose early and went to bed early by candlelight, too pleasantly tired to do any-thing but sleep. We lived mostly on wholemeal wheaten bread and porridge of our own grinding and growing, mutton, milk, and butter from the farm, and coffee. A bath was taken at night once a week, the water being heated in empty paraffin-tins on the kitchen stove. Once a week the post was fetched from Molteno. I learnt the unimportance, at least in a good climate, of material comforts. I learnt to thatch, to make or repair fences, to cover roofs with corrugated iron, to sow broadcast, to do simple black-smith's or carpenter's jobs, to cut up a sheep as deftly as any butcher could, and to make bread, and I used with my own hands to make up to sixty pounds of butter every week. As for sheep, I learnt all about them, in theory and practice, their diet and their diseases, their points and prospects, and we used to dock the tails of a couple of hundred lambs and castrate them before breakfast and think nothing of it.

Not the least of my pleasures was to wander in the mountains, where the solitude was complete and the wild flowers new to me — tree heaths, curious liliaceous plants, and canary-yellow dwarf arums. I discovered some caves adorned with spirited and elegant Bushman paintings, ritual and hunting scenes carried out in black, white, and red and yellow ochres. So I lacked neither a garden nor a picture gallery. What I did lack was society — but in a place like Marsh Moor half a century ago one couldn't expect it.

Once a week Fred Pope drove to Molteno to buy provisions, collect the letters, and do business. I seldom went with him, generally having more urgent things to do. In any case there was little inducement; the sleepy dorp had few amenities. I didn't even bother to go there to get my hair cut, but ordered a pair of clippers and with these and a couple of looking-glasses learnt to do it myself. A mile away from Marsh Moor was a farm belonging to some relations of Fred Pope's, and we saw them now and then; but other farmers, three, five, or ten miles away, were Afrikaners, and the Popes were not on visiting terms with any of them. Why was that? Because birds of a feather flock together, and this law of nature is itself a form of apartheid. Because it was only twenty years since the South African War, and there was no compulsion for persons of either race to like or trust each other. If I had been born an Afrikaner I should have regarded persons of English descent as grasping and overbearing intruders, and I might have felt revengeful towards them. If I had been born Fred Pope, I might perhaps have found no compulsion to like or trust Afrikaners and have done no more, at chance encounters, than show superficial civility. But I must say I longed to get to know some Afrikaner families, and I know how much I missed by being cut off from them. At the same time, apart from the friendly intercourse of working together out of doors, anything like social intercourse with Africans was taboo.

Visitors were rare. A friendly Afrikaner mounted-policeman would call on his rounds; somebody would come to buy sheep; occasionally a relation or two of the Popes would come for a short stay. It was quite an event when two carpenters came for a couple of weeks, an Englishman and a young Afrikaner full of life and mischief and bearing the Horatian name of Posthumus. Another time several men came to do some repairs to the house. They were spoken of as 'Totties' (Hottentots) but called themselves the *Bruyn Mense*, or brown folk, though they were in fact pale buff or primrose colour, with a strong strain of Malay in them. They seemed to evoke the atmosphere of Capetown a century before I was born, with their simple and winning manners and clear, soft, seductive voices.

Best of all was a grand old Scotch wanderer, who turned up from nowhere. Born a gentleman in Scotland, round about 1855 or 1860, he had come to Africa when young, and had led an easy-going, drifting, improvident life, much like my father's in his early African days, only begun earlier and continued permanently. Gathering no moss, he seemed quite content. With the air of a *grand seigneur* and easy manners, he got some sort of living as a journeyman blacksmith, and was invited to stay long enough at Marsh Moor to mend some farm implements and make some useful things of wrought iron. A fine figure of a man, with a flowing golden moustache and a ruddy face, a cheerful sceptic with entertaining anecdotes of his earlier days, when the country was freer and wilder and full of odd characters. In spite of his rough life he had retained many of the little as well as the stronger prejudices of his class. 'I do *wish* they wouldn't say "serviettes",' I remember him saying plaintively. It was the sort of thing my mother might have said, and it sounded funny coming from him. While I kept the forge going for him he built up for me out of his past, both ancestral and personal, a world of legend, and I grew fond of him as one might of a benevolent uncle. He left abruptly after giving offence by failing to show, in a particular instance, colour prejudice.

Everything came back to that in South Africa, and at Marsh Moor the colour bar was stronger than the iron he had hammered on the anvil. I remember when I first arrived I made a gaffe by suggesting that I should learn to milk the cows. No white man, I was told, ever milked a cow: evidently it was not 'The Thing'. If the Xhosa farm-servants, who worked faithfully and well, lived at a low standard and were paid a pittance, that was the custom. They weren't treated in the least harshly, but there was no conspicuous human touch in their employer's attitude towards them, or of the paternal care which had sometimes been shown by benevolent owners long before in the days of slavery. They were there, they were necessary, they must do what was expected of them, and that was all there was to be said: but to me their strength and grace, patience and humour, sad songs and cheerful banter, were a consolation and allurement. Once, when the Popes were away for a fortnight, I only saw African faces—but I only saw them across a great divide.

The Eastern Province had its literary associations, and the knowledge that two distinguished writers had grappled success-fully with the solitude of intellectual exile among such rocky peaks as those of the Stormberg gave me comfort. One of the original 1820 Settlers was Thomas Pringle, a lively Scotch cripple, who had come out to Africa at the age of thirty, with the blessing of Scott. He wrote, among other things, 'Afar in the Desert', a poem Coleridge declared to be among the two or three most perfect lyrics in our language. Pringle was only in Africa for six years, but it was long enough for him to leave a record of his sojourn there in prose and verse, to champion the Africans and the freedom of the press, and to defy with real courage the tyrannical administration of Lord Charles Somerset. Returning to England, he became less active in literature than in philanthropy. He did what he could to encourage the talent of the youthful Ruskin, who afterwards wrote patronisingly of him in *Praeterita*, but his chief activity was as secretary of the Anti-Slavery Society. Pringle was that rare thing, a good man. He was the first white poet of his briefly adopted country, and if his subject-matter was on the whole more original than his approach to it, he managed to strike some bell-like notes, and is still read. He fought against injustice, but deluded himself in believing that 'the dragon Slavery' having been destroyed, 'its odious brood, the prejudices of caste and colour, must ere long also expire.' The odious brood is still very much alive.

As a place to abide in, Africa defeated him as it later defeated Olive Schreiner. She had died at the Cape only a few months before my arrival in the Stormberg, and had been buried on the top of a mountain not very far away, as distance is reckoned in those parts. I wish I could have seen her, if only once and in her last days. I did meet people who had known her, including an old woman who had known her when they were girls together, and who happened to die while on a visit to Marsh Moor. This informant told me that once, while employed as a governess, Olive lost this post because, after listening to a pious scolding from her female employer, she replied with a scornful 'God, indeed!'

I had with me *The Story of an African Farm*, and knew her as one who had given lasting shape to forms of life hitherto unperceived or unrecorded and who, therefore, was still living. Such is the power of the written word that she was in fact a closer companion to me than those beings with whom my life was then being passed. Later I was to read, with increasing sympathy and admiration, all her published writings and most of what has been written about her. A creative artist at odds with her environment, she had one thing in common with my father—she was a highly temperamental asthmatic. Formed by her Evangelical background and upbringing, she was a passionate protestant. To protest is not merely to protest against this or that; it is, in the first place, to affirm solemnly; and in both senses her life was one long protest. She protested against war, predatory imperialism, the oppression of minorities, racial and social injustice, political chicanery, and private spitefulness; and she solemnly affirmed the everlasting need for the opposite of these things. In Europe she dazzled some of her contemporaries and impressed others, but when she came to Europe did not strike new roots and was not made fruitful. Then she returned at last to South Africa—'a whole nation,' she had called it, 'of *lower* middle class Philistines'—and there she left her bones. It was a life of restless struggle—physical, intellectual, emotional, social, and literary; she was hounded from place to place by asthma, and animated by a hopeless passion for truth and justice.

At Marsh Moor there was scarcely any time for writing, but I once sent some verses to Harold Monro, the leading poetic impresario of the day. I told him that I had for a time been taught at St John's by an elderly schoolmaster, Simpkinson by name, who had formerly taught him at Radley. He wrote me an encouraging letter in reply, and I reminded him of it when we met some years later.

I didn't have many books with me. For poetry, Blake, Rimbaud, and D. H. Lawrence's *Look! We have Come Through*; a selection of Van Gogh's letters; two or three books of stories by Maupassant and Bunin; some French and English periodicals. It may be true that it is only by being alone that a man can find himself, but it is not by being alone that he can find his proper level. It is certainly not by being alone that an adolescent can find himself, and I felt strongly the lack of congenial society of my own generation.

There was much that enchanted me about the Stormberg, much that I enjoyed in the life I was leading. I kept a big notebook in which I wrote useful prescriptions for the diseases of sheep, the measurements of cowsheds, and particulars about silage, fertilisers, and such matters; but alone in the radiant mountains, out of earshot of anybody, I could have been heard intoning, in the most powerful voice I could produce, the whole of 'Ah, Sun-flower! weary of time'.

What was the next step? How could I, by myself, start a farm of my own at eighteen? Did I really want to? Could I not now spend a year on a fruit farm in the Western Province to find out if it might not be better to grow peaches than breed sheep? Suddenly a perfectly different project was put before me.

16

A Perfectly Different Project

By 1922 my father had wound up the affairs of the Africans recruited for labour in France during the war, and had returned to the Native Affairs of peacetime. His prospects were uncertain. Not being an Afrikaner Nationalist, he was likely to be got rid of quite soon. Only just over fifty, he would receive only a very small pension. Would it be better to stay in Africa or go back to England?

He and my mother were inclined to go and see for themselves whether there were any prospects of a livelihood in post-war England, but were more hesitant than formerly about drawing on capital to pay for the voyage. They must have thought I had some sense, because they asked my opinion. I advised them to go and reconnoitre. This they accordingly did, taking my brother with them in order to leave him at a preparatory school. They had a lively send-off. Just as they were leaving, Johannesburg was in the grip of a revolutionary strike, and soon after they had left the station they had to lie on the floor of their compartment while bullets cracked and whistled through the windows.

When they came back my father was promoted Inspector of Native Affairs and gave his experience to the welfare, as it was called, of Africans working in the gold mines. The task was congenial, but didn't last long: he was, as he had expected, 'retrenched'. He felt a slight sense of grievance. For twenty years he had given his best energies to the public service; he was active for his age, and would gladly have continued. He had a soft spot for the Afrikaners and had often defended them against their traducers, but now felt, understandably, less cordial towards

148

them. The sudden obligation to begin a new life with a pension about one-seventh of that with which his father had retired from the Indian Army caused him anxiety.

The visit to England had not convinced him and my mother that it would be prudent to return there for good at that time. If they had only had themselves to think of, they might have done so, but in the goodness of their hearts they tried to put the interests of their children first. Their chief and generous wishes at this time were to provide my brother with what they thought a proper education and to give me a good start in life, and to do these things it seemed necessary to make some money.

The only one of us with any ability in that direction was at that time my father. He had been thinking of his early adventures in trading with Africans, when he had seen Europeans — including quite unbusinesslike English gentlemen — making their own living at it, an adequate and honest living, while remaining their own masters. He had also been wondering how my newly acquired knowledge of farming could be turned to account. He now thought of a plan. This was to take over a 'native trading-station', colloquially known as a 'Kaffir store', with some land attached, where I could live with my mother and him, our combined energies being given to a happy blend of agriculture, commerce, and home life. The main flaw in this plan was that it did not allow for the amount of continuous hard work it would involve.

Having made enquiries of an old colleague in the civil service in Natal, he received details of a place which seemed promising. This letter he sent on to me, with the suggestion that if I liked the idea I should meet him in Natal; we could then go on together and see the place for ourselves. The first and most startling fact was that the place was described as 'one of the oldest trading sites in Zululand'. Zululand! That was a word to quicken my interest, and raising my eyes from the letter to the bare and ochreous mountain over against the house at Marsh Moor I seemed to see a softer, warmer landscape of sub-tropical verdure springing from a more generous soil than that of what Pringle had called 'Stormberg's rugged fells'.

Entumeni, said the letter, was in a fairly densely populated Native Reserve. And the Zulus, I said to myself, are a distinguished nation. Entumeni, the letter went on, was some dozen miles west of Eshowe, on the main road to Nkandhla and the middle drift of the Tugela river. It was about 1500 feet above sea level. The climate was very healthy, the place itself being in 'a fine mist and rain belt'. There were a hundred acres of land and the soil was good. There were several acres of natural forest on the site, with permanent water from a spring. There was a fair-sized house of wood and iron, besides the store and various outbuildings. There were grazing rights in the Reserve for a hundred head of cattle. The place was not freehold: there was a 99-years' lease, of which about fifteen years had run, with a virtual right of conversion to freehold at the expiration of the lease.

Fifteen from ninety-nine, I said to myself, is eighty-four, so when the lease runs out I shall be a hundred and two. The words which haunted me were 'Zululand', 'Zulus', and 'natural forest'. Clearly words meant more to me than speculation on the scope for agriculture and commerce. I wrote at once to my father and agreed to visit with him this earthly paradise. Sanguine, curious, impulsive, what did I expect?

We travelled north up the Natal coast from Durban by train through the cane-fields. The platforms of the little stations were thronged with Indians, and sometimes through a clearing in an orange grove or mango orchard could be seen some white temple, small and ornate. After we had crossed the swirling Tugela the landscape became flatter, more open and less populous; then the train wound up the serpentine line through the fertile hills and a tunnel of 'natural forest' to Eshowe, the capital of Zululand.

Eshowe, by the way, is a word of three syllables, with each 'e' as in 'end' and the accented 'o' as in 'show'. The name is onomatopoeic, to evoke the sound of a wind among leaves. A conspiracy of leaves, whispering, sighing, and muttering, surrounded the hotel where we spent the night. In the morning they were seen to be as dense as in a tropical scene by the Douanier Rousseau. The verandahs were caves of ferns, creepers, and flowering plants, and an immense avocado tree was covered with heavy and innumerable fruit. The continuous dulcifying rain, pattering among stiff or flexible foliage and dripping and dropping into overflowing cisterns, had gradually ceased, the hot sun rose, and while steam and fragrance rose from the earth we climbed into a rickety flivver with a young Norwegian, and drove out to Entumeni with chains on the tyres, churning at times through deep clay, red and gluey, up gradients of a remarkable steepness.

Perhaps Entumeni bewitched my father and me: it brought us into harmony for once. Someone described us, after we had returned to Johannesburg, as 'the two enthusiasts'; perhaps I had inherited from him something intense and excitable. My mother, like us, and for our sakes, was prepared to give all her energies to an undertaking that seemed justifiable, but she was not an enthusiast. With characteristic scepticism and common sense, born of bitter experience, she opposed our rhapsodising with a few practical questions.

Was the road good? Was the house habitable? It could be made so. Had we seen the books? No; the sub-tenants said they had been sent away for audit. (A wry smile from my mother.) Did I think the land likely to be productive? Possibly; but it was completely different from the hardy, heathy country I was used to and was certainly unfit for sheep-breeding, the only branch of farming I had learnt. Was there any white society? We had heard that there was a mission station a mile or so away, and that a few white farmers had settled here and there outside the Reserve. Had we, any of us, the least idea what we were letting ourselves in for? Probably not, but if we didn't make a success of it, that wouldn't be for want of trying.

My mother sighed. She had made her bed, and as usual she had to lie on it in some outlandish and inconvenient setting. Some women might at this point have said, 'My God, why on earth did I ever marry you? If only I had known what I was being let in for!' But she didn't say it—at least on this occasion. She folded up her needlework and put it away, like a Prime Minister putting away a map of Europe that wouldn't be needed for a long time.

Her friends and my father's were even more sceptical. How could we possibly expect to make a success of our project? Weren't we used to a civilised existence? Could we even speak Zulu? Did we know the first thing about trading? Could we stand the exertion, the isolation, the lack of all amenities, the inevitable loss? Enterprising perhaps, those Plomers, was the general opinion, but foolhardy.

The first thing we did was to clinch the contract. The second was, for us, even more extraordinary: we bought a large, new, and handsome American touring car, a Buick, 'cherry-black' like the highwayman's horse in Harrison Ainsworth's song. None of us had ever taken the slightest interest in machinery, except my brother, much the most practical of us, who was now at school far away in England. Up to now, when in need of a car, we had hired one with a chauffeur. I learnt to drive, we made all our preparations, and off we went with a hired driver by way of Durban.

It was the rainy season, and north of Durban, about half-way to the Zululand border, we came, late one afternoon, to a place where the road forded a stream. It had been raining heavily in the hills, the stream was swollen, and we stopped to see if it was safe to cross. Our driver judged it so, but in the very act of our crossing, the volume of water suddenly increased, and the laden car, awash and half afloat, wobbled as if about to overturn and be swept away. We three males jumped into the water, which was nearly up to our necks, and with some effort shoved the car out on to the road on the other side. My mother, who had been in danger of being trapped in the car and drowned, had sat as calmly as if at a tea-party. She and my father, though at times unduly excitable about trifles, were both commendably cool at moments of real danger or crisis.

Our driver discovered that the carburettor was flooded and we were short of oil. The district, called New Guelderland, was fairly populous, we were on a main road, and an inconspicuous Indian of middle age was watching us with some curiosity. My father asked him civilly, but with the directive air of a white man addressing a coolie, to fetch us some oil. The Indian then gravely turned and with an imperious wave of the hand summoned another of his race and gave him a peremptory order. The irony of this small incident, as we learnt later, was that the first Indian was a very prosperous sugar-planter, far richer than we had ever been.

Even more important than oil was the need of dry clothes and shelter for the night. Luckily there was a small wayside hotel not far off, so we squelched towards it, the water running out of our boots as fast as they were filled by the busy rain which had come on once more. 'Hotel' is an imposing word for the sodden bungalow which stood back from the road in a grove of eucalyptus trees. There were no residents or casual visitors except ourselves. Drinks were brought by the proprietor and his wife. He had evidently come out from England in the South African War, and had remained in 'the coming country'. Perhaps he had been a sergeant. With his white gym-shoes, his big chest outlined by a tight white sweater, his red face with his moustache waxed into two points like needles, he had the air of being about to take a class in physical training. One almost waited for him to shout, 'Knees—bend! Up—down! Up—down!' His wife could only have obeyed such an order with difficulty. She was notably plump, with a gold tooth, fluffy hair like gold wire, very high heels, and a white satin blouse enclosing, but only just, an ample bust. She had the air of a retired barmaid and spoke with a charming Midland accent which took me back to Spondon.

This happy and hospitable pair almost took our thoughts off the deluge outside. After supper she entertained us with popular songs at her piano, but every now and then, while singing

> I'm for ever blowing bubbles,
> Pretty bubbles *in* the sky,
> They fly so high,
> They nearly *reach* the sky,
> Then like my dreams they fade and die—

she struck a muffled chord, which she excused on the grounds that the piano was little used and had been affected by the weather. Later, lying in a small room, a little uneasy about a very large and motionless black spider, like something out of a horror film, on the whitewashed wall, and reflecting that it was still a long way to Entumeni, I fell asleep to the sound of big raindrops beating a spasmodic tattoo on the corrugated-iron roof.

It was perfectly fine by the time we got to Entumeni and took possession of the shabby and neglected wood-and-iron house. There was no fence round the garden. A couple of gaunt cows were scratching their pelvises against the trunks of some handsome tree-ferns. Famished-looking chickens, light-headed from hunger and looking disillusioned, tottered feebly in and out of the house in search of food. Everything looked rubbishy and unkempt. Besides the sad fowls, we took over, by agreement, some cattle, a white horse of middle age and little character, and several dusty donkeys. In fact we took over the whole place as a going concern — going downhill, it almost appeared, at a Gadarene pace.

The interior of the store, which was the *raison d'être* of the whole outfit, was discouraging. It was lofty but dark, musty, and cluttered with old, outmoded, and unsaleable goods. Having seen, without regret, the last of the outgoing tenants, we set to work to reduce dirt and chaos to cleanliness and order. We fenced the garden. We made a kitchen garden. We painted the house and built on to it a pillared concrete veranda. We improved the outbuildings and built new ones. We hacked away undergrowth and grubbed up rank and sinewy weeds. And this 'we' includes our good African helpers, for whom we provided decent quarters. We struggled with the store, with the house, and with the hundred acres. Entumeni means 'the place of thorns', and thorny were those early days — as formidable in some ways as those at Louis Trichardt years before. My mother would have been justified in saying to my father what Hardy (of the comic duo) often used to say to Laurel, 'And *now* look what a mess you've got us into!'

The donkeys made straight for mud-holes in an adjacent valley, sank in them up to the eyes, and were extricated only with difficulty and ropes and some expense of time and labour, and then in some cases too late. The horse, which nobody had the time, the need, or the inclination to ride, ate (as they say) its head off, without, strangely enough, any marked effect on its physique or spirits. The cows either strayed into other people's cultivated fields and gobbled up what was growing there, which then had to be paid for, or they behaved oddly, bellowing like fog-horns in the middle of the night for no discoverable reason, or contracting rare diseases with disquieting symptoms. The chickens, un-accustomed to a proper diet, collapsed from surfeit, or else grew strong enough to deposit their in any case undersized eggs in the 'natural forest' (which we always called the Virgin Bush), where nobody had time to look for them, or, if there had been time, any earthly chance of finding them. Altogether it seemed to me that there was much to be said for wool-gathering in the Stormberg.

We were not too busy to enjoy very much the surrounding landscape. Open, fertile, and undulating, with clusters of dome-shaped African woven huts, with groves and thickets and streams and patches of cultivated land here and there, it was haunted by distinguished birds—toucans, hoopoes, humming birds—and by small mammals like the galago. It invited saunters of the 'nature trail' variety which we were not free to take. From the very first we were pleased with the climate, which never ran to extremes. Almost perpetual sunshine one took for granted, but at the end of a hot summer's day, a dense, refreshing mist would sometimes rush upon us from the south and steep everything in an opaque and silvery silence.

Although physically less strong, my mother slaved in the house to ensure that we had good food, clean linen, and such things. Helped by our robust, good-tempered handyman, Mose Qwabe, I struggled with the outdoor work, the perverse livestock, and the neglected garden. As for the Virgin Bush, I left it almost intact. Weary-bones, I wrestled at night with Bishop Colenso's Zulu dictionary and grammar, and in the daytime lent a hand in the store to get the hang of things. My father's energy, early experi-ence, and love of order were soon improving matters, and we had hired a white assistant who was supposed to be expert, but soon chose to do without him. There was more than enough to keep two men busy with the trading, so I soon found myself almost wholly taken up with that.

For many months on end we worked very hard to make a success of what we had undertaken, to win the confidence of the Africans by honest dealing and to meet their needs and tastes. They soon understood that we didn't intend to exploit or take any unfair advantage of them, and that we liked them and enjoyed their company. The result was that the place became almost like a club, and Africans of all ages and both sexes would drift in for a gossip. Even so, we had to run the place for a year or more at a loss before this diminished and turned into a useful profit.

The Zulus brought us their handiwork or their money, their labour or their produce – maize, millet, chickens, eggs, vegetables, hides, skins, and so on – and could obtain in exchange an extra-ordinary variety of merchandise. It ranged from ploughs, lanterns, textiles, parasols, and musical instruments, by way of many kinds of food and clothing, to love-philtres, aphrodisiacs, and *cache-sexes*, the last-named in assorted sizes. At first we were much en-cumbered by an accumulation of unwanted or demoded goods, but as we got rid of them we replaced with better stuff. From time to time I went to Durban for a day or two, and used to go round the great and fascinating warehouses of the wholesalers, buying imitation jewellery from Czechoslovakia, textiles from Lancashire, bales of American military clothing left over from the world war, tinned beef from the Argentine, penknives from Sheffield or Solingen, mouth-organs and jews'-harps from Germany, silk handkerchiefs from Japan, kettles from Birming-ham, and heaven knows what besides.

The Africans were mostly quite primitive, but some had been superficially 'Europeanised' by the missions or by spells of work in Durban or Johannesburg, and some were betwixt and between. The most primitive were generally the most dignified and grace-ful, and the most suspicious. If one played them a Zulu record on the gramophone their astonishment and pleasure knew no bounds and were constantly renewed. Older women, hearing the thing for the first time, would recoil from it in terror. Sometimes they would peer round it as if they expected to surprise some cunning midget vocalising behind it. Often they would exclaim, 'It's bewitched!'

The physical beauty of the Zulus was conspicuous. Many of them went about all but naked, and their presence was to me deeply and agreeably disturbing. Well-developed young girls would long remain chatting and chaffing each other, their prominent breasts almost under one's nose, or they would playfully divert themselves and each other by removing their scanty coverings in order to reflect their buttocks in a pier-glass near the door, but some were more modest. The young bucks, descendants of Chaka's braves, ornamented with a few beads and little else, and moving with superb grace and upright carriage, were often models of bodily perfection. They used to remind me of Herman Melville's comparison of the beautiful Marquesan islanders with the inhabitants of New York:

> Stripped of the cunning artifices of the tailor, and standing forth in the garb of Eden—what a sorry set of round-shouldered, spindle-shanked, crane-necked varlets would civilized men appear!

Among the more primitive Zulus there was extreme conventionality in matters of custom, conversation, and personal adornment. We sold or bartered large quantities of beads of various colours, which they were very fond of making up into ornaments to wear, but there were certain colours among the old stock we had taken over which no girl would now have accepted as a gift—they were no longer 'The Thing'.

Convention imposed certain taboos in ordinary conversation, but I never expect to hear better talkers. Zulu voices are euphonious and finely produced, and they know all the arts of oratory and conversation—the skilful maintenance of tension in leading up to a point, the vivid description, the harangue, the formal speech, the quick repartee, the dry and ironical comment, the perfect metaphor, mimicry, and so on. Bishop Colenso claimed that the Zulu language could be used to express the most subtle philosophical ideas. It could certainly be used to express a kind of affectionate amusement, as it was by a most good-humoured and handsome man of about my father's age, called Nkiyankiya. Bare-legged, wearing nothing but a leather loin-cloth and an old army tunic, he had such natural style that no grandee dressed by the best sort of London tailor could have looked more distinguished. His shopping was done by his womenfolk and he evidently came to Entumeni because he liked talking to me. I shall never forget his half-affectionate, half-ironical salutation '*Sa'u-bona, umtwana ka Kwini Victoli!*' ('Greeting, child of Queen Victoria!').

Some of the Christianised Zulus were inclined to give themselves airs, especially the women, who tended to have names like Tryphena and Sophonisba. Perhaps they felt 'saved' and therefore a cut above their less enlightened sisters. They tended to adopt European-style clothes, to wear shoes, drink tea, do crochet, use strongly scented soap, and air their ability to read and write. In between the naked primitives, daubed with fat and stained with ochre, and the occasional prigs turned out by the mission stations were nondescripts caught between two worlds—charming backsliders who would take off and roll up their trousers and carry them on their heads when going for a long walk; or demimondaines, christened but not yet confirmed, who would go straight from church to a wild party, and were more able perhaps to 'enkindle wantonness' by enclosing their ripe curves in a loose-fitting calico pinafore than were their stark sisters in nothing but a G-string of blue and white beads. It was not uncommon to see a girl in a neat print dress with the lobes of her ears distended in the primitive style to admit decorative circular plugs as big as the top of a teacup.

The Prince Imperial was said to have ridden right past Entumeni to his rendezvous with death, and there were local place-names which commemorated officers in the British Army who had taken part in the Zulu War. Such white neighbours as we had were of a different kidney. Once a week either my father or I would drive to Eshowe to do business and buy food, and we made acquaintances there – the local magistrate, the parson, and so on – with whom we exchanged occasional brief visits. Our nearest and most congenial neighbour was a stately old Lutheran missionary, a Norwegian, and what used to be called 'a gentleman of the old school'. A distinguished survivor from Victorian times, educated, courtly, and benevolent, and clad always in a frock coat, he made one realise how strangely exotic, how almost Martian, the early missionaries must have seemed to Africans. A widower, he was helped in his labours by two or three Norwegian spinsters or widows, who looked as if they had walking-on parts in some lost, unfinished play by Ibsen, and by cheerful and contented-looking African converts.

Of most of our other white neighbours (none of them very near) it cannot be said that their outlook was liberal, their treatment of the blacks good, or their behaviour to one another polished. Some of them cheated and oppressed the blacks as a matter of course, were at times cruel to them, and would even boast of it to one another, but not – after one attempt – to us. Some of them disliked us a lot, and their dislike was mixed with envy; but if they disliked us, some of them detested one another. The worst of them would assassinate each other's livestock, remove their neighbour's landmarks, and take away the characters of their supposed friends. One man drove a long way to visit another merely to fling a dead dog in his face. As it was no lapdog, the gesture was vigorous.

We did not need these people in any way, either for our livelihood or for social intercourse, but when we first arrived, one or two of them hoped to batten upon us, imagining that we should be naive enough to grant them credit. Some of them came to call and were entertained to tea on the veranda. Either the tea or the unwonted strain of polite conversation appeared to have a laxative or at least a diuretic effect upon them and more particularly upon their wives; after fidgeting they would excuse themselves and make for a little edifice at the back of the house. We had built it ourselves in the interests of hygiene and called it the Pagoda, but in fact it was purely functional in style—of plain brick, whitewashed within, and having a concrete floor. We were at first puzzled by the repeated pilgrimages to this place of convenience, but presently it appeared that it had become the talk of the countryside and that our visitors—who were not 'poor whites' but quite well-to-do farmers—wished not so much to use it as to see its splendours for themselves. It was perhaps partly because of the harmless, necessary Pagoda that they spoke derisively of us among themselves as 'the Royal Family'. It was also partly because we kept aloof from them and had in general a higher standard of living; but I think the chief reason was our unforgivable car.

Again, we merely thought it a necessity, like the Pagoda. Admittedly it was roomy, black, and glossy, and had a contented purr when in motion. I suppose it was I who taught my father to drive it, because he had certainly not driven any car before. After he had been driving it now and then for about a year, I discovered by chance that he believed it went by steam. His conviction was that the petrol, which he knew to be inflammable, was ignited by something called a sparking plug, and then, on the principle of a spirit lamp, boiled the water in the radiator, which then gave off steam to provide the motive power. I saw the logic of this but knew it to be incorrect. I didn't laugh at him, I thought it really distinguished and endearing of him to be so indifferent to the banalities of a mechanised age. In view of his quite unmechanical mind, it is hardly surprising that the car once broke down with a horrid grinding noise when he was at the wheel: great was the joy of our white acquaintance to learn that this hated symbol of what they thought our sense of superiority was stranded on the road miles from anywhere for several days.

To the more primitive Zulus, again quite logically, cars were objects of terror. I must admit I used to drive very fast; it was for my own pleasure and not because it gratified me to see, as I occasionally did, some frantic woman—with a cylindrical coiffure as tall as Madam Arden's and a pot-bellied baby strapped on her back – throw up her lean brown hands with a gesture of *Chacun pour soi*! and then scramble madly up a steep bank by the roadside, her pendulous breasts flying over her shoulders like the ends of a scarf, long before I was anywhere near her. Once, more usefully, I made use of the car to remove a sick French *réligieuse* from the trackless hinterland and nearly lost my life from heat apoplexy in doing so; but I delivered her safely to her destination near the coast.

One of our diversions in Entumeni days was the visit to Zululand of the Prince of Wales (later Edward VIII). We were invited to stay at the residency at Eshowe by the magistrate and his wife. It happened that the Prince's secretary, Sir Godfrey Thomas, had married a cousin of ours, and the settlers round Entumeni were further acidulated when they somehow got to hear of this fortuitous connexion.

When the royal train drew into Eshowe in the late afternoon sun a slight, hatless young man emerged from it, discarding a cigarette only just lighted, then fidgeting his tie with lean, boyish fingers. He looked strained, like an athlete too long keyed up to the top of his form, this errant servant of staring mobs and shaker of innumerable public hands. One had only to see him to understand that the immense volume of cant continually poured out in the press about this 'Prince Charming' who was 'the Empire's best ambassador' was based upon the truth that he was young and to most people appealing, and that he did his duty with energy. The revulsion against him at the time of his abdication seemed a typical *volte-face* of a mob. Whatever the political and constitutional reasons for the abdication, it seemed that British moral indignation, which still used to cause pleasure – especially that of other people – to be puritanically hated, could not forgive him for finding and sticking to private happiness, and so rose up and swept him away.

The whites in Eshowe, as elsewhere, ran after the Prince, staring and jabbering excitedly as if trying to round up a rare animal. The chief event was a gathering of the Zulu clans, in

6

somewhat Scottish style, for a war-dance *en masse*, a fine barbaric spectacle which at moments got a little out of hand. Owing to some fault in what would perhaps now be called public relations, the assembled Zulus largely failed either to see or to show curiosity about seeing the heir of their sovereign, and their attention was diverted by the presence of the heir of their own former ruling house. For the evening the whites had arranged a small dance for the Prince, and there I admired my mother for being able to step out of the tough obscurity of Entumeni and without effort look as if she were in the heart of European civilisation — if it ever had a heart.

We were not dinner-jacket backwoodsmen, but the fact that we were able to live virtually in the orderly way to which we were accustomed was due chiefly to my mother and her faithful Zulu maid, Josephine. To be able to sit down to a proper meal at the end of a hard day, with decent linen and silver, and to see from where I sat a cabinet containing some good miniatures, the candlestick which Byron had given Miss Pigot at Southwell (and which, more than forty years later, I presented to Newstead), and books in fine old bindings — Shakespeare, Milton, Pope — all this didn't make me feel rooted at Entumeni, but it did make me feel that wherever I might go I should be grateful to be able to draw from my roots in England any good sap that might rise from them. All the same, some of our inherited relics seemed incongruous with our present life and prospects. We were only keepers of a 'Kaffir store' in Zululand, and it seemed absurd to have with us a quantity of plate (including a bag of crested livery-buttons) and an enormous seventeenth-century bedspread, with sumptuous Stuart embroidery, which had come down to us from the Ardens. My parents had preserved these inherited objects for their children, but their children had to live in an austerer and unsettled world, so whatever seemed superfluous was sent to England for sale.

If we prospered modestly, it was due chiefly to extremely hard work by my father, and after a time we took on a Zulu assistant. Lucas Makoba was an educated Christian, and was a good companion to me. He had some concern about the position and prospects of his people. He thought they were too resigned to their position, too easy-going and pleasure-loving; they were 'fast asleep', he said. He deplored their lack of unity and their habit of envying, decrying, and pulling down any one of their number who tried to lead or unite them.

He had strong views about the desirability of domestic steadiness and concord, and did not hold with the old Zulu tradition of despising women. He advocated temperance and conjugal fidelity in the male, and deprecated the old Zulu habit by which a man roams or idles ('doing his glories', as Lucas put it) while his woman works in the fields. Even more he disapproved of the custom by which a bridegroom pays a sort of inverted dowry, called *ilobolo*, to his father-in-law. In consequence, he said, a man tended to be always thinking what he had paid for his wife, so had a good mind to make her work to repay him. Lucas looked yearningly to the achievements of Negroes in the United States and wished that his own people could work to be like them. He thought too many young African boys and girls aspired to be teachers instead of learning some useful trade or profession. 'When a teacher teaches,' he said, 'he follows the syllabus. His mind is tied up in a bag. He doesn't worry about little lives.'

17

Look Elsewhere for your Bedtime Story

When the time came for Lucas to leave us, my parents surprisingly decided to send for my brother from England. He had been at a preparatory school and was now just at the age to go to a public school, but my father thought he would do better to come and make his life in Africa: possibly there was a shortage of money. Now that Entumeni was a going concern, I think my father indulged in a fantasy that both his sons might in time take it over and expand it, perhaps running it in conjunction with a farm and a hotel. In fact the life was too much of a strain for my mother; I had put my back into the work, but not my heart; and there was no reason whatever to suppose that it would ever interest my brother.

An odder transition for a boy of thirteen can hardly be imagined, but my brother, who from early childhood had been of a cheerful, sensible, and independent nature, took it well. As I was the elder by eight years we were not exactly companions, though we were on affectionate brotherly terms. He was now sent to school in Durban and came to Entumeni for the holidays.

In some notes which Lucas made for me, he wrote:

Our paper, *Ilanga*, is not taken into sufficient consideration. The man who founded it and built up a school for boys at Ohlange has done a great work, and we do not appreciate it.

This was my own opinion. I had for some time been in correspondence with the man alluded to. *Ilanga lase Natal* was the only Zulu newspaper, and the first periodical, I think, ever to print a poem by me. John Dube — more formally, the Rev. John L. Dube — who had founded and edited it was a man of great worth. The Ohlange Institute, which he had also founded, produced the late Chief Luthuli, the Nobel Prize winner, and it was Dube who, with Africans from other tribes, established the African National Congress for the political advancement of the African people.

Dube invited me to visit him, and I did so. He sent a boy with a white horse to meet me at Phoenix, and I ambled up to Ohlange through that often rather Indian landscape of the north coast of Natal. Dube was a kind, fatherly, gentlemanly host. He was serious without being ever dull or pompous, and we sat up late talking. In the morning he showed me his school and then took me to visit a Tolstoyan settlement near by, one of two founded by Gandhi in his African days.

Gandhi's son, Manilal, who seemed about my own age and had, I think, been born there, received me with great courtesy; he was graceful, gentle, mentally alert, and of finely bred appearance. We found him superintending the production of an Indian newspaper. It was a strange meeting, this, between the son of a great man who had been kicked, stoned, and imprisoned for defending his own people in this harsh and radiant country, a representative of a recently barbaric race who was seeking to better his oppressed and disorientated people by helping to adapt them to a 'Western' civilisation of a sort, and then myself, a mere youth, a member of a ruling race who was there to show he regarded it as a misruling race.

In forming my ideas about the world and my standards of behaviour I had been much influenced by my mother. Intelligent and observant, she had the gift of curiosity, particularly about the manners and motives of all kinds of people. Her Evangelical background, no doubt, had helped her to do what she could for their well-being and to long for more justness and mercy in their dealings with one another, racially, socially, and personally. She was well aware that her education had been hopelessly inadequate, but she never said a word against her mother, who had been responsible for it.

To me it seemed that there must be something fatally wrong with Christianity, if a civilisation which called itself Christian had actively created and enlarged what seemed to me the greatest crime against civilisation, that is to say, the First World War. I also thought that puritanism, whether Catholic or Protestant, had falsified, misled, and distorted human nature. My mother saw the force of my objections but argued that, whatever harm Christians had done, their creed was a force which had made much more for good than evil; and that any creed which tended to make men less inhumane towards one another was deserving at least of tolerance. She certainly believed, and so did my father, even if in a 'paternalist' way, in the human dignity and human rights of Africans.

I myself had been tenderly cared for in infancy by Africans, and as I grew up was conscious not only of feeling protective towards them but of warm admiration and affection for them. I wanted to be with them and to get to know them as fellow-beings. I would gladly have spent weeks or months living, working, and playing with Africans, and could easily have adapted myself to unfamiliar or uncomfortable ways of living. Two things made this impossible. The first was the Berlin Wall of racial and social segregation which barred any but furtive or guilt-burdened intimacies. A feeling of guilt might arise, on the part of a white, from knowing that, presuming on his status, he was exercising, with impunity, some sort of *droit de seigneur*. The other obstacle was that earning one's livelihood in the Entumeni way made an almost whole-time demand on one's energies. Nevertheless, my strong flow of feeling had to shape something, if only a protest. The shape it took was on paper.

In the Sixties and Seventies of this century the frustrated, life-hungry, idealistic, and disillusioned young have tended to join in public demonstrations and to utter their own inner turmoil in some kind of poetry. In the Twenties it was more usual for them to write a novel. A literary historian with nothing better to do might find it curious to trace, in the minor English novel-writers of the period, the workings of revolt against the society to which they had been brought up to conform.

When I began my novel I was nineteen. I had been largely deprived by circumstances of the direct influence, correction, and guidance of my intellectual equals and superiors. They might have made me more diffident. As things were, I had the false confidence of inexperience and a kind of youthful priggishness. I finished the book when I was twenty-one, and sent the manuscript to Leonard and Virginia Woolf at the Hogarth Press. Why? I had no personal connexion with them whatever, but I had liked their own writings and (no wonder) had been impressed by some of the writers they had published. I had written with a hard pencil on thin paper, and the Woolfs must have had a strong curiosity to read the novel at all. It must certainly have surprised them to be hearing from Zululand. They not only read the manuscript but expressed a lively interest in it and accepted it for publication. So sure of myself was I that I believe I had almost taken this for granted. My mother showed more pleasure than my father at the news. If he was ever pleased by anything done by his sons, he kept it to himself.

Turbott Wolfe bears the date 1925, but owing to a printers' strike — not caused by their being asked to print this book — it didn't appear until the following spring. In the meantime, in June of that year, a mutual acquaintance told me that the poet Roy Campbell had come back to Durban, and urged me to get in touch with him. Royston Dunnachie Campbell was a son of the Dr Campbell who had taken good care of my mother when she had been ill in Durban at the beginning of the century. He was two years older than I, and had spent several years in England, where he had married a beautiful girl, Mary Garman. In 1924 he had produced a long poem, *The Flaming Terrapin*, which had been published by Jonathan Cape on the recommendation of T. E. Lawrence, and which I had read.

On my next visit to Durban to buy useful and ornamental things, for the supposed benefit of both the Zulus and the Plomers,

I invited him to lunch with me at Twine's Hotel, where I used to put up. With its shady balconies overlooking the palm trees of the Esplanade—nowadays crammed with traffic, but quiet enough, in June 1925, for the passing jingle of a rickshaw-puller's ornaments to be audible—the hotel had, like the Durban Club next door, an air of Victorian Colonial homeliness. We had much to talk about and got on well, and after lunch we walked on the sand in the Bay, the tide being out, and talked for hours. I told him about my novel, and he told me of a project to produce a literary magazine and asked me to help him with it, which I gladly agreed to do.

I don't remember why Campbell had come back to South Africa. Perhaps it was to introduce his wife to his family and to South Africa, and perhaps to consider the possibility of remaining there. They were not living in Durban, but had been lent a house on the so-called south coast of Natal (i.e. south of Durban), and he at once asked me, with characteristic warmth, to go and visit them. Before long I was able to do so. Umdoni Park, at Sezela, was an estate belonging to a rich sugar-planter called Reynolds, who lived, some way inland and apart from the cane-fields, in a house something like a smallish late-Victorian country house in England. It was approached by a drive and surrounded by a park, with well-kept lawns, spiky palms, and ornamental sub-tropical trees and shrubs, poinsettia, hibiscus, and bougainvillaea. Inside, it was solidly and comfortably furnished: one had an impression of panelling, deep leather armchairs, antlers, decanters, and cigar smoke. It was the planter's son, Lewis Reynolds, who was the backer of the proposed magazine. He was an amiable young man who had been up at Oxford and later attached to General Smuts as some sort of aide at the Versailles Conference. He collected books, and was a keen reader of Aldous Huxley, then much in fashion. I remember him, young and boyish-looking, with a new copy of *Those Barren Leaves* in his hand and speaking appreciatively of the book's format.

Among the features of the estate were a golf course; a hilltop house given by the senior Reynolds to the nation as a holiday residence for tired Prime Ministers, and occupied at that time by the widow of General Botha; and a swimming pool constructed among the rocks on the seashore, there being a danger from sharks to bathers in the open sea. A few hundred yards further south, in the bush above the sandy beach, from which it was separated only by the railway track to Port Shepstone, stood a bungalow sometimes occupied by a locally well-known painter, Edward Roworth. It was in this dwelling, which I think had been lent to them by Roworth, that the Campbells and their infant daughter were living. It had a veranda on three sides and was built on a seaward slope overlooking the Indian Ocean. There was no garden: the house stood in a clearing in the bush, and steps led down in front to the railway line and a path of deep, dry, white sand through the bush to the beach, only a few yards away. It was an ordinary Natal house of the late nineteenth century, with a corrugated-iron roof and boarded interior walls covered with shiny varnish. At a short distance from the house was a *rondavel*, a round room standing alone, used by Roworth as a studio, and now adapted as a guest-room for me. I was no stranger to this coast and its perfect winter climate, and felt anything but a stranger to Roy and Mary Campbell, who were very good to me and very good company. Campbell and I had in common a sense of isolation and alienation, and we were both high-spirited. Each was dedicated to imaginative writing and to the recognition and perpetuation of the first-rate in literature. We liked the same sort of jokes, and agreed that the cultural pretensions of English-speaking South Africa at that time were mostly absurd, mediocre, or contemptible.

From the moment that *Turbott Wolfe* appeared, Campbell championed it most generously, both in private and in print. He told me he thought that, after publishing Eliot, Herbert Read, and Graves, such an orgasm had never been experienced before by the 'elegant and accomplished' Hogarth Press. The book is still in print, with a long Introduction by Laurens van der Post, so I will avoid describing it. Forty years after it appeared Cyril Connolly included it in *The Modern Movement: A Discussion of 100 Key*

6*

Books from England, France, and America, 1880–1950, the key to that movement itself being the spirit of revolt.

Yes, it was in a spirit of revolt that *Turbott Wolfe* had been engendered, and I should have been surprised if it had been received locally with rapturous applause. I was pleased by the violence of the reactions it provoked. After Flaubert had published *L'Education Sentimentale* George Sand wrote to him, 'They go on abusing your book. It has shown too well the disorder that reigns in people's minds. It has rubbed the open wound; people recognise themselves too well in it.' *Turbott Wolfe* had rubbed the open wound of South Africa racialism.

Leading newspapers devoted long leading articles to vituperation, and Campbell wrote to me in Zululand to say that the editor of a Durban paper had been seen by Reynolds 'with his jaws chattering together with rage' after reading it. In writing about it these rattled journalists borrowed their vocabulary from the backyard. They said the book was nasty, it was garbage, it was pornographic, and ought to be burnt. They wrote in the same way as before long Nazis would be writing in abuse of 'degenerate' art. How horrible it would have been if they had praised me! Then I should have had something to worry about. The chorus of vilification was not universal. The book had its champions, and I heard of two instances of men coming to blows over it in public. There were even one or two favourable reviews and some courageous letters in the papers. 'He has defied public opinion and fusty usage,' said one of them, 'and has made us see the larger issues with a poet's vision.' Us? Very few of us.

Clearly the book had dragged into the sunlight some of the guilt and fear and self-deception of the whites in regard to the blacks. Some years later I was amused to hear that *Turbott Wolfe* was being kept under lock and key in the public library at Durban, sharing a shelf with Rabelais, Boccaccio, *The Origin of Species,* and some illustrated books on classical sculpture; but, as Herman Melville once remarked, 'Those whom books will hurt will not be proof against events.'

While the hullabaloo was going on, I received a sparkling letter from my Uncle Franklyn, who had settled for good in Spain. 'You have managed to catch an effect,' he wrote, 'where tedious people only catch malaria.' Then the reviews began to come in from London and New York. In England the book was first noticed by Desmond MacCarthy, who said it had prevented him from looking out of the window of a train for three hours. What more could a writer ask? There was a wise warning in the *New York World*, which wrote 'Look elsewhere for your bedtime story.'

Even my father couldn't help beginning to be impressed. There were some passages in *Turbott Wolfe* which amused or interested him because we had shared some mood or experience from which they derived. And although he felt some concern at my having, as he put it, 'stirred up a hornet's nest,' he had, after all, always been regarded as negrophile, and perhaps took some sort of pride in his rebellious child. My mother was openly pleased with my sudden emergence. In any case, parents who feel that their own lives have not given them full scope for their potentialities may reasonably enjoy signs of what seems like promise in their children. At the same time it became obvious that although I might remain some time longer at Entumeni it could not be my destiny to stay there. My father took this well, in view of all the trouble he had taken over the place, largely for my sake. He had no belief in writing as a means of making a living, but saw that I meant to go on with it.

'If you want to go to the Devil,' he said quite affably in his archaic idiom, 'you must go to the Devil in your own way.'

The plans for the magazine were taking shape, and it became clear that if I was to help Campbell with it I must go and settle for a time, as he urged me to do, at Umdoni Park; so I went. There now began a short phase of intense activity and enjoyment, which was remarkably fruitful. The first number of the magazine, *Voorslag*, appeared in June 1926. The title signifies a whiplash: we intended to sting the mental hindquarters, so to speak, of the bovine citizenry of the Union. Most of the first number was written by Campbell and myself, either under our own or fictitious names. It also contained a philosophical article by General Smuts, which advanced the proposition that 'beauty would be there even if we were not there to behold it'.

Literate South Africa was somewhat puzzled by *Voorslag*. It had been prepared to welcome Campbell's reappearance as a poet, for it thought, in its fatuous way, that poets lived in a dreamy cloud-cuckoo-land and had nothing to do with everyday life, but it was disconcerted to find him exuberantly praising *Turbott Wolfe* and collaborating with its author. The tone of the press was on the whole respectful, bewildered, and slightly cautious. The second number, again mostly written by Campbell and myself, was more satirical than the first. Differences arose with the promoters as to the future policy to be pursued, and not choosing to compromise with their timid philistinism we left them to pursue their own fancies. The magazine dragged on for a few months, but without us had not enough horse-power to sustain it. We had derived a good deal of amusement from the enterprise and perhaps, like twentieth-century Bushmen, had left a few vivid paintings on the walls of that dark cave, the mind of the white South African. Certainly nothing remotely like *Voorslag* had confronted its readers before, nothing so European, so cultivated, so forceful, ironical, and direct. It was too confident, too new, too lively; and the journalists, beginning to understand what fools they had made of themselves over *Turbott Wolfe*, tried to be respectful, to stick to their prejudices, and to hide their ignorance. Naturally they floundered.

Special circumstances had brought Campbell and me together. It seems unlikely that we should have been mutually attracted at Oxford or in London; the differences in our backgrounds, temperaments, outlooks, ambitions, and tastes were great. Now the sun warmed us, we were full of energy, and conscious of doing things never done before. I felt free and forward-looking, but for Campbell this was not altogether an easy time. He was suffering from what was then called neurasthenia. I think we might now call it hypertension. I suppose it may have been partly hereditary, and partly to do with uncertainties about the immediate future of himself, his wife, and his two infant daughters. He seemed much affected by the death of his father but much more by his environment. His native land had got on his nerves. 'The whole of this country,' he said one day, 'has an acid smell, and all the white people have khaki faces.' It is the function of a poet to say things for effect, sometimes in a teasing way, but when, on 18 August 1926, he remarked, 'One must be theatrical at all costs,' I felt, in view of his already noticeable tendencies to rodomontade and fantastication, a sudden chill—even though to condemn the irregularities of a poet's behaviour may be a failure to recognize that they may condition his ability to write his poetry.

This was not a phase of his life in which he was thinking how glorious it would be to take bulls by the horns: we were too busy twisting the tails of asses. And that reminds me that his often-quoted epigram which ends with the line

But where's the bloody horse?

was the admirable outcome of a casual remark by me. We were speaking about a certain South African novelist, in those days much reviewed in England, but not read with any respect by us. I said I thought it odd that English reviewers constantly praised her for 'restraint', that I couldn't see what she was supposed to be restraining; and that the only one of her novels I had read seemed to me like a dog-collar without a dog inside.

Campbell wrote at night, slept in the morning, and appeared at lunch-time. He ate only scantily and at odd moments, took no exercise to speak of, had a great many baths, and was often sucking lemons or smoking cigarettes. He sometimes went fishing, or flew a kite from a fishing rod, and he liked making a bonfire at night on the rocks near the sea, which seemed to me the sort of thing Shelley might have done—not that he took after Shelley. He was much under the influence of Nietzsche and somewhat under that of the French Symbolists. We sometimes read Baudelaire and Rimbaud aloud, and amused ourselves with twenty stout volumes of Chalmers' *British Poets* which had been given to him. I don't remember his speaking with warmth of any English poets except Marlowe, Pope (for *The Dunciad*), and, oddly, Robert Nichols, in whom he found a congenial romantic streak. I think, as I look back, that English tradition and English life were quite alien to him, and that he neither understood nor responded to them. He was a wild Highlander.

Sometimes we went for a swim, or strolled in the bush, or along the railway track to the store at Sezela. Once I was going there alone in the afternoon and passed three or four whites, male and female, going the opposite way. I took no notice of them and had perhaps given them what seemed a disdainful look, because, after they had passed me, one of the females called out, 'I am! I am!' Campbell was much amused by this, and said I should take it as a compliment.

'The *I'm nots*,' he said, 'salute the *I am*.'

In the evenings Mary Campbell sometimes gracefully played the guitar, watched by blue-headed lizards with the cold eyes of music critics, and Campbell would sing sea-shanties like *Shenandoah*, which were popular in the Twenties. In my mind they are associated with the rediscovery in the same decade of Herman Melville. Since then Melville has been the object of such a cult in America, and of such innumerable theses and sterile academic combings, siftings, proddings, and probings, that his very name must have set up reader-resistance. But in those days he burst upon many a young imagination as a splendid original. His romantic voyagings in the last haunts of noble savagery, his isolation, his grandeur, and the neglect he suffered in his lifetime all appealed strongly to Campbell, by whom my own interest in Melville was much fostered and stimulated, with the result that in later years I wrote introductions to reprints at various times of *Redburn*, *Whitejacket*, and *Billy Budd*, and also edited a selection of Melville's shorter poems.

The short period of our close association was in fact remarkably fruitful for both Campbell and myself. Among other things, he widened and enriched my understanding of poetry. At the same time, an evident intensity, which at first surprised him, in my feelings about racial conflicts in South Africa, and my open sympathy with Africans, were not without an effect, a temporary effect, upon him. At Umdoni Park I wrote, among other things, a long story, *Ula Masondo*, which was more coherent and objective than *Turbott Wolfe*, and gave, I think, an original perception of the impact upon a tribal African of being immersed in an industrial revolution.

Every moment seemed fertile. A writer going through a strongly creative phase may find he has developed a more than ordinary power of immediate assimilation. A few words over-heard, a chance incident or encounter, a paragraph or even a phrase in some book or newspaper, stray facts or current ideas may hurry forward and offer themselves just when and where they are wanted: earlier or later they might be useless or un-noticed. In this state of acute impressionability the distinction between living and writing seems almost to disappear: every action, every impression, seems integrated in a single function and purpose. So it was with us.

Under the stress of neurasthenia, rows over *Voorslag*, uncer-tainty about the future, and perhaps my negrophilism, Camp-bell's poetic faculties were in full swing. On the night of 28 July, just after I had gone to bed in the *rondavel*, he came hurrying in with the manuscript of 'The Serf'. He was very excited, and said it was the best thing he had ever done. I think he was right. In the morning I told him I thought both this poem and the splendid 'Zulu Girl', also new, ought to be printed in England. I asked him to let me send them to Leonard Woolf so that they could become known in London as soon as possible. Leonard Woolf arranged for them to be printed in the *New Statesman* and the *Nation* — ironical settings, in view of Campbell's later hostility to all forms of liberal and leftward opinion.

On the night of Saturday 31 July he finished both 'To a Pet Cobra' and 'The Making of a Poet', and the next day read them aloud to me. On Thursday 5 August I read aloud to him some passages from a letter addressed to me from Oxford in February 1922 by my old Rugbeian schoolfellow, Darsie Gillie. In one of them was a translation of part of Kuhlemann's 'Tristan d'Acunha'. This so enkindled Campbell that he began to write a poem on the same subject. He worked at it all night and brought me the first version just after sunrise. It was not until Saturday 14 August that he read me the completed version. He read it so well that I was moved to the verge of tears. This poem also appeared in the *New Statesman* and drew an appreciative letter from T. S. Eliot, which besides being a well-deserved compliment was an instance of Eliot's knowledge of poetry: he wondered, he said, whether Campbell had heard of a poem on the same subject by a German called Kuhlemann.

Campbell and I do seem to have been the forerunners we felt ourselves to be in those days. Forerunners of what? Of a stronger consciousness of the functions, status, durability, and influence of imaginative literature than had (for obvious reasons) been previously conspicuous in South Africa—in English-speaking South Africa at least; and forerunners of fine and various and courageous efforts made by South African writers to apply themselves to the hidden forces in the heart as well as to the patent conflicts and complexities of their country.

In later life Campbell and I were estranged. I blame myself, and am ashamed to have been an unfaithful friend to one who had been so generous to me, but there was too sharp a divergence in our opinions and affinities and in what might now be called our life-styles. It was from him that I first heard the generic term 'Bloomsbury', uttered with a touch of contempt. Knowing that *Turbott Wolfe* was being published by 'Bloomsbury' he had no doubt expected it to be mild and polite and imbued with Cambridge-bred, rationalist superiority. It surprised and impressed him and when I was attacked he defended me. I think a romantic idea of himself as a wronged and persecuted hero had already recurred in his writings, and perhaps he didn't quite like the idea of my drawing *all* the fire, so in his 'Poets in Africa' we appeared as 'twin Sebastians', each in his 'uniform of darts'. Well, I had woken up one morning to find myself notorious, but hadn't at all rehearsed the role of martyr.

Until Campbell found how strongly I had reacted against accepted ideas about what used to be called in those days 'the Native Question' he had, I think, tended to share the prevalent white South African attitude to the black South African—a variable amalgam of tolerance, indifference, and impercipience, at its extremes tending to contempt and brutality in one direction and affection in the other. My obsession with the situation of the black African, whom I had been brought up to regard as a human being with a head and heart and vast potentialities, and whom I had seen frustrated and humiliated, perhaps attuned itself for a while to his feeling, and attitude, of conscious isolation and pugnacious independence.

Preparations were made for leaving the house at Umdoni Park, and we departed for his mother's house in Durban on 29 August. The Campbells were thinking of going back soon to England, and I was thinking that I might go with them. In fact they didn't leave until early in 1927, and in the interim Campbell had ideas about bringing out a successor to *Voorslag* to be called *Boomslang* (Tree Snake), but it remained unhatched. As for me, I had by then left in an opposite, perhaps symbolically opposite, direction.

In the early days of *Voorslag* we had heard from someone in Durban who wished to contribute something in Afrikaans. As I was going to be in Durban, Campbell suggested that I might meet this prospective contributor and encourage him or not, as I might think fit. I had no hesitation in thinking it fit to encourage a young man of uncommon distinction and intelligence, who seemed to me modest yet confident, and imaginative, and who had perfect manners. His name was Laurens van der Post. One of the thirteen children of an impoverished nobleman who had emigrated from the Netherlands and had become a landowner and State official in the old Orange Free State, he was at this time a journalist—but in spite of that a defender of *Turbott Wolfe*. He had duly visited Umdoni Park and had made his contribution to

Voorslag. He now, at this uncertain and critical turning-point of my life, came to me with an extraordinary piece of news.

In the course of his work Van der Post had made the acquaintance of Katsuye Mori, the captain of a Japanese merchant-ship at present berthed at Durban. He had told Captain Mori about me, and Mori had said he would like to meet me. On 30 August, Van der Post visited him in his ship and had a long talk with him, the upshot of which was an invitation to both of us to sail with him to Japan as his guests. He would be there a fortnight between voyages and that would be long enough to take a tourist's glance at the country. I was so surprised that you could have knocked me down with a *netsuke*.

Van der Post had no difficulty in getting leave from his newspaper. As for me, I had to make up my mind quickly, since Mori was sailing in three days' time. I knew that, if I accepted, I could never be content with a mere fortnight in Japan, and that if I refused, such a chance would not recur. On Thursday, 2 September 1926, the *Canada Maru*, a small cargo ship, left Durban for Kobe with Van der Post and myself as the only passengers.

I heard in later years that Campbell was supposed to have said that he had been left 'to face the music': but there was no music, and the *Voorslag* episode was over.

At Entumeni the news was taken philosophically. My brother was just fifteen, and his ambitions were no more fixed in Zululand than mine had been. He soon decided to go to the United States, my parents paid his passage, and without any other help he was soon earning his living in New York. After some years he chose to become a Canadian citizen and was to have a distinguished career as a sailor, retiring eventually from the Canadian Navy with the rank of Commodore, a great many decorations, a charming English wife (his second), and three fine children.

Both the young birds having left the nest, my parents felt neither inclined nor able to carry on the establishment at Entumeni, so they sold it and returned to England.

18

A Passage to Asia

I was twenty-two and Laurens van der Post was even younger. He was then unmarried, and I had no compelling ties. He could make the voyage an exercise in his profession. I had no money, no degree, no trade or profession; I had my mother's curiosity and my father's restlessness. Captain Mori had been pleasant and persuasive, and evidently had some confidence in our characters and prospects. What needs explaining is why he had pressed us to go with him to his own country.

He was in his thirties. He came of the Samurai class in the southern island, Kyushu, had been educated at Etajima, the Japanese naval college, and had entered the Imperial Navy, with which he had served in the Mediterranean and elsewhere during the war of 1914–18. His upbringing, education, and experience had been determined by duty, tradition, and convention, by 'custom and ceremony', and had produced a balanced and capable man with formal manners and of dignified appearance. His mind was serious and active, his behaviour prudent and deliberate, and his body vigorous. He was sturdily built, not particularly short, very erect, with an ivory skin (occasionally flushed by alcohol or excitement) and a broad face with regular features, the eyes rather far apart ('always a good sign', my mother used to say), the bony structure strong but not heavy, and the maxillary muscles noticeably developed. To support his dignity he wore a sparse moustache and beard. He sometimes joked about this with a touch of boyish playfulness. He gave the impression of being in control of himself and of his surroundings, his ship was as spotless as his person, and from his allusions to his family it was plain that he was as good a husband and father as he was an affable companion. Van der Post and I were anxious to make what amends we could for the insults to which he had been subjected at Durban because of his Asian aspect, and which he had suffered with dignity.

The *Canada Maru* belonged to the Osaka Shosen Kaisha, one of the two leading Japanese shipping lines. It had chosen Mori to open up a new and regular cargo service between Japan and East and South Africa. Since he had been charged to open the way for closer trade relations, his task was to some extent diplomatic. He was confronted in both countries with a strong racial prejudice and with commercial distrust as well.

On his very first voyage to Africa (this had been the second) he had scored a diplomatic success. The evidence hung on the wall of his cabin in the shape of a framed and signed photograph of an obviously English couple—a tall man, dressed in an expensive-looking suit, standing on a lawn, with his wife beside him in tweeds, both of them hatless, and, I think, with some kind of terrier at their feet. If, in a dentist's waiting-room, one had noticed this photograph in the *Tatler* one would not, except for some personal reason, have looked at it twice—but this was not a dentist's waiting-room, it was Mori's cabin, and the photograph was a trophy, almost a scalp. It represented, he explained, the Governor of Kenya, who had (by Mori's account) been gracious and cordial, and had gone so far in promoting 'good relations' as to consent to accompany Mori as his guest and passenger on a short coastwise voyage.

This triumph at Mombasa had no doubt won Mori the commendation of his employers and his Government, and he had no doubt been anxious to achieve at Durban some comparable feat. I suppose Van der Post and I were the best he could do. He seemed to be bearing us off to his far country very much as in the days of Captain Cook exploring navigators used sometimes to carry home for exhibition in Europe natives of the Pacific islands. We were very young, it is true. We had no official status. I hope we seemed polite. We had at least one quality very rare among whites in South Africa, a complete absence of racial prejudice—and that emotion was perhaps the greatest obstacle in Mori's way. Rarer still, we showed a sympathetic curiosity about Japan. Also, he judged us to be not without influence. Van der Post was on the staff of the principal newspaper in Natal, and I had written a book and helped to produce a magazine, both of which had become widely known there and had been noticed in England and the United States. Mori knew the potentialities of the written word.

Since Mori thought we might be useful to his country by helping to lessen difficulties in his way, he naturally made himself very agreeable to us, but I believe he liked us for our own sakes. If he was making use of us, he was delightfully enabling us to make use of him. There was no deception on either side, there were no commitments: this was a case of mutual aid. If we had not both liked and trusted Mori we should not have launched ourselves on this unexpected adventure.

My ignorance of Japan and the Japanese was flagrant. I had given them little thought. In the far-off Spondon days, during a visit to the Isle of Wight, I had seen a large battleship, a complicated structure, gliding through a golden morning haze.

'Look at the pretty flag, Billy,' somebody had said. 'The rising sun! That great big ship belongs to the plucky little Japs who beat the Russians. Yes, they're our friends, and perhaps some day you'll go and see their pretty country, where the houses are made of paper and the ladies wear chrysanthemums in their hair.'

If I had later occasionally seen Japanese in London, I had never spoken with them. One had simply grown up with this romantic, period conception of their race as 'quaint', 'plucky', 'clever' little people, who lived in picturesque surroundings, their womenfolk dainty and petite, with names like Nanki Poo, fluttering silk fans all day and mincing about at night with paper lanterns. Later on, from Loti, one had gathered that daintiness was happily united with easy virtue. I had read a few books by or about Lafcadio Hearn, two or three travel books, and a couple of metallic sonnets by Heredia. These were all right as far as they

went; now one must begin to learn. It appeared that it must have
seemed to the interest of the Japanese to make the most of
Western sentimentality about them, and that behind a barrage of
cherry blossoms the militarists had built up their heavy industries
and plans to expand abroad.

Our first port of call was Kilindini. Mori went ashore in a
topee and a well-cut suit of cream-coloured silk and carried an
ebony stick with a silver top. These did not make him look
dandified but very much the *soigné* Samurai. While he was
attending to his business and cultivating 'good relations' to
prepare the way for Japanese trade, Van der Post and I explored
Mombasa. We asked a pleasant young Englishman, retrenched
from the Indian Army, if there were any good books to be had
about Kenya. Glancing furtively over his shoulder, he admitted
the existence of *Kenya*, by Dr Leys, and offered to lend it to us if
we would promise not to tell anybody. This made us laugh,
because we knew the book well. Dr Leys had sent me a copy of it,
I had reviewed it in *Voorslag*, and it had largely formed our ideas
about Kenya.

Van der Post and I played tennis on a concrete court; through
its fissures tropical weeds protruded; and the balls had long lost
their bounce. The game was therefore in slow motion and full of
hazards. Evidently at Mori's behest, we were entertained to a
lavish dinner by a Japanese merchant and his wife. As course
succeeded course and drink followed drink, we grew more and
more conscious that we were being made much of.

Mori naturally wished to sustain and cultivate his 'good relations' with the Governor, announced that he was going to
Nairobi to see him, and invited us to go too. What next? From
the train we watched springy antelopes, cantering zebras, and
leisurely giraffes which regarded it with a mild incuriosity, their
heads protruding through the tops of trees against a background
of the sun-dazzled equatorial snows of Kilimanjaro.

In Nairobi, which then seemed a sort of tropical version of a
Middle Western pioneer township, the hotel in which we stayed
was as good as a play. Among those taking part were an American

professional big-game hunter; boyish settlers from the lesser English public schools; an adventuress in a cloche hat and jodhpurs who, out of bravado, rode into the dining-room on a spanking chestnut mare, dismounted airily, and tossed the reins to the nearest waiter; tanned but anxious-looking young couples of the stranded gentry who rattled round to the banks in Ford cars to try and increase their overdrafts; a dressy but superannuated lady novelist looking round with haggard eyes for copy and a new husband; well-bred young women out from England to visit landowning relations; a Balkan speculator; a touring bishop. The partitions between the bedrooms were thin, and at night the drowsiest ear might receive lessons in biology. And where were the Africans? They were in the future.

In the morning Mori invited us to go shopping with him. We went with him to the premises of an Indian taxidermist, to whom trophies of many a safari were brought to be mounted. Picking his way among horns, tusks, and antlers, bottled serpents, trays of glass eyes, and huge hairy stuffed carcasses, Mori gravely approached the proprietor, and we heard him say (since the Japanese sometimes have bother with the letter 'l'), 'I desire some rion's whiskers.'

Van der Post and I looked at each other enquiringly, but the taxidermist, a stately person in flowing robes, took the request as the most ordinary thing in the world, and presently handed over an envelope in which he had placed some long bristles. Mori explained that he had a friend in Japan who possessed a lion's skin but the whiskers had moulted and been swept away by a maid: it had been much hoped to replace them—but only by the real thing.

Mori made it known that he wished to pay a courtesy call on the Governor and asked if he might take us with him, no doubt meaning to introduce us as Japanophils. Hanging about the hotel, gnawed at by dwindling expectancy like a middle-aged man waiting for an unfaithful young girl under a station clock, Mori waited for a pleasant message of invitation: then the shattering news came that the Governor was ill and couldn't see him. Was the indisposition genuine or diplomatic? We knew what Mori thought. We gathered that the telephone message he had received from an A.D.C. had not been soothingly worded. He took it as a rebuff, perhaps as an insult, that the man whom he had entertained in his ship and who had been so cordial should now refuse to see him after the long journey up from the coast.

It is a mistake to believe that the Japanese are adept at hiding their feelings. They can be disciplined, but they are temperamental. On the journey up to Nairobi, Mori had been calm, confident, and playful; on the journey back to Mombasa he was silent and broody, and for him the zebras now trotted and the antelopes pranced in vain. All this safari had brought him was an envelope full of somebody else's lion's whiskers.

When we got back to Mombasa we learnt that the ship's carpenter had died suddenly. The dead young man, Mori resolved, should not be cremated or buried at sea or, equally obscurely, in some cemetery for 'coloured' people. No. He should decompose among the remains of some of Japan's former allies as an equal.

> Sceptre and crown
> Shall tumble down
> And in the grave be equal made
> With the poor crooked scythe and spade.

Difficulties were raised, but Mori the diplomatist got to work, and so it happened one sultry evening that the Anglican burial service was read over the corpse of a Japanese peasant by a hot and cross-looking Anglican clergyman in a surplice, while Mori and Van der Post and I stood by with the crew of the *Canada Maru*, well behaved and in spotless white ducks, and looking slightly spellbound, like shy children at a grand wedding. Japan was vindicated as a Great Power, and Mori had such a look of solemn satisfaction that he might have been burying a rich and childless uncle.

Dreamy Indian Ocean days. In the afternoons Mori used to shut himself up in his cabin (the Governor's photograph had been removed) and indulge for an hour or so in solemn ritualistic chanting from the Japanese classics: this was evidently not merely a cultural exercise, his voice sounding like a lion's roar, to the benefit, he assured us, of his internal organs and nervous system. The purser was reading Bergson and the wireless operator Einstein, and in the evenings one of the officers used to play the haunting *shakuhachi*, a bamboo flute, and as the masthead of the ship stirred rhythmically about among the stars on those calm warm southern nights, the long-drawn notes seemed a lamentation, exquisite and resigned, for some irrecoverable age of primordial peace, an evocation of what the Japanese call *awaré*, which has been translated 'the ah-ness of things'.

In an empty hold, displays of *judo* and *kendo* ('sword-way') were put on, and Mori, dressed in a masked helmet and a jerkin with breastplates, wielding a two-handed sword and uttering blood-curdling yells, not only became barbaric and medieval but revealed himself as a formidable athlete. One night by full moon a feast in Japanese style was held on deck, with singing, and much *saké* was drunk. Presently Mori, flushed with drink, performed with great vigour what was obviously a war dance, and his clean and muscular feet looked as if they wanted to plant themselves on the neck of a defeated enemy. A moment atavistic, a moment ominous.

At Singapore we were given a Chinese banquet. Off the precipitous eastern coast of Formosa, where the sea is inordinately deep, we were tossed about like a paper boat in a typhoon of surprising violence, but in due course we glided, on a clear autumn day, to our anchorage off the port of Moji. The ship was instantly infested with forewarned reporters, each equipped with a smile, a visiting card, and, as we learnt later, with powers of invention. Almost the first thing we noticed when we went ashore was a shrine at which a Russian shell taken in the Russo-Japanese War had been mounted on a pedestal. We were being introduced to the cult of patriotism in its Japanese form.

Our first evening was the beginning of the most strenuous fortnight I have ever spent. It was to be devoted to night-life in an elegant pleasure-house. Formerly a rich man's villa, it stood in its own grounds, formally laid out in the traditional style. Everything was gracefully organised. Mori was our host: we hoped he was to be reimbursed by his employers or his Government, because even by the standards of a sailor long absent from home the night must have been expensive. Deprived of our clothes and provided with clean kimonos, Van der Post and I went off to take a hot bath and then joined Mori in the best room, where we sat on silk cushions on the floor round a low table of red lacquer.

There were three other guests, local friends of Mori's. One of them had just returned from mushrooming in the country. Unlike any Japanese we had yet seen, he was a *gros gaillard* in a white shirt and shorts, six feet high and strongly built, with a smooth tawny skin and a neck like a young bull's. Like so many toughs he had a poor head for liquor, and long before midnight was rolling about the floor and rather too playfully worrying, like a young but overgrown dog, one of the little prentice geishas, who was perhaps a little alarmed but didn't lose her head. These doll-like creatures had their faces thickly made up with wet white, their tiny tongues now and then peeped out of their painted mouths, their eyes and the pretty ornaments in their coiffures twinkled and sparkled, and their movements were as studied as their clothes were sumptuous.

Mori had evidently primed the most attractive and intelligent of the fully-fledged geishas to make up to me. She was pretty, gentle, quick-witted, and had none of the affected ingenuousness which was sometimes to make geishas boring. Perhaps his idea was that I should fall heavily at the outset for Japanese womanhood and accordingly for Japan, but matchmaking is such a gamble, and just as people often give as presents what they themselves like rather than what the recipients want, Mori had chosen the bait he himself would have taken. She was a very nice and obliging girl, and had been trained to please.

We had been eating an excellent and leisurely Japanese meal and drinking enough *saké* to float a sampan, and in between times there were songs, dances, fun and games. At some unearthly hour a dapper local photographer appeared with a camera, a tripod, and magnesium flares, and after quite a struggle (especially with the mushrooming hearty, who was at last propped up in a semi-recumbent position of which he was probably unconscious) we managed to form a more or less coherent group. The result is a credit to the photographer: Mori looks perfectly self-possessed, Van der Post relaxed, and Plomer has a deceptive air of innocence.

In the morning we were offered some sinister-looking segments of a fish called *fugu*, which is supposed to be a delicacy—unless you eat the wrong bits, when it is lethal. In fact, we were assured, a well-known athlete had died of eating *fugu* in this very town only a week ago. It was not quite the thing to tempt a 'morning after' appetite: too suggestive of a breakfast with the Borgias. Although we ate some of it, this act of politeness was an effort. We falsely expressed ourselves grateful for being offered a dish so unusual and so appetising.

Later in the day we sailed through the Inland Sea for Kobe, admiring islets covered with pine trees, seeing distant factory chimneys smoking addictedly, and in due course looking through Mori's binoculars at Mori's own house on the beach at Tarumi and at his wife and child waving to us as we passed. From the moment we set foot ashore we were caught up in a whirl of entertainment and sightseeing.

At Osaka we were taken by Mori to be introduced to the heads of the shipping company, who gave us another slap-up dinner with urban geishas in attendance. Excursions to castles, temples, and 'beauty spots' were designed to attune us to the picturesque; other excursions were arranged to impress us with what was modern. What was described as a model hostel for workers in a textile factory seemed deeply depressing. We were taken over the premises of the *Osaka Mainichi* very much as foreign delegations visiting London might have been taken to Printing House Square. We were shown over a mammoth department store: accommodated in a brand-new American-style hotel with waffles and maple syrup for breakfast and iced water on tap in every bedroom; repeatedly photographed—on the roofs of high buildings, in groups, and even in bed; and interviewed not only by the leading newspapers but by those less well known, such as the *Yorodzu Choho* and the *Jiji Shimpo*. The reporters continued to show rare imaginative power, attributing to us opinions and intentions of which we were amazed to read. We hoped they might divert for a moment or two some of the millions of tired commuters in the industrial cities.

It was a relief to spend some quieter hours pottering among the faded splendours of Nara and Kyoto and tasting in ancient surroundings the tranquillity and cool melancholy of the Japanese autumn. It was a relief to rest our eyes on moss and the reflections in still water of scarlet maple leaves, to refresh our ears with the sound of running water in wooded valleys, and to contemplate, in the intervals of feeding the deer in the cryptomeria groves of Nara, superb ancient sculptures whose gilded faces seemed to 'fill the hushed air with everlasting love'. But then Tokyo was waiting, with more reporters and photographers, more sight-seeing, luncheon with a millionaire, an interview with a Cabinet Minister, and something strange, a gathering of the Rotary Club, not made up of bluff, back-slapping tradesmen but of formidable and silent tycoons, to whom I was constrained to make a speech. Goodness knows what *they* made of it.

It seems almost unbelievable, but by the time the fortnight was up we had visited Nikko, the most conspicuous of 'beauty spots', Isé, the most sacred national shrine, Arashiyama, Momoyama, Hiyei-san, Hakone, and Miyanoshita. Most of all we had enjoyed an early morning in a boat on Lake Chuzenji, where in perfect stillness a few red and yellow leaves fell like dead butterflies and floated on the clear water, through which we could see the lake-bed of coloured pebbles.

It is interesting for a private person, just once in a lifetime, to go through the sort of routine that may be arranged for public persons on official visits to distant countries. We must have had much physical and nervous energy to visit so many different places and meet so many people. Both of us had received strong, various, and enlightening impressions. Van der Post was able to go away much better informed than any ordinary tourist could have been in the time. Perhaps it is not too much to say that what we had learnt saved his life when, only a few years later, he became a prisoner of war of the Japanese in Java.

Mori's hospitable abduction of us, the immense trouble he took to show us and teach us so much, and his continuing friendship and interest in us, which continue to flourish, like himself, nearly fifty years later, have been a rare treasure to us. I made up my mind, when the fortnight was over, to stay in Japan.

19

'Gone Native'

Having seen off Mori and Van der Post (to whose initiative I owed the journey) on the departing *Canada Maru*, I found myself, so to speak, alone in Japan. I had enough money to live simply for two or three weeks, no friends or influence, and only the merest smattering of the language. I returned from Osaka to Tokyo, hoping to earn a living by teaching English. It didn't occur to me to apply for help to our embassy or consulate, or to call on any of the bigwigs to whom I had been introduced. I had a letter of introduction to Edmund Blunden, and made use of it. That fine poet and sensitive, good-hearted, courageous man was then occupying the chair of English Literature at the Imperial University and, I think, already at work on his *Undertones of War*.

Blunden received me kindly and suggested that I might like to stay for the time being in the unpretentious Japanese hotel where he was established. I could not afford such 'Western' amenities as the hotel might provide, and was obliged to take at once to the Japanese way of living, sitting and sleeping on the floor, eating Japanese food, and suffering a little from the cold. With Blunden's help I obtained part-time work, as a stop-gap, on the staff of an institution with the name like the croaking of a frog – the Gwaikoku Go Gakko, or School of Foreign Languages. Perhaps I was accepted as the author of a novel published by the Hogarth Press. My only qualifications were a love of the English language and possibly some natural aptitude for teaching. The students were almost as old as I was, alert and friendly, easy to teach, and pleasant to know. Marquis Hirohata kindly proposed that I should tutor his children, and offered me a house in his grounds. This might have been an agreeable post, but I felt that to isolate myself with one family, however charming they might be, might limit my freedom to explore Japanese life.

I found myself with plenty of time to explore Tokyo, but needed a better-paid and full-time job. The excellent Blunden made this known at the university and before long an opening presented itself. I went to see Professor Sanki Ichikawa, a philologist of international repute who was head of the English faculty. Sitting with his back to the light, he looked at me as searchingly as if he were an oculist and treated me to one of his characteristic silences, long, inscrutable, and slightly disconcerting. Whatever he saw in my right and left eyes fortunately didn't prevent him from offering me a post at the Tokyo Koto Gakko, or Higher School, which, it was explained to me, might be called the Eton of Japan.

At this juncture a genial student at the university, Sumida by name, attached himself to me and asked if he might be my factotum in return for the chance of bettering his English. It was a useful arrangement for us both.

Encouraged by Sumida and my new job, I took a house near the village of Kami Nerima, on the Musashi plain outside Tokyo, out in the fields but within reach of a speedy electric train. The winter was delicious. Dry, sunlit snow like sugar lay thickly on the landscape and outlined the bare branches of paulownia trees and the evergreen, red-berried nandina bushes in the garden. Not far off stood a grove of cryptomerias, cocoa-brown at this season, and thickets of tall and graceful bamboos, curving under their burdens of snow.

In the nearest house lived a family named Shimoju. By a remarkable coincidence they were connexions of Mori's, the head of the family, an ex-officer of the Imperial Guards, being Mori's wife's uncle. They were a most cheerful family, and while Sumida (whose standards were somewhat exacting, for a speck of cigarette ash on the floor would send him scurrying for a brush and dustpan) was trying to get us a suitable servant, Mrs Shimoju and her daughters insisted on coming to do all the housework for us, even the cleaning of shoes and the scouring of pots. It was difficult to know how to show proper appreciation of such extraordinary kindness.

Unfortunately my acceptance of a post at the Koto Gakko had led to unpleasantness. There was a feud in the educational world of which I knew nothing, and the Gwaikoku Go Gakko accused the Imperial University of having seduced me from its service. It seemed that I too had incurred the displeasure of the authorities at the Gakko by giving them notice of my departure.

Some time later I learnt that this had led to my being slandered to my former students. They came to me in a body of their own accord to tell me they would believe nothing against me and to apologise for the behaviour of their principal. I was greatly touched by this instance of Japanese loyalty. Whether I had behaved rightly or wrongly, I was a foreigner, and in some quarters xenophobia was slightly on the increase. The day after these young men had first been to see me (they often came again) one of them wrote to me:

I am now very grateful for your yesterday's warm reception ... To tell the truth, I expected that we should meet with more starchy, formal treatment which is usual between people who belong to other nationalities, so I was rather afraid of seeing you. It was interesting for me to find you accustomed to the Japanese manner of living, and seeing you live in a simple way like a man who was thoroughly acquainted with the world I couldn't help smiling. But I believe the life you are leading now will not be unpleasant for you, because I perceived that you have something of the genuine Japanese character in your spirit—that is, the indifference about the world's affairs, the despise for social talents and a calm and self-possessed attitude.

I was pleased not to be found starchy, and pleased to be thought at ease with the Japanese way of living. The fact is that I was now able to do what I had always wanted to do and never could do in

William Plomer with Roy and Mary Campbell, 1926

Captain Mori

Africa, that is to say, to live at ease with people of an extra-European race and culture, and I was happy to be doing it.

Was there not in the letter a faint resemblance to an Englishman's praise of a foreigner for not behaving like a foreigner? The Japanese, like the English, did seem to feel that they were on a loftier plane than other races. The inflated self-esteem of the English (by no means yet extinct) came partly from insularity and partly from a long history of security and wealth, and a superstition of invincibility. It was comparable to that particular kind of self-assurance which can be found in persons with a family history of the same kind.

The Japanese sentiment of superiority was also that of an insular people, but a people far more homogeneous and for many centuries far more isolated than ourselves. Suddenly finding themselves exposed to a large, powerful, and dangerously aggressive world, it was natural for them to cling together and feel different: they *were* different. They often argued that the Western races had been their superiors in technological achievements but that they themselves had been spiritually on a higher level. They sometimes argued that it was their national mission to combine the best of both civilizations. Having proved, in much less than a century, and by unprecedented feats of concentration and adaptation, that they could master and use the mechanical arts of the West, they continued to believe that their own traditions were glorious, so it was naturally tempting to believe that they were a superior race and to instil that belief into their young. All the same, I felt that my students treated me, so far as possible, like one of themselves, and I loved them for it.

In February 1927 Mori came to stay a night or two at Kami Nerima. He was much vexed at my having been caught up in the pedagogues' vendetta and most solicitous for my welfare. Though not at all a rich man, he most generously offered to maintain me at his own expense if I cared to abandon teaching and stick to writing, and Sumida said he would serve me without any recompense, but I thought it better to earn my own living. So many kind attentions made me happy. A friend of Mori's lent me

7

a seaside villa at Kamakura, and before Mori himself went to sea again I went to stay with him and his family at Tarumi, on the Inland Sea. He said I could stay there as long as I liked, or for good. Was there ever warmer hospitality?

His house was on the beach, among clean-smelling pine trees contorted into formal growths like ideographs, and with a view of the island of Awaji between a calm sky and the calm sea. Waking in the morning and lying in bed listening to the wavelets lapping at the shore, and watching the sun scattering early spangles on the untroubled water, one felt that Tarumi might be a good place to live and die in.

Before going back to Tokyo, I spent a night with an acquaintance at a place not far away. In the evening we were sitting quietly with several other people in the main room of the house, which was open to the garden, and I was looking admiringly at a vase upon a shelf. Suddenly the vase seemed to move—yes, it began a little dance, tottered, paused, righted itself, pirouetted, and then rolled over. This seemed unaccountable, but the floor was moving too, and then the whole house creaked, swayed, and shuddered, there was a sound of glass breaking, then a universal dull rumbling, followed by distant shrieks; then a deep silence. I found myself alone in the room; everybody else had rushed into the garden. This was my first experience of a considerable earthquake. Luckily the epicentre was a good many miles away. Two thousand people, the papers said, had been killed, and more than four thousand injured.

It was springtime at Kami Nerima. The fields round the house were green with young corn, larks performed overhead, and violets came out by the wayside. A whole field of sumptuous peonies were soon in splendour; beyond the terminus of the electric railway was a hill covered with pine trees, and under them were thickets of flowering wild azaleas; and at the foot of the hill ran a broad stream over which dangled long, long bunches of white wistaria. In the opposite direction lay the vast wilderness of ever-growing Tokyo, infinitely spread out, soon to be the largest city in the world, with innumerable lines of little shops, each overstaffed with polite and eager assistants apparently thriving on next to nothing. It was a city electrical with life and, at least to me, of inexhaustible variety.

Before I began work at the Koto Gakko I was taken to a licensed fortune-teller, the widow of a novelist of some notoriety, I forget why. She was a very old woman with very thick spectacles and hands like a turkey's claws. She told me among other things that the middle of my life would be the happiest part and that I should not stay more than two or three years in Japan, but, she said, 'Even though you were born of a good family, your life will always be very complicated.'

The Koto Gakko looked like a new factory. In most of the masters was that touch of boyish innocence which often made the Japanese endearing. It was naturally even more evident among the students. The curriculum was stiff, and as they grew up the boys tended to get tired and a little desperate, their adolescence strained by overwork and a sense of exacting duty. That they should have had to learn so difficult a language as English, on top of everything else, greatly increased the strain. It seems unjust to cite their little mistakes instead of their achievements, but even their howlers commend the agility of their minds. Here are two answers to examination questions. The first question was 'What do you know of Robert Louis Stevenson?' 'He was a famous Scotch poet,' the answer ran, 'who invented the steam engine, and because he suffered from a disease of the lungs he was always known as Puffing Billy.' Another student, asked what he knew of *Moby Dick*, answered that it was a nickname given to Charles Dickens, because he was always moving his lodgings. In commerce, as well as in education, both English and French were sometimes surprisingly adapted. There was on the market an alleged whisky, labelled 'Rabbit Brand, as supplied to the Nobleman'. (Nothing was said of the Nobleman's opinion, or his symptoms after drinking it.) I long preserved a label from a bottle of soy, got up to look like Worcester Sauce. The inscription on the label was partly in French, but it had been copied from a bottle of hair oil, so one learnt with surprise that the consumption of this delicious sauce, containing the choicest oriental spices, would not only remove undesirable *pellicules* from one's *chevelure* but would impart to it suppleness, brilliance, and an agreeable perfume.

There was much in our civilisation which to the Japanese student, whose view of it was bound to be distant, scrappy, and distorted, appeared absurd or unaccountable or merely barbarous, but there was much that seemed enviable, particularly the freedom of the individual. The contrast between the two civilisations was conspicuous in education. An English boy used to begin his life with endless 'dos' and 'don'ts'. At his preparatory school he used to be ruled and regulated in all things. At his public school he gradually began to feel a little freer, to have more time to himself, and to be able to begin to follow his own inclinations. At the university, or wherever he went after leaving school, he enjoyed as a rule something very like freedom in his spare time. With the Japanese boy the process was reversed. As a child he seemed as free as a cherub, prattling and roaming about at his own sweet will, seldom lectured, nagged, or corrected, and apparently behaving well because he was happy and wished to please others. Directly he went to a primary school he was popped into a little uniform, and was liable to wear one for the rest of his life. At a secondary school, like the Koto Gakko, all was work and obligation, and by the time he got to the university or out into the world he had to be a cog in the national machine or perish.

Though a trifle older and more variously experienced, I was in some ways younger than some of my students, some of whom seemed more mature for their age than English boys. Between them and me was the bond that links persons of the same generation, and I was able to associate with them as among friends in school and out. I never had to keep order, because they never behaved in a rowdy or slovenly way; and I never had to keep my distance, because I had no motive for doing so. They came from various backgrounds, and among those I was fond of were Honda, whose father was a diplomatist, and who had spent part of his childhood in England; Shidehara, whose uncle, when Foreign Minister, had brought honour upon his name by advocating a civilised policy towards China; Shiomi, whose father was a small farmer, and with whom I am still happily in touch; and Fukuzawa, of whom I shall have more to say. I first got to know them well in the summer holidays, part of which I spent with them at a hostel belonging to the school. It was at Ikenodaira, in the Japanese Alps, and was used in winter for ski-ing and in summer for walking and climbing.

A large room on the ground floor had been built to house a wide, shallow bath through which a hot spring flowed all the year round. We spent much time quietly wallowing and gossiping in this benign water. Nothing stimulates well-being and good temper like a sociable hot bath, and since hot springs exist all over Japan and I spent my holidays travelling about the country, I passed much time in them. They are best perhaps in winter when the sun is shining on the snow, or when plum trees are coming into blossom a few yards from one's nose, the rest of the body being under water, and a congenial companion by one's side. At Ikenodaira there was a mountain to climb, with a rest-house to sleep in half-way up, and at the top, at dawn, one could enjoy a prodigious view. This region, fresh and temperate while Tokyo was sweltering in the *nyubai*, was graced by the flora and insects which have to be known in order to appreciate Japanese poetry and painting. Flowers like the *hagi*, or lespedeza, and birds like the *uguisu*, the so-called Japanese nightingale, have to be seen or heard before their delicate and varied associations for the Japanese mind can be even guessed at.

Later in the summer I went to stay with Sumida's family at Hiroshima, on the Inland Sea, and so learnt something of provincial life and hospitality. Among the ornaments of the house was a large wooden plaque engraved with a single gilded ideograph. This object hung over a sliding door leading to the lavatory. When I asked what it meant I was told it meant *Perseverance*. Further enquiry revealed that it was intended as a moral precept, not as an encouragement to the constipated. Back in Tokyo in the autumn I ran into an English businessman I knew, who asked where I had spent the summer. When I said I had been staying with some Japanese friends at Hiroshima his astonishment was great.

'Well,' he said, 'I've been fifteen years in this country, and no Japanese family has ever asked *me* to stay with them.' I am sure this was not because he was stuck up. He was amiable, but all his social or business contacts with the Japanese had been at places of business or public entertainment. I suppose that Japanese business-men in England may find themselves equally segregated by habit rather than by inclination.

From Hiroshima we had crossed over to Miyajima and given ourselves up to the joys of swimming, using the same beach as the cadets who had come over, as they did every year, from Etajima, the naval college. Burnt to an apricot colour by the sun, they were extremely hardy and athletic, but they had serious, anxious faces as the result of too much brainwork and too intense an addiction to duty. I suppose many of them were destroyed in the war in the Pacific about fifteen years later: memory makes them seem like phantasms.

When not bathing or idling we used to go out in a boat or stroll about in the village or the pine woods. I remember the astonishment of two Indian visitors at seeing a young European dressed in a Japanese fisherman's hat, a cotton kimono, and high clogs; I supposed they had been used to seeing Anglo-Indians, stiff-necked and Poona-minded, who would have thought it 'not The Thing' to relax among what their poet, their only poet, called 'lesser breeds'. Later in the same summer I made a wonderfully enjoyable journey with my friend Honda to Hokkaido, the northern island, and to the then remote and unfrequented Lake Towada, in the north of the main island, a journey I have recorded in my book *Paper Houses*.

This was a good life—periods of not uncongenial work, for which I was well paid and which allowed plenty of spare time, alternating with long holidays in which to explore and savour Japan and the Japanese. If I was largely concerned with Japanese culture, I gave much time to reading European literature, both ancient and modern, because Marsh Moor and Entumeni had kept me back from it. I didn't feel I had much in common with the sort of English people who, in countries not their own, used to huddle together, play golf or bridge, and stick, as if defensively, to their national customs and attitudes. I hadn't been long in Japan before I was amused to learn that in such circles I was reputed to have 'gone native'. In fact I had neither the wish nor the need to cut myself off from all European society, nor did I do so, but I put the Japanese first, and somehow felt nearer to them.

20

Dangerous Thoughts

According to what was then the custom in Japan, Sumida's parents had found a bride for him. In any case I was finding Kami Nerima rather far out, so I decided to leave my Sabine farm — as Blunden playfully called it — and move into Tokyo. I took a house in Higashi Nakano, then a peaceful quarter, with quiet byways among gardens full of evergreens.

The house, of one storey, had one room in 'foreign style', which I turned into a study; otherwise it was entirely Japanese. When you came in, you took off your shoes and left them in the hall. The rooms all led into one another. They were separated by sliding partitions covered with thick white cardboard lightly sprinkled with motifs of gilt pine-needles, or silvery sprigs of flowering grasses. If one wished to give a party or to air the house one could remove all these partitions and turn the whole building, with the exception of the entrance hall, kitchen, bathroom, and lavatory, into one large room. Japanese rooms not being cluttered with furniture, any room could be adapted for any purpose at any time. At bedtime, the maid opened the sliding doors of a built-in cupboard, took out the bedding, unrolled it, and spread it on the springy grass mats, or *tatami*, which covered the floors and seemed to have a faint scent of hay. After getting used to sleeping in this way, the thought that throughout one's life so far one had climbed at night on to the back of a wooden quadruped seemed grotesque.

On the garden side was a narrow veranda of polished wood. Between this veranda and the interior were sliding wooden screens covered with paper, known as *shoji*, with glass panels let into them. Between the veranda and the garden were sliding glass doors, and outside these were sliding wooden shutters.

According to the weather or your mood, you could shut the whole house up like a box and be entirely snug and private, or you could throw it open to the sun so that to sit indoors was virtually to sit out of doors. In a changeable climate there is much to be said for an adaptable house. The chief bother in those days was the inadequate heating in winter: charcoal smouldering in large china cauldrons was not exactly central heating, and if unwary and unventilated one was liable to asphyxiation by carbon monoxide.

I had now set up house with Morito Fukuzawa, whom I have already mentioned. A year or two younger than me, he was handsome, of a slightly melancholy or disillusioned nature, but with an agreeably ironical sense of the absurd, and of a hedonistic and sceptical disposition which I found perfectly congenial. His tastes were literary and he spent much time initiating me into Japanese literature, ancient and modern. We read much poetry and much contemporary fiction, in which there were strong influences of Russian and French naturalism, mingled at times with a peculiarly Japanese strain of the morbid and horrific. We also read Saikaku, the seventeenth-century novelist, who was so candid that twentieth-century prudery tended to translate him into asterisks.

We also went to the theatre. Japan was said to be a country where the drama, in all the successive forms of its evolution, was alive and flourishing — as if in England one could at any given moment have chosen to see a medieval mystery-play, a Punch and Judy show, Shakespeare, a Restoration comedy, Chekhov or Ibsen, or the latest art-theatre experiment. The three main kinds — the Nō, the Kabuki, and the Bunraku — depended for their effects upon tradition, stylisation, and the great accomplishment of actors who came of acting lineage and seemed to have hereditary poise. I was surprised to learn that Lafcadio Hearn (who so far 'went native' as to become naturalised as a Japanese and who had his academic salary heavily cut in consequence) apparently never went to the theatre; perhaps this was because of his bad eyesight. The Kabuki used to be called the 'popular' theatre; its appeal was the most direct. In the Bunraku, or puppet theatre,

7*

there was no dangling of puppets on strings. The dolls were manipulated with extraordinary skill by visible men who gave such life to these creatures that they themselves soon became invisible men. How was it that the dolls became more real than people, and that the dramas in which they were involved became intensely dramatic? That perfect mastery of movement and gesture—were the men merely attending the performance as stage-hands to see that all went well, or were they in fact creating it? The dolls had it all their own way; they had perfected their art; and because, unlike flesh-and-blood actors and actresses, they had no personalities or personal fame to exploit, this was pure art. And what was the Nō play? To this the European brought that total ignorance which, in its way, made him specially impressionable. One didn't understand the archaic language, the completely strange chanting; one knew nothing of the symbolism, and the briefly outlined plot was so steeped in the mysteries of antiquity, of a remote and venerable culture, of esoteric Buddhism, that one had to rely on little but the evidence of one's senses to perceive the great beauty and refinement and agelessness of a wholly non-popular tradition and convention, which, in present-day jargon, would perhaps be sneered at as 'élitist'—whatever that may mean. Perhaps, for those who use such a term, the best is too good.

Apropos the censoring of the novels of Saikaku, prudishness seemed to have been a recent import from the West. It had made rapid headway in bureaucratic circles, which seemingly detected a connotation of sexual with political liberty. It sometimes took remarkable forms. At an exhibition of sculpture in modern Western style by young Japanese artists the middle of the hall was occupied by a nameless something covered by a dust-sheet, to which was affixed the following notice:

> This figure is improper. In order to view it
> visitors must lift the covering.

Needless to say there was a long queue waiting to inspect what turned out to be a banal and dumpy nude: the only impropriety was its creator's lack of talent. Then, one summer in the country, a friend of mine was reproached by the local policeman for exposing his back at a window. He was in fact wearing a loincloth and was merely sitting on the window-sill to enjoy whatever coolness there was in the air. This incident was all the stranger because the Japanese were not prudish about nudity and bathed together as a matter of course.

'You Europeans think it disgraceful to expose your bodies,' a Japanese once said to me, 'but you shamelessly expose your minds. Everybody knows how men and women are made, so we see no shame in uncovering our bodies. We think it improper to uncover our thoughts.'

Another exhibition in Tokyo was of so-called 'proletarian' painting. In the mid-Twenties in Japan, what were officially classified as 'dangerous thoughts' could still, up to a point, express themselves with impunity. The paintings were not good; they were large, crude, realistic, and enthusiastic. The subjects were heroic portraits, or allegories, or scenes of riot designed to glorify the struggles of the working class for political power. One canvas, crowded with embattled figures, attracted particular attention because a number of small flaps of white paper were stuck on to it here and there, but only by their upper edges. On lifting up these flaps one saw that in each case they were covering representations of wounds or blood. They merely drew attention to what they were meant to conceal—dangerous thoughts. It is a curious fact that so mild a book as Gissing's *The Private Papers of Henry Ryecroft* was banned for its supposed power of promulgating such thoughts. It advanced little more than a solitary, world-weary hedonism, but that has long been a temptation to many Japanese, and could never be 'The Thing' to militant nationalists; it was neither more nor less than a dangerous thought.

At about this time the Japanese Government set aside three million yen—then a lot of money—in a single year 'to improve national thought'. A third of this sum was assigned to the Ministry of Education to develop a system of spying in the schools and universities. The spies were to smell out socialistic and communistic tendencies, particularly where these had led to the formation of secret societies. There was at that time a vogue for communism among the young, and the *marukusu-boi* ('Marx boy') was no rarity. It often looked as if this type was more conspicuous for long hair, a Bohemian or drop-out way of life, and a restive, protesting attitude to the growing authoritarianism than for any real grasp of *Das Kapital* and other canonical works.

It was not until after I had left Japan that the official repression of dangerous thoughts reached its greatest intensity. Six years after I had gone, one of my former students wrote to me about the fate of two others. The writer had, and still has, a singularly sweet nature.

'My dearest friend, M.,' he wrote, 'had been working secretly for labourers and farm-workers against the present policy of the Government. He was somewhat successful, but he worked too much. A physical crisis fell upon him. He lay in bed unconscious for about two months. Afterward in this February he was captured in a police station and is yet at present. Also O., a dearest friend, came out this September from the confinement of a year and a half in prison.'

The writer himself had become tubercular and had been sent to a mountain resort to recuperate. 'There,' he wrote, with an exquisite choice of words, 'I realised for the first time the sweetness and delicacy of breathing air in.'

If adherence to a so-called communism became frequent among those young Japanese who felt rebellious against the narrowing, reactionary, chauvinistic régime, it was by no means their only heresy. Some sought escape or relief by adopting some aesthetic or contemplative or idealistic or escapist formula, modern European or ancient Chinese, by which to guide their lives. As one of my friends wrote to me:

Men have shut themselves in material mechanism, not organism. They have forgotten and lost their own souls. In this condition, how can men examine their own selves and respect each other? A revolt against mechanism or universalisation is the creed of some young Japanese.

By 'universalisation' no doubt he meant uniformity. Clear-sighted, these young idealists were to have innumerable counter-parts in the coming years, pacifists and anti-Fascists and resisters in Europe and America, volunteers in the Spanish Civil War, the Bible Christians and victimised Jews of Germany, the flower-people and hippies and yippies and yogis of California, the protesters against the war in Vietnam, who thought and behaved as if war and destruction were not the best way to save us from ourselves.

What did I believe? How did I influence my Japanese friends? And how did they influence me? Young as I was, I was at least old enough to have formed some views about life in general and about such matters as religion and politics. In Tokyo I was able for the first time to enjoy and profit by those long discussions and arguments on all kinds of topics which I might have enjoyed if I had gone to Oxford, those talks which so greatly help a young man to find his level and develop the muscles of his mind. In a sense, Japan was my university; and I had the rare and valuable advantage of being placed among intimates in a remote civilisa-tion. This helped me to understand that Europe was not every-thing, and to see Europe from a distance through Asian eyes.

I have made it clear that I was bred an Anglican. Largely thanks to my mother, to the Fathers of the Community of the Resurrection, and to innumerable associations with English literature and architecture, I have never lost an affection for the Church of England, a kind of belief in it, and a kind of unfaithful attachment to it, but the Christianity of Beechmont I had rejected as poisonous. I disliked particularly the Christian attempt to reconcile suffering with virtue. As Darwin remarked, 'the number of men in the world is as nothing compared with that of all other sentient beings, and they often suffer greatly without any moral improvement'. I know of no better condemnation of Beechmont Christianity than Edmund Gosse's, in *Father and Son*:

It divides heart from heart. It sets up a vain, chimerical ideal, in the barren pursuit of which all the tender, indulgent affections, all the genial play of life, all the exquisite pleasures and soft resignations of the body, all that enlarges and calms the soul, are exchanged for what is harsh and void and negative. It encourages a stern and ignorant spirit of condemnation; it throws altogether out of gear the healthy movement of the conscience; it invents virtues which are sterile and cruel; it invents sins which are no sins at all, but which darken the heaven of innocent joy with futile clouds of remorse.

In this permissive age, all that may seem self-evident; but for those who had to reach such conclusions through bitter frustrations and struggles there was an extraordinary sense of triumph. Yet I have never felt in the least like an atheist. It seems to me even more presumptuous to say one doesn't believe in God than to say one does. Before the immense mystery of the universe our opinions tend to be absurd. How can one explain a world which appears too beautiful to be an accident and too hideous to be a design?

Had I perhaps become a determinist? When, in Japan, one was woken up in the night, as often happened, to feel the house gently rattled or abruptly shaken by an earthquake, one did not proclaim that one was the master of one's fate or the captain of one's soul: whistling in the dark does nothing to disperse it. In any case, my sense of heredity weakens my belief in the independence of the individual. I used often to think that the things which happen to us, including our deaths, are the appropriate things. Deciding that I was what she called a fatalist, a woman once said to me, 'Don't you brush your teeth, then?' by which she no doubt meant that if you think what will be will be, why bother to do anything at all? I said she misunderstood me if she thought me negative and inert.

The idea of progress was one in which I had been brought up to believe, but I had already discarded it. Progress implies perfectibility, which appears incompatible with life as we know it. The conception of utopias seems only useful as a form of criticism of the way the world is being managed and as a possible influence leading to some local or temporary improvement. 'Liberty begets anarchy,' said Balzac, 'anarchy leads to despotism, and despotism back to liberty. Millions have died without securing a triumph for any one system. Is not that the vicious circle in which the whole moral world revolves?'

These remarks I have set out more clearly than I could have done in my early twenties in Tokyo, but I had already, perhaps by nature, a somewhat detached and sceptical attitude to both religion and politics, and happiness seemed largely a matter of luck. 'The happiest man in the world,' wrote Natsumé Saseki in his copy of *Also Sprach Zarathustra*, 'is he for whom necessity becomes freedom itself ... All is fate and all is freedom at the same time.'

The nature of happiness was something my Japanese friends liked to discuss. I remember once suggesting that clear headed-ness, a highly developed consciousness, might make for one form of happiness: it ought to provide much entertainment, and would at the same time enable one to free oneself from many illusions about both oneself and the world. But those harassed young men, crammed with lessons, already feeling the pressures of duty and responsibility, and contrasting their lot with that of the peasants among whom some of them had grown up, were inclined to believe that it would be happiest to live like a frog at the bottom of a well, knowing nothing of the outside world and keeping cool in peaceful isolation. But, talking on into the night, we would agree that happiness might consist in belonging to a community confident of its identity; in feeling respect for that community and being respected by it; in doing the work, both of hands and head, for which one was most fitted, and yet having enough leisure; in being neither rich nor poor to the point of annoyance; in being free from envy and spite; in having good health, being happily married, and feeling confidence in the future of one's children; in the consciousness of loving and being loved; and in being able to enjoy some variety and surprise. We agreed that nobody could expect so much, and that happiness is likely to be partial and intermittent—so we passed round the *saké* bottle and sent for more, growing mellow and bland, and gathering rosebuds while we might.

If I influenced my Japanese friends, it was probably in much the same ways that they influenced me—in the direction of pleasure and doubt, but even more in the direction of a heightened perceptiveness, of creativeness, or towards support of the individual or the community against doctrinaire repression. There was one convention against which I did try to influence them, that of suicide. It was commonly resorted to by the Japanese— sometimes singly, sometimes in pairs, even in groups—for reasons which to a European seemed trivial and insufficient. In those strata of Japanese society with which I was associated suicides were annoyingly common. They often seemed a waste of promising or potentially happy and useful lives, and I lost no chance of saying so. Today I might more readily hesitate to dissuade an intending suicide, and there are circumstances in which I might regard it as proper to help someone to bring about his or her departure, but I still cannot sympathise with a patriotic, theatrical, or face-saving suicide.

I was told by Fukuzawa that a young man who was staying in our house in Higashi Nakano took about among his toilet things a cut-throat razor and a bottle of arsenic in case he should feel the need of them. I persuaded him to hand these lethal objects over to me and got rid of them. Fourteen years later he was a prosperous businessman, inclined to plumpness and with a thriving family of children. I don't know whether that was a good thing or not, particularly in the light of a letter which I received in England, about ten years later, from a Japanese acquaintance on a visit to London.

'How do you do?' he wrote. 'I hope you are quite well. I am quite well now, but my death is coming nearer and nearer, because I must leave Europe about the end of this year and then work as a slave for my family, which is quite the same as to die.'

Another of my Japanese contemporaries wrote to me, some years after I had left the country, to say that after a sudden and violent haemorrhage from the lungs he had had to spend five months in bed, but had now recovered.

'While in the sickness bed,' he wrote, 'very often I thought of you, remembering that at Higashi Nakano we talked with you on suicide and you showed the different opinion from ours ... Your opinion had much to do with my heart. As you well know, the Japanese people think very slight of life ... I also might have done the same at the expectoration of blood if I had not heard your opinion.'

The house at Higashi Nakano was a home to me in the best sense. I should define that as a house to which you return in the dark, and see a lighted window, and where you know someone you are fond of is looking forward to your arrival. I added to my income by university lecturing, and could live as I like, modestly but not meanly. I enjoyed entertaining young men or women who needed a temporary refuge from family or other troubles. Space was limited, or they might have been many instead of few. Two permanent members of the household were a cat called Bimbo ('Poverty'), who had sprung from nowhere, and a girl with a baby face and a childlike disposition who had had a stormy adolescence and was glad of a haven. She was subject to hallucinations—her father's face would appear suspended in the hedge, supernatural cats lived in the cupboards, she saw fireworks at midday and heard bells at midnight—but she was a cheerful little person and quite a good cook.

I did a great deal of reading and writing in that house and a great deal of merrymaking. A married woman who came to live with her husband next door, had attended an American university, and now lectured either to sociologists about Buddhism or to Buddhists about sociology, once politely asked me, when I met her on a train, why such *dramatic* noises came from my house. When I hoped that they didn't disturb her too much, she only tittered and bowed several times from the waist; I suppose she had heard us larking about, or one of our *saké* parties had been a little wild. Admirable drink! Never did it leave anything the next morning but a feeling of well-being.

Among our neighbours was a poet and art-historian called Yoné Noguchi, lean and sardonic-looking, with an air of having burnt his candle at both ends. As a youth he had emigrated to California, where, soon after his arrival in San Francisco, he had been gazing into a shop-window, when a heavy hand gripped his shoulder and spun him round. He found himself face to face with a burly Californian who, to show his racial antipathy, spat in Noguchi's face. It was an attack as unexpected as that on Pearl Harbour in 1941.

After a period of dish-washing and so on, the young man was taken up by a local poet, Joaquin Miller, who encouraged him to write in English. The result was a book purporting to describe autobiographically the adventures of a Japanese girl in the United States. This ambidextrous production had some success, and after a time its author appeared in London and issued a quantity of verses in an English of his own. They were invertebrate but had a certain novelty, and serious pronouncements were made upon them by the writers and critics of the day, from Hardy downwards. Today they are probably forgotten, but monographs by Noguchi on Utamaro and other artists may be more durable.

An occasional and important visitor was Mori. At Durban, during one of his periodical calls at that port, both my mother and brother, before leaving for England and America respectively, had had the pleasure of meeting him. He had in fact become a friend of the family. My mother was greatly impressed with his courtesy, charm, and intelligence, and he seemed to find the same qualities in her. They were perfectly at ease. Good manners are an international language. Both had had formal upbringings. My mother found him a polished man of the world, like, yet unlike, a European of that sort. Mori told me that my mother reminded him of a Japanese lady and was superior to any other European woman he had met. He was pleased with my brother for being tall, humorous, and sensible. My brother rightly thought him 'deep'.

At Durban the local attitude to the Japanese had improved, partly by Mori's own efforts and partly by those of Laurens van der Post, who, in the press and on the radio, had been giving his impressions of Japan and gently hinting that the Japanese were highly civilised before white South Africans had ever been dreamt of. In East Africa, too, things were better, and in April 1927 Mori had been able to write and tell me that the hotels at Mombasa, partly as the result of a *démarche* by himself, now accepted Japanese guests. The *Mombasa Times* had helped by referring to him editorially as 'an old friend of ours'.

All was not yet well. On 13 January 1928 the *Natal Advertiser* reported an 'unfortunate incident' in a Durban tea-shop. It appeared that 'a well-known and popular Japanese gentleman, widely respected as a cultured and courteous man', who had the entrée to 'the leading restaurants and hotels', had nevertheless been 'placed in a very delicate position', or, more bluntly, publicly ordered out of a tea-shop by an ignorant virago. A few days later the paper printed a letter from Mori, describing the incident with restraint. Being a seaman by profession, he said, he had been all over the world but had 'never met such a manner before'. He ended by asking, 'Is not the world changing day by day, and everything exposing its intrinsic value, disregarding its race value?' But wasn't it an undue regard for 'race value' which drove Japan to attack Pearl Harbour?

It was nearly always possible for me to see Mori during his brief interludes in Japan, and at other times his letters from distant places always contained pleasant touches. Returning a book I had lent him, he wrote, 'Please excuse damage done to the cover by my pet rabit [*sic*]. He was given to me by an Indian friend in Mombasa, and seeing me with the book so much he must have known it was something good.' His letters mingled affection and anxiety. He called me 'the genious, the world-wide treasure,' and wondered always if I was still getting on all right in Japan, and hoped I wasn't feeling lonely and neglected. 'I have done very little to you during your stay in Japan,' he wrote, after I had been there a year. In fact he must have been lonelier than me, and during his long voyages I feel sure he used to turn over many things in his mind which he did not discuss with his subordinates.

He was impressed by the renewed hullabaloo in South Africa over the second book by 'the genious', *I Speak of Africa*, and began to compare his career with mine. Nearly old enough to have been my father, he went so far as to say that I had so far made better use of my time than he had. This was odd, or modest, of him; his career had been full of courage and enterprise, and he was accomplished in ways beyond my attainment.

Addressing me as his 'dear friend', he wrote to me somewhat wistfully on his thirty-ninth birthday, remarking sadly that the Japanese expectation of life is short, and that he had perhaps only a dozen more years to live. (I'm delighted to say that he's still going strong.) He compared himself to an ephemera, 'which fulfilled the meaning of his life, there is nothing to be grieved for ... Therefore only concern of mine is to have a flight even for a day, but not a mere longelity [*sic*]. Indeed, how innumerable ghosts scrambling on in this world!'

Once at Higashi Nakano, as I lay awake in bed, *more japonico*, between Mori, who had come to visit me, and Fukuzawa, who lived with me, they both being asleep, I thought how different they were. Awake, they were a trifle formal in their manner to one another. They could hardly have approved of each other, and they had perhaps little in common except a special claim on my affection. Mori was the dutiful man of action, perfectly self-controlled, a patriot who believed in the destiny of his race and its military qualities. Fukuzawa was an intellectual, moody, ironically sardonic, an aesthete, interested in personal relationships, not patriotic dreams. He stood for peace and quietness, for living and letting live, for the immediate and tangible good, for everything (as William Allingham put it)

                                        we prize
For mirthful, gentle, delicate and warm.

My two friends seemed to typify the dualism of the Japanese

nature, the two tendencies of the Japanese double life, which were often to be found commingled in one person. Every Japanese, I was to hear it said, is a split personality; and though we may shrink from such a slick generalisation, one cannot forget it.

Such understanding and observation of Japanese life as had been attainable by me had been given shape in a book of stories, *Paper Houses*. This reached Japan when I was still there and was soon afterwards translated into Japanese. It had a dust-jacket which Leonard and Virginia Woolf had had designed by Roger Fry, and among its contents was a piece of satirical buffoonery called *Mother Kamchatka*, ridiculing the cult of emperor-worship. If this had been read and understood by some chauvinist fanatic, he might have put a violent end to me. Mostly it consisted of stories written under the influence of Maupassant, Chekhov, and Bunin. My Japanese acquaintances politely congratulated me on my understanding of the female of their species, on whom they traditionally looked down. Of the Japanese male they thought me less understanding, no doubt because, conscious of their superiority, they did not like being analysed or criticised. (I had already heard exactly the same criticism of a novel about Japan then being widely read, *L'Honorable Partie de Campagne*, by a Frenchman named Raucat.) My book, I thought, implied, as it was meant to imply, that Japan would be in the future, as she had proved herself in the past, formidable as an enemy, but nobody in the West wanted to know that then. It was not, all the same, a book with a political purpose, but a fictional celebration of the great privilege and pleasure I had enjoyed in being accepted by the Japanese and enabled to live among them, after the long frustration of not being able to live among Africans.

21

Not Through Eastern Windows Only

With habit and increasing knowledge, travel and the theatre, the social pleasures of the bath, the café, and the geisha-house, enjoying the changing seasons, each with its own flora and formalities, the life of the streets and of the remote countryside, popular festivals, the company of children, the fine and applied arts, I was becoming more and more adapted to Japanese life and ideas. The slow gesture of a masked actor, the gnomic poem of a Zen sage, the lonely shrine in an autumn forest carried one away into mysterious spheres where the arsenal and the stock-jobber seemed non-existent. So absorbed had I become in my surroundings that several times, when writing to my parents, I remarked that it was two or three months since I had spoken to a European.

When I caught sight of stray Europeans, they often looked odd or grotesque, and I could understand why, once or twice in remote villages, the population had hurried excitedly forward to stare, muttering, 'Seiyojin, seiyojin!' ('A foreigner, a foreigner!'). Even to me the mongrel features of Europeans or Americans looked irregular in comparison with the stylised Japanese face — not that Japanese faces were always beautiful. The complexions of Europeans were often not clear, their gait was sometimes ungainly, their manners could be casual and uncouth, their voices too loud, their opinions too self-confidently outspoken. Once or twice, at close quarters, they seemed to *smell* peculiar. But I was one of them myself, therefore I too may have seemed odd or grotesque but I trust not odoriferous, to those who shared my daily life. One was stared at in public, not least in public baths, as if newly arrived from Mars, and could only reply with 'the smile extending'.

Yet in photographs where I appeared among groups of Japanese I wasn't particularly outstanding. True, my fair hair hadn't grown straight and black, but my cheekbones and raised eyebrows were not unlike theirs and my eyes looked *mi-clos*. The Japanese had given me a happy sense of community with them. I lived with them and felt I belonged to their society. I worked for them and played with them. Love and habit had made them part of me. And yet, and yet ...

Even then I was aware of the anomalous existence of exiles everywhere and of their inevitable unbalance and distorted perspectives; and I felt, intermittently, the pang of isolation from my own kind and their culture. Talking occasionally with local European acquaintances I could chatter freely and didn't have to talk English in a simplified way and with a deliberately clear enunciation, like a teacher of elocution, carefully avoiding unfamiliar idioms, obscure allusions, and slang.

I saw that it might be possible for me to go on living happily in Japan, to make a good livelihood without excessive effort, to learn much and perhaps to write creditably about the country and the people, but I felt this could not be my destiny. I must return to Europe and whatever trials of poverty, patience, and obscurity might await me, simply because I belonged there, not to Asia, not to Africa. Against this was the prospect of separation from Fukuzawa: we understood each other, we were used to each other, we were fond of each other. But if he came to Europe with me he would only be postponing his own proper evolution and a suitable marriage to protect him against the threat of an innate sadness in his temperament.

> Put the torch to ties though dear,
> If ties but tempters be,

wrote Melville sternly, but for me the stronger temptation was from stronger, atavistic ties. It would no more have been probable for me to remain in Japan—though in some ways it was to me an earthly paradise – than it had been possible for Melville to remain in the Marquesas.

The decision was not taken early or irrevocably; I wavered and wondered. I refused the offer of a chair of English Literature in a provincial university, because I didn't want an academic career. After a year and a half in Japan I had made a new contract extending my stay by another year. I still didn't know whether, when that extra year was up, I should return to Europe only for a visit or for good.

My hunger for European culture grew with the books it fed on. It was sharpened by occasional sights of European paintings acquired by Japanese collectors, especially by a show of modern French pictures which included the first painting I ever saw by Rouault. But when, in 1928, an exhibition was held at Veno Park of ancient Chinese paintings, my hankering for Europe went into eclipse. The exhibits included the rarest and most splendid masterpieces obtainable from both Japanese and Chinese collections (the two countries were then not at war, and Chiang Kai-shek had been on a visit to Tokyo). Most had never been shown in public before; some had been illustrated in the best monographs on Chinese painting; all had been selected with the highest discrimination. Among them was Yen-Hui's *The Wizard T'ieh-Kuai*, an extraordinary masterpiece.

The noble profundity, the symbolism, the directness, the plant-like grace and freshness of these paintings gave me the strongest inkling of the grandeur of Asian civilisation, and I wished I could spend some years in China to learn even a little of what it had to teach. It seemed disturbing that one might die without so much as a glimpse of, let us say, China and Persia and Russia, the Mediterranean countries, or Latin America. Yet I could understand the futility of globe-trotting. One must build up images out of the little one could know and could guess; there could be fruitfulness within narrow bounds. It might be better, perhaps, to be like the Japanese poet Basho, or like White at Selborne, and to hear with a thrill of pleasure a frog jump into an evening pond (that now hackneyed but still immortal frog) than to diffuse energy in vain and spread one's faculties thinly over more than they could cover. The important thing was never to lose the appetite for art and life, never to lose curiosity, never to lose heart.

In the summer of 1928 I went with Fukuzawa to Lake Kawa-guchi, and while there visited the house of a decayed Samurai family in an old, weird, and secluded village. The heir, reported locally to be slightly eccentric or degenerate, was reported to be disposed to sell some of the antique bibelots and works of art he had inherited, and we went to see him. A pale, tallish, and haunted-looking young man of about my own age, wearing a kimono of faded blue silk, he received us with elegance of manner and an appearance of pleasure, and entertained us to a meal, which was served by an elderly maid with a face as impassive as a mask. Afterwards he took us to see an ancient temple rich with carvings and gildings but slowly rotting under a mantle of mosses and ferns. When he produced his treasures he said nothing at all about selling them, but asked me to choose whatever I liked and he would give it to me. It seemed proper to choose something not too rare or precious, so I picked out a pair of *saké* bottles which seemed to fulfil this condition.

My choice seemed to please him and we three fell to drinking together. He behaved rather strangely, and the uncanny atmos-phere of his house and garden and of the old temple beyond it was not in the least dispelled by the warming effect of the liquor. One seemed to be living in an unwritten poem by Walter de la Mare. The sibilant sound of a sliding *shoji* somewhere in the house, followed by a low-voiced argument and a sound of weeping, suggested the presence of a neurotic invalid or *séquestrée*, some victim of tragedy or domestic tyranny. Our host listened for a moment, smiled resignedly, said 'It's always the same in this house,' and then, 'I'm glad, very glad, to meet a foreigner,' and poured out some more *saké*. He was in the end reluctant to let us go and wished me to come and stay with him. So I might have done, had I remained in Japan, with a mixture of uneasiness and fascination as the de la Mare poem gradually changed into a novel by one of those living Japanese novelists—

Akutagawa, perhaps—to whose work I had been introduced by Fukuzawa.

Before I left Japan I received from Mori a *kakeji*, or scroll, inscribed in the admired calligraphy of one Rai Kyohei. It was a treasured family possession. Here is a translation:

> To make oneself pure in heart,
> To reach the essential reality of things,
> To let others think of themselves,
> Not to envy the merit of others,
> Not to boast of oneself,
> Not to think oneself wise,
> To try and find good people and at once reject bad ones,
> To help merciful government, and to uplift the degrading
> customs of the world.

A difficult programme, but a specimen of conventional Japanese idealism, derived from ancient Chinese tradition, and hard to reconcile with patriotic dogmas. There is surely something aesthetic rather than moralistic in this prescription for gentlemanly behaviour.

From Singapore, Mori wrote to say goodbye:

> The three years sojourn of you in Japan, I expect, will be remembered by the world for ever as the epoch-making of the genious. It was a blessing for me to have met you at Durban and contributed something to this matter, but I must be ashamed for having undone my duty for the genious.

How could he possibly have done more for me than open his heart, his house, and his purse? He brought me to his country. What I learned to love there has been an infinite enrichment. The dislike I felt for Japanese imperialism and militarism was surely justified by their explosion a few years later. Suppose we reach 'the essential reality of things' and it appears twofold, what are we to do then? What can we do then except be glad of the times when it reveals its singleness and singularity?

Any traveller who is happy in some pleasant place is likely to play with the thought of staying there for good, even when he knows he cannot. So it was with George Wheler, who travelled in Greece in the seventeenth century. Nobody who has known and loved Greece can fail to sympathise, reading how Wheler, visiting a hermit on the slopes of Helicon, was by him brought

> delicate white Honey-combs, with Bread and Olives, and a very good wine: to which he set us down in his Hutt, and made us a Dinner, with far greater satisfaction, than the most Princely Banquet in Europe could afford us. For the Quiet and Innocency of their Life, the natural Beauty of the Place, the Rocks, Mountains, Streams, Woods and curious Plants, joyn'd with the Harmonious Notes of Nightingales, and other Birds, in whole Quires, celebrating, and as it were, welcoming that forward Spring, to speak the truth, so charmed my melancholick Fancy for a time, that I had almost made a resolution never to part with so great a Happiness, for whatever the rest of the World could present me with. But, in conclusion, it prov'd too hard a task for me, so soon to wean my self from the World.

If I had decided to stay in Japan and make my life there, it would have been the double life of the exile. I should have seen the disgusting rise of militarism to supreme power and the total eclipse of freedom. I should have seen some of my friends persecuted and if I had tried to help them should presumably have been penalised or deported. If I had been able to remain there until the country, in the hands of its war-lords, was committed to its desperate expansionist war, I could then, because of my 'dangerous thoughts', or merely because of my nationality, have expected to be expelled to a Europe from which I should have become greatly estranged.

In Japan I sometimes complained about what seemed to me the

shortcomings of Japanese life, but it is as common for a traveller to do that in a foreign country as it is for him to praise it when he returns to his own—which also has its shortcomings. Civilisation has many dialects but speaks one language, and its Japanese voice will always be present to my ear, like the pure and liquid notes of the bamboo flute in those tropical evenings on the Indian Ocean when I heard it for the first time, speaking of things far more important than war, trade, and empires—of unworldliness, lucidity, and love.

22

A Passage to Europe

On a fine, dry, starry night in the early spring of 1929 a Japanese steamer began to cast off from the quayside at Shimonoseki. She was the regular boat on her way to the port of Fusan in Korea. Clean and brightly lighted, she was quickly brought round with a wash and skirmish of water astern, and was about to head rapidly and purposefully westwards. The passengers were few. Only two were Europeans. They were strangers to each other, and I was one of them.

Standing alone on deck, I could feel through the soles of my feet the accelerated throbbing of the ship's engines, but my attention was fixed elsewhere. Like a bare stage brilliantly lighted, the receding quay was as clean as the deck, unencumbered with gear or goods, and now deserted except for one human figure. It was Morito Fukuzawa, who had come all the way from Tokyo to see me off. From that lonely and lessening form under the arc-lamps there presently came, in a voice made strong by emotion and enlarged in the empty night by the high roof above him which acted as a sounding-board, the Japanese valediction, that forlorn word 'Sayonara!' He uttered it four times, at what seemed long intervals, and four times over the calm sea I called back those four sad syllables. The last time I was surprised by the volume of my own voice, but I knew that by the time the word reached him it would be faint, ghostly, final. Long after Shimonoseki was out of sight I seemed to hear him still.

It was not an easy parting. We had lived on terms of close friendship under the same roof, and had travelled about the country together, understanding one another perhaps as nearly as the barriers of tradition, race, language, and education would allow. I cannot judge for which of us the parting was less easy. It might have been harder later. At this time we were both young. We had our separate destinies, and possibly I was the more fortunate of the two: I seemed more hopeful by nature, freer, more forward-looking. But he had a kind of wisdom, disillusionment and resignation, which was not mine. He also had the advantage of remaining on the soil to which he belonged and knew he belonged, whereas my young allegiances had been dispersed between Europe, Africa, and Asia.

From that moment I went into a kind of trance. It was not simply because I missed my familiar companion and had torn myself from the life in Japan I had grown accustomed to. It was also a matter of disposition. Those who are not bent upon what is called 'getting on' fall easily into trances, into a mood that may last through a lifetime of semi-indifference, of habit fitting as comfortably as an old overcoat, of dreamy resignation: and such a state, though its causes are no doubt partly physical, is by no means incompatible with activity of body or mind. Contributory to my trance was an enormous ignorance—of politics, economics, languages, geography—which made it impossible to see things, places, and people in proper perspective.

The next morning, when the express began rushing northward through Korea, unfamiliar scenes, caught in glimpses, began to succeed one another too rapidly to be apprehended, and fragments of literature, geography, and history eddied through my mind like straws in a wind-tunnel. Sudden perceptions of contrast, like unexpected juxtaposition of sound in a smooth piece of music, often startled me out of my trance. In the new and well-equipped train Japanese businessmen in white collars, black coats, and striped trousers sat about smoking, reading newspapers, and talking about stocks and shares. Outside it the bare mountains of Asia, rocky and remote in the pale sunshine, glided past in silence, as if floating or changing places according to some predetermined manœuvre, and beneath them from time to time could be seen stately Korean gentlemen of leisure wearing full white robes and tiny top-hats of black gauze tied with ribbons under the chin, *as if nothing had happened* – as if there was no train, no line, no Japanese expansion, no next war germinating. The whole of our time – if by our time we mean the whole period since the Industrial Revolution – has abounded in such contrasts between formal survivals from the long ages of what may be called the Hand-Made and manifestations of what is called progress.

As a child I had seen Chinamen wearing pigtails; at Mukden I saw in the street a richly dressed Chinese woman tottering along on tiny bound feet, a belated martyr to an uncommonly perverse fashion. I supposed it was the mingled appearance of helplessness and affectation which these broken, crippled, trotter-like feet gave to the gait that had caused them to be thought beautiful. Possibly for the male the sexual attraction lay in the certainty that, if pursued, no woman with such feet could run away. But behind this woman loomed smoking factory chimneys. On their black stilts the Satanic mills were after her. They would soon overtake her. She would never be seen again.

While blue-shadowed snow still lay in shady places, the early spring sun was already bright on the biscuit-coloured plains of Manchuria, and those blue stains were repeated in the people's clothes, often faded or washed out to a smoky or chalky turquoise. Whole tracts of fawn-coloured country opened out from the train like fans decorated with little knots or dots of blue that were peasants at work. But at Harbin the sky was overcast, and for the first time I had the feeling of being in Russia – not Bolshevik Russia, not Czarist Russia, but a sort of Russian no-man's-land in some unwritten novel. From the uncomfortable glitter of fixed bayonets at the station I stepped into the street and saw that it was not Russia: a dignified elderly Chinese, dressed in black, was giving money to a flaxen-haired young Russian beggar standing in the gutter.

In some ways Harbin did look like a Russian provincial town. The presence there of many White Russian emigrés fostered the illusion. Other displaced persons of many varieties gave it at the same time a certain cosmopolitanism: there was a Viennese restaurateur who said he made the best coffee in Asia and was affably fluent in several languages. Extremes of poverty and patches of luxury were in evidence, and over everything hung an atmosphere of suspense and uncertainty. There were indications of intrigue, of the sinister and the corrupt. In the daytime the streets were drab and lethargic, but late in the afternoon the town yawned and stretched itself. Lights were turned on, faces were painted, and the febrile night-life of a lonely city, without morale and with the most precarious outlook, began to throb.

I paid a morning call on Madame S., half-Russian and half-French, to whom I had undertaken to convey a message. I found her in what could only have been called a boudoir, the sort of room in which a ham actress might have delighted twenty years earlier. It was full of lacy hangings, braided trimmings, and crowded bibelots—so full that one could scarcely move without ducking or sidling. The draped shawls, framed photographs, and hanging yataghans seemed to have huddled together for safety, as if inanimate things too were driven by some herd-instinct to resist change by hiding from it. But with joy I recognised the samovar: it called up for me the enchanted world of Russian fiction, which had meant more to me than English fiction. I hoped the denizen of the apartment would be like somebody out of Dostoyevsky: voluble, and in a spiritual ferment. She proved to be much more like a Chekhov character.

Her talk was largely about how she had set out for Paris after the Russian Revolution, had got as far as Harbin, where she had found herself saddled with various responsibilities and tethered by various frustrations, and was still bound for Paris—if only she could get her husband to leave Harbin. This was already more than ten years after the Revolution. Perhaps she was still there years later, scanty-haired, toothless, bent double among the fringed antimacassars and darkening icons, still hoping, still clasping her hands, and quavering in a rapturous whisper, 'Ah, Paris!'— her husband, perhaps, having collaborated or pretended to collaborate with the Japanese, the Japanese puppet regime,

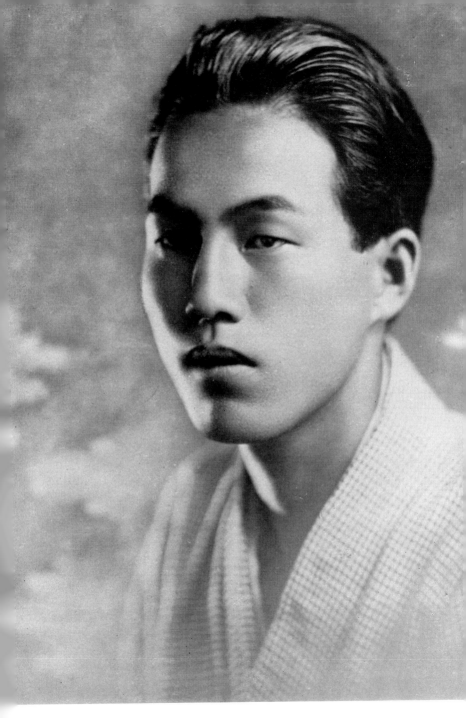

Morito Fukuzawa

Portrait of William Plomer by Edward Wolfe, 1929

Soviet agents, White Russian refugees, Nationalist Chinese, Communist Chinese, in turn, or all at once, in order not to leave Harbin. But I doubt if she dresses now as she was dressed when the bead curtains clashed apart and she stepped forward to greet me. The fashions of those days often lent even a chaste woman a look of wickedness – but the wickedness of a precocious and delinquent schoolgirl. There was something furtive and adolescent about those brimless beehive hats that all but hid the eyes; there was something of the gym-tunic about those short dresses, cut loose and square, with the waistline round the pelvis, and the skirt ending at the knees. Ah, Madame S., your Paris was behind your mirror! It was not bound feet that were your trouble or your fascination, but the bound psyche of the displaced person.

One afternoon I was taken to a brothel which was evidently not at its best in the daytime. My companion and I were shown into a large, unaired parlour with sleazy red-plush divans round the walls, on which were gaudy frescoes of pairs of heroic sun-burnt lovers, more than life-size, in a fancifully tropical setting. There was a stale miasma of last night's fumes of tobacco and vodka, and a general air of seedy hangover. The girls were asleep or resting, but one or two were up and about. We went upstairs, where the air was better, drank Kirin beer, and tried to make conversation. A young Russian girl, a mousy blonde of about seventeen, drew my attention to a gaudy postcard pinned to the wall. It must have come from Natal and showed a handsome Zulu. The consequences of being oneself are unpredictable: that he should have become this girl's pin-up man could hardly have been imagined. From the window I could see a tough-looking Chinese man-servant sweeping the yard; above and beyond him, over the roofs, the wide and mournful river Sungari, like a vast width of dark grey silk, was being endlessly unrolled between its snowy banks, for ever and ever. There was no wind, the air was chill and dry, and lights were beginning to be turned on for the town's awakening to another night of night-life. I felt that I was seeing life, but I would rather have seen it gayer.

It was time to take the Chinese Eastern Railway through the

8

Great Khingan Mountains and over the Barya steppe to the Siberian border. Somnambulistic, I was gently guided by a fellow traveller, an amiable Czech. If he did not break the trance, he let some light of consciousness in. It was a valuable service, yet I can't even remember his name: such is the gratitude of the entranced. He spoke fluent Russian and English, and willingly interpreted for me when we conversed with Russians. He had been here ten years earlier, in the Czech legion that had fought, I believe under Koltchak, the Bolsheviks. He was without prejudice against them, and was anxious to see what they had done and were doing to make a new Russia. From the train we looked out over dune-like wastes of a most forbidding loneliness to the sunless Gobi Desert. At Manchuli, in those days a one-horse, one-storeyed frontier township, we had a drink of kvass, and when, in the slushy street, we stopped to talk to a much-wrapped-up and bearded old man who smelt stronger and cheesier than anybody I ever met, I knew that I had entered the world of Gorki, where distances were in versts, payments in kopecks, and souls naked and tormented. So real had Russia been made to me by the Russian writers I had read in translation that it was impossible to feel like a stranger.

We found ourselves enclosed for the journey in an ancient *wagon-lit* decorated in the *art-nouveau* style with fancy woodwork and figured dark-blue velvet. The atmosphere was stale, so I made as if to open a window. In my ignorance I did not know that for nine months of the year it was forbidden to open the windows because cold air would rush in, and for the remaining months it was ordered that they were to be kept shut because of the dust. There was a dining car, more remarkable for its vodka and excellent macaroons than for lavish meals, and we had been warned to supplement our diet by buying food from the peasants at wayside stations. So we did. We bought all sorts of things, the most notable and lasting of which was a cold roast goose, tender in spite of its ostrich-like dimensions. We also bought honey enclosed in a container made of a hollowed-out section of a young birch tree. This rustic receptacle proved not wholly satisfactory. When our backs were turned, honey exuded into our

pyjamas and socks, and when we tidied our hair we found quite a
new meaning for the phrase 'honey in the comb'. At the rare
stations boiling water was on tap, and the overcoated passengers
queued with teapots: my Czech, like a wise virgin, had provided
us with one before leaving Harbin.

The next excitement was Lake Baikal. One morning there were
mountains, wooded mountains, some of them six or seven
thousand feet high. Handsome conifers towered above the train,
which presently began running in and out of short tunnels round
the southern edge of the lake. Baikal, on which there were small
distant boats, extended there below us in the sun, not a lake but an
inland sea more than three hundred miles long. It was like a
secret sea, because one had never thought about it. Like all this
hardly imaginable northern world it had only the vaguest place
in one's conception of the world as a whole.

Siberia, even on a modern map, was much like some *terra
incognita* on an ancient map, and marked similarly with place
names outlandish and few—Ushumun, Amazar, Sungor, Turu-
chansk—but with this difference, that through it ran this thread,
this clue, this nexus of railway, leading the traveller through
steppe and tundra and taiga to Europe. And now the clue had
brought us to Baikal, the deepest lake in the world. It was said to
be full of delectable fish, and in a capitalist world would soon
have become a millionaire's playground. It was restful not to see
vulgarians in big sports cars but Mongol fishermen in fur caps
minding their own business in a vast silence. Originally, it was
said, the Trans-Siberian railway stopped abruptly at the western
shore and began again on the eastern, the trains being ferried
across in the summer and in the winter driven over rails laid on
the ice, until one winter the ice gave way and a train was drowned.
I doubt if the story is true, but it can only have been at a great
expense of time, money, and labour that the railway was taken
round the southern shore and tunnel after tunnel driven through
the mountain buttresses.

Beyond Irkutsk the ice was breaking up in a rapidly flowing
river of crystalline water rushing eastwards. Chunks and slabs

of ice tilted, swam, or piled up against obstructions, and showed their emerald and sapphire tints to the whitish but strengthening afternoon sun; and on the further bank groves of young silver-birch trees, quite leafless still, gleamed and trembled as if with a consciousness of returning sap. By now we were getting used to the vastly spaced-out stations, where we left the train once or twice a day to buy food, make tea, and stroll about in the cold, pure air. When one left the train the silence struck the ear like a blow, and then each casual sound – the panting of the engine, the snatches of dialogue, the barking of a dog, or crowing of a cock – was enlarged into a monstrous nearness and exactness.

The sensation of space, silence, and emptiness I had known in Africa, but never quite this feeling of immensity. I had read that Russia's Arctic coastline extended to something like seventeen thousand miles, and at Irkutsk we were still far more than a thousand miles from the Arctic Ocean. To someone coming from the swarming warrens of Tokyo and bound for the drab agglom-erations of London the pure and silent Siberian air was like a new and unknown element, and when one saw some solitary man driving off in a troika, or two women with kerchiefs on their heads and wearing big felt boots trudging away into a landscape at times so featureless that it seemed nothing but a perpetual motion of slowly receding horizons, their journeys seemed acts of courage.

The stations and towns at long intervals – Chita, Krasnoyarsk, Novosibirsk, Omsk – had been witnesses of war and revolution, and before that of enforced exile: in their past their future was implicit, of growth and change. Certain buildings put up in Czarist days, solid and well-proportioned under their light-coloured stucco, owed their style to Italian influences in Russia in the eighteenth and early nineteenth centuries. They now wore Bolshevik emblems, stars and sickles and hammers. There were still traces to be seen of the fighting after the Revolution, and already there were signs of that huge expansion of strength to which the Revolution gave the first great impetus and which has since transformed many places in Siberia.

Among the passengers was a lean, lone American who only travelled part of the way with us. Something between a prospector and a mining engineer, he seemed to be more ignorant of Siberia and the Russian language than was right for a prospective resident. He was an ingenuous, credulous, boyish man, and was very anxious to know what was before him when he left the railway to travel by cart or sleigh, or both, to a gold-field in the far north. His male fellow-passengers — and among us was a cynical young Frenchman — were tempted to tell him tall stories. Like heartless, teasing boys we competed to see how much we could make him swallow. We told him gravely of myriads of wolves and bears, aggressive and perpetually hungry, man-eaters all. At this time of year, we said, only a small percentage of northward-bound travellers could expect to get through unscathed. If they did get through they would soon be tormented by three months of extreme heat and perpetual daylight. Sleep would in any case be impossible owing to the mosquitoes. Mosquito nets and insecticides, we explained, were not merely unobtainable but unknown, and the insects, though fortunately not malarial and admittedly smaller than wolves and bears, surpassed them in numbers and in appetite for human blood. Owing to the high intake of ice-cream in the United States, we said, mosquitoes were known to be particularly partial to the blood of Americans. With the first breath of autumn, we went on, the temperature fell abruptly — so abruptly that the mercury had been known to fall out of thermometers not stoutly constructed; by mid-winter the cold was so intense that speech became impossible — it froze on being uttered and fell clattering to the ground. The winter diet was little varied; tallow was the mainstay, because it was an antidote to cold; there was also black bread, soggy and coarse, with a high proportion of the roughest roughage. Radio and newspapers were unknown.

And what, he asked, were the people like? What did they do in their spare time? Exchanging resigned looks and shrugging our shoulders, we competed in gravely inventing deplorable domestic manners and embarrassing sexual customs, to which he would of course have to conform. His eyes grew big with apprehension and he seemed paler under his weathered skin. His relief when we managed to persuade him, before he left, that we had been kidding him all the time was a pleasure to watch. Or was he perhaps a splendid actor, kidding us that we were kidding him? I think not. Innocence is so rare that it is not easily mistakable.

After the American had left us we were joined by another engineer, a Russian from Semipalatinsk, where he had been working on the building of the Turksib railway. He was in his thirties, animated, voluble, shrewd, and humorous, with a refined face and a smart, embroidered blouse. Thanks to my Czech companion's interpreting I was able to carry on long conversations with this agreeable man, the first real Bolshevik I had met. It was obvious that he enjoyed life, because he was full of confidence and hope in his own and his country's future. He did not preach, he did not even talk politics: he exulted. Every now and then he broke into song, and if there had been room I suppose he would have danced. More than once I thought of the exiled girl in the brothel at Harbin. I felt that she might have been happier in Semipalatinsk.

Night after night, day after day, Siberia was rolling past the windows, not monotonous and by no means always bleak. There were fine rolling green steppes, and birch forests, and prairies where the soil looked fat and fertile. The frozen marshes of the taiga came nearer to the Siberia one had imagined, a Siberia of exiles and misery. The considerable town of Sverdlovsk, formerly Ekaterinburg, was under snow when we reached it, beneath a dark grey sky. It was of a forbidding aspect, the more so because one knew it to be the place where the Czar Nicholas II and his family had been done to death. The public rooms of the station were frowsty, and crowded with people who sat or lay about the floor with bundles of possessions, some asleep, some lethargic. They looked as if they had been there a long time, waiting without hope for some long overdue train, and with nowhere else to go. There was a strong smell of old clothes and dill pickles. I stood at a window looking at the town in the leaden afternoon: it seemed lifeless, as if under a curse.

The journey across Siberia itself had taken nine days and nights: it was the longest train-journey in the world. As we approached the Urals and European Russia we seemed to be returning to winter. The whole country was deeper in snow under a dark sky. A derailment somewhere ahead caused us to be held up for the best part of a day at a small station on the way to Kazan. Near the station was a village where it was apparently market day. The peasants came down to the station and took much interest in us passengers. In spite of language difficulties there was cheerful fraternisation. My Czech companion persuaded a friendly mujik to take us for a ride in a horse-drawn sleigh. We went off at a tremendous pace, and it was almost disappointing to see that the train was still in the station when we got back. The interlude was one of those delightful accidents of travel which bring one for a moment much nearer to what is strange.

As the landscape became flatter and slightly more populous and one saw ancient-looking villages with clusters of houses and clumps of trees round churches with gilt, onion-shaped domes, and small wooden manor-houses with pillared porticos, I realised how clearly my ideas about Russia had been formed by Gogol, Tolstoy, Dostoyevsky, Aksakov, Turgenev, Chekhov, Gorki, and Bunin—so formed that I seemed to *recognise* what I saw, as if returning from a long absence. Even in Moscow itself, though awed and excited, I strangely did not feel like a stranger. It was a place where I had often lived and suffered vicariously, and it was haunted by characters whom I felt I had known, whom I almost felt I had *been*. Such is the power of literature.

We went one evening to the Bolshoi Theatre to see a popular spectacle called *The Red Poppy*. The splendid interior, formerly a setting for jewels, uniforms and *grandes toilettes*, was now filled with an audience in working clothes, homely, serious, respectable-looking people, conventional-looking too, in a lower middle-class, yes, a bourgeois, sort of way—though in the former Imperial box a woman with a kerchief over her hair gnawed an apple until the curtain went up. The scene was laid in Shanghai. The plot was simple, but developed by a battalion of performers, ballets, choruses, spectacular lighting, and loud music. An apparently English naval officer, abetted by a few Chinese, tried to induce a Chinese courtesan to offer poisoned wine to his rival, the commanding officer of a Soviet ship. She refused, and was murdered. On her death-bed she kissed a red flower previously given her by the Russian officer, and then, although *in extremis*, managed to preach a revolutionary homily to a group of Chinese children. A crimson map of China appeared in mid-air, and the curtain came down in a perfect frenzy, to which both audience and orchestra contributed their loudest.

The walls of the Kremlin reflected in the river, the Red Square, the views over the roof-tops of solid, early nineteenth-century buildings, the absence of traffic and advertisement, the ancient droshkies, the encrusted ecclesiastical splendours, the evidence of religious feeling and of poverty, the sad, ancient, barbaric atmosphere, the sensation of grandeur, of the world's most enormous hinterland behind this muffled, mysterious, tragic town, the underlying pulse of new power and purpose, little outwardly evident at that time — all this made an overwhelming impression of being in one of the nerve-centres of history.

The museums seemed to be of two kinds, those where remains of past cultures were preserved and those which celebrated the Revolution. They were then being much used to indoctrinate the young, who could be seen going round in eager squads at any time of the day and being lectured to on the usual lines. At the Tretiakov Gallery there were some unpleasant realistic pictures of the misdeeds of the Czars. Before a large canvas showing Ivan the Terrible immediately after the act of killing his own son, a group of silent people stood staring as in the Middle Ages people might have looked at a cautionary picture of Hell. At the Historical Museum, in a room devoted to illustrations of life in the early nineteenth century, I came across a copy-book used in those days by a young nobleman. He had been required to write out the following sentence in Russian, French, and English:

The sense of Honour is of so delicate a nature that it is only met with in Minds that are naturally Noble or in such as have been cultivated by good Examples or a refined Education.

While I was reading this, a class of some forty adolescent boys and girls were being given a purposeful lecture by a buxom young instructress, who was showing them a series of prints depicting the various corporal punishments used in the wicked old Czarist days upon prisoners in Siberia. For all I know, she may have been saying that there would never be any more prisoners sent to Siberia.

As I sat down to dinner that night in the Grand Hotel I unfolded a table napkin of the finest linen, woven with the crown and monogram of the Czar Nicholas II, and out of it ran a cockroach.

23

Mrs Fernandez and Dr Pood

To cross the frontier between Soviet Russia and Poland was in those days to go from shabbiness and gloom to neatness and order. The change was immediately noticeable. Fields, gardens, and houses were well cared-for; the inhabitants had a more upright bearing, more open faces; the customs officials and railwaymen were spruce and civil. It would be too easy to say that to cross this frontier was to cross from Asia into Europe. Frontiers are false, inconstant things. This one no more divided Europe from Asia than do the Ural Mountains. There is no hard and fast barrier between Europe and Asia, and Europeans have lost the right — if they ever had the right — to regard barbarism as something that begins where Europe, or European civilisation, has its ostensible boundaries. If there is one thing clear to any thinking person who has survived the first half of this century it is that there are no limits to human violence and cruelty.

To speak of Warsaw as it was then is to try and look back through a chaos of cruelty and suffering to a city whose civilisation seemed balanced and comprehensible, though it was neither perfect nor secure. The Roman Catholic religion, the survival of a landowning class, the links with France, and the elegant eighteenth-century architecture all contributed to the grace and order of the city. The pleasure of perceiving something of its quality I owed to my old schoolfellow, Darsie Gillie, later the Paris correspondent of the *Manchester Guardian*. He was then living in Warsaw. Even as a boy at Rugby he had shown a more than ordinary appetite for knowledge and power of assimilating and applying it. I forget how long he had been in Poland, but he seemed to have completely mastered the language, and I remember the cheerful firmness with which he corrected some fault of usage or pronunciation made by an imperfectly educated Pole. He also showed great kindness in taking me about, showing me the sights, and introducing me to various forms of Polish life. The Lazienki Palace, the Jewish quarter, a cabaret, a literary salon, the best place to drink mead or borsch, and patience with an ignoramus—he displayed them all.

By way of Berlin, to which I was to return a year later, I came at last to Ostend. The winter of 1928-9 had been more than usually severe, and although the sun was shining, a wind which seemed to have followed me from Siberia did not make the crossing to Dover something to look forward to. It was still early in the day, and the prospective passengers, congregated in the open air just before embarkation, were not in a jovial mood. We were a mixed lot, by no means all English, and among us was a tall English woman with a figure like a cricket bat—straight, narrow, flat in front, and only slightly convex at the back. Her tweeds, her long shanks and feet, her managing nose, and her big front teeth would have made her perfect raw material for some virulent German or French cartoonist of the Anglo–Boer War period. Her supercilious yet carrying voice was in keeping. To borrow a phrase of my brother's, it could only have been evolved 'behind the Tweed Curtain'. It had in it more than a hint of arrogance, as if its function was to convey that her position in life was so assured—racially, socially, and economically—that she had no need to worry about her want of feminine grace. It was the kind of voice that helps to destroy empires: no doubt something like it was once heard in Byzantium.

The owner of the voice might fairly have been classified as an upper middle-class ungentlewoman. After glancing round at the wind-bitten, bluish, resigned faces of the other passengers, she said to her male companion (possibly a son or nephew) in an ineffably condescending drawl, pitching her voice so that we could all hear her:

'Everybody has an expression as if they were just going to take the first fence.'

This was perhaps her idea of a *bon mot*. It was in its way true, and issuing from some jolly, saddle-bashing riding mistress would have been harmless enough. It did not seem harmless to me. It seemed as if she wanted us all to know that the language of the hunting field was natural to her, and that if it was not natural to us, so much the worse for us, whatever we were.

Anybody may make some casual remark, in keeping with his nature and without harmful intention yet liable to make a bad impression when overheard. The bad impression made upon me by this particular remark has as much to do with me as with its utterer. Being young, I was (I hope) suitably intolerant, but she had struck more of a chill into me than the east wind. I must try and explain why.

One of the effects of having left England when very young and of having been long absent was that although I came back with many pleasant memories of English people, places, and things, I came back as a displaced person. Displacement had enabled me to understand, as I could not otherwise have understood, something of the strangeness a foreigner approaching England for the first time might feel, especially if he lacked the comfortable backing of a settled political and social background, a substantial capital, and secure prospects. Such a foreigner, even if unprejudiced, might feel some apprehension about the English character and about some of the traits he might have heard attributed to it. I for my part harboured disagreeable memories of a certain English attitude to life against which I had from early childhood been in rebellion. And having sometimes seen this attitude disagreeably and one might almost say indecently exposed abroad, to the detriment of our national reputation, I was even more sensitive to it and even less ready to make allowances for it.

As a child I had perceived though I could not then have defined this attitude. Having been a boy in the period called Edwardian, I am now of the opinion that it might almost as well be called Late Victorian, and that up to the year 1914 there was no very significant change in English ways of life and thought. If the adults I liked least as a child were complacent, insular, and hypocritical, their habits of mind had certainly been made possible by their having been born and brought up in the second half of the nineteenth century. Some of them were concerned, among other things and other people, with bringing me up, and I saw them as large as life and quite as ugly. Their religion did not seem to have warmed their hearts; their principles seemed too narrow and rigid; their culture, though grounded on the classics, was of a deplorable thinness and poverty; their conventionality was unquestioning; they were dominated by materialism, and their imaginations had atrophied under the sheer weight of national, social, family, and personal complacency. Any but athletic pleasures enjoyed by other people or by the young were liable to incur their disapproval and vindictiveness, and their ignorance of the non-British peoples of the world was more than tinged with contempt. In the lady of the first fence I had recognised instantly a female of the species. Each of us might have tickets to London; but my destination was quite different from hers. Her London would have been more alien to my temperament than some of the remote places I had known, than Hluhluwe or Noboribetsu.

What on earth I seemed like when I returned to England I find it hard to imagine. I think I retained for some time the formal and I suppose defensive manner to which I had become accustomed when living with the Japanese. I may also have brought with me some traces, still adhering, of protective colouring.

'You've come back with a golden face,' my mother said as soon as she saw me.

Going about without a hat in Japan may have given my fair skin a tinge of the local complexion. My eyes were not slanted 'at ten to two', as they say, nor had they developed the epicanthic fold, but they were sometimes as surprised at what they saw as Japanese eyes might have been. I remember for instance noticing with astonishment how well dressed the younger English working men and girls were. They did not seem to be wearing working clothes at all. Was England now becoming a standardised lower middle-class nation, with the rich being impoverished at one extreme and the poor enriched at the other? As a child I had seen glimpses, through loopholes in the solid ramparts of Late Victorian comfort that protected me, of ragged tramps, barefooted urchins, and drunken viragos. I saw none now.

I continued my habit of not wearing a hat. It was then exceptional, even eccentric. Some allusion being made to it at a luncheon party in London, an amiable man next to me said, 'Oh, but don't you think it looks a little *shoppy* to go about without a hat?' I was puzzled by this, and asked what he meant. He explained that he meant '*like a shop assistant*'. I said it had not occurred to me, and I should not really much mind if I *were* mistaken for a shop assistant. He died a year or two later of pneumonia brought on in winter at his wife's funeral. Instead of standing bareheaded by the grave he would have been wiser not to have taken off his hat. It may have been necessary to suffer in order to appear respectful, but death was a severe penalty for having taken the appalling risk of looking like a shop assistant.

I cannot say I was deeply interested in my own appearance, but I remember my old friend the painter Enslin du Plessis said at this time I looked like 'a mixture of Puck and Buddha', so I suppose my evident but unconsciously acquired Eastern aspect was enlivened by gleams of Western playfulness. I had already learnt that many people expect a writer to look like the image they have formed of him in their own minds. I had hardly set foot in England before somebody or other exclaimed, 'Oh, but you don't look in the least like your books!' or 'You don't look at all as I had imagined you!'

Several times since then strangers have come up to me and begun a conversation, mistaking me for a doctor—each time a different doctor. A serious-looking man in a club once took my hand in his and told me how glad he was to hear of my new appointment at Bart's. A year or two later an eagerly friendly refugee couple, perhaps Austrian, clung to me in the street, beaming and exclaiming, '*Ach, sind sie wirklich Doktor Gruber?*' And I have actually been congratulated on my successful treatment of a difficult case of hydrocele. I have thought these mistakes gratifying, because a doctor may be expected to have some insight into human nature and some powers of diagnosis, prognosis, and analysis.

To have called myself a displaced person is perhaps to appear to angle for sympathy. It would be more exact to call myself a repatriated person. My parents had returned for good from South Africa and I went to spend the summer with them in their house, which was far enough from London for nightingales to be heard in the garden, but not too far to prevent my dining in London and returning home by a late train. I write 'their house', not 'their home', because they were never long enough in one place for it to be regarded as a home, either by them or their children. But their great kindness, and the trouble they took to make me *feel* at home, provided perfect conditions in which to write. I was working at my second novel, and when it was finished I moved to London. What were my motives? First, the need to function as a writer, and to exercise and try to develop whatever talent I might possess, in what seemed the best environment. Next, curiosity about people and about London itself, and the impetus to unlock a London of one's own. I had at that time no responsibility for contributing to the support of others, no intention of marrying, and almost no interest in trying to make more money than was needful to keep myself clothed, fed, warm, and clean, and to perform such small acts of charity or present-giving and make such modest returns of hospitality as might be possible for an indigent bachelor. I had no wish to impress anybody with my manner of living. I felt no need to own or use many of the things that most people found indispensable, like a telephone, a car, or a club, perhaps because I had lived quite happily without them elsewhere. I had not the faintest ambition to write best-sellers. I should never have thought that my cast of mind was at all fitted to engage the interest of a large public. Nor was I set on any particular literary form. I wished to write prose or verse in various forms, as the spirit moved me, and, I hoped, in such a way that

everything I wrote would be part of a gradually evolving interpretation of life in terms of my own art.

As for the business of making a living, I have never been
pushful, and would not have dreamed of soliciting any kind of
favour or help from the eminent or the rich, from relations or
friends, or of asking for any kind of job. Such ambition as I had
lay entirely in the twin spheres of literature and of personal
relationships. Both are impossible without leisure. As J. B.
Yeats, the father of the poet, said in one of his letters: 'A society of
poor gentlemen upon whose hands time lies heavy is absolutely
necessary to art and literature.'

My family had had associations with London for at least four
centuries, and I myself had often stayed there as a child. Now, at
twenty-five, I entered it alone.

The first question was whereabouts I was going to live. It
would not have occurred to me to settle in Bloomsbury. Chelsea,
which I knew of old, seemed now to have a new, floating population of well-to-do culture-vultures. Kensington was too sober,
Mayfair too smart; and when I saw in some paper an advertisement of 'chambers near Hyde Park' I followed it up.

I envisaged one of those quiet, clean, comfortable, old-fashioned
establishments not far from the Marble Arch, kept by some urbane
ex-butler whose wife had been a housekeeper or a lady's maid, the
sort of house in which before 1914 my parents had sometimes
taken rooms on visits to London. I was quite mistaken. Imagination could hardly have allowed for what lay in hiding beyond that
advertisement.

The house was in Bayswater, to which I was not at all disinclined. My grandfather, while still serving in India, had taken a
house for his wife and children in Stanhope Street in the 1860s.
My parents had been married at St John's Church in 1901. And in
1918 I had tottered light-headedly out of a Bayswater nursing-
home after recovering from the Spanish influenza. I liked the
quarter. It was quiet and near central London, and in 1929 not so
gloomy and decayed as it became later. The afterglow of Victorian
prosperity had not yet wholly faded and I liked the Victorian

atmosphere and architecture; I have always taken a great interest in the social history of the nineteenth century.

As soon as I saw the house containing my prospective 'chambers' I was pleased by its looks. There was nothing mournful or faded about it. Perhaps built in the 1850s, it was villa-like, not tall and gaunt but with a cheerful light stucco façade, some pretty leafage behind the massive iron gate and railings, a balustraded balcony and parapet, and some graceful ironwork enclosing the window-sills on the ground floor. The front door was approached by a flight of steps under an important-looking glass and iron canopy.

The door was opened by a lively, pretty, fresh-looking Jewess in her early thirties, and I told her I had come in response to her advertisement. In the hall there was an air of bareness and improvisation, and there was no carpet on the stairs. She explained that she had not been long in the house and was still getting it ready, but she showed herself anxious to welcome me as a prospective lodger. She made some passing allusion to her husband, but he didn't appear. She showed me a large unfurnished front room on the first floor, with a bathroom adjoining it and a view of a roseate Swedenborgian church on the other side of the road. I liked the room, took it, soon furnished it with a bed, a desk, and other necessary things, and moved in.

I was out a great deal and busy when in, and only saw Beryl Fernandez occasionally. I have given her a false name. She had done the same herself, it later appeared, because her husband, who apparently wasn't her husband, was not using his real name.

Mrs Fernandez was inclined to take me into her confidence. With the help of a woman friend, unmarried and formerly a nurse, she had the running of the house. It was not clear how her husband, as she called him, spent his time: he didn't go out to work and had no visible occupation. From the first I felt that there was something enigmatic and furtive about him. He was more than twenty years older than she was, and they had a little girl of six, Betty, to whom he was intensely devoted. I only once or twice had a fleeting glimpse of him. He didn't make himself known to me, but looked at me with an unfriendly eye. A tomahawk look, I thought: I had heard that he was supposed to have Red Indian blood.

There was an atmosphere of emotional tension, and partly from Mrs Fernandez's confidences and partly from other sources, I began to understand something of its nature. The couple were evidently infatuated with each other, but his passion for her was distorted by jealousy. He felt ferociously suspicious of any male who might even set eyes on his wife—the milkman, the newspaper boy, any shop assistant, any man in the street who even glanced at her, and in particular (I learnt later) myself.

When his jealousy came to a head, as it often did, he used violence and threats towards the pretty wife who was young enough to have been his daughter; and while fascinated by him she was terrified by him; so that clean and orderly house was charged with high explosive.

She told her woman friend she was afraid he might do her a mortal injury. The friend was equally afraid, and urged her either to leave him or seek the protection of the law.

'Why don't you?' I said.

'Oh,' she said, 'I *couldn't*.'

His suspiciousness grew until it became a dangerous delusion, and one night in November he butchered her in the presence of the child. I have good authority for saying that if I had not happened to be away for the weekend he would have butchered me in my sleep.

Coming back to London on the Monday afternoon I noticed news-bills saying *Shocking Bayswater Tragedy*, and when I saw them I had suspicions of my own.

The poor, deluded woman was dead. The poor, deluded man had attempted to do away with himself, but was prevented. I did not attend his trial at the Old Bailey two months later. Mr Justice Avory, whose appearance and reputation were far from attractive, was presiding. In spite of medical evidence that he was suffering from delusional insanity, Fernandez was sentenced to death. An appeal was dismissed, but the death sentence was commuted to penal servitude for life. It had come out at the trial that he was an American citizen and had been a vaudeville performer of some kind, and that she had been a milliner and the daughter of a fancy-goods merchant who had died in Brighton a year earlier.

Later I wrote a novel based on the circumstances of the crime. *The Case is Altered* had some success and was chosen by the Book Society, then a fairly new institution. After the book had been in circulation for some time I received a letter from a man whose name was vaguely known to me. Let me call him Zebulon Pood. He wrote from Harley Street. He said he had been reading *The Case is Altered* with keen interest. After come compliments he said the book had a special significance for him, because it was evident to him that it had been based upon the life and death of his unfortunate cousin, Mrs Fernandez. He said I had given such a sympathetic and understanding account of her character and situation that I could no doubt tell him things he did not know about her. On the other hand, as she had not only been his cousin but one of his patients, he thought it likely that he could tell me things about her which I did not know and which might interest me. He would be so pleased if I would come and see him.

This seemed to me a faintly irregular letter. I was naturally curious to know more about the woman who had been caught up in that terrible doom, a woman whom I had known, liked, and admired, and with whom I had co-existed – and nearly died – under the same roof. But why should the writer assume my readiness to swap reminiscences with him? And in Harley Street! I looked him up in *Who's Who*. Dr Pood had been born in a distant country, was unmarried, and had had much and varied experience in his profession. He described himself as a sexologist and an associate of specialists and organisations concerned with sexual enlightenment and reform. He was strong on gynaecology, obstetrics, and contraception. He listed many of his articles and essays. (If we all did that, *Who's Who* would no longer be portable.) He had also written books, among them a monograph about some contraceptive contraption he had invented. I made one or two inquiries about him from worldly-wise friends about town.

'What can you tell me,' I asked, 'about Zebulon Pood?'

'The most indiscreet man in London,' was the first answer I got. It was confirmed by others. The natural curiosity of a fictionist to meet a man with that reputation was damped down. I wrote Dr Pood a civil reply and was easily able to excuse myself for not going to see him, because I was about to go abroad.

Two or three years later, when some other book of mine had come out, Dr Pood wrote to me again. He had just read my new book, he said. Again there were compliments. He was still hoping, he said, that some day he would have the pleasure of meeting me and exchanging recollections of his cousin, Beryl Fernandez. Well, I thought, why not? And I made an appointment to go and see him.

It was on a dark November afternoon that I found myself standing on his threshold in Harley Street. The door was opened by an uncommonly large and handsome butler. I said I was to see Dr Pood. With a slight bow, the beginnings of a Mona Lisa smile, and a pregnant silence, he ushered me into a waiting-room. It was furnished with the usual impersonal opulence of such places, intended no doubt in this instance to have a calming effect upon the many persons who came to Dr Pood to have their sexological uneasinesses ironed out. Back numbers of journals about eugenics were to be seen interspersed with nice fresh copies of the *Tatler*, suitable for an invalid. Almost immediately the butler ushered me out, shut me up in a coffin-like lift, and fired me off like a guided missile to one of the upper floors.

As I stepped out I was greeted with the remark, 'You're not at all as I imagined you! I thought you would be pale and gloomy, and here you are, bursting with vitality!'

The speaker was dark and had a longish, whitish, rather flabby face, with the alert expression of a trained observer who had seen a lot of life, in this instance mostly below the belt. His figure was notably pear-shaped, and enclosed in the appropriate black coat and striped trousers.

The room he led me into seemed hardly likely to be a consulting room, unless he was a sorcerer as well as a sexologist. It looked more suitable for the smoking of imitation opium, to the strains of *Chu Chin Chow*, being furnished in bad Chinese made-for-export style. It looked like a setting for a melodramatic film, an English film, about some Dr Fu or Dr Wu in Limehouse or Shanghai, with moustaches drooping like rats' tails on either side of a cynical mouth, with a diabolical urbanity, nails as long and pointed as skewers, and an abducted blonde, gagged and trussed up like a chicken, squirming behind the bead curtain. I looked instinctively for the bead curtain, but in vain. The other properties were there – the excessively carved furniture and screens, the joss sticks burning in a big porcelain vase before an image of Buddha, and the bronze sconces in the form of dragons, from the mouths of which dangled the dried and spiky skins of globe-fish, enclosing electric-light bulbs. But Dr Pood was no Fu.

'Do sit down. Ah, here's tea,' he said, as a tray was brought in by the big, observant butler. 'Do you mind helping yourself? I never have tea myself: I prefer ginger beer. I'm very glad you've come to see me at last.' And as I poured myself out some tea he actually filled a glass with (of all things, on a black November afternoon) ginger beer.

'You realise, of course, that my cousin's husband was suffering from general paralysis of the insane?'

I said I had supposed it might be something like that.

'And that she was passionately in love with him? She used to come and borrow money from me. She started that place, you know, on nothing ... He was useless, useless to her. By sticking to him she threw her life away.'

The cold suds of ginger beer made him eloquent. Her private life, her husband's sexual habits, the very questions she had put to Dr Pood about them were now communicated to me. A man of more principle than myself would perhaps have said, 'But why are you telling me all this? It was told to you in confidence. These ought surely to be consulting-room secrets. Isn't this a breach of professional etiquette as well as of personal loyalty?'

What seemed to me more important was that we had something in common – that we had both liked Beryl Fernandez, had both been, in different degrees, in her confidence, and had both wished to help her. Dr Pood *had* helped her, with professional advice, with money, and with sensible worldly advice, as her kinsman. From what I had learnt of him I knew that he was something much more than indiscreet. He was a man, so far as I could judge, entirely without puritanical prejudices, a man of great experience, with great knowledge of what used to be called human frailties — or, to be more precise, the dreadful physical and psychological muddles, fears, frustrations, and pains into which men and women are dragged by the sexual instinct. His hard-working life was devoted to easing or preventing these things.

I saw him as a benevolent and beneficent man. It seemed to me that his specialised view of human life and human nature was uncommonly clear and direct. And he was amused, yes, amused, by human folly, by the grotesqueness of thought and behaviour into which we are led by the sexual impulse. Whether my doctor-like appearance made him more candid than usual I do not know, but he talked to me as if I was his equal in knowledge and under-standing of gynaecology and the whole bag of tricks. Indiscreet undoubtedly, but without discernible malice.

From the subject of Beryl Fernandez and her life with her husband, we passed to a wider examination of life in London — the aspects of life to which Dr Pood's attention was drawn by his patients. He began to tell me of some divagations of the sexual instinct that had come to his notice. He was amused by some of them — and justifiably. Unless a doctor has got beyond being shocked, angered, or disgusted by what he sees and hears, he must surely be wanting in professional poise. If he has the capacity to be amused and saddened at the same time, he is likely to be a healer. Perhaps the same is true of a priest. And how the human race needs healing, inside and out!

I recall a story of Dr Pood's about a youngish man who came to consult him and admitted to a perversion that surprised even Dr Pood a little, and would to most people have seemed grotesquely unappetising.

'Yes, I see — of course, of course,' Dr Pood said blandly, as if it were the most ordinary proceeding. 'But don't you find it rather difficult to find anybody who is willing to join you in that?'

'Oh, very difficult,' was the answer. 'And when I *do* find anybody, of course, they're *never* my type!'

It requires imagination as well as tolerance to arrive at anything like a sympathetic understanding of strong emotions aroused in others by agencies that can only arouse strong distaste in oneself. Dr Pood did not seem to me an imaginative man. It was in the physiological aspects of his case-histories that he showed his understanding best, and he had that intuitive appreciation of character which is often a Jewish trait. One ludicrous, yet pathetic story he told me had to do with a man well known to the public and professionally eminent. Dr Pood did not tell me the man's name, but from a fortuitous detail he let slip I was instantly able to identify him. Dr Pood might have foreseen that if I should take it into my head to go to the patient and tell what I had heard and from whom I had heard it, tremendous mischief could result, with serious consequences to this indiscreet consultant. But Dr Pood's mind evidently did not work like that. His indiscretion and trustfulness were, so to speak, part of his method as well as of his character. He did not hear the music of humanity in muffled tones; he did not see life, and he did not expect his patients to see it, in a dim religious light. He seemed to treat them as fellow actors in an outrageous comedy.

His directness and candour helped to make him not at all a bad specimen of a twentieth-century man — scientific; seemingly untroubled by racial or social or some professional conventions; functioning independently and well in advance both of public opinion and of the average in his own profession; unspiritual, materialistic; inclined to make much active propaganda for what he believed helpful; and in working to save or improve human life obviously opposed to those destructive — or, rather, self-destructive — tendencies in mankind which in this century have caused such incalculable suffering.

24

Tavistock Square and Gower Street

When I got back to my 'chambers' after the fatal weekend, the woman friend of Mrs Fernandez was bearing up against distress and shock. Upon her had devolved for the time being the need to maintain the house. One of her most immediate worries was that the conjugal bedroom had not yet been put to rights. Since the police had seen it she had kept it locked. To save her a painful task I undertook to put it in order myself. She gave me the key, and with the help of the young house-man I set about removing the traces of the crime. They were copious.

Those of my friends who knew something of what had happened took it for granted that I should at once be leaving the house, but I saw no reason for hurrying away. The harm had been done, and I was no longer in danger. Besides, I had sent out invitations to a small evening party and was disinclined to put off my guests.

When I had left England more than ten years before I had been too young to form any very close or settled or habitual friendships, and had had no settled home in England. Although a repatriated person, I lacked threads to take up. I had no circle to re-enter. This was not surprising; and in view of my tastes and inclinations I did not try and base my social life upon relations and connexions but was drawn more to the new acquaintances my writing had made for me.

Among the guests at the party was Gyles Isham, with whom I had been at school. In Rugby days we used to bicycle about looking at churches. At Oxford, in the interim, he had distinguished himself as an actor, and was to appear later with Greta Garbo in *Anna Karenina*. He brought his sister Virginia, and I had asked them to meet Virginia Woolf, to whom they were related. She duly arrived with Leonard Woolf, and with her acute sensitivity to atmosphere she looked about her with interest.

We were assembled in a somewhat cavernous room with moss-green walls and one of those enormous Bayswater chimney-pieces made of great slabs of Italian marble. This was Victorian London all right; Frith had had his studio only a few doors away; and near at hand was Westbourne Grove, where some of the shops, and some of the shoppers, had hardly altered since the Nineties. Engaging her fellow-guests in conversation, Virginia Woolf must have found them somewhat mixed. Among them was the ever-lively Edward Wolfe, whom I had known in Johannesburg, and who was painting my portrait, and a new friend, Anthony Butts, about whom I shall have more to say, with his mother, Mary Colville-Hyde.

I was now twenty-six. Several years had passed since the manuscript of my first book had travelled six thousand miles to the Hogarth Press. I had since produced two books of short stories, which had been well received. The welcome which the Woolfs gave me when I came back to England, and their subsequent friendship, were much valued by me. Soon after my return I dined alone with them in Tavistock Square: it was the first of a long series of evenings and conversations, during which they were good enough to introduce me to many persons of character and literary distinction. For a young writer, obscure, somewhat reclusive by nature, poor, and curious, these evenings were of great benefit and pleasure: and Leonard Woolf, then literary editor of the *Nation*, gave me practical help by sending me books for review.

In the upper room to which we withdrew after dinner the lighting was fairly subdued, otherwise attention might have been unduly distracted by the mural decorations from the hand of Virginia Woolf's sister, Mrs Bell. In fact those rough trellises and wavy lines, two-handled vases, guitars, fans and sketchy floral motifs, made their contribution to the unsolemn atmosphere of a room not quite like any other. Virginia Woolf, equally adept at entertaining and being entertained, unobtrusively kept those present as active, or attentive, as an orchestra, and unless some visitor was awkward, shy, or moody, the tempo was lively and the tone gay.

A card would have reached me, and her handwriting, sharp, delicate, and rhythmical as her prose, was pleasing in itself—the more so because it had formed an invitation; and there was often added, as if by way of an afterthought, 'X is coming.' X was almost always somebody eminent in the sphere of writing. Only a week or two after the murder a card of invitation had reached me. 'Lytton Strachey is coming,' it said.

Strachey was then still in his forties, but his beard and spectacles made him look older. They seemed to create a certain distance between himself and others. About Strachey's eyelids, as he looked out through the windows of his spectacles over the quickset hedge of his beard, there was a suggestion of world-weariness: he had in fact just two more years to live. I did not think of him in terms of a sum of years but as an intelligence alert and busy behind the appendage of hair and the glass outworks. A glint came into his eyes, the brain was on the move as swiftly as a bat, with something of the radar-like sensitivity of a bat, and when he spoke it was sometimes in the voice of a bat.

Quite a different voice from Strachey's came crackling, dry and vibrant and precise, out of the intellectual head of Roger Fry, whose spectacles seemed to magnify both ways. To look him in the eyes was to look through twin lenses at two keen and magnified visual organs, and simultaneously to be conscious of exposure to expert scrutiny. If one had been anywhere overpainted, or badly varnished, or if one had been wearing the exasperating label of a false attribution, one could hardly have gone on looking him in the face. His devotion to 'significant form' is pleasantly illustrated by the story that he was seen in the National Gallery lecturing about the composition of a large religious masterpiece to a docile squad of gaping self-improvers. Indicating with his long wooden pointer the presiding figure of God the Father, he was heard to say, 'Now, this important mass ...'

Fry's own pictures have generally seemed to me saddish confections, like those of an amateur cook with sound training and well-tried recipes but without the least spark of inspiration. He had been engaged by the Hogarth Press to design the dust-jacket for my book of short stories on Japanese themes, *Paper Houses*. Though not at all Japanese in feeling, it was a pleasing design in blue and white, and aroused regret that dust-jackets are such perishable things.

It was at Tavistock Square that I first met Lady Ottoline Morrell, who, once seen, could not be forgotten. Her bearing was impressive. As was not unusual with women of her generation and of orderly upbringing, she held herself so straight-backed that she gave an impression of being taller than she was. There was style and dignity in her movements, even if the style of her clothes and ornaments was sometimes that of fancy dress. The first time I saw her she was wearing in her frizzed-out, reddish hair several quoit-like rings of what looked like reddish amber, and very full and stiff and sibilant shot-silk skirts, which set up a tremendous whispering campaign every time she moved. Her large-boned head, held rather high, with its commanding nose and chin, and her long, bony fingers helped to give her an air of authority. Her voice, nasal but not unpleasant, and with a curious and indescribable timbre, confidential and almost conspiratorial, caught and held one's attention.

If she had a streak of unwisdom, if her interest in writers and painters and in their personal affairs was held to be sometimes intrusive, or even scheming, that didn't trouble me. I was purposely not very responsive to direct inquiries about my private life, and when Stephen Spender once asked her what she thought of me, she said, according to his account:

'A very nice man – but he's just like a pump! I *pump* and *pump*, and I can't get *anything* out of him!'

She had, all the same, got Stephen Spender out of me. With her flair for creative talent she had taken note of his name and work at a very early stage in his career; she knew I knew him; and she had urged me to introduce him to her at one of her afternoons in Gower Street. I had accordingly done so, and they enabled us to meet Yeats and Eliot (whom I had already met with the Woolfs), and to hear the fluent speech of the one and the carefully weighed and measured utterance of the other.

'And do you often go back to America?' a friend of mine asked Eliot in my hearing at about this time.

'Not very often.' A pause, while he looked at the floor with great concentration: his answer mustn't offend any of his principles, nor militate against truth, logic, or the established religion. 'On an average,' he said, and then again paused, perhaps to consider the possible ramifications of the effect of what he was about to say, 'I should say about every twenty years.'

At Gower Street he was sometimes accompanied by his first wife. I couldn't help noticing her neurotic behaviour and what seemed a morbid fear of being slighted. When I came to sign the visitors' book just after her one day I was disturbed by her tremulous and conspicuous signature, 'Vivienne Haigh Eliot.' Why bother, I thought, about the Haigh? I felt sorry for her and more sorry for Eliot.

More than thirty years later, on a crowded, sunny afternoon in Worthing, of all places, I suddenly caught sight of him with his second wife. He was wearing a white cap of the kind golfers wear, they were arm in arm, looking at each other and smiling happily. Eliot's sacramental view of marriage is nicely indicated in Robert Sencourt's memoir, which tells of Eliot heard telephoning, apparently to a social secretary:

'Will you please tell her ladyship that I am unable to come to lunch with her because I don't accept invitations from ladies I have not met, nor from one who invites me without my wife, nor from one who is divorced.'

So strenuous a life, intellectually and spiritually, whatever its putative reward in heaven, surely deserved its happy ending on earth.

Lesser poets were to be seen at Gower Street—Yeats's friend Sturge Moore, for instance, whose demeanour and harmless writings (which 'may seem', according to a reference book, 'to

lack concentration and tension') had caused him to be spoken of as
'The Sheep in Sheep's Clothing'. It was said that in one of his
poems the two following lines were to be found:

> She was as old as any rose,
> And older than most sheep.

I cannot vouch for the truth of this, but the lines somehow remind
me of Queen Anne's opinion that the goose is an unsatisfactory
bird: 'It is too much for one, and not enough for two.'

At Gower Street, too, could be seen a gnome-like Irish writer,
James Stephens. Seated in a corner one afternoon, Stephens was
heard by me to say, in a thickish brogue and apparently to clinch
an argument, 'After all, the Little People always know best.' This
piece of Celtic twaddle was too much for the strict Cambridge
rationalism of Leonard Woolf, who happened to be present, had
been listening to Stephens with obvious and mounting exasperation, and now said testily, and with unconcealed disgust, 'Nonsense! *Nonsense!*' There are moments, all the same, when
imagination, intuition, perhaps even superstition are wiser than
self-confident reasoning, but whether they are properties of the
Little People I am not Celt enough to know.

These afternoons in Gower Street, with their celebrities and
often good conversation, could I suppose be described as a salon.
They were valuable for a young writer. I am not ashamed of
having been pleased by the interest Lady Ottoline expressed in my
writings. When Eliot lent her my novel *Sado* she took the trouble
to write and tell me what she thought about it, and when I sent
her *The Case is Altered* she wrote to me at length with an appreciation of character and incident that seemed as genuine as it was
detailed. Her letters, written in brown ink, a rococo script unlike
anything else on earth, and in a style which seemed to owe
something to Mr Jingle and something to Ronald Firbank, have
been well described by Stephen Spender in *World Within World*.
I had in those days some aptitude for graphological analysis, which
later went into abeyance, and even if I had never seen her or

known her I should have found them revealing of a character both original and impressive.

She was, I suppose, the only person I am likely to have known who began life with the 'double blessing' (as her half-brother, the Duke of Portland, put it) of being kissed both by the Prince of Wales (later Edward VII) and Disraeli. I have sometimes thought of this when passing Disraeli's house in Curzon Street, and also of my father as a boy being sent across every morning after breakfast from my grandfather's house in Chesterfield Street to read the bulletins outside the house when the great man lay dying. I like these links and fortuitous associations with the past. They lend perspective to the great turmoil of life.

Of Lady Ottoline it may be said, in a phrase much hackneyed by amateur obituarists, that we shall not look upon her like again —but then, who had ever looked upon it before? That she was not a type but an individual was the primary thing her handwriting proclaimed. Style, warmth, enterprise, and a passionate respect for creativeness in the arts were among her attributes. She was easy game, or rich material, for satirists. She is said to have been a mainstay, a breadwinner almost, for certain satirical novelists of the Twenties who had made use of her hospitality and friendship. Something of an anthology could be made of fictional characters who might be supposed to be gay traducements of this un-common woman. Perhaps not enough has been made of the courage she showed in being a rebel against the tyranny, in her time and class, of 'The Thing'. Without knowing it, she occasioned one of the most old-world or feudal remarks I have ever heard. Far from London an old noblewoman, hearing Lady Ottoline praised as a patron of the arts, said with some severity, 'But she has betrayed our Order.' I remember Virginia Woolf's astonish-ment when I repeated this anachronism to her.

Once when Virginia Woolf was sitting beside Lady Ottoline on a sofa their two profiles were suddenly to be seen, one in relief against the other, like two profiles on some Renaissance medal — two strange, queenly figures evolved in the leisured and cere-monious days of the nineteenth century. Each, by being herself, won an allegiance to herself in the twentieth. Both faces were aristocratic, but in that chance propinquity Virginia Woolf's appeared much the more fine and delicate. The two women admired one another, with reservations on one side at least; and they were affectionate in manner when together, though one appeared more affectionate than the other. They had a good deal in common. Both had what old-fashioned people used to call *presence* — a kind of stateliness, a kind of simple, unfussy dignity. Lady Ottoline Morrell, not always discriminating about people, recognised the uniqueness of Virginia Woolf. Virginia Woolf spoke admiringly of the independence and force of character which had enabled Lady Ottoline to emerge from the grand but narrow world into which she had been born (and of which she retained the panache) into a more varied world in which ideas and talent counted more than property or background.

Both had an insatiable curiosity about their fellow-creatures, and both a love of gossip and the capacity to be amused or astonished which goes with that virtue. In the exercise of this curiosity the difference of approach was as striking as the difference in their profiles. Lady Ottoline would ask the most personal, direct questions, not in a hectoring way, but without the slightest compunction, and with the manner of a feudal grandee who had a right to be told what she wanted to know. Because most people like talking about themselves to a sympathetic listener she often got what she wanted, but not, as I have indicated, from me.

Virginia Woolf's approach was less blunt and more ingenious. With a delicious and playful inventiveness she would often improvise an ironical fantasy about the life and habits of the person to whom she was talking, and this was likely to call forth protests, denials, and explanations which helped to make up something like a confession. Lady Ottoline, less tense and less discerning, was an easier mixer: Virginia Woolf sometimes frightened people by aloofness or asperity, for which they had sometimes their own clumsiness to blame. Yet she could show the most graceful restraint. In the course of several hours of the company of an individual who, she afterwards told me, caused her alternating emotions of anger, laughter, and utter boredom, she showed no sign of the first two and only a faint trace of the last — which is the most difficult of the three to hide.

The fact that Virginia Woolf did not make, either in social life or in her books, any concession to vulgarians, or offer any foothold to a banal understanding, or bait any traps for popularity, probably helped to create a legend about herself among the uninformed, the envious, and the ignorant, that she was some sort of precious and fragile being, ineffably superior and aloof, and quite out of touch with 'ordinary' life — whatever that may be. This legend has been completely dispersed. It is now understood that her life was rich in experience of people and places, and that her disposition, as is sometimes the case with those who are highly strung and have an inclination to melancholy, was genial.

Her biographers, so far from having to chronicle the life of an etiolated recluse, may be embarrassed by the quantity and variety of their material. Clearly no adequate biography will be possible until her immense diary has been published in full. From her conversation I recall many interesting glimpses and facets of her earlier life — how, as a young girl, in an agony of shyness, she drove alone at night in a cab with straw on the floor to a ball at one of the great London houses, wearing no jewellery except a modest string of pearls ('but they were *real* pearls'); how she had Greek lessons with Clara, the sister of Walter Pater, in Canning Place, in a setting of blue china, Persian cats, and Morris wallpapers; how she took part in the Dreadnought Hoax, one of the world's great practical jokes and a superb piece of acting, a demonstration that high-ranking hearts of oak at Portsmouth were accompanied by heads of the same material, since they were unable to see through a bogus Negus of Abyssinia and his preposterous 'suite'; how she went bathing with Rupert Brooke, whose profile was not quite lived up to by his legs, those being perceptibly bowed; how she sat up all night in a Balkan hotel reading the *Christian Science Monitor* to cheat the bugs; and how there was a murder under her window in Euboea.

Speaking of writing as a profession, she once remarked to me that one is bound to upset oneself physically if one works for more than two hours a day. She put so much of herself into her work that it must have taken much out of her, and she was in fact a prodigiously hard worker. The volume of her published and unpublished writings, including her letters and diary, is as impressive as the sustained high level of all that has so far been printed. She was as energetic as her father, to whom mountains were no obstacles, nor mountains of fact either.

To be so active, one's nature must be integrated. In each of us there are two beings, one solitary and one social. There are persons who cannot bear to be with others, and turn into hermits or something worse; most cannot bear to be alone, and become common or shallow, or both. In Virginia Woolf the two beings seemed to have an equal life and so to make her into a complete person. She could be detached and see things in perspective; and she could enter into things, into other people's lives, until she became part of them. The two beings can be perceived in her writings, sometimes distinct, sometimes merged. The special genius of her rare and solitary spirit reached its purest expression in *The Waves*, an exquisite, subjective book nearer to poetry and music than to what is generally meant by 'the novel'. The social being in Virginia Woolf, and (in my opinion) the novelist, can be seen most clearly not in her fiction but in *The Common Reader*. Those essays are full of shrewdness and knowledge of the world and of human nature, qualities which, though discernible in her novels, are less important to them than her own sensitivity, as an instrument to the vibrations of the external world.

The old masters of fiction — Shakespeare, Balzac, Tolstoy — are such because, besides all the other gifts, they are imaginative men of the world with an exceptional robustness and gusto. They have also an extreme preoccupation with sociology. This, when it goes more with finesse than with animal spirits, produces novelists like Jane Austen, Flaubert, or Proust, and it was to such writers that Virginia Woolf was in some ways akin. It may be argued that her myth-making faculty was chiefly applied to sensation rather than to characters, and that her passion for sociology was in a

9

sense scientific. Although she enjoyed embroidering facts about people, sometimes in a poetic or a fantastic or a censorious or an ironical way, she was really devoted to the facts themselves. The solitary being was a poet, the social being was a sort of scientist: the former discovered poetic truth, the latter anthropological truth.

During the last ten years of her life Virginia Woolf several times told me how much more she enjoyed reading autobiographies than novels. She once said she thought almost any autobiography more satisfying than a novel. When autobiographical memoirs were written by people she knew and found congenial —Lady Oxford, for instance (and what a sharp profile there!), or the bluff and breezy Dame Ethel Smyth—she not only had the pleasure of getting to know them better, but her appetite for social knowledge and reminiscence was much gratified. A passionate precision in collecting data about society (very strong in Flaubert and Proust) made her delight in anything that helped it.

At those evenings in Tavistock Square she was at her best with persons who, like herself, were not merely articulate but articulate in a new way. She had a gift for making the young and obscure feel that they were of value too. She admired physical as well as intellectual beauty. She could charm away diffidence, and, since she was something of a feminist, could be notably sympathetic with young women, in particular young women from Cambridge. A strong sense of the proper functions of literature and a highly and constantly cultivated taste gave her a proper pride (derived in part no doubt from her literary father and background) in her own gifts, but she was without arrogance, and wore her rare beauty without ostentation.

It is not enough to say that she was a hard-working writer, and that she always read a great deal. She also worked as a publisher, and even at times as a printer, with her husband. She examined a great number of typescripts and even of manuscripts for the Hogarth Press, books from which rightly bore the imprint of 'Leonard and Virginia Woolf'. As early as 1930 she and her husband expressed some annoyance at the way the Hogarth Press was developing. They even seemed half vexed by the increasingly profitable sales of Hogarth Press books, and were seriously considering reducing the press to its original and remarkable dimensions — a hand-press in a basement at Richmond, worked by themselves as amateurs. This was before John Lehmann was inducted into the business and began his long and conspicuous career as a publisher and editor. From the time I first saw him he showed an interest in my writings which has continued to this day, and I am only one of innumerable writers whom he has helped.

Virginia Woolf loved London and the country, her relations, and friends; she loved her domestic surroundings; she loved the written word. She liked good talk, good food, and good coffee. I see her in a shady hat and summer sleeves, moving between the fig tree and the zinnias at Rodmell; I see her sitting over a fire and smoking one of her favourite cheroots; I see the nervous shoulders, the thin, creative wrists, the unprecedented sculpture of the temples and eye-sockets. I see her grave and introspective, or in such a paroxysm of laughter that the tears came into her eyes. But her eyes are shut, and I shall never see her again.

25
Grand Chain

I have said that I lacked a circle to re-enter, but the word 'circle' is distasteful, with its suggestion of clique or coterie, and I have an innate disinclination for hunting in a pack. Not everybody I met at Tavistock Square was new to me. I remember Virginia Woolf being surprised, when she introduced me to the beautiful Rosamond Lehmann, that I knew her already. A straight and slender neck supported a head carried with an adventurous tilt. The hair springing from the finely modelled forehead, the high colour on the salient cheekbones, and the eyes with their prevalent expression of attentive amazement seemed an embodiment of eagerness and expectancy. But sometimes the mouth lost its playful tenderness and looked sad and resigned, and the eyes were fixed in a blank, faraway look. Her brother and sisters are all physically impressive and unlike one another. Perhaps they owe their unusualness to their mixed ancestry, of which John Lehmann has spoken in *The Whispering Gallery*. I never saw their father, but their mother, even in old age, was uncommonly handsome. Of John Lehmann's light-blue eyes, sometimes disconcertingly narrowed in moments of scepticism, inquiry, or disapproval, and set in a head without fleshy padding, someone had said, 'Those eyes! Like forget-me-nots inside a skull!' His svelte sister Helen has so deep a voice that it never ceases to be a delightful surprise every time she speaks. And his sister Beatrix, whose vibrant performance in *Mourning Becomes Electra* almost made one forget the poverty of its author's language, has a face upon which the masks of tragedy and comedy succeed one another so rapidly that they become one, just as the wings of a hover-fly vibrate so quickly that they almost, but never quite, appear static.

Virginia Woolf's discovery that I already knew Rosamond
Lehmann aroused her highly characteristic professional curiosity.
She was agog to know *how, when,* and *where.* Writers of memoirs
often say nothing about the most usual process by which acquaintance is extended. It is like the movement in the Lancers which
used to be enjoyed by children of my generation at their dancing
classes and was known as 'the Grand Chain'. I first met Rosamond
Lehmann with Stephen Spender, then still an undergraduate at
Oxford. His home was in Frognal, at Hampstead, an establishment he has described in his autobiography. Directed by remote
control by a rather formidable grandmother – a troglodyte in the
comfortable gloom of a mansion flat near the Albert Hall – it was
managed by a pair of devoted but perhaps rather strict family
servants who had developed a composite personality. These two
excellent women had therefore been given a composite name and,
to an occasional visitor, had an inseparable identity. They maintained at Frognal a clinical cleanliness, and exercised a sort of
jaunty strictness over the orphaned Spenders. The eldest brother
seemed to be away a good deal; the quiet Humphrey and the
sister, Christine, with her enigmatic smile, listened in fascinated
and affectionate silence to the gay and spontaneous talk of their
brother Stephen, in which acuteness mingled with a certain
naivety, innocence with sophistication, unworldliness with
ambition, benevolence with a strain of satire. No wonder their
attention was held: here was a young poet 'bursting' (to repeat
Dr Pood's phrase) 'with vitality' and aimed at the future like a
rocket. The freshness, candour, and newness of his early poems
has re-emerged in later ones. It is one of the advantages of middle
age to have been able to watch the development of the characters
and talents of one's friends. Sometimes success and maturity fit
them out in the hard, crustacean shell of the impatient public
man, so that their early tenderness becomes little more than a
memory. Sometimes bitterness of experience, or the influence of
a wife or mistress, changes their nature or inflates their self-
importance. Sometimes they deteriorate, through loneliness, or
drink, or vagabond desires, or illness, or disappointment. But

none of these things has happened to Stephen Spender. Happy in his wife and children, he pursues his course without a sign of diminished energy or gaiety.

I had first met him in Egerton Terrace, at the flat of René Janin, who was the son of a French general and who had what may be called social curiosity. He was able to exercise this even when young with what seemed an innate knowledge of the world but was in fact an aplomb seldom to be seen in an Englishman of his age. With his good looks, his intelligence, and ability, he might understandably have been a little vain, but he seemed without illusions: any melancholy that may have resulted (as it may from such a cause) was made almost imperceptible by his rare capacity to amuse and to be amused. He seemed to have a fixed standard of traditional beliefs in political matters. Compared with, let us say, Stephen Spender, he seemed a reactionary surviving from some *ancien régime*, but that put him in the strong position of mistrusting the loud-voiced demagogues, villains, and madmen of our time who were trusted by millions and ruined Europe. He moved and still moves with equal ease and amusement in social, intellectual, diplomatic, and commercial spheres in any country where English, French, German, or Spanish are spoken, and like most of his contemporaries he has needed fortitude to bring him through to the present day.

René Janin I had first seen in the company of Laurens van der Post, who was now married and a father, and had settled in London—if settled is the word for one who had a long way to go before he found full scope for his energies. In the early Thirties he wrote a novel about South Africa, for which I had the pleasure of finding a title in the Bible. *In a Province* is a book with a place of some significance in the interesting evolution of the South African novel, but in those days it attracted less attention than many less valuable books later, when South Africa had again become more topical. Then his natural inclination to the open air and his liking for animals took him, a few years later, off to the Cotswolds, where he acquired a farm and where I used to visit him.

Sometimes I encountered persons with whom I had made

contact by post. When still very young I had sent poems to Harold Monro, who had written encouragingly to me in Africa. And now, in a mixed gathering one evening in London, 'There's Harold Monro,' said one of his contemporaries, and then called out to him in a mocking voice, 'Monro! Miaow, *miaow*!'

Monro turned, looked displeased, and said in a serious tone: 'That's a *good* poem, Z. That's a *good* poem.'

The allusion was to a poem of Monro's called 'Milk for the Cat', which in those days was widely familiar and had earned him, so he told people, a then surprising sum of money in anthology fees.

I looked at Monro with respectful curiosity, and was introduced to him. His poetry is by no means all so gently domesticated and descriptive as the poem about the cat: it used to seem to me like the voice of someone somehow encaged or immured and trying in vain to get out. As a boy at Rugby I had bought 'rhyme sheets' from the Poetry Bookshop to hang on my wall, best of all Walter de la Mare's 'Arabia' with gaudy decorations by Lovat Fraser: I soon knew it by heart. The successive volumes of *Georgian Poetry*, breaking in upon the post-Victorian twilight, had been quickening to many readers of my generation. I had lately visited the Poetry Bookshop for the first time, with its temple-like atmosphere and its polychromatic lining of 'slim volumes'; but it seemed already to belong to the past. Guerrilla warfare had broken out in the earliest printed poems of W. H. Auden.

It would be untrue to say that I was wholly engaged in dancing the Grand Chain. I was often alone. For some writers it may be enjoyable to be steeped in alcohol, it may be necessary: but not for me, who had other weaknesses. I was in any case shy, and had not yet adjusted myself to English life. For some writers, when young at least, it is habitual to go into a huddle for twenty-four hours out of every twenty-four with half-baked devotees of the arts, persons of both sexes, often with no visible means of subsistence or fixed abode (who make up the fringe, pretty frayed in places, of the serious world inhabited by serious artists), in pubs, clubs, studios, and beds. Again, not for me. I was more inclined to haunt picture galleries, old and new. I have a visual, or pictorial, imagination, and it needed training by looking at all sorts of pictures very often. In Africa I had been deprived of this exercise, in the Far East I had accustomed my eyes to Chinese paintings and the decorative arts of Japan. Much as they had helped me, they had not been enough. I had craved for the arts of Europe, and now I pursued my visual education with lusting eyes. Of all European painters the two who stirred me most at this time hardly made a pair — Millet and Poussin. In London and Paris I pursued them both. In Millet a kind of earthy goodness, wholly West-European, and in Poussin the classical myths, the rigid, immortal gestures, and the yellow draperies in an eternal-seeming golden light combined to appease some appetite in me; they took away the feeling of impoverishment, of aesthetic displacement. And for a stimulant there were the newest Picassos.

Is there such a word as re-occidentation? The process it denotes was not altogether easy for me, the process of re-adapting myself to life in England. In many ways it seemed to me an alien country, in some ways it does still, in certain beliefs, habits, pleasures. What irregular features and physiques the English had! How dirty most of them were! How peculiar they smelt in public places! Why were they often cruel to children? Why did they in any case bring them up so badly, too strictly or too neglectfully? Why were they cynomaniacs? And why, being so, did they treat their dogs with such a lack of understanding? Why had they made a cult of cricket? There was no end to my questions. Daily life was strange enough. How clumsy to eat with a great metal implement in each hand instead of with chopsticks in one! And how strange not to sleep on the floor, but nightly to be extended, Mazeppa-like, on the back of an inanimate quadruped with a tendency to squeak or creak!

Perhaps what shocked me most was the theatre. It was not that I was an addict, but I was less of one when confronted with imbecile plays of what might be called an unreal realism. The curtain went up on a room with a door at each end and always a

french window at the back, and the entrances and exits were so
obvious that one could generally foresee them. Use was made of a
telephone on a table, and there was nearly always a servant, who
was represented as comic—too dignified or too vulgar or too
uneducated. No wonder domestic service, which is an honourable
calling, became despised. It would have been intolerable to work
for these men with falsely hearty and women with falsely genteel
voices. Evidently strangers to acting, they spoke lifeless words
strung together by some uninventive hack and leavened with
cheap or puerile witticisms. One's attention was dragged through
some anaemic succession of stale contrivings and blatant in-
significance, and, if one happened to be the guest of somebody
one did not know very well, the effort of keeping the jaws
clamped against the giant yawns continually trying to escape
almost led to lockjaw.

I was not used to this sort of thing. I was used to the tension, the
visual splendour, the stylised diction and posture, and the
schooled, hereditary actors of the Kabuki. I was used to professional acting that could make an old man in the part of a young
girl more like a young girl than any young girl could possibly be.
These English offerings had not the remotest connexion of any
kind with the even more stylised, the noble and hieratic Nō plays,
where an actor standing masked and motionless in a formalised
envelope of stiff sumptuous brocade seemed on a supra-human
level, until, to a palpitation of drumbeats, he slowly, slowly
raised one waxen hand, with the fingers joined, and held it in
front of his face to signify grief, and one's whole being was
agitated and torn by the extreme pathos of the moment and the
movement, which brought out the inmost humanity of this
unrealistic figure and joined it, as if electrically, to the inmost
humanity of the audience. No wonder, I thought, that the
Japanese regarded Europeans as barbarians and went for them
(barbarously) with two-handed swords.

As for the snobbish, would-be satirical plays of the period, and
the wet, sickly, sub-romantic musical fantasies, they seemed
decadence itself. And I remember no critic then who had, for

9*

instance, the directness, sharpness, and verbal dexterity of Kenneth Tynan in dealing with them. But in the music-halls and cabarets there were to be found studied, finished, original performances perfect in their way—Nellie Wallace with her insecure aigrette and trapped in her too-tight silver lamé evening dress, or Douglas Byng with his grotesque impersonations and improprieties:

> In two yards of tulle I could break every rule
> And still keep the censor at bay,

or

> A bit hard to go wrong on a marble chaise-longue,
> But never too hard for me.

Perhaps in a moment of irritation—and not only irritation but exasperation must at times be allowed to exiles—an Englishman in Japan had said to me, 'The Japanese will never be civilised until they have a Mozart and a Middlesex Hospital.' All he really meant, I suppose, was that he himself had a longing for the best of the West, in whatever form. That same longing had brought me back to Europe, to England, to London, and how wonderful were the achievements with which, in fact, I was surrounded! Gyles Isham took me to see Gielgud in *Richard II*, and although it was too evidently a one-man show, the play seemed made for the actor, the actor for the play. With a temperament, a technique, and a sense of the sublime language he had to use, he played his part as a musician of the first class plays a first-class instrument. And when I took my mother to hear Edith Sitwell reading her own poems to a small public audience, all was well again. A rare nature with rare bones; a face and hands that might have belonged to a daughter of one of those 'Angevin dim Kings'; a manner without the least taint of affectation or pomposity. There was a dignity that seemed as if it might sharpen into asperity; an underlying compassion in the voice and in the shape of the eyelids; an easily accessible sense of the ridiculous, the impertinent, and the

commonplace. The poetry of Edith Sitwell was not new to me.
It must have been about 1920 that I had sent to England from
Johannesburg for *The Wooden Pegasus*, and when the book
arrived, in its bright magenta cover, it confirmed that she had
obeyed the summons of the ninety-eighth Psalm, a summons
which only a poet is able to obey:

> O sing unto the Lord a new song: for he hath done
> marvellous things.

Not long after this I heard her reading with her two brothers at a
full-dress evening gathering in a private house in Mayfair. This
time there seemed a slight lack of *rapport* with the audience, as if
performers and hearers did not quite trust one another. There did
not seem any reason why they should, nor was it possible to
imagine a bridging of the gulf between them. The three profiles
made a memorable ensemble. A commando troop, the Sitwells
had originated and led a resistance movement against the philistinism of their own class. The distinction of their own writings is
inseparable from their devotion to the fine arts, and it is not often
enough remembered how much they have done to help, to
appreciate, and to draw attention to the works of writers younger
than themselves. It was not until later that I came to know them
personally, but I had been the more gratified at an early stage by
Osbert Sitwell's interest in my writings because I already admired
his own. As a wit, a satirist, a writer of fiction, and an autobiographer, he has maintained an independence that can best be
called aristocratic. During the Second World War, when a good
many people suddenly took to reading Trollope, my preferred
authors were Gibbon, Balzac, Gissing, Firbank, and Osbert
Sitwell.

I have been lucky in the friends I have made through my
writings, and there was one who played a special part in my
re-adaptation to Western life. While living in Japan I had received
a fan letter from an Englishman whose name was new to me. He
wrote from Taormina. It was an effusive letter, full of adjectives.

The writer evidently did not see life – or literature – in half-tones. He kept using words like extreme, profound, deep, amazing, blinding, extraordinary, sheer, exquisite, dynamic, icy, terrible, immense, superb, vast, penetrating, hideous. I hasten to say that they were not all applied to me and my fictions. But if he lacked moderation, most people, after all, lack anything else. And he had understood what I was driving at in my earliest published writings, and had on the whole approved of the way I drove. What had most interested him was what he called my analysis of the impact of the European upon the African. He had seen, he said, something of the effect of Western materialism in Asia, and he thought it was beginning to make life unliveable even in Europe and had failed to evolve any belief by which men could live in the future. He felt that the African could only try and maintain his identity by taking over the white man's techniques, and yet that in doing so he would in fact cease to be himself. He thought Africa ought, all the same, to revert to the African. His name was Anthony Butts.

There are a good many people living who knew him, but I doubt if anybody knew him as well as I did. I wrote and told him of my return to England, and a close friendship began which lasted to his death. In many ways he was unusual. A descendant of Sir William Butts, who is a character in Shakespeare's *King Henry the Eighth*, he came of a family of Norfolk origin. His great-grand-father was Thomas Butts, the friend and patron of Blake. He himself was born in 1900, the son of an old man with a young wife. His own father had in fact been born in 1830, and his grandfather could remember having been held up as a child in the arms of a nurse who showed him the portrait of a lady and said, 'That is the poor Queen of France, whose head was cut off the day before yesterday.' So Anthony Butts, almost my coeval, was rooted in the already remote past. I suppose that being an old man's son must have affected his physique, appearance, and disposition. His premature baldness, large luminous eyes, and at times eccentric behaviour or conversation caused persons who did not like him to think him a booby or zany. I did not find him that, but his character was admittedly somewhat extravagant.

After his father's death his mother had married again. He had not liked his stepfather, Freddy Colville-Hyde, and his early experiences of family life had made him cynical. A complication was that he had an elder sister, Mary, who hated her mother and was neither liked nor trusted by Anthony himself. She wrote books. They had a tone of precious knowingness, and the fatal limitation of being too much of their period. In a sense they were vulgar: J. B. Yeats, writing of the paintings of Orpen, defined vulgarity as 'the excess of the means of the expression over the content'. I do not mean to imply that the writings of Mary Butts had anything like the technical brilliance of Orpen's paintings, but they did show excess of manner over matter. They had for a time a certain vogue. She also wrote an autobiography, about which the most memorable thing was not modesty, nor good sense, nor veracity, but the frontispiece—a reproduction of a drawing of the author by Cocteau.

As a very young man, her brother found himself rich, lively, and without responsibilities or clearly defined ambitions, or any one strong bent. He was fond of pleasure and travel, and had some knowledge of music and literature and much of painting, for which he had marked talent. He was sociable and a brilliant raconteur, and it cannot be said that in his late twenties, when I first knew him, he had done much except amuse himself. But he was not merely a playboy. He was entirely serious in his intention to develop his talent for painting, and he had an instinct for what was sound in people or creative in the arts. Underneath the sometimes wild frivolity and immoderate satire of his conversation he was haunted by a sense of the tragic future. This too may have had something to do with his having been the offspring of an old man, but I believe it had much more to do with imagination and intuition. He had an acute sense that the society which had produced him was dislocated and doomed: so had many psychologically or socially maladjusted young men and women in those days, and it made some of them look to what they believed to be communism as what they believed to be the hope of a better world. If he was maladjusted, that very fact is a criticism of his background and education; if he was early disillusioned, it was not his fault. Even before the Twenties were out he had no doubt that there would soon be another world war. It was perhaps his sense of the destructiveness, and self-destructiveness, of Western civilisation which had reinforced his admiration for other races and cultures than those of Europe and North America.

It would be false to suggest that there was anything obsessive about his negrophilism, but I think it worth some further comment. Many men and women in London and elsewhere in the West during the Twenties were attracted by coloured people. Coloured singers and dancers, jazz music and dancing from America—African in remote origin and best executed by performers of African descent—had been making a strong impact, and personal acquaintance with them was for many youngish English men and women something new and exciting. To the young and frivolous such acquaintance promised new sensations and a chance to startle the staid, or to annoy their own parents; and the cultivation of coloured acquaintances, even to the point of intimacy, became a fashion. It would be a mistake to suppose that to be young and well off in the Twenties, or the Thirties either, was necessarily to be wholly frivolous or merely fashionable. When a strong sympathy with the coloured races, amounting to partisanship, showed itself in some persons of intellect and sensibility, this was put down by those who could not understand it to unbalance or a perverse sexual attraction. But it is at least possible that this sympathy may have been something more than an attraction of opposites, of white skins to black, or of nervous and complex natures to natures supposedly simple and comparatively carefree. Did it not perhaps foreshadow the collapse of what has lately come to be called colonialism, and the emergence of that entirely fresh attitude to racial differences which necessity now demands? That such a sympathy, with arguments of some weight to justify it, should have arisen in Anthony Butts, a lively young Englishman of the propertied class, schooled at Eton, and with no boyhood experience of any country but England, seems to me to have much to do with the fact that he was a child of the century with something of the unconscious prescience that is found in visionaries.

Under his roof, or that of his mother, Mrs Colville-Hyde, I was to meet a number of interesting people, but only one Negro, in the shape of Paul Robeson. He was then at the height of his vocal powers, and his imposing physical presence and candid manner seemed to be the index of largeness of outlook and a genial humanity. He was accompanied by his lively wife, who later made a tour of Africa and wrote a book about it.

When Stephen Spender asked me to Oxford to address the English Society, Anthony Butts travelled with me and we put up at the Mitre. The next day we took Julian Green, who was with us, round to see the sights of Oxford—a town to which I was no stranger, and which I remembered well in the sinister tranquillity of summer during the first world war. When we were back in London, Julian Green wished to see the Crystal Palace, and off we drove one afternoon to look at it. The sky was of grey flannel— it was early in March—the air was raw, and the palace, though open, was deserted. It ought to have been haunted by the glad ghost of Victorian confidence, by the excitement of the wondering millions who had visited it, by the organ recitals, and soulful vocalising and junketing visitors of later years; but though still imposing, those glassy walls held only a cold, dirty, and lugubrious emptiness.

After walking a long way we found a sort of indoor watergarden at one end, in a faintly Moorish enclosure and overlooked by assorted Victorian statues, dead white, with dust in their crevices. In the water were tubs, and in the tubs were funereal aspidistras. A bored, elderly workman in waders was going over the leaves with a nailbrush. Another workman on some steps was resting one foot on the back of a large figure of Diana or somebody, from whose shoulders he was straining to remove epaulettes of accumulated filth. Suddenly his foot went through her plaster thorax into the interior of Diana. Anthony Butts burst out laughing, and so did I. But Julian Green looked gravely at this scene of English life inside one of the great monuments of English architecture. His manner was always cautious. It matched his almost prim and wholly correct appearance, which gave little indication of the sombre and smouldering imagination that had already excited interest in his writings.

I turned to go. I was already thinking of the *Criterion* party which its editor, T. S. Eliot, was giving that night, and at which I should meet far weightier contributors than myself, though I did not think I should feel for any of them quite as much respect and admiration as I felt for the author of *The Waste Land*.

26

Moderately Grand Tour

I set off with Anthony Butts early in 1930 on a European tour. We were away for the best part of a year. In Paris, to which he was no stranger, we met a number of American expatriates of the so-called 'lost generation'. Perhaps they were not representative, but those we met seemed prosperous and self-possessed. From Poussin to Picasso, I looked at a great many pictures, and in between times soon came to understand how easily Paris can attract alien as well as native allegiance.

At Bonn we had the pleasure of getting to know Ernst Robert Curtius, to whom I had an introduction. Of this learned and weighty critic, who seemed as deeply understanding of French as he was of German literature, André Gide had written three years earlier, '*Je trouve en lui, dans son regard, dans le ton de sa voix, dans ses gestes, une douceur, une aménité, une bonté comme évangéliques ...*' His and his wife's kindness and hospitality to us mingled happily with other impressions to give an insight into some lasting aspects of German life. The unruffled Rhine, the pink-flowering chestnuts, the calm walls of the Bishop's palace, the well-kept gardens and houses made an outward harmony, but conversation with university students showed uneasiness and uncertainty. If any reminder were needed that harmony is not easily won, there it was, in a collection of nightmarish shapes – the devices with which Beethoven had tried to conquer deafness.

In Berlin we were plunged into the feverish atmosphere that preceded the dominance of Hitler. It was the world upon which our friend Christopher Isherwood was already beginning to focus his camera-eye. Acute political and economic uncertainty and tension were not concealed by the flashy up-to-dateness of life in the centre of the city. Naked ambition and naked despair were both conspicuous. Two strong currents, often intermingling in a puzzling way, especially puzzling to someone unfamiliar with the German character, were earnestness and cynicism. And resentment was visibly gaining over disillusionment.

The atmosphere was certainly stimulating — much too stimulating to be healthy or lasting. The kind of cleverness which, in the Twenties, had produced that surprising periodical the *Querschnitt* was much in evidence, and the then notorious night-life was something well worth seeing. Blatant impudicity on such a scale was certainly exciting to youthful senses, but there was something desperately sad about it — and at times something grotesquely funny.

Conscientiously going the rounds of private and public entertainment, of picture gallery and *Nachtlokal*, whom should we encounter but Gide himself, apparently taking his pleasures with his usual seriousness. There is a rather obscure entry in his *Journal* at this time, about hoping to wake up and find himself somebody else, and about hoping to find a new country at the end of a long tunnel. More explicit, in the same month and place, is his saying '*Je voudrais déguster cet été fleur à fleur, comme si ce devait être pour moi le dernier.*' Substituting '*premier*' for '*dernier*', I could have said the same myself.

At Verona we saw Ezra Pound and his father. Coatless and in braces, the father was haranguing the son with an evident consciousness of knowing best which strongly resembled the manner of some of the son's more polemical writings. We had already spent a day or two in Milan, but it was at Verona that I first felt that veneration for the splendour and antiquity of Italy which northerly barbarians are expected to feel. It can be an exalted and yet physical sensation, in which consciousness of the past, sensitiveness to atmosphere, and the sight of the perfect proportions of ancient monuments are made more actual by bland sunlight, by food and wine, by the looks and manners of the people, inheritors of so tremendous a tradition of enlightenment and humanity.

It was too early in the year for Venice to be thronged, but already the water at the Lido was like warm saliva, cigar butts were floating on it here and there, and through the open windows of a large hotel came the African rhythms of a *thé dansant*. An hour in those surroundings was enough: the rest of our days and nights were given up to the splendours and surprises of the city, of which many aspects were so familiar from painted, photographed, and written images that one had the feeling of returning there, not of being there for the first time. The great monuments of Western civilisation, like those of any other, are part of the consciousness of those who have been born into it.

And so to Athens. If I had a son or daughter just grown up, and if either had a suitably responsive or impressionable nature, it would be my wish that he or she should spend a year in Italy and a year in Greece, with as much freedom as possible. I would like my child not only to pay attention to works of art and to mix with educated people, but to get to know some uneducated people or peasants. My hope would be that emotions would be awakened while knowledge was being extended, and that the influence of climate and culture would be heightened by feelings of tenderness as well as of excitement. I should hope that in Italy it might be possible to learn what Dante meant by the expression *anima cortese*, and to appreciate the tactile sense of this nation of artists and craftsmen. And I should look to the dry, white light of Attica to burn away any lingering shreds in my child's mind of puritanical or suburban British fog. It is easy, of course, to be sentimental about Latin or Mediterranean countries: a writer in *The Times Literary Supplement* lately made some sharp comments on the canting ecstasies of travel writers about Greece; even the Parthenon, he said, had become a 'howling cliché'. But there are other things in Athens besides the Parthenon. Some contact with good society in a small capital might be instructive as well as pleasant. Being more compact than in London, Paris, or New York, such a society can be more easily understood; and the conventionality, passions, intrigues, illusions, eccentricities, and scepticism observable in Athenian society could no doubt still arouse, as they aroused in us, liking and admiration as well as amusement.

While in Greece we sought no contacts with anybody but Greeks. There was therefore a language problem. Educated Greeks spoke English or French, but we did not spend all our time with educated Greeks, who were sometimes shocked by our glib use of some low colloquialism we had picked up in unrespectable surroundings. Unless one is a linguist it is necessary in one's travels to employ interpreters or struggle with phrasebooks. I have always remembered a sentence that occurred in an elementary manual of conversation which I used in Japan: 'Is this purple pencil convenient?' Not really a thing one would often want to say. And there is a wonderful sentence in a nineteenth-century phrase-book for English travellers in Portugal, or Portuguese travellers in England: 'Bring me a wand and some hooks, I wish to angle.' As I had 'done' Greek for a year or two at school, and as Anthony Butts had been in Greece before, we managed fairly well in a simple way, but when we were together and in need of some particular colloquial phrase, our little book used to fall open at the sentence 'She is always well dressed.' When we wanted to inquire about a journey to Mistra, we found 'Are their nieces tired?' And trying to work out a complaint to a laundry we came upon 'If you had heard Mrs B you would almost have fainted with delight.'

One afternoon we heard a phrase in English which I have never seen in any manual of conversation, though it might have its uses. We sat down at a café table in the Syntagma, the central square of the city, just as a convoy of cars drove up and off-loaded a swarm of dusty and sweating tourists from the Middle West. *Study Tours in Bible Lands* said a label on each windscreen, and the inquiring pilgrims, footsore, thirsty, and querulous, came swarming into the café. To see the waiter (who knew us) taking our order and making them wait their turn was too much for a formidable matron among them, and in raucous accents which seemed addressed to Providence itself she cried, '*Can't* they wait till their betters are served?'

I should hope that my offspring would have enough imagination to try and see how life might look to American tourists as well as to Greeks, and that a sustained effort would remove whatever vestiges might remain of insular complacency or arrogance—but not that it would weaken the proper pride that may be taken in being English. I should not wish him to think that his forefathers had all wasted their time. And I would wish the young creature to feel something approaching the acute pleasure I myself felt in Greece in my twenties. Alas for the fantasies of parents! Their children are not made in their own image.

Acute pleasure can hardly be described. A little before midday on a morning in early summer I was swimming a good way out in the bay of Phaleron with an inhabitant of Athens of my own age with whose physical beauty I had become infatuated. In the warm sun and the light breeze a small boat with a sail came gliding and prancing past. In it was an old fisherman. When he saw us he asked if we would like to climb in for a sail with him. We said yes, climbed in, and settled down, and while he guided the lightly dancing boat over the sparkling wavelets and glanced back at us now and then with the fatherly playfulness of an old triton, we happily embraced one another with naked arms that the sun had quickly dried, and kissed the saltiness from one another's smiling lips. This, I thought, is happiness—to be young, to be healthy, to be free, to love and be loved in the sun, in the radiant light, flying along over the water in the flawless visibility of early summer in the Aegean.

> What hour shall Fate in all the future find,
> Or what delights, ever to equal these:
> Only to taste the warmth, the light, the wind,
> Only to be alive, and feel that life is sweet?

Neither in sentiment nor in diction are those lines of Binyon's of a kind at all fashionable nowadays, and fault can rightly be found with them; but they do at least hint at the intensity of those moments when one is not 'warming both hands before the fire of life' but conscious of being a flame in the fire itself. I felt a kind of amazement that life could rise to such a pitch, that circumstances could combine to produce and sustain for more than a moment such perfection.

After a time our lives in Athens took on a certain regularity. Anthony Butts was painting seriously; I had begun to write a book. Both in our working time and our leisure time we led independent existences, though living under the same roof. In the mornings I usually put on black spectacles and sat writing out of doors, on a seat in a secluded corner of the Zappeion Gardens. We generally lunched together. During the siesta I was not always alone. In a high white room, shuttered against the heat of an Athenian afternoon in July and against a fine view of the 'howling cliché', the flame that had sprung up in the Bay of Phaleron was often rekindled, while no sound was heard except the plaintive voice of a hawker below in the burning street chanting, in that sad, haunting, but tempting tone of street cries in many parts of the world, the cool, sweet names of melons, grapes, and fresh figs:

Πεπόνια! Σταφύλια! Σῦκα φρέσκα!

Late in the afternoon, or sometimes in the morning, we went off to Glyphada or Vouliagmeni to swim and then to come out and sit in the sun and drink retsina under the pine trees. The colour and salinity of the sea, the piny fragrance of the shadows and the piny tang of the wine, the clearness of the wine and of the white-wine-coloured sea-water, the salty warmth of the skin and of the blood, the warmth of the sun and of the sand all seemed inter-fused, as if the elements of earth, air, fire, and water were one element, in which life was immortal. As often in those parts, a sensuous experience of a certain complexity seemed also a spiritual or at least a suprasensory experience.

Late one afternoon we came back to Athens in a country bus, in which we noticed a peasant pair — the woman for her Madonna-like placidity and regularity of feature, the man for his fierce, bristly, brigand-like aspect. The man took no notice of his wife. In one hand he held a white carnation and on his lap a white rabbit. From time to time, alternately and unselfconsciously, he would smell the carnation and kiss the rabbit, to which he murmured endearments. The mixture of fierceness and gentleness seemed essentially Greek, and more manly than the assumed 'toughness' so common (in every sense of the word) among the English and the Americans.

In the evening, when the Zappeion Gardens, where I had been almost alone in the morning, became exceedingly animated, I was busy seeing, at various levels and as opportunity offered, what can only be called life. To dine late out of doors, outside a restaurant or at some hospitable villa at Psychiko, or in some simple resort by the sea; to see something of night-life of the obscurer sort in the Piraeus; to sit late in an alcove of oleanders in the warm semi-darkness and buy sprays of strong-smelling white jasmine from an old woman with a basket; to be alone with that one other person very late, when there was velvet silence and a moon, and soft dust among the rocks, and a consciousness of very old surfaces of marble, and of layers of lost secrets stratified in the air of Attica for two or three thousand years, was to be as if under the unimaginably agreeable influence of a drug.

Lotus-eating, if that is what I was doing, did not keep me from working. I wrote with concentration, as a rule for several hours a day. I had come to a point where, in my myth-making, I was impelled to try and resolve some of the conflicts and harmonise some of the contrasts of my dispersed earlier years. What happens when a child does not grow up in a settled surrounding, in a fixed home, in the bosom of its own family, and constantly surrounded by other families of the same race, class, tradition, and habits as its own? When it finds itself controlled, cherished, or ignored by various kinds of grown-ups of differing social backgrounds, beliefs, and habits? When it has been involved in a series of disjointed contacts with different worlds, like scenes from different plays made to succeed one another but not composing a single play? It is likely to have been over-stimulated and unsettled. It will have learnt in some ways too much, too soon, and too superficially. Precocious and independent in some ways, it will be backward and unsure of itself in others, because it has missed the steadying, ripening effect of a fixed environment, a single tradition, and a homogeneous society. It may resemble a plant too often transplanted, putting out what flowers it can while it can. From such a child I was still evolving, and in the fiction I was trying to compose I was being too ambitious, straining such talent as I possessed, and aiming at something beyond my scope. I had miscalculated—but did not yet know it.

I thought my work was going well, I felt happy in my environment, and it was possible to see something more of it than Athens itself. '*Vous aurez beaucoup de figues,*' said an Athenian lady who, like a number of our acquaintances, seemed a Firbankian character. She had a villa on the island of Spetsai and had suggested we should take it for a time: the figs were a symbol of plenty, to go with the envisaged peace. We voyaged there, by way of Hydra, but Athens drew us back.

Greece was for the time being a republic. I forget why, if I ever knew. It is a weakness of the Greeks to get excited about their politics, but they failed to excite me. Voluble explanations about Venizelos or the Bulgarians, delivered with equal energy and variety of gesture at two o'clock in the morning as at two o'clock in the afternoon, seemed to me as much a national failing as English conversations about runs, wickets, and batsmen. I said I was a monarchist and complained because Athens was not more Byzantine, but that only led to protests and fuller, much fuller, explanations. Part of the Royal Palace was open to the public. It lacked magnificence, but the monarchy had not been affluent. Such things as a faded enlargement in a bamboo Oxford frame of a snapshot of Queen Alexandra gave one little more than a feeling of intruding upon the always precarious privacy of royal persons. Nor did I much like it when a charwoman in the Royal Chapel, anxious to explain things to us and no doubt hoping for a tip, picked up the nuptial crown used at weddings and held it over her own head to demonstrate its use. She was only being playful, but the gesture was too much like the playfulness of a *tricoteuse*.

I do not know if there was any truth in the following story. It was said that when King George and Queen Elizabeth of the Hellenes were still on the throne they had been visited at the Palace of Tatoi, outside Athens, by an American lady. The visitor was so much pestered by flies and other insects that she asked her host and hostess if she might send them some insecticides, squirts, powders, mosquito nets, and so on, from America, so that they could get rid of the nuisance. They said they would be pleased. But when she got back to America the lady found there would be various difficulties about sending off the things, so she wrote and suggested that they should be bought in Europe, and enclosed a cheque for $5000. This offering was received at a moment when the Royal funds were low—twenty-four hours, in fact, before the revolution—and it enabled the royal pair to get away. Flit-money, so to speak.

If one is conscious of intense happiness, one is a fool to trust it. Anthony Butts and I received different and unexpected kinds of bad news from England. We could do no good by returning there at once, but in the autumn we began to move westwards. We spent some weeks in Corfu, where we were conscious of a more recent past than in Athens. There were many charming vestiges of the English occupation of the Ionian Islands in the nineteenth century, and we were taken to see the Achilleion by a man formerly attached to the Empress Elizabeth of Austria, whose refuge it had been—so far as there was any refuge from such a destiny as hers.

Anthony Butts painted two or three landscapes of solitary places with ruins or very old buildings, the weather was sultry and still, and huge accumulations of thunderclouds hung in the afternoons over the mountains of Epirus and Albania. One morning we returned to the town in an open carriage by an unfamiliar road which passed for a time between two cactus hedges. Then there was an open space and not far from the road a whitewashed cabin by itself. The door was partly concealed by a rustic pergola entirely covered with a profusion of convolvulus in flower, in many different colours. A girl in a red skirt appeared in the doorway, and a young man in a white shirt standing under the pergola looked over his shoulder at us as we went by. It happened that my friend had a very strong liking, almost a mania, for convolvulus, and he at once said he must paint the scene, which was strikingly beautiful. We arranged to come back the next morning, but when we did come back there was no trace of the house, or the flowers, or the two people—simply an open space. It was not only disappointing but disconcerting. The hallucination—if such it was—had been shared by the driver, who was as disquieted as ourselves to find nothing, and I do not know how it can be explained.

Swimming too far out to sea as usual—from habit, not bravado —I narrowly missed bisection by a steamer. I have said that I was not addicted to drink, but I was addicted to water, a craving for which seems to be transmittable from father to son: after all, President Kruger had compared my father to a fish. I was a leisurely and far less accomplished swimmer than my father, and spent far more of my time in the water than he did. I understand now that swimming, and the basking that follows it where climate permits, is a drug—one might almost say a dangerous drug. That agreeable but essentially purposeless movement in another element, away from the world, as it were; that abandonment to muscular rhythm, to the seeming use of all the muscles; and that lulling sensation of well-being that follows, with the nerves comforted and the mental processes subdued, are all part of what moralists might call an escape. Water being a feminine element, probably to swim in it means that one is trying to return to the womb. I make no excuses; even if my addiction to swimming showed a weak or retarded character, I enjoyed every moment of it.

I had been reading a good deal about the Greek War of Independence, and in Corfu I saw a painting of the Suliot women about to throw themselves and their offspring over a precipice rather than fall into the clutches of the tyrant Ali Pasha. It was only an anecdotal painting of no great merit, but the image so haunted me that a few years later I wrote his life. After it was published I was reading a story by Balzac and found that he had written these words: '*Allez, Ali, pacha de Jannina, est un homme incompris, il lui faudrait un historien.*' As I had no pretensions to being an historian, it was perhaps forward of me to attempt such a book, but it has been tolerantly and even kindly spoken of by professional historians. As they sometimes seem to be members of a narrow and exclusive sect, favourable notice of an outsider or amateur seems quite a trophy. The theme seemed to me to have a certain topicality: the book is in fact an account of a dictator's misuse of power, and it attempts to show how a cruel monster can exert charm and can seem both execrable and likeable – to some.[1]

One afternoon in Corfu, Anthony Butts and I were having a drink in the house of a Corfiote lady. Somehow or other he had launched into a scandalous satirical tirade against Mussolini. It was extremely funny. Before it was done the lady, who seemed 'not amused', leaned sideways in rather a strained attitude and raised one finger to point over her shoulder. Immediately behind her was a large signed photograph of that distasteful individual, floridly inscribed by him to herself. It was an abrupt reminder that we were in the Thirties now.

[1] *Ali the Lion* (1936) was reprinted in 1970 as *The Diamond of Jannina.*

27

The Good Sir Hugh

At intervals in my life I have been drawn towards South Wales and the Border Country, to the landscape and some of the people there. As a boy I had spent an idyllic summer with my friend Bob Synge at Cwmbach, the home of his family in Radnorshire. And now I felt drawn in that direction again: I wanted to be alone in the country and get on with my work. I spent a winter at Lingen in Herefordshire, staying at the inn, where I was made comfortable by a friendly family. I was able to write in peace, and to explore on foot the region round Knighton and Presteigne. In those days there was hardly any traffic on the less important roads, and walking made it possible to enjoy country details and casual encounters. In a country place characters emerged 'in the round' and in variety. If I had been less occupied, I might have wished that I had been born and bred in such a place, where everybody knew or knew about one another, and felt their roots entwined.

When my book was finished I went to live in Pimlico, where nobody had roots. While there I discovered that the book did not form a proper unity: it remained episodic. Some parts were the result of a truly creative process; everything between them, everything that was supposed to hold them together, seemed mere contrivance. The discovery did not make me dejected. I was relieved to be able to see (with the help of a total stranger from America) how and where I had failed. There was no sense of wasted time or effort. I knew there were good things in the book, and saw that some of them, rewritten, could stand by themselves. I rewrote them, and they stood by themselves, and appeared in print as short stories, or as what are so oddly called 'long short stories'. These were thought well of by persons whose opinions I most cared for.

There must always be a gap between the imaginative writer and the reader. The writer, if he is any good, is working out a new interpretation of life; the reader holds a variety of accepted ideas. Collaboration between them is not always easy: it may take a long time to be possible. A taste for the work of any original artist is an acquired taste. Goethe speaks somewhere of how one often takes no pleasure in a work of art at first sight, because it is too strange. But by trying to perceive its merits one may discover new faculties in oneself. He says that an artist can show no greater respect for his public than by never bringing it what it expects, but what he himself thinks right and proper in that stage of his own and others' culture in which he finds himself. But what was my public, and where exactly did I stand in relation to it? When a writer feels he does not belong wholly to the environment to which he chiefly belongs—in my case, England—as he would if he had never left it when young, uncertainties must arise in his mind. Early experiences elsewhere will have made him still more unlike his potential public than he would have been in any case. His own view of life will certainly differ more from that accepted unquestioningly for the most part by most of that public: his very subject-matter, by its remoteness, may be not only strange but with little or no appeal to them. Among the things that had aroused me most and found expression in my earlier writings had been racial conflicts in South Africa and the duality, or divided nature, of the Japanese. However lacking in weight or ripeness those writings had been, they had contained clear foreseeings of such things as the intensifying of the racial crisis in South Africa, and the intensifying of racial fanaticism and militarism in Japan. How could I expect English readers then to know or care about these things, though they were to me of great urgency? And how could I now understand the stage of my own and others' culture, or estimate the width of the gap between them?

Chance brought me into contact with a popular novelist for

whom no such gap appeared to exist, and it was interesting to learn something of the workings of such a writer. At Tavistock Square one evening I was surprised to be introduced to Hugh Walpole. I wondered what he was doing there. I had read one or two of his early books but had felt little or no curiosity about their author. I now saw before me a pink, portly, restless man who seemed to be enjoying himself but on the defensive—which was not surprising, because Virginia Woolf was teasing him. He made himself agreeable to me, and when we were leaving invited me to lunch. I accepted the invitation. I did not then know two things that are plainly shown in my old friend Rupert Hart-Davis's admirable life of him: that he was an untiring encourager of any indications of talent in writers younger than himself, and that his life was not just a quest for a perfect friend but for any number of perfect friends. To be a perfect friend to anybody would be difficult, and much as I came to like Hugh Walpole and to have reason to be grateful to him, I never felt myself destined to intimate or confidential acquaintance with him. Nor did I feel easy in his company: it was no good being oneself, because the romantic novelist in him saw one as somebody very different, whom one was neither able nor willing to impersonate.

When in London, Hugh Walpole occupied a first floor above Piccadilly. The entrance was just round the corner in Half Moon Street; and from his high french windows there was a view down an avenue in the Green Park towards the Victoria Memorial. So central a situation seemed fitting for him. His flat seemed like the setting for a character in one of his novels; he himself was more like a character in a novel by somebody else. A keen acquirer, he at once showed me some of the latest things he had bought—a rare and ancient book, a modern bronze figure, a jade carving, a Sickert, a Renoir. I was the only guest, and the interest he expressed in my writing was obviously more real than that of a politely affable host. When he said, 'What are you writing now?' I told him that I had just scrapped a long novel I had been working on for some time. His reply is recorded in Rupert Hart-Davis's biography; I repeat it here.

'Marvellous, marvellous! What courage! *I've* never had the courage to destroy anything!' Then, after a pause, 'Do you know, you make me feel just like a little girl taken to see the elephants for the first time.'

I did not know him well enough to be sure whether he was being ironical or not. I had not thought it an act of courage to do away with the novel, but hoped it was a sign of improving judgement. Because Hugh Walpole himself wrote with facility he was apt to be fascinated by the hesitations of writers less fluent and less sanguine than himself. I, for my part, was astonished to see a popular writer at close quarters. In a book of reminiscences called *The Apple Trees* he has told how he deliberately put into his first novel 'everything that would, I hoped, help it. Cornish scenery of a very coloured kind, a noble long-suffering hero, a beautiful heroine, a female sinner who repented, a theme apposite to the day.' I think he went on writing as easily as he had begun because he knew precisely, by instinct, what the large and not acutely critical public he wrote for would like. People were sometimes irritated by his ebullience and air of assurance, but he was more understanding of his own weaknesses than he appeared. His pen would race ahead, he hardly ever paused to make a correction, he never destroyed what he had written, but, he told me, the buoyant optimism he felt about whatever book he was writing, *while* he was writing it, was liable to collapse as soon as he had finished it, and to give way to doubts. If those doubts had been stronger, or had set in sooner, he would have written fewer books, and his books might have had smaller circulations and more serious appraisal than they have had. If I, on the other hand, had had fewer doubts and a tenth of Hugh Walpole's fluency, I should have written more and oftener and been better off and better known than I am. Not that I have anything to complain about in the responses my writings have met with.

'There's one thing I *have* got,' he would say defensively, as if one was about to attack him. 'I *have* got the narrative gift, I *can* tell a story.'

He was quite right. His gift for inventive narrative was quite out of the ordinary. A Balzac without copiousness would not have been Balzac; but here was copiousness without Balzac, and this was Walpole. His understanding was acute enough to enable him to see that his gifts as a novelist were incomplete, and behind his air of assurance was a most uneasy awareness of the fact, and an uncommon vulnerability.

His little joke about the elephants was not without point: if he had called me a rogue elephant, it might have had even more, because he was speaking to someone rather deficient in the herd instinct. A nomadic early life may make a man inured to a certain independence, yet adaptable enough to attach himself now to this herd, now to that, as opportunity offers or occasion or inclination demand. If a novelist, he is likely to be of an eccentric, marginal, or occasional kind. To produce a large or solid body of work, even today, it still seems necessary for a novelist to have and enjoy an essentially uninterrupted relation to one background and the environment of his earliest years – like Hugh Walpole. Otherwise one can only expect his novels to be few and spasmodic, the product of some special stimulus or phase of development.

These indications of the difference between Hugh Walpole and myself are confirmed in a report on a manuscript of mine which I saw some years later. It was written by Edward Garnett. After a statement which modesty prevents my repeating, he wrote:

> Plomer is emphatically of the minority, i.e. of the section of writers, the real intelligentsia, the unconventional, critical-minded, literary artists whom the British Public in general don't *like*, and therefore only buy in restricted quantities. He is a Left-winger in popularity, i.e. what D. H. Lawrence was to Hugh Walpole.

If this was true, then all the more credit to Hugh Walpole for doing all that he did to help and encourage creatures of the same species as myself. But patronage and encouragement of writers and artists do not necessarily make those who exert them liked or respected, especially if they are envied for their position, their success, or their fortune. Their hands are liable to become deeply indented with scars caused by bites from those they have fed. In the case of Hugh Walpole, his enthusiasm (with which, as he once wrote, he 'always had trouble'), his excitability over manifestations of creativeness, his longing to be liked and to attach people and things to himself did *seem* to make him un-discriminating. It would be truer, as well as kinder, to say that he was eclectic. If his abode at 90 Piccadilly had a somewhat museum-like aspect, the various things in it had been chosen because he liked them as examples of their kind. It was well known that he was a keen amasser of pictures, books, other works or objects of art, and bibelots, and his enemies said that he was gullible and that his gullibility was taken advantage of by sharp dealers and anti-quaries in Bond Street and elsewhere. But when his collection of pictures was shown after his death these same traducers were surprised to see that he had either been well advised, or had shown a flair, or both, because he had often bought remarkably good and sometimes surprising examples of the work of some great painters and some interesting or neglected ones. Similarly, though his range of acquaintance was extremely wide, I have never known or known of anybody he liked who was without some distinction of character. Some persons who were fond of him were of the utmost distinction: to have won in early life, and not to have lost, the affection of Henry James was no common thing.

Hugh Walpole had tendencies observable in other best-selling writers. However successful, popular, and prosperous, and however confident of undiminished ability to continue so, such writers incline, even more than other writers with more obvious cause, to be touchy and uneasy. They seldom seem as contented with their success as might be expected. Not only their talents, ambition, and hard work have made them successful, but their pandering to the accepted ideas, romantic sentimentality, stupid prejudices, and complacent woollen-headedness of mediocrity in the mass, their willingness to put into their work 'everything that
10

would help it', or some 'theme apposite to the day'. It seems un-reasonable, therefore, that they should feel injured because they have failed to receive the praise of those not necessarily choicer but 'choosier' spirits who by their nature must always be in a minority. Yet they do. Their vanity is wounded—and an author's vanity, as Chekhov wrote, is 'vindictive, implacable, incapable of forgiveness'. (About Chekhov, be it remembered, there was nothing wistful or dreamy: as Shestov wrote, he had a 'pitiless talent'.) In those ostensibly 'normal', breezy, man-to-man types a form of persecution mania is apt to germinate. They imagine themselves to be the victims of conspiracies either of silence or of denigration among persons or (often imaginary) coteries who are simply not interested in them. They are then in danger of adopting a scornful attitude against highbrows or aesthetes or eggheads (or whatever the current term of abuse happens to be for those who seem to qualify for it), complain that they are stuck-up, or precious, or out of touch with 'ordinary' people (meaning their own public) or with the events 'apposite to the day'. But when some favourable notice is taken of them by these despised beings they are apt to go abruptly into reverse.

When secretly tormented by a knowledge or a suspicion of their own limitations—like a stone in the shoe, or an ant in the pants—it is surely because they do not accept that it is their own limita-tions that have made them what they are. They want to have their cake and eat other people's too. Even Hugh Walpole was not without this appetite. Only a mean spirit could have grudged him his pleasure in making a great deal of money and spending it in ways he enjoyed or upon objects he coveted. But he did seem a little inconsistent when, for instance, at one moment he would express a laughable anxiety lest the current sales of his latest book might be surpassed by the latest book of Brett Young, a then successful writer of popular fiction; and at the next moment show acute anxiety to please somebody more concerned with matters of taste than those of circulation.

The fact that Hugh Walpole had a kind of veneration for Virginia Woolf and was constantly anxious to write something she might approve of was in itself evidence that he was not entirely complacent about his own writings. There was something winning about his anxiety to please. She teased him, and since we do not bother to tease people unless we like them, she obviously felt a kind of affection for him. I think she was fascinated by his energy, by the way he lived and worked, and by the candour with which he could, to a sympathetic listener, talk about his own experience or people he had known, revelling as he did so in a freedom, a plain speaking, he could never allow himself in addressing his public.

If tape-recordings had been as easy then as they are now, I would have tried to persuade him to record some of the stories he had to tell. They were sometimes scandalous, but none the duller for that; and he told them with a lively humour and a kind of worldly scepticism that are not, I think, conspicuous in his books. I remember particularly an extraordinary account of a visit paid to Conrad by Robert Hichens, accompanied by an intimate friend who was male, large in body, a cook by vocation, and Russian by nationality. The radar-like sensitivity of Conrad to the intrusion into his domestic sphere of a Russian became even more agitated by what seemed to him the social solecism of causing it and by his instantaneous suspicion of what seemed to him an equivocal relationship; and the combustion set up in the great man by the duties of a host, the prejudices of a Pole, and the antipathy of a heterosexual almost caused him to explode. Mrs Conrad, a faithful pourer of oil upon waters more often troubled than not, found on this occasion that all her years of practice were of very little help. It is sad to think what golden harvests of scandal are lost because the reapers do not, for various reasons, record them. And it is pleasant to think that Hugh Walpole was once kissed in public by Conrad, who recorded in writing his feeling that thanks were due to a 'Higher Power' for the friendship of which that was a token. The man who won that tribute is not to be written off as a nonentity or an ass.

A few doors away from 90 Piccadilly was the Ritz, where a man had been pointed out to me as a regular frequenter with an unusual habit. He was what used sometimes to be called a well-groomed man, and of middle age. His thinning white hair was parted in the middle of a symmetrical scalp. There was nothing plethoric about his complexion, which was of a neutral tint. A rather full moustache, in an Omdurman or Majuba style but well cared-for, seemed to emphasise the suavity of a face upon which neither a single thought nor a single emotion appeared ever to have pencilled its signature. His head was supported by a starched collar of a height then no longer customary: it might have come from his shirtmaker in 1910. And his shirtmaker, like his tailor and his shoemaker, was probably not far away: he was perfectly dressed, in a style that would have been unobtrusive twenty years earlier, but was by this time dated. His grooming was less interesting than, so to speak, his oats: the story was that he came to lunch alone at the Ritz every day, and having eaten his way through the meal, stopped short of coffee, and ate his way through the same succession of courses a second time. This was a solemn thought. Whether he was actuated by appetite or gluttony, the thought of, say, a meringue with an extra dollop of whipped cream being followed by turtle soup, and of another similarly enriched meringue rising into view beyond the second rounds of lobster and jugged hare, was gruesome enough to make one's palate creep.

A few hundred yards eastwards, in Denman Street, there was an inconspicuous basement I had discovered and often visited. In it was a small Greek restaurant where one could be sure of eating well at a proper cost. That is something important for a self-employed young man on his own in London. I remember Dr Pood telling me that in his day he had relied on the cheapness and goodness of one meal a day at a small Chinese restaurant near this very place: it was there perhaps that he had formed his less commendable taste for Brummagem chinoiserie.

Honest Mr Stelios did the cooking himself and would take one into his savorous little kitchen to show what he had in preparation and to guide one's choice. I introduced two or three of my closest friends there, under a strict promise that they would tell nobody else: the place would soon have lost its character if invaded by knowing male and female twitterers from the westwards. That so good, so homely, and so secret an eating place should be almost within arm's length of Piccadilly Circus, and as good as invisible, gave meals there almost the sweet taste of stolen fruit. I remember how pleasing it was one day to notice, hanging from three adjacent hooks on the coat rack that served as a cloakroom, an overcoat, a side of lamb, and a guitar. This Levantine islet was a whole continent away from Pimlico, where many of the floating population seemed to sustain themselves with clammy oddments out of paper bags and greasy improvisations over a gas ring.

'I do hope you've got nice rooms,' said one of my aunts with affectionate considerateness. She was sitting in her Cotswold garden under a bower of buddleias: on each fat flower two or three velvety peacock butterflies, drugged with the warm odour of honey and the honeyed warmth of the sun, seemed like mounted specimens. There seemed no reason why they should ever move, or why the flowers should ever fade, or my aunt ever grow older or less lively.

'Very, thank you,' I said. It would have seemed somehow priggish to explain that my 'rooms' amounted to only one, and that it was no hardship to me to be occupying it. My room might very well have been a model for one of Sickert's Camden Town interiors. Its large brass bedstead would have served equally well for cheerful nights or hopeless dawns, and no doubt the shining metal globes with which it was ornamented had reflected in their time a variety of domestic tragedies and comedies, like tiny scenes cut from a lost film, scenes that had been more amply reflected in the large and mottled Victorian mirror with the carved frame over the fireplace. To this succession of little dramas I had visitors who contributed. Of special interest to me just then was the table, covered with a mohair cloth in spinach green, upon which I was writing a novel based upon the misfortunes of Mrs Fernandez, *The Case is Altered*.

If I had been obliged by illness or some other cause to spend all my time in this phrontistery, or if I had felt it to be more than a temporary expedient, I might have felt gloomy, but I doubt it. In fact I found it intensely interesting. To live in such an environment was quite new to me, and what I observed of the life of the quarter began to excite my curiosity about some of the many Londons unknown to me. I had already seen enough to understand that there were many survivals not only in architecture and furniture, but in the ways of life of some of the inhabitants, from Victorian and even from Dickensian London. I have never understood the term 'ordinary people', and I could see then that there was quite as much eccentricity at lower economic and social levels as in Mayfair or Bloomsbury or Bayswater. And what of the vast unexplored tracts of London extending in all directions? I longed to know more about the lives that went on in them and was to be found sampling the life of Islington or the Elephant and Castle.

Poverty is easily supportable when it is not a whole-time occupation and one is young and active. If I was going out to dinner and wanted a bath beforehand, I had to go to the public baths, because there was no bathroom in the house where I was living and I did not care to sponge either at or on my friends. My only regret was that public baths in England were not sociable as in Japan, but solitary.

Moving on various social levels, I was learning and enjoying much, and becoming more acclimatised again to London and to English life, but my interests and connexions were too diverse to be harmonised. A constructive life implies a tying together of loose ends, but mine were so many and various that the knots themselves tended to be peculiar.

A little later on, when Peter Davies asked me to contribute to his pioneer series of short biographies a life of Cecil Rhodes, I readily agreed. I felt that I had the right to attempt to define Rhodes's character and career in terms which would have been impossible at an earlier date and which, though not likely to be popular, would be in keeping with my conviction that Africa in the future was likely to prove something more than the sterling area of his fancies. It already seemed urgent that the West should pay more attention to deserving goodwill than to annexing territory. I said in the introduction to the book that I did not intend either to try and prove Rhodes a scoundrel or 'to affect a gross impartiality'. The book pleased and annoyed exactly the persons, or kinds of persons, I expected it to please or annoy. On completing it, I had decided to dedicate it to Hugh Walpole. This was a chance to pay him a compliment in public, and, as he was a collector of such things, I presented him with the manuscript. But what an odd conjunction of names! Although Rhodes was a hero to many of Walpole's public, I think the novelist himself can have had little or no interest in the subject, and the book itself could only, in those now far-off days, have been regarded as almost subversive or at least outrageous by the more jingoistic old memsahibs in the circulating libraries of Truro or Tunbridge Wells. Can there have been in the dedicator, besides a genuine wish to pay a compliment, just a suggestion of mischievousness?

28

The Shield of Achilles

A change in the fortunes both of Anthony Butts and myself
decided us to set up and share the expenses of a joint establishment
in London where he could paint and I could write, and where we
could entertain our friends — who were not always friends of both
of us. We found a house we liked, one of those old white houses
in Canning Place, off Palace Gate. It was in good condition, quiet,
and not cut off from the sun; it had room for us both to pursue
coexistence without clashing; and the garden had been occupied
once and for all by a single species of wild flower. Beneath the
sour London soil its roots proliferated like an inexhaustible supply
of half-cooked spaghetti, and in the summer the leaves swarmed
up and mantled everything, putting out a vast number of large
flowers: it was a white convolvulus. And far from attempting to
extirpate it, we gave it every encouragement, as if to make up for
the Corfiote mirage.

I have twice mentioned Walter Sickert. He told me that
Anthony Butts was the best talker he had heard since Degas. They
had known one another for some time, and used to have tremendous jokes together. For a time my friend became Sickert's pupil,
though I think without much benefit to his painting. His natural
inclination was towards a smooth and thickish impasto, a Courbet-
like sumptuousness, and the squared-up canvases he prepared in
the Sickert manner and began to cover patchily with thin paint
came to nothing. His inclination was to something more monumental than the translated photographs of Victorian variations,
however brilliant, of the later Sickert.

I seem to remember that one of the Georgian poets wrote some painfully winsome verses expressing gratification at having heard a cuckoo while looking at a rainbow. His pleasure cannot have been so rare as ours at the synchronised presence one evening in our little drawing-room of Walter Sickert and Lady Ottoline Morrell. I should hesitate to say which was the cuckoo and which the rainbow, and it may have been by contrivance and not by chance that they came together under our roof. It was an evening worth more than all the collected and combined poems of Geoffrey Smallbeer and Roland Milk.

Our two guests got on like a house on fire. After a time they began swapping recollections of the music halls, and became so enkindled that they rose to their feet and performed from memory a music-hall turn, with a *pas de deux* and a duet. Neither was young, so their animation was the more glorious. Sickert, wearing a Harris tweed frock-coat with trousers to match, and doeskin spats, held out his arms to Lady Ottoline and performed what was almost a series of high kicks. She, strikingly dressed as usual, with a flying scarf of flame-coloured chiffon, jingling ornaments, and hoop-like earrings, held out her long arms to him and repeatedly raised and extended a stork-like leg until it was almost parallel with the ground. And together they sang, or rather declaimed, with tremendous gusto and emphasis:

I *throw* my affection
In *your* direction,
You're just my size and style!

'Le fond du caractère anglais,' according to Taine, 'c'est l'absence de bonheur.' I wonder.

Another of our visitors at Canning Place was Christopher Isherwood. He was a letter-writer of exceptional brilliance, and when he moved on from Berlin, original observations made in Copenhagen, in Lisbon, or later from China (literally, as they say) to Peru, arrived in a very small, regular, and evidently imperturbable handwriting. If, as he pretended, he was a sort of camera eye, then the eye of no camera can ever have had a more diamond-like twinkle in it. And when he appeared in person, his conversation continued in exactly the same tone as his letters. 'Amazing' was one of his favourite words, and his capacity to be amazed by the behaviour of the human species, so recklessly displayed everywhere, made him a most entertaining talker. I have an impression that the young, or youngish, English intellectuals in those days were, when high-spirited, somehow freer in their high spirits than the conscientious and understandably troubled ones of today, who seem much concerned with what was called in Victorian times mutual improvement. Christopher Isherwood, compactly built, with his commanding nose, Hitlerian lock of straight fair hair falling over one bright eye, and the other looking equally bright under a bristly eyebrow already inclined to beetle, an expression of amusement in a photo-finish with an expression of amazement as he came to the conclusion of a story, and almost choking with delight at the climax, also made Taine look silly – or would have done so, if one had been thinking of him.

And then there was Nancy Cunard. Arriving slender and trim on a piercing day, she peeled off, as she came into the room, onion-like layers of elegance – a close-fitting jerkin of soft suède, then inner skins that seemed wisps of silk or wafers of wool, until she was slenderness's own self, showing a cat-like appreciation of the fire, and turning her steady and uncompromising gaze upon ourselves. Her eyes, like those of some cats, were lucent among their dark lashes, a pale and precious enamel in which had been fused a suggestion of gold dust – a sentient enamel. And when she moved to put a cigarette or cup or glass to her lips, attention was inevitably attracted to her thin, fine-boned arms, both encased in such a concatenation of wide, weightly armlets of rigid African ivory that the least movement produced a clacking sound, as of billiard balls or the casual cake-walk of a skeleton.

Already, with her courage and independence, she made no bones (as we seem to be on that subject), whether in the United States or in Europe, about her complete indifference to the colour-bar and her partisanship on behalf of those who were suffering most by it—like the victims of the Scottsboro trial. Anthony Butts had known her for some time and they seemed fond of one another. She had come this time with a particular purpose—to talk about a projected book. Among some old press-cuttings of the early Thirties I notice this, from a literary weekly:

> Nancy Cunard arrived this week in London from France with the manuscript of her forthcoming anthology *Negro*, which contains 475,000 words and 400 photographs of contemporary Negro personalities. Among her 150 collaborators are Norman Douglas, Augustus John, George Antheil, William Plomer, and Professor Westermarck.

It was an honour to be classed as one of her collaborators, though my own contribution to this impressively conceived and edited book was not a weighty one.

I saw much at this time of Lilian Bowes Lyon, who was a near neighbour, living then in Courtfield Gardens. Her grip on life was intense but always seemed somehow precarious; as it became more precarious it grew more intense, but it was not the grip of rapacity. She had a passionate concern for right relationships between human beings, and it extended far beyond the boundaries of nationality, class, or convention. She had, with it, the instincts and the courage of an artist, and in later life a long fight to the death with prolonged and exceptional physical pain.

She could find no abiding place in this world. In later years I used to go and see her in a succession of temporary homes—in Gloucestershire, in Hertfordshire, in Surrey, at Holmbury St Mary, later at Ham Common, and finally in Brompton Square. My first and last impressions of her (and I believe I was the last person to see her alive) were of her gentleness of manner and intensity of feeling. Her gaze—now withdrawn, now direct and glowing—was without subterfuge. The bones of her face, delicate but strong, suggested her firmness of purpose and the fineness with which she exerted it. She spoke with strong emphasis, but always in a very low and pleasing voice. Her firmness was to be needed: though pity and consideration for others were with her always, it was in her own being that fortitude was demanded of her.

Lady Ottoline Morrell, when I introduced them, remarked to her that they were connexions. Though very different natures, they had more than a link of blood in common. The younger woman was, in her way, no less unconforming and independent. She had torn herself from her home in Northumberland and a segregated family life (of a nineteenth-century type) to launch out on her own, to live in London as she thought fit, and to write. She produced a novel, which rattled some of her older and less flexible relations, not because it was libellous or indecent or politically tendentious but because it did not conform to their conventions either that she should write, or that she should write fiction, or that, if she did, she should write fiction suggesting that life was not a wholly comfortable proceeding. Her first novel was not her last: perhaps to spare those objectors from renewed vibrations, she put out another under a pseudonym. Jejune writers about 'the novel' have not understood clearly enough how often in the inter-war years a novel was the form in which it was most convenient for young men and women to express and record their consciousness of finding themselves in a world of changing values. It gave them a chance to challenge or flout or protest against what seemed to them stale or sterile, and to advance their own ideas of emancipation, progress, rightmindedness, or leftwingedness. So far as the vast output of first novels in that period is concerned, it is probably true to say that while very few are of enduring literary value a good many are of some sociological interest. It was, however, in the writing of poetry that Lilian Bowes Lyon was best able to try and communicate some of the stirrings of her spirit and the complexities or simplicities of her view of life.

I have always been interested in heredity. On her mother's side Lilian Bowes Lyon was related to Lady Anne Barnard, who wrote *Letters from the Cape*, a masterpiece of the early colonial period of

South African literature. And the history of the Earls of Strathmore is anything but dull, and includes that of *The Unhappy Countess* and her demon lover, so effectively told by Mr Ralph Arnold in his book of that name. Augustus Hare, in his fascinating autobiography *The Story of My Life*, makes much of his connexion with the family. Excessively, even painfully, class-conscious and cousin-conscious, even by Victorian standards, he had the virtue of curiosity and collected many anecdotes that would otherwise have been lost. He gives a pleasing description of his occasional visits to Ridley Hall on the South Tyne, which was later the home of Lilian Bowes Lyon. I asked her whether she thought his account of the supernatural mysteries at Glamis Castle was to be taken seriously. She told me that very soon after her parents were married her father took his bride to Glamis for the first time. They went there in daylight; he was driving, I think, a dog-cart; and she was seated beside him. As they were approaching the castle he was startled to hear her utter a sound of distress. Instantly turning to ask her what was the matter, he pulled up. She had covered her eyes with her hand.

'Oh!' she said, hardly able to speak. 'That poor, poor woman!'

'What woman?'

'There, just there beside the drive! She was running! You must have seen her!'

'I saw nobody,' he said gently. 'There was no woman there. You must have imagined it. What was she like?'

Lady Anne Bowes Lyon could hardly speak, but she said:

'She had such an *agonised* expression on her face. She was running, and holding out both arms in front of her, but—oh!— her hands had been cut off, and the stumps were bleeding!'

'Ah,' said her husband, as if now he understood. 'I didn't see her, but I know about her. I know she has been seen.'

There are other stories or legends of troubled spirits associated with the house, but none so painfully memorable. Atrocities in Scotland in the Middle Ages cannot have been worse than those in England, but were no doubt just as bad. Nightmarish visions of desolated or outraged humanity may still appear, lifelike in the dark caves of history; and history is not merely a matter of records, or of records interpreted; those caves are part of the endless underground system of unconscious memory.

I do not wish to suggest that Lilian Bowes Lyon was fey, or preoccupied with the supernatural. She was not remote from this earth, nor from other people, nor from what was going on in countries not her own. A kind of criminal negligence is sometimes attributed by a younger generation to those who were flourishing in the Thirties. That is not surprising: children always think they know better than their parents, and their own children too will be wise after the event and will formulate against them charges of folly, stupidity, mismanagement, and irresponsibility. I should hesitate to say that those who are generally classified as intellectuals would govern better than politicians. They would probably be too reasonable. But if some of my friends were classified as intellectuals, they were none the worse for that. It seems to me that they saw further, sooner, and more clearly than most people, even than most of those whose business it was to look ahead. Before the Twenties were out, Anthony Butts regarded another world war in the near future as a matter of course, and our visit to Germany confirmed him in an opinion that really needed no confirmation. In the early Thirties I would sooner have had a report on Germany from Christopher Isherwood than from Sir Nevile Henderson: fresh from his observation post there, he told me he thought a war between Germany and Poland inevitable. But who would ever have taken any notice of him then, if he had said so in public? Leonard Woolf explained to me that the international situation was a repetition of what it had been some years before 1914, and foretold almost exactly the date of the beginning of the second world war. But to take such serious views then was to risk being called a crank, a bore, an alarmist, or a defeatist. Stephen Spender, now in Hamburg, now in Vienna, and later in Spain, had gone so far as to adhere to what seemed to him then the only effective opposition to the forces of reaction and oppression. If it was a mistake, it was an honourable mistake.

I did not myself then regard it as an obligation to be involved in politics, to advocate policies, to join parties, and to protest against injustices in every part of the world. For one thing, I was not politically minded. For another, because I had been living when younger in Africa and Japan during the most emotional and impressionable time of my life, their problems were still nearer to me than the confusions and ferocities of Europe. Furthermore, I was chiefly interested in the pursuit of literature and in personal relationships. Also, I was not yet thirty, and my education and even my re-Westernisation were far from complete.

I suppose it is a flat truism to say that the greatest force in education is example. There was one visitor to Canning Place whose example and personality aroused an admiration and affection which were immediate and lasting. This was E. M. Forster. Although he had a perching-place in Brunswick Square and seemed to be on good terms with that group of friends and acquaintances whose similarities of social origin, outlook, interest, and habit, to say nothing of early influences at Cambridge, had caused them to be spoken of as 'Bloomsbury', he never seemed to me to be quite one of them. I saw him, and see him, as an independent.

During the years that followed I saw him often and got to know him better than any other writer of his generation. His liveliness, charm, insight, understanding, and unlikeness to anybody else made his friendship the rarest of treasures. In appearance he was the reverse of a dandy. Incurious fellow-passengers in a train, seeing him in a cheap cloth cap and a scruffy waterproof, and carrying the sort of little bag that might have been carried in 1890 by the man who came to wind the clocks, might have thought him a dim provincial of settled habits and taken no more notice of him. When I said as much in an essay written during the second world war for the French review *Fontaine*, published in Algiers, I sent him a copy for his approval or disapproval before it went to the printer. He showed it, or read it, to his mother, who said, 'There! You see what Mr Plomer says. How often have I told you, Morgan dear, that you really ought to brush your coat?'

Crouched in a corner of that imaginary railway compartment, he would have worn a kind of protective colouring, like an oak-egger or a stick insect—or, rather, like a retired booking-office clerk from a station on a branch line. It can never have been said of him, as it was said of another literary man of my acquaintance, 'Nobody could possibly be as distinguished as X looks.' But one might have said that only an uncommonly distinguished man would have taken so little trouble to look like one. The moment he was engaged in conversation with anybody in the least congenial, or potentially congenial, he lighted up. First the vivacity of his mind became apparent, his openness to new impressions; then some comment, softly yet sharply striking exactly the right note, would seem to be striking the very note that nobody else would have touched upon at that moment; then gradually it might become guessable how his variety of experience and interests had combined with his originality of mind to form his powers of judgement. His is essentially a critical mind.

One did not think of him in terms of age. Recalling him in absence, one thought of certain quick darting movements and bird-like inclinations of the head; of the intense blue of his eye in certain lights, as if it had changed colour; of the sweetness of his smile; of the little puffs and spasms of laughter that rushed out beneath his untidy moustache; and of his real and not officious politeness, his winning considerateness to the shyest and least self-important persons in mixed gatherings. He often varied his surroundings and his company, but no man could be more tenacious of associations once cherished.

Years later, in a book about him, Lionel Trilling was to write that in a world at war E. M. Forster reminded us of a world of true order: 'he is one of those who raise the shield of Achilles, which is the moral intelligence of art, against the panic and emptiness which make their onset when the will is tired from its own excess.' Rose Macaulay, that staunch independent with an impassioned concern for the abolition of cant and for the proper use of words, listed, in her book about Forster, some of the things he believed in and disbelieved in. He believed, she said, in personal relationships, in individuality, in beauty, in affection, in liberty, and in democracy; he disbelieved in nationalism, empire, militarism, catchwords, Christianity, oligarchy, dictatorship, big business, schoolmasters, 'and a number of other things'. And Forster himself, in a pamphlet called *What I Believe*, provided his own explanations. It is a good thing that he did, because it must be said that words like 'beauty', 'liberty', and 'democracy' are elastic: they have been so abused by stretching that what they ought to describe may wrongly be assumed to have perished. The stretching process is not new. I have no note of the source of the following quotation, but it dates from 1799:

> Facts teach us, that *liberté* signifies the most horrible tyranny, silencing all law, and violating all property; that *égalité* signifies murdering sovereigns and the higher classes, and putting over the people men the most low, ignorant, and wicked, invested with power to insult, enslave, and drive them in flocks to be slaughtered, and placing them at a greater distance than there existed before between them and their superiors by birth and education. *Fraternité*, in France, signifies being a Frenchman; applied to other nations, it signifies forcing on them a government, plundering their property, and taking their wives and daughters. *Philanthropie* is professing a general love of all mankind, and practising cruelty to every individual. *Philosophie* signifies the commission of every crime without remorse; the extinction of every sentiment religious or moral, of every generous and social feeling; the dissolution of every tie of kindred and affection; the annihilation of every quality which ornaments and distinguishes the gentleman, the scholar, and the man of taste; the banishment of chastity, modesty, sensibility, and decorum from the female sex.

Who, giving a moment's thought to what has been done in our own time in the name of 'democracy', could possibly support it or give it two cheers? E. M. Forster could. He found it less hateful than other contemporary forms of government; he credited it with the assumption that the individual is important, and that it takes all sorts to make a civilisation; he found that it allows criticism, and some degree of liberty to the creative. But order, for him (it later appeared), was 'something evolved from within, not something imposed from without'. For him, yes, because he is an artist; but unfortunately what is called democracy tends more and more, like any other form of government, to impose what it calls order upon as many of the people as possible, as rigidly as possible, from without. It is a mark of E. M. Forster's energy and honesty that, instead of assuming an air of superiority and roosting more or less contentedly in the snug debris of liberalism, he has constantly tried to adjust himself to the phases of the revolution through which he has lived, without deserting what he has believed to be true, and without relaxing that 'moral intelligence', without lowering that 'shield of Achilles'.

It is a commonplace that the artist, especially since the Romantic movement, has tended to be a solitary, an independent, an anarchist, or even a misanthrope. But the notion has become more and more accepted that it is now not only the artist's duty but his function to commit himself to public affairs. In the Canning Place days I should have been even less interested than I am now in theorising on such a topic: but I do know that one of my main reasons for admiring E. M. Forster was that moral intelligence of the artist with which he had observed, felt, imagined, and embodied the relations between races in India. From the nature of my earliest life, I had been driven to observe inter-racial contacts and social incompatibilities, and, as I said in the preface to *Four Countries*, most of my own fiction reflects the age 'by isolating some crisis caused by a change of environment or by the sudden and sometimes startling confrontation of members of different races and classes'. It was, therefore, natural that I took special pleasure in being with him. Many of my closest friends have been unconformables, and of all my unconformable friends he has had, I think, the clearest, subtlest, deepest mind, the most generous understanding, and the most fruitfully revolutionary influence.

29

The Summer Robe

Anthony Butts's path and mine diverged, but our friendship lasted until his death, which occurred in 1941. After we gave up the house in Canning Place I removed to the two top floors of a house in that region near The Boltons which is not quite of Kensington, turns its back to Earl's Court, holds aloof from Chelsea, and a hundred years ago was called New Brompton. The road was quiet and had a neutral atmosphere that I found congenial.

When I went to the post office I used sometimes to encounter a lady of the upper middle class with whom I had a nodding acquaintance. She was evidently advanced in her views, because she hung about offering copies of the *Daily Worker* for sale. A little earlier, she would have been a suffragette; a little later, an existentialist. To advertise what she was selling, she had a news-bill fastened near her navel with a safety-pin. The first time I saw her there, she was about to proffer a copy of the paper when the news-bill came adrift and slid to the ground. 'I'm afraid you've lost your poster,' I said, much as one might say, 'Excuse my saying so, but your slip is showing.' And I picked it up for her. By some fatality, certainly not by design, this doctrinaire apron collapsed twice more at the very moment when I happened to be the person nearest to her. The third time, while she thanked me almost effusively and showed what light novelists used to call 'a pretty confusion', I had to pin the thing to her jumper because neither of her hands was free. And talking of hands, I think it may have been on that very day that the news-bill carried the slogan *Hands off China*! I believe these brief encounters were the nearest I ever came to communism, which some English writers of my generation appeared to regard as hopefully as a new star in the east.

It is part of the intention of this book to sketch or suggest its author's relationship to a few of the persons he has admired and places he has known—to a few, not to all. If, in doing so, he has so far happened to give any impression of detachment, of equanimity, or even of urbanity, let these things be attributed to a retrospective mood, not to a pose. If he has said little or nothing about being lonely, or needy, or downcast, or anxious, that is not because he was a stranger to any of those conditions. He knows what it is to be ill, to be in pain, to be disappointed, to be mis-understood, to be cheated, to be insulted, to be frustrated: we live in a world where such things occur. But he has no inclina-tion to compile a hard-luck story; and if he does not dwell upon actions of his own that were foolish and others of which he is ashamed, that is because his way of writing memoirs is not to turn them into a public confessional or a parade of vain regrets.

To look back is all very well, to select, to weigh, and to measure, but there was plenty of folly in my life in the Thirties. There were things I wanted to find out, and I found them out. If I were to survive into old age and retain my faculties, and feel inclined to contemplate 'the ash of all I burned' when young (the phrase is Wilfred Owen's), I should hope not to moisten it with useless tears but to recall happily the fires of which it is the residue. I wore what Jeremy Taylor called 'the light and phantastic summer robe of lust'. Much time and energy were used up by me in the pursuit of chimeras—and exceedingly magnetic some of them were. Obsessively, and sometimes recklessly, I pursued illusions—and sometimes caught them: sometimes it was bitter to lose them, and sometimes it was a relief. I asked more of life than it could reasonably have been expected to give; but I was not guided by reason. In a letter I wrote to my parents at this time I find:

By the way, Joe says he has never seen anyone so up and down as I am—so choppiness is evidently hereditary. He says he doesn't know how I can write, because I'm 'always in an emotional storm'.

Joe was J. R. Ackerley. He was then living in a cottage of character wedged in between the Mall and the river at Hammersmith. I had first seen him at Savoy Hill in the summer of 1929, in connexion with some broadcast. There was a heat-wave, and he looked so cool and self-possessed in his white silk shirt that I was a little frightened of him. Elegant to the point of dandyism, and fine-featured, he had (like Herbert Read) the gentleness of manner that sometimes goes with strong convictions, independence, and pugnacity. The mixture of directness and vagueness in his manner made me nervous of being a bore.

By the time I was living in New Brompton I had begun to know him better. His book *Hindoo Holiday* was and is generally admired. To me it had a special appeal. Together with *A Passage to India* it seemed truthful in a new way, and a new approach to Asians on the part of an Englishman. I was magnetised by its freedom from preconceived notions, its unwincing directness, and its surgeonlike delicacy. It was delicate, but it probed. Again, like the work of E. M. Forster, it suggested a character in some ways formidable. Then there was his play *The Prisoners of War*, an early idiosyncratic work in the huge literature of imprisonment which this age of persecution and punishment has produced. How fortunate I was that so humane a heart should put up with my vacillations of mood, and that such an unsullied eye and understanding should perceive and not condemn my pursuit of chimeras! His patience gave me shelter in my then unceasing 'emotional storm'.

Chekhov says that love is 'either the shrinking remnant of something which once was enormous; or else it is a part of something which will grow in the future into something enormous. But in the present it does not satisfy. It gives much less than one expects.' It is because love is never wholly satisfying that a man without weighty ambitions or responsibilities can so easily make a cult of sex, the more because of those moments when love seems to attain perfection, as if disclosing what it once was or some day may be. Such moments may be but are not necessarily those of coition, or of physical contact or mere proximity, and they seem closely related to those other moments of religious or artistic experience when an extraordinary equipoise or harmony is reached and sometimes sustained, when it seems as if the world were properly, or ideally, organised after all; or as if the sky itself had suddenly opened, and the ear had caught hitherto un-imagined harmonies. A line of poetry can open the sky, or a flourish of Handel's, a serenade with fiddles and flutes in the dead of night on a Greek island, a solitary prayer, or, if one is attuned to it, anything in nature, any work of art. All the world is open to the senses, and more than the world to that extra sense that transcends them.

To intervals of solitude I was accustomed but not always reconciled. If you never find yourself alone, said Gide, you will never find yourself at all. But as soon as you *have* found yourself, he might have added, it is time to hurry back to others. If you overhear solitaries talking to themselves, you seldom find them saying anything worth hearing. There is often a tone of complaint in their utterances. They rely too much upon themselves in their judgement of others, and because the world seems to have abandoned them, their judgement of the world is unfavourable.

In the late Thirties, on fine afternoons, there was a lady who used to sit on a particular seat on the front at Brighton, facing the sea and the strolling promenaders. Even when other persons were sitting beside her, she was conspicuously alone. In her late fifties or early sixties, she was respectably (as they say) but not fashion-ably dressed, and rigidly corseted in the Edwardian style. On her head she always wore the same hat, a toque trimmed in front with a pair of rampant white wings. Pointing skyward, north-west and north-east, they were faintly yellowed with age and exposure, and not very securely fastened; they wobbled slightly.

'Men!' I was startled to hear her exclaim gruffly the first time I saw her. I was passing by, but slowed down, leant on the railing within earshot, and looked intently out to sea for the ship I was not expecting. '*Men!*' she cried. 'I hate them all!' A pause. Then, with withering contempt: '*Husband!* He *called* himself a husband! The dirty, lowdown, sneaking, deceitful *rotter!*' Then a mumbling, then crescendo: 'Men! *So-called* men! *Rotters,* that's what they are! *Rotters!*'

I moved on. I often saw and heard her again. One day I heard her say, with an ineffable disgust that might have given hints to Mrs Siddons, 'Sold my furniture!' Other people constantly saw and heard her too. In the tolerant way of the English they would nudge one another, give her a glance, and stroll uneasily on, as if ignoring an almost indecent exposure. Children, or coarse oldish women, would sometimes stare and giggle; men, feeling stigmatised, would slink past or, indifferent, stride past.

On and on went the tirade, and she nodded her head vigorously. She was like an actress putting herself wholly into her part. But it seemed a part in a morality play. Perhaps she represented Death itself. The wings in her hat looked steely in certain lights, they were blade-like, a pair of abhorred shears. Would they suddenly, softly, irrevocably close? Or would a more than usually energetic nod one day unhinge them, making the blades fall uselessly apart? If that happened, she would cease to protest; she would collapse like a puppet; she would at last surrender; with the falling apart of those exalted emblems of her will and personality, both would disintegrate; arthritis, suddenly tightening its screws, would keep her indoors for the rest of her time, and never again would she be able to harangue the gusty breezes bustling up the Channel from the Atlantic, the expressionless southern sky, or the promenaders pretending that she could be neither seen nor heard.

Then one day, just as I was going past, she accidentally dropped her tall, thin umbrella. I picked it up and as I handed it to her I smiled. She beamed as if electrified.

'Oh, thank you! Thank you so much! How very kind of you!'

Gracious, radiant, benevolent! The poor soul was suffering from something quite different from the pleasure of solitude, she was suffering from the disease of loneliness. Can it have been that all she wanted was a male in her life, any male not a 'rotter', a male who, instead of making away with her furniture, would occasionally bring her a cup of early morning tea, tell her she needed a new hat (and how she needed it!), notice it when she had bought it, and take her out to the pictures, or to church, or to inhale the sea air? But the likelihood of such a male presenting himself seemed fanciful.

Solitude is not the same thing as loneliness. No man could have seemed more sociable, less solitary, than Laurence Oliphant, that strange Victorian full of the energy and enterprise so characteristic of his time: but he was isolated, madly isolated. His biographer, Mr Philip Henderson, records his having written:

> The world, with its bloody wars, its political intrigues, its social evils, its religious cant, its financial frauds, and its glaring anomalies, assumed in my eyes more and more the aspect of a gigantic lunatic asylum.[1]

There is an Oliphant in all of us, and a century later any of us could say the same: but how dangerous to say it! To feel wise alone is to feel oneself superior to the rest of mankind: one thinks the world mad when one is mad oneself. And that is the time when people are tempted to rely upon and submit to the discipline of some system claiming absolute authority, like Roman Catholicism or Marxism. To crave for absolute authority is a form of infantilism, and no system, whatever its claims, possesses or can maintain absolute authority. Yet if one is left to one's resources they will sooner or later be found inadequate.

It is the fate of more people, it appears, in the twentieth century than in previous times to move about, to live in exile, and to share the material advantages of some community with which they have little in common and little or no sense of community – particularly in urban or suburban surroundings. Persons with no strong religious or political adhesions, without assessable property, or children, or even a settled family life, and either self-employed, casually employed, or unemployed, may find themselves living in

[1] *The Life of Laurence Oliphant,* by Philip Henderson (Hale, 1956).

a state of fatalistic suspense that cannot be called good. Such was the condition of many people in England between the wars, and such, in the Thirties, was mine. Perhaps if I had understood it more clearly, I could have snapped out of it; perhaps not.

'There can clearly be now no question of our meeting in Munich', I find in a letter to my parents written in 1933, about a plan for one of our meetings abroad. We were already confronted with what David Gascoyne has called those 'years like a prison-wall', and perhaps no English poet has commemorated more exactly that poisoned atmosphere of the ineluctable:

> ... night by night the same
> Weary anabasis
> Between two wars, towards
> The Future's huge abyss.

Some people valiantly tried to prevent what could not be prevented, some to cure what was incurable. The majority, as usual, were blindly indifferent; without knowing it, they were afflicted with moral drought, with a partial eclipse of the will. Without understanding it, I was in the grip of the same affliction. Now that I think I understand it, I do not see how I could have been in any other condition. At the risk of boring the reader, I must say a little about the more personal reasons for my having succumbed to it. Who knows? A chance word may help somebody somewhere to avoid something of the same sort.

Looking back from a distance, I see that the first world war, at the beginning of which I was still a child, produced a deep trauma in me. What! Have I the face to say that, of a war in which millions were killed? I have. Is it not indecent to draw attention to private woes in a time of general calamity? It may be, but I have had to live with the consequences of both. I had been brought up in atmospheres where it was generally accepted without question that one belonged to a race that enjoyed, as if by Divine right, a moral and material superiority which gave it the leadership of the world. Under the *Pax Britannica* the world would go radiantly forward under the guidance and dominance of Englishmen imbued in church from an early age with a sense of fair play and the team spirit, and, from reading Kipling, with a sense of their own high destiny. Pervading everything was an ideal, seldom explicit, of gentlemanliness, which included such things as not boasting, not hurting other people's feelings, never letting others feel inferior, being kind to the weak, the poor, and the old, and regarding cruelty and falsehood as the greatest of evils.

In a disposition naturally critical it was natural that scepticism should put out early shoots. One does not have to be very old to see that not everybody practises what he preaches. At a very early age I could not help having difficulty in taking cricket seriously. What was all the fuss about? Like other games it needed practice and skill, but it seemed slow, and an elaborate way of wasting time in fine weather, when one might be doing much more enjoyable things, or doing nothing in particular. The tedium of spoken or written discussion of cricket scores or the form of its players seems to me as colossal as the fond freemasonry of the game's addicts seems incomprehensible: some of my best friends are batty about cricket, but we never meet at Lord's or crouch together to attend to what the wireless calls 'a ball by ball commentary'.

I suppose it was the smug assumption that cricket-playing was a sign of racial superiority that helped to put me against it. The same grown-ups who treated cricket almost as a religious exercise, and religion as if it were a form of cricket, spoke of Kipling's works or read them aloud as if they were the Gospel itself. Christopher Isherwood has told how they were read aloud on Sunday afternoons at his preparatory school, almost as if part of the curriculum, and how the things Kipling approved of seemed to him aspects of an Enemy he knew he would have to fight for the rest of his life. I understand this perfectly, but it does not wholly blind me, any more than it has blinded him, to the great gifts of the man who could write a line like

I have paid my price to live with myself on the terms that I
willed.

I could not know that Henry James, in a letter written several
years before I was born, had said of Kipling, 'Almost nothing
civilised save steam and patriotism—and the latter only in verse,
where I *hate* it so, mixed up with God and goodness ...' Defini-
tions of God and goodness had not been kept from me, but I
could not reconcile them with jingoism or with war, though my
grandfather was a professional soldier and so were two of his
sons, the third being an amateur. At a very early age I was shown
a portrait of an uncle. 'That is poor Uncle Durham,' said my
mother, 'who was killed in the war.' I said 'Why?' and am still
waiting for an answer: he was killed in the Boer War.

No child of my generation of even minimal intelligence or
sensibility could have remained untroubled by what went on in
France from 1914 onwards. What had it to do with peace, or
loving one's neighbour, or with forgiveness of one's enemies?
Were torpedoes, tanks, and poison gas linked in some way with
fair play and not hurting other people's feelings? 'Thou shalt do
no murder,' said the commandment. But what was being done in
France? Was not Cain killing Abel over and over again? For
those of my generation in whom these questions had laid their
eggs, the temperature of the Twenties could only promote a
hatching. I could remember all the wishful cant about Tommy
Atkins, and the Russian steam-roller, and the war to end war, and
making the world safe for democracy. How could we look
forward with hope, with another and probably far more destructive world war in prospect? Whom and what were we to trust
in? Military judgement, political wisdom, the ill-defined 'man in
the street?' How could war promote peace?

At this point it seems right to summon up poor Uncle Durham.
He was poor only in the sense that it was thought a pity he had
been killed in the prime of life. The son of a kindly and fairly rich
father, of decent birth and conventional upbringing, at ease in any
society he might find himself in, established in the military

profession, a healthy extrovert, good-looking, good-humoured, athletic, fond of women and attractive to them, he was a fortunate son of a civilisation apparently at its climax.

'What's all this rot,' I seem to hear him say, 'about disillusion-ment, and cricket, and Kipling? You're alive, aren't you, and free? If other men hadn't given up their freedom and allowed themselves to be deprived of their lives, you mightn't be either alive or free. Kipling? Not much time for reading, myself. Or inclination. But they say he's good ... I played cricket for Cheltenham, and enjoyed it.' (At this point he gives particulars of an innings in some match.) 'When my regiment was sent to South Africa, I naturally went with it. I happened to stop a Boer bullet, and that's all. Bad luck, perhaps, but I didn't have a bad life; I enjoyed almost every moment of it.'

'If I may say so,' I reply, 'you were shoved into the Army because your father thought it the best place for you. You were a good soldier, you did your duty, you were killed in action, you were missed, and for a time you were grieved for. An inscribed stone was put up over your corpse ... But there is another side to all this. You did what you were told, because your profession demanded obedience. But whom were you obeying? You probably had no doubts of the wisdom of those who had made British troops invade so distant a country. But their wisdom and their morality were questioned by many of your own con-temporaries, who thought that war unnecessary, unwise, and unprincipled.'

'Ugh!' he replies. 'Pro-Boers!'

'What good do you suppose that war did? Do you think it made England loved? Do you know the Boers call it the Second War of Independence? Did you think you were helping to make South Africa a permanent colony? Today, in all but name, it's a Boer republic ... In *your* time you were so confident. This is *my* century, and we're not so cocky and light-hearted as you were. Our doubts are precious to us. Without them all that is still left of what you imagined you fought for will be destroyed, and man-kind itself may come to an end.'

'But you've got to believe in *something*,' he says gently. He wrinkles his forehead. He is puzzled and yet not hostile: he sees that I seem to mean what I say. 'If you give in to doubt, surely you won't want to do anything at all.'

It would be difficult to explain to him that at an age when he was bursting with energy and hope at Sandhurst, I had been isolated in the altogether remote and alien atmosphere of Tokyo, and much influenced by the outlook of my Japanese friends and coevals there. Smiling sadly, I shake his cold hand, and let him fade back into the hero's grave at Nooitgedacht ...

The importance of maintaining my own being did not seem to me, I dare say, any greater than it had to poor Uncle Durham, or the importance of maintaining European civilisation any less. But I believed that if it was to be done with weapons, the weapons most immediately appropriate were doubt and disgust. If these machetes, I felt, were in more general and strenuous use, ways out of the encroaching jungle might be steadily hacked: but time was short, and the more nearly a State became totalitarian, the stricter the taboo upon their use, and the rarer the skill and courage to use them.

I was not without beliefs. I believed in art and literature and the devotion of those who produce them—though what I meant by art and literature was far from the cheap or precious meanings with which those words are sometimes invested. I loved individuals. I saw this belief and this love, which together had led me to live as I was living, conjoined as one creative function, outside which I had no ambition. I do not say my way of living was virtuous, or the best possible for my purpose, but the increasing tension and despair of the world's prospects did not leave the spirit free or the judgement calm. To be deficient in hope is unchristian. I was deficient in hope, and a lapsed Christian.

30
Not Alone in London

From New Brompton I had removed to a quiet ground-floor flat in Maida Vale. On one side was a house with a plaque to commemorate Sir John Tenniel. On the other gleamed the leafy Regent's Canal, where a grimmer fantasy than his seemed to be at work one morning when a casual angler mistook for a 'bite' the waterlogged body of an unwanted infant.

To judge from the reactions of certain ageing types to any mention of Maida Vale, the quarter was thought louche. It had the reputation of having abounded in the nesting places of kept women, generally of a lower status than those who had been set up earlier in the pretty villas of St John's Wood. By my time economic and social changes had made it more conspicuously a quarter of unkept women—unkept, but not unkempt. Even before lighting-up time, prinked-up figures swathed in silver-fox capes and hoisted on high-heeled shoes were to be seen stationed all along the pavements, at regular intervals like lamp-posts. So clearly demarcated were their spheres of influence that one could hardly help knowing one's own strumpet. The occupational hazards of scandal and crime were such that the local newsagent, if asked for the national Sunday newspaper most given to reporting such things, used to say sardonically, 'You mean the *Maida Vale Gazette*.' All the same, the quarter was largely what used to be called respectable. There were houses not yet divided into flats, inherited and still occupied by retired lawyers or old rentier spinsters, sub-Forsytes stuck fast, it appeared, in a habit of life as dull, fusty, and outmoded as what could be seen of their heavy furniture or as the blackish laurels in their gardens. The gaslight

and gloom, the silent back streets with noisy, baroque public
houses at each end, and the heaviness of the architecture all helped
to maintain the late-Victorian atmosphere, which for me had
strangeness and a kind of glamour.

There was one place in London where it was possible to indulge
less vaguely my taste (which was not fashionable but personal) for
the energy, oddity, and variety of England in the nineteenth
century. That was the Caledonian Market. In the pale light of
some Friday morning in autumn that great open space and its
adjacent buildings, with its groups and strolling couples and
absence of motor traffic, had the very tints and ambience of a
scene in a Victorian lithograph, and there, spread out at one's
feet, were long, long avenues of treasures and treasurable trash.
It is perhaps as well that I lacked the cravings, the means, the
leisure, and the storage space of a collector, otherwise I could
easily have accumulated a whole museum. Down those avenues I
loitered, looking perhaps like the last of the *flâneurs*, but animated
in fact by an almost suffocating and quite unrational excitement:
it was the appetite—one of the appetites—of a poet. And this
appetite was fed, but never appeased, by the pleasure of seeing
and touching sauce-boats and sovereign-purses, fans and cigar-
cases; a Gothic chair, or an old, well-made chest of smoothly
sliding drawers; a banner-like firescreen, worked in turquoise and
white beads with a flying angel; a cross set with agates, or a pair of
coral earrings carved in the shape of a hand holding a Grecian
urn; a discarded group-photograph of a family, showing a virgin
in a bustle, a little aloof from the rest under an ivied rustic arch,
her eyes big with frozen hope; or a stereoscopic view of Leaming-
ton in the eighteen-seventies with a stationary cab immobilised
and almost, but not quite, immortalised by the camera. To enjoy
a sense of the essence of the vanished age from which I had
derived and in the last phase of which I had come to consciousness
—I suppose this might be written off as escapism or a psychologically culpable reversion to something or other. I do not see it like
that. I was too much amused by the ingenuities of craftsmanship
and the aberrations of taste, and too touched all the time by a

peculiar sense of the transitoriness of life. I have always been a keen escapist from the banal and the fashionable, and enjoy ignoring the dogmatic assertions of half-baked doctrinaires and being left free to follow up clues to social history. And, by the way, not everything at the Market was Victorian; it was just the place to pick up cheaply a handsome pair of curtains, a set of bookshelves, or other useful furniture.

Under my nose—and indeed above it, on the upper floors—and all around were change, decay, and new life. In a house not far away lived a then well-known film star, who was to be seen stalking about now and then with a long upper lip, a walking stick, and a self-consciously proprietorial air. The fact that he was chosen to impersonate legendary nineteenth-century characters, the Duke of Wellington probably, Disraeli certainly, and I dare say Gladstone as well, was in itself a measure of the gulf that already separated us from their time. It was the fictionist rather than the poet in me who took a keen interest in the social revolution going on all round me, and I regarded with the utmost curiosity the types and individuals of everyday life in this and other parts of London.

Not all the living that went on in Maida Vale was loose, probably only a very small proportion of it. There were plenty of inconspicuous and thrifty couples, and single persons, of office-going or shop-owning habit; and there were marginal or un-accountable figures, seedy or showy, about whose invisible means of subsistence it was tempting to speculate and instructive to learn. The landlady of that house over there let out her rooms to hopeful students of drama and ballet. Clearly a dog addict, she could be seen towing a wan Bedlington to the greengrocer's. 'Isn't he a lamb?' she was heard to say—and he almost was. Another of her sayings was addressed to a young girl who asked if she might receive a male visitor in her room. 'I don't care what you do in your room,' said the landlady, 'so long as you don't set it on fire.' She was said to be a failed contralto, and I should like to have a tape-recording of her making that pronouncement. That man with the military air of twenty years earlier was said to

Anthony Butts

Four Friends: René Janin, Laurens van der Post, Lilian Bowes Lyon, Stephen Spender

be a cashiered ex-subaltern basking in the false afterglow of a manufactured past. He had been seen at Somerset House, and was rumoured to get a living by manufacturing other pasts, in the shape of pedigrees, for the socially aspiring descendants of emigrants overseas. That poor wight with a stoop who goes often to the pillar box might perhaps be doing precarious hack-work as a translator; he looks as if he were maintaining an invalid wife who no longer gets commissions for those sugary miniatures of children she used to do.

There had always been a cultural element in these parts, from the days when Browning and Edmund Gosse had lived in houses overlooking the canal basin, which the author of *Sinister Street* was said to have overlooked rather later. And now among my notable neighbours were Joe Ackerley, Stephen Spender, and Air-Commodore (retired) L. E. O. Charlton. A joke was current about our constituting a 'Maida Vale Group', but we were all too independent, too obviously barking (or refraining from barking) up different trees, or too deficient in team spirit, even to want, let alone attempt, to form anything like a group. Stephen Spender, with his mingled air of surprise, self-confidence, and ruddy health, was by now turning his attention ever more closely to European continental politics: he was not at all of the kind of solitary, introverted, doomed poets of the Romantic tradition, but an example of a twentieth-century kind that feel it necessary to be if not in the news at least not behind the times.

General Charlton (as he was usually called) I had first met at one of T. S. Eliot's *Criterion* parties. The author of an autobiography written in the third person, he had in fact been a general in the army before the first world war. He had served with dash and bravery in the Anglo-Boer War, had served in West Africa, and had so distinguished himself in the Royal Flying Corps that he was later believed to be all set to rise to a great altitude in the Royal Air Force. Posted to Iraq in 1923 as chief of staff at R.A.F. head-quarters, he found that on grounds of conscience he could not support what he regarded as a policy of indiscriminate bombing of unarmed villagers, including women and children. He made it known that he considered it 'a species of oppression which tended to render infamous the British name for fair dealing throughout the world'. He accordingly asked to be relieved of his duties, deliberately relinquishing his professional advancement, and before long had retired into private life. Independent, high-spirited, and well-bred as a racehorse, this honourable man came of an ancient Northumbrian Roman Catholic family, the Charltons of Hesleyside. The *Memoirs of a Northumbrian Lady* which he later edited and published are of uncommon historical, social, and regional interest.

Joe Ackerley had, I think, already been promoted literary editor of the *Listener*, a post in which his taste and conscientiousness were to be brought to bear for many years. I had now become familiar with his unique personality. Brushing aside what seemed to him inessentials, going straight to what seemed to him the point of any subject or situation, impelled by a logic of his own, unhindered by ordinary usage, convention, or prejudice, rendered acute by the workings of an inquiring, literal, totally uninventive yet artistically selective mind, and independent by unworldliness and a kind of innocence, he made an impression of troubled candour and rare purity – troubled, because his face often wore a look of anxiety. When interested, his powers of concentration were those of a burning-glass, but his trains of thought, as obstinate and as surefooted as mules, seemed often to lead him far from the place where he was and the person or persons he was with – over almost inaccessible paths, one imagined, with an abyss on one side and the threat of a landslide on the other. His introspective processes of inquiry, analysis, judgement, and speculation often gave him an abstracted air.

With all the detachment of a somnambulist he once went into a tea-shop at Shepherd's Bush to drink tea. He sat down at a table for two. The chair opposite his was already occupied by an elderly woman. If his attention had been caught by her he would at once have registered every detail of her appearance and bearing. Like Gogol, he might have said, '*Je ne parvenais à deviner la nature d'un homme que lorsque je voyais clairement les moindres détails de son extérieur.*' But his thoughts were far away, and quite without knowing it he was gazing at her as intently as if she were an aircraft pin-pointed high up in a cloudless sky.

'Oh!' she cried, under the gimlet of his scrutiny, 'what piercing eyes!'

Slowly returning to consciousness, he said with the utmost surprise, after looking round over his shoulder: 'Is it possible that you mean me?'

'Yes, I do,' she said. 'I think you must be a customs officer.'

'Then,' he said, with his usual quick-wittedness and charming smile, 'I can only ask if you have anything to declare.'

It was the valuable policy of the *Listener* to pay much attention to the art of painting. He was a constant visitor therefore to new exhibitions and became a discriminating appreciator not only of pictures but of art critics. Before lunching together one day, probably at the Café Royal, we looked in at Burlington House for a preview of one of the great special exhibitions, which had just been hung. As the galleries were almost empty we could see the pictures without being distracted by the pleasure of meeting friends or the bother of being obstructed by a crowd. But he seemed to have something on his mind. He was carrying under his arm not a parcel but a round object as big as a croquet ball and untidily wrapped in some loose and crumpled sheets of the *Daily Mirror*. I knew what it was, because I had asked him: it was a cauliflower he had bought on his way. He had said that he wasn't altogether happy about it. He suspected that it wasn't quite fresh. As happens with the Brassicae in such a condition, it was making its presence perceptible—or he thought it was. Telegraph wires of anxiety appeared on his forehead, and it was evident that the place where he had bought the vegetable, the bona fides and manner of its vendor, its destiny, the possibility that his suspicion was after all unfounded, and so on, were all engaging his attention to the exclusion of the successive masterpieces upon which his eyes were turned, as if searching for contraband or, Roger Fry-like, for evidence of a false attribution.

As we moved into one of the larger galleries, a distant and

solitary figure, dressed (as novelists say) 'immaculately' and in the style of a banker or diplomatist, was to be seen gazing at a picture.

'Ah!' Joe Ackerley exclaimed, and hurried forward. It was a cry of recognition: the solitary figure was the Director-General of the British Broadcasting Corporation. This important person, after acknowledging our presence with a restrained greeting, looked with unconcealed distaste at the untidy sheets of the popular newspaper so ill-wrapped round what might have been something inappropriate, unclean, or even sinister.

'Do you know anything about cauliflowers?' he was charmingly asked without preliminaries. 'The reason I ask is——'

And a moment later the important man was to be seen half unbending to pretend to catch whatever effluvium might be rising from the proffered object, now half unveiled. The natural-ness of this proceeding reflected credit on both, but the third person present found it, in those surroundings, characteristic and exquisitely incongruous.

A migrant life has its advantages, but among the things against it are that it tends to disrupt some personal relationships – those, for instance, of a domestic kind. Both my parents, who, as I have indicated elsewhere, led nomadic lives, used to win the hearts of their servants, white or black, not by spoiling them but by treating them in the traditional old English way as persons in their own right. It was taken for granted that obligations were mutual. A servant did work and was paid for it, but it was the employer's function to help and protect the servant, in health or sickness, in happiness or trouble. Each did his best to promote the well-being of the other. From my earliest days in Edwardian England and South Africa I had seen admirable examples of the master-and-servant relationship, beautiful when it brings out the best in the nature of each and creates an equilibrium of trust, security, and mutual aid. But even at an early age I had seen tears running down a good black face and the sight of them causing tears to blur the eyes of my mother at one of those all too frequent moments of necessary parting. In my own life, too, besides the pangs of parting from persons more intimately beloved, I had felt the sadness of losing the services of others who had looked after one's daily needs, faithfully and without complaint. And so it was in London.

At New Brompton, as at Canning Place, I had had the help of what was called a daily woman. She was not in the least like the type of charwoman so standardised by cheap plays and radio plays that charwomen now try and live up to the conventional level of big-breasted, never downhearted, wise-cracking, synthetic Cockney trollophood. No, Mrs Lydamore was small, neat, delicate. She had to be helped to lift heavy weights. She was neither shabby nor genteel, but clean as a cat, was never heard to complain or say an unkind word, and was sustained in her widowhood by one idea — the well-being of her young and only son in Canada — and by one prospect, that of seeing him again. In Maida Vale, to which it was not possible to bring Mrs Lydamore, I took on, during my first sojourn there, a daily man called Rainbird. He, too, I am glad to say, conformed to no type. Punctual, sober, deft, clean, tolerant, and a good cook, he was a married man, but spent all his spare time, when the weather allowed, flying kites which he had made himself. I do not understand well the attractions of this obsession, which I had also noticed in Japan, but I suppose it gives a feeling of solitariness, of power, of freedom, tranquillity, and soaring exaltation which may be of healing value to the bruised and constricted spirit of an urban man.

I was to return to Maida Vale about 'the time of Munich', to unusually large rooms in Randolph Crescent, which I left only after they had been damaged by bombing and looted. Between what I may call my first and second Maida Vale periods I was absent from London. At the beginning of the second I interviewed a number of prospective daily men, hoping for another Rainbird. I was impressed by their individuality. One was too emotional and perhaps hoped to be more than a servant. Another would do anything but cook. A third seemed to have been born in a tiny green baize apron; his pride and joy, he explained, was to clean silver in all his waking hours. His feeling for silver seemed as instinctive as that of some men for horses or pigeons, and my few spoons would soon have built up in him a terrible frustration. For a moment I almost wished my parents had not got rid of some of those inherited objects, silver candelabra, or the soup tureen which had been used by one of my forefathers when Lord Mayor of London in the seventeen-eighties. Instead I engaged Utting.

At an early age Utting had been injured in the first world war. A smallish, stocky, compact man with a veiny complexion and small eyes, he was a most helpful and unfussy maintainer of a simple domestic rhythm. We never had more than brief colloquy, but when Utting did speak I had the impression that his view of the universe and of the immediate foreground was very much his own. He lodged in or near Lisson Grove, in Marylebone, and one day seemed anxious to tell me about something that had gone wrong at his lodgings. I listened attentively.

'It's my landlord,' he said.

'Oh, yes.'

'He's troubled with boils on the neck. And his wife, she's got boils on her feet.'

'What a nuisance,' I said. 'Perhaps they're both a bit run down.'

'No, it's not that. He says it's because they were both born in October.'

'Libra, or Scorpio?'

'Pardon?'

'Oh, nothing,' I said.

'But she won't have it,' said Utting. 'She will have it that it's the water.'

'The water?' I echoed.

'It's not that,' he said. 'I know what it is. It's the smell from the animals.'

'The animals?' I seemed cast for the part of Echo. 'Why, Utting? Do they keep a lot of pets?'

'No, no, it's not that. It's the zoo.'

His belief was that the wind, when it blew from the direction of the zoo, more than a mile away on the far side of the Regent's Park, brought with it a contagion which caused boils. This did not seem scientific, but rather the theory of a man conscious of the pressure of strange natural forces around and within us. It was not strange to me; it was the sort of belief one might have found in Zululand, but I should not have expected to find it in London.

I found many unexpected things in London. It should not be thought that I was so disengaged from the life of the time that I had retreated into a Victorian dream-world. Not at all. In the mid-Thirties I brought out a novel, *The Invaders*, which was a fruit of curiosity about the answers to such questions as what might happen to a girl from the country who came up to London on her own to make her living and drifted into different employments, and to a boy who came to London and joined the army, and how the lives of such 'invaders' might interact with the lives of persons of a different class or different racial origin. As in *The Case is Altered*, I was concerned with what happened to a variety of persons brought together in London by changing social conditions, and with their feelings. Some people thought it the best of the four novels I had written, some did not. I was confident that I had written a book that was not superficial, and I knew it was full of truth about people and what happened to them; it was presented, I hoped, with a certain freshness. The inside view of military life in London in peacetime caused the leading non-commissioned officer of a well-known regiment to place a copy of the book before the colonel commanding it: he deferentially suggested that it would help that officer to understand better the lives and conditions of the men under his command. The book was also thought well of by those of my friends who had experience of social work and a better idea of the gulf that separated South Kensington from the purlieus of the Edgware Road than had certain literary intellectuals of the know-all type.

It is the business of the novelist not so much to see life as to see it from the point of view of others — one might say of *any* others, so far as that is possible. In England this often meant learning to see members of one class from the point of view of another. A good friend of mine was Jack Carey, a roadworker, or navvy, of about my own age. He was not a Londoner, and it was interesting to see the people of London through his eyes, and to notice how the little things that happened to him and his mates in the course of their work sometimes indicated social change – or no change. He had no political views and, being of an independent nature, no class consciousness.

He found that the public were mostly ill-mannered and in-considerate; that motorists were the most selfish and insolent people, and that the worst of them were taxi-drivers or women. It was nothing unusual for a motorist to knock down the road-men's poles and trestles and drive on without apology. Twice my friend had himself been knocked down by impatient motorists. Once when he and his party were repairing a pavement (which he called a 'footway') in Mayfair a tall military-looking man came out of a house and said:

'What's all this mess?'

'It's all right, Captain,' said one of the roadmen civilly, 'we'll soon be finished.'

'Colonel to you!' the man bellowed.

'Oh yes?' said my friend quietly. 'We're not living in those times now.'

The man glared and snorted, got into his car, and slammed the door in a rage.

Only once in my friend's experience had a rich person shown any consideration: that was when a lady sent her maid out to ask if the men would like some tea. One winter's day in a residential street it came on to rain very hard. The only shelter was in a door-way, and three of the roadmen stood in it. Suddenly the door opened and out came a woman who said, 'Get out of my doorway and don't make a mess with your muddy boots on my step!' They got off it, and one of the men said to her, 'You should have told us that in 1914, when we were looking after your interests. We had mud up to our necks then, and you called us heroes.' She had no answer, and banged the door in his face. He still had pieces of shrapnel in his body.

It is sometimes suggested that the writers of the Thirties were sentimental about what was still called the working class. What if they were? If Stephen Spender or George Orwell appeared to some to idealise or falsify the lives of persons of a lower level than that into which they had been born, perhaps that was necessary to their art and thought. Every considerable poet I have known has had some unusual concentration of interest, some fantasy or obsession or predilection which has been an essential motive force in his work. It may be a passion for a person, place, or thing; for a vice or a virtue; for Hindu mysticism, or neo-Gothic architecture; for the past or the future; for a civil war in Ireland or Spain; for a dangerous political creed, a bad writer, or a deaf giantess; but whatever the fantasy, it has been more or less closely related to the significance of his own time or of the time that is to follow it. Every considerable poet opens a window, or even several windows, that nobody has ever opened, or even noticed, before: the greater the poet, the more wonderful and unfamiliar the view. But people don't take easily to unfamiliar views and visions; they like the shelter of cosy prejudices and accepted ideas.

It was not only radical politicians, social workers, or left-wing intellectuals who were conscious of the fate of the unemployed — of their numbers, and of the disintegrating effect of their condition upon personality as well as physique. Unemployment, as Archbishop Temple wrote later, is a 'corrosive poison', of which the worst effect is 'the moral disaster of not being wanted'. I found out by chance that my parents, whom I did not see very often, had been brooding over the problem. They had heard a bad account of South Shields, where they had never been in their lives, and they wrote to the Anglican incumbent there and asked him to put them in touch with a family suffering from that poison. This he did. My parents were no longer young. One was in the lifelong grip of a nervous illness, and the other in the tightening grip of a mortal illness; and through no fault of their own they were much less well-off than they had been. Yet they were now prepared to do without things they would have liked and perhaps really needed, so that they could send from time to time small sums of money or material comforts to the family in South Shields. Scrupulously avoiding as far as possible the semblance of being charitable, they tried to vary the nature of their

11*

gifts and wrote letters inquiring about the welfare of various members of the family. They hoped to convey as unobtrusively as they could the sort of stimulus that may help those who have been feeling useless, unhopeful, undernourished, and unwanted, to feel that they matter in their own right. The warm response of the widowed mother of the South Shields family was without false pride or servility: she showed the proper dignity of one who needs help, and is helped, and is pleased.

Anything my parents did for the betterment of that family was small and temporary. Born in mid-Victorian times, faithful but not fanatical Anglicans, they believed that it was an obligation to help those less fortunate than themselves, as a matter of ordinary humanity and Christian charity. Their forebears protected dependants and servants and poor neighbours; they themselves were displaced and migrant, and the world was their parish. It may have been too late to try and restore that sense of community which had been weakened or destroyed by industrialisation, overpopulation, mobility, bureaucracy, and so on, but I felt nothing but respect for the thought and the action.

Extract from a letter to my parents:

I was present at the Means Test riot, which you have no doubt read about, and got banged about by a mounted policeman, although I was merely looking on, not 'demonstrating'. I hear that the authorities had actually ordered the Guards to stand by. This seems rather a Czarist approach to the misery of the unemployed. Nearly forty policemen are said to have been injured. A shop was broken into by the crowd and looted. It had large notices advertising a 'Great Clearance Sale—everything Must Go!' Everything did.

31

A Broken Chain

Of the pleasures of London none was sweeter than leaving it. After taking a train, being met by a car, and driven to some country house or house in the country, the visitor was immediately astonished, shocked, by the grassy silence. It fell on the cars like a blow: but the shock was therapeutic; the clean air was perceived by nose and throat and lungs, and by the skin itself, like a cool draught on a thirsty palate. A starving and parching time was suddenly known, by its temporary interruption, to have existed. The sky and its phases were visible and open; the feet were conscious of pressing on the earth; and a moment had come to wonder why on earth anybody not under compulsion should go on living in London. This moment of speculation did not last long, because I did in fact then feel myself still under a compulsion of habit, curiosity, and supposed necessity.

Thinking of those vividly remembered moments of sudden and grateful immersion in country air and country silence puts me in mind of an observation by Norman Douglas. 'A retrospect of life,' he wrote in his own flavoursome and well devised retrospect, *Looking Back*, 'is a chain, a broken chain, of remembered moments.' Not a very fresh or striking image, but a true one where a wandering and fragmentary life is concerned. A diligent and regular diarist (I know of several now living) has no need of retrospect; he is constantly spinning his *aide-mémoire*. The non-diarist must shuffle through the snapshots capricious memory has fixed. He can only collect links or irregular strands of the broken chain.

So far as I was connected, or my relations and friends were

connected, with places and regions, these were seldom remote or northerly. Escape from London was nearly always southward or westward. The Cotswolds, the Chilterns, the Thames Valley, South Wales, Kent, Surrey, and Sussex were the usual settings for chance groupings, glimpses of other people's lives and standards of taste, relaxed pleasures, sudden intimacies, and spontaneous confessions. Rooms opened on to gardens aloof from the car-infested roads. In quiet rooms, old gardens, and easy conversation there was healing and renewal.

I know more about Sussex gardens now than I did then. The arboretum at West Dean can hardly be called a garden; it is more like a secret entry into Nepal. Numb with wet moss, the hillside paths wind among banked or tree-tall shrubs; May switches on myriads of many-coloured rhododendrons and azaleas, and the luminous glades are suffused with a sleepy fragrance; far above them soar the stiff spires of giant rare conifers from Asia; turn a corner, and there, yes, surely, is a dak bungalow. May is also the time for Sir Frederick Stern's miraculous paradise in a chalk-pit at Highdown. But Rodmell has always seemed to me at its best in late summer, with the fig trees expansively southern, the pear trees weighted with abundance, the zinnias glowing in pure scarlet, yellow, and magenta, a heat haze over the valley of the Ouse at midday, and evening opalescence lending a nuance of autumn to Mount Caburn. In a work-room in that garden Virginia Woolf did much of her writing, overlooked (it seems a little ironic) by the tower of Rodmell Church.

Once at tea-time indoors in the summer the click of the gate was heard, and a second or two later there appeared in profile in one of the windows a stylish panama hat, sporting in cut and tilted slightly forward on a determined, military-looking head with a granite chin, the head itself set rigidly on a square, parade-ground chest and shoulders which, lacking epaulettes, looked undressed. At a glance one might have thought this the top part of a Prussian field-marshal just back from shooting chamois in the Carpathians. The purposeful progress of this animated bust, in vivid relief against the old yew hedge, and without a glance to left or right, was as resolute as that of some old man-of-war, called perhaps *Immitigable, Indomitable,* or *Impregnable,* carrying a great many guns and under urgent orders to ram and board a cornered enemy. But there was no enemy, this visitor was not on any hostile intent, and, just as a man-of-war used to be called *she,* was in fact of the feminine gender. The baton in her knapsack was more wandlike than that of a field-marshal; she was a composer; and the only English one with whom I was then acquainted.

As the figurehead, pressing on steadily towards the front door, appeared in a second and then a third window, Virginia Woolf looked up and exclaimed, 'Good heavens, there's Ethel!' Her exclamation seemed to signify 'What fun!' and anybody who looks into the memoirs of Ethel Smyth can easily discern why. This high-spirited woman addressed herself to life with a gusto more often seen in her generation than in ours. If her sensibility had been as conspicuous as her energy, her music might have been as attractive as her enjoyment of life. Perhaps it is; but what I have heard of it has suggested to me collision and grappling-irons and war-cries, or repeated discharges of firearms in a Central European mountain landscape; the rocks reverberated, the knickerbockered field-marshal clapped his Zeiss glasses to his battlefield eyes, but there was never a sign of the nimble chamois; it had been too quick for the hunter.

She now snatched off her hat and cast it on to a table, revealing, clamped to her thinning grey hair (with which no coiffeur could be envisaged as having busied himself for some time), what looked like a headphone, as if on her way to Rodmell she had been determined not to miss a first performance, in Serbo-Croat at Zagreb, of *The Wreckers.* But the thing was only a device to alleviate impinging deafness.

'This damned contraption,' she cried in a tone of voice that cannot have been much like Beethoven's, 'is not the slightest good!'

And she snatched it off and flung it beside her hat. As I turned to follow her I noticed that the gesture had cost her a sizeable wisp or hank of grey hairs, which had been caught in a joint of the contraption as she wrenched it from her scalp, without, so to speak, turning a hair. A moment later, she and Virginia Woolf were seated knee to knee and *tête-à-tête* on a couple of upright chairs. The composer had a lot to say. The writer was almost immediately speechless, because laughter, uncontrollable laughter, had taken possession of her. She quivered, she vibrated; every time she attempted to speak, her throat seemed to close up, and she touched it with one of her beautiful long hands as if to free herself from choking.

'But, Ethel——' she said, and got no further. Tears of laughter coursed down her face, while the composer, as sure of this good listener as of an orchestra in full cry, unswervingly pursued her theme ...

Summer in Sussex, summer in Surrey—that part of it which faces south from the slopes between Guildford and Dorking. In a William Morris-papered bedroom a brass can of hot water, covered with a face towel to keep it hot, waits patiently in the basin on the washstand. Time to wash, yes, but how to stop looking out of the window of this quiet house at that quiet view? Such things are not to be enjoyed in London: those who enable one to enjoy them in the country are more than friends, they are life-givers. The late hot afternoon light gives an almost African look to Hackhurst Down and its old wild black yew trees of the Pilgrims' Way, and the heat has drawn out from the flower-covered cistus bushes beyond the lawn a Mediterranean fragrance, suggesting goats, rocks, and lizards. The peaceful warmth seems deepened by the passage of an airborne stag-beetle on a drowsy cruise towards the wood.

Downstairs Mrs Forster, the novelist's mother, is sitting near a window facing south. She is overlooked by the Richmond drawing of her son's great-aunt, Marianne Thornton. It is earlier in the afternoon, or it is another afternoon in an earlier or later year, and from the window can be seen a flourishing tree-of-heaven, and further off, down at the end of the sloping garden, the distant figure of Bone, the gardener, stooping among the raspberry canes. Perhaps the novelist is only a young man, perhaps this is the nineteenth century still, or the early twentieth (which is much the same thing), when ladies sit in drawing-rooms with silver spirit-kettles and cakestands, sit quietly recalling the past and noticing the present instead of rushing about. The door opens, admitting Agnes with the tea. Thin, kindly, and formal, she wears the light armour-plating of a parlourmaid, her perceptibly starched cuffs and apron and the biretta-like cap on the top of her head all dead white, all crackling faintly like the talc of a dragonfly's wings. It might almost be tea-time at my grandmother's in Buxton in 1909, the tempo is so tranquil and the atmosphere so much one of safe-seeming, immortal-seeming seclusion. Mrs Forster and Agnes seem to have their being in a perspective that shuts out the great garish world and greatly magnifies details in the foreground. Some discussion was held between them earlier today about the precise whereabouts, colour, and function of a pencil; it was conducted with a quiet care and stately thoroughness that suggested conformity with an almost Confucian system of order and appropriateness.

The tea ceremony is certainly in the style of 1909, but the small wireless-set at Mrs Forster's elbow is not—nor is her son, who presently comes into the room. He brings with him anything but a feeling of troubling this peace: he is part of it. The house was designed and built by his father. It is his home (this word has special potency for the nomad guest) and there can be no question that he loves it. In 1909 he was already a novelist, but if his early novels are charged with an aroma of their time, they are charged also (the point need not be laboured) with the dynamite of non-acceptance. This is his home, but he is only intermittently here; he belongs to the world and the present, to the future too; he is a harbinger of change.

In this last half-century of violent and in some ways total change it has sometimes been more than usually the mark of a superior understanding not to be what my father used to call a stick-in-the-mud, not to get stuck with any rigid formula of life or belief but to show curiosity about change, enough adaptability at least to recognise it, and enough understanding to discriminate between its fertilising and its transitory or stultifying tendencies. Curiosity, adaptability, and independence are some of the qualities that have kept E. M. Forster in touch with quite other aspects of the world than this, his mother's drawing-room in Surrey. But it is something much more, the indefinable motive power of his personality, that has put him in revolt against much in his time and enabled him to follow his negatives with a positive creed, attitude, and theory of conduct. I have heard superficial people praise or condemn his early writings for 'period charm' or for 'dating a bit'; they were too stupid to recognise the direct blasts of a mind that has sometimes worked like a flame-thrower, scorching up some falsity held to be truth. Unfortunately falsity grows again, however often it is cut down.

The small tabby cat at my feet, I notice as I drink my tea, has a wry neck. I ask if this is a natural deformity or the result of an accident.

'Poor Toma,' he says, 'had a stroke. It happened while he was listening to a broadcast of *The Flying Dutchman* ...'

And now it is November, at a farmhouse in Wharfedale. My host's father, telling me what a lot of rabbits there are on the fell, says, 'On a summer's evening you can see millions of them. If you clap your hands, why, you'd think the blessed earth was moving.' Language is not often so perfectly used by non-literary persons. Hearing us speak of Haworth, he unexpectedly says, 'Ah, Haworth. That was where they raked the moon out of the pond, so they used to say when I was a lad.' This was not a joke about the Brontës, who were no more than a name to him, but just a stale country whimsy.

His son, Norman Carr, took me to see Haworth. No day could have been more propitious. It was November, and the climate gave us the full treatment. We drove off after lunch in semi-darkness and a wind that was strong, damp, and piercingly cold. The clouds were low, tearing along with maniac speed over the austere, deserted fells and stained the same sapless tint as the withered heather. This deepened to a depressive dark grey with tinges of puce and khaki, as if the clouds were the effluence of satanic mills not far away; and then there would be a sudden, livid, whitish area among them, as if some horrible flare were being dropped above. For an instant everything was blurred by rain; a few gritty handfuls of small hailstones were flung contemptuously against the windscreen; then these turned soft and were seen to be sleet. After this we drove without surprise into a swirling theatrical fog, not very thick but of an uncommonly sulphurous khaki colour. By the time we reached Keighley the fog had dispersed and the wind had gone down a little; the sky had turned blackish, and a few chilled and rugged souls, hunched under shawls and black umbrellas, were scurrying along, as if to sit for early drawings by Van Gogh.

To find a funeral procession preceding us up the hill to Haworth was a real stroke of what in the theatre is called production, on the part of Fate. We were obliged to slow down and follow it. Anything more stagey can hardly be imagined. The pathetic fallacy was working overtime: the sky loured and threatened, the wind wailed and wuthered, gutters wept copiously. A mournful bell was tolling from the church, and before we got to the Black Bull soft, squashy flakes of snow had begun to fall. As soon as they touched the glossy black roof of the hearse they dissolved and ran down it like the tears of an Ethiopian princess.

We had the immortal house to ourselves. The silence and semi-darkness and solitude left the body free to manœuvre in those haunted rooms and the imagination free to try and enter into those lives that had flared up in them and given out an unprecedented radiance, now light-years away. The window of the room on the ground floor which had been Charlotte Brontë's husband's study was framed in ivy leaves as black and shiny as patent leather. It looked straight into the churchyard, the surface of which was well above the level of the floor, and the thought of the very juices of mortality seeping almost into the foundations of the house was not wholly comforting.

I will not swear that I caught sight in Haworth of a tea-shop called Emily's Pantry, but I was credibly informed that in summer months a great many trippers were conveyed to the place in motor coaches marked 'Brontë Tours Ltd'. It is very easy to deplore the commercialisation of a place with such associations and of the memory of the rare spirits who gave rise to them, but such is fame. Foreign visitors apart, Stratford-on-Avon may be presumed to be visited by semi-educated hordes of litter-droppers; but perhaps such people are part of the backbone of this industrialised England. If one does not care for the sight of vertebrae, or of other people enjoying themselves, one can always stay away; but it is priggish to condemn and impossible to prevent their attempting to improve their understanding of the environment and civilisation in which the most eminent of Englishmen long ago exerted himself ...

The scene changes to Tiger Bay, the dockside quarter of Cardiff, and, by a slight transition, to a 'depressed area' in the mining valleys behind it. I would not say that nothing but a hope of self-improvement took me there; curiosity has in it an element of pleasure. Among its rewards were evidences of Welsh temperament and Welsh brains triumphing wonderfully over unemployment, and varieties of night-life in strong chiaroscuro and with crude musical accompaniment, suggesting dramatic waterfronts in French films. In Wales, as in Ireland, it was possible to feel very far from England; there were moments of total foreignness.

To Ireland I went, to visit Elizabeth Bowen at Bowen's Court, and as the boat from Fishguard slowly made its way up the estuary towards Cork, the light mists that dangled or drifted over the trees seemed sub-tropical. The disposition of the landscape, and the colour-washed houses, pale pink, blue, or buff, and the stray fishing-boats on the silky water, and the men in them, and the cormorants on the buoys, suggested an approach to a remote island. A pink ruin glided by, as if on a pivot. It was said to have been a hotel. But there were no numbers now on the bedroom doors, because there were no bedroom doors. On the long road by the shore two or three cars passed; across the water one could hear the swishing sound of the tyres on the moist asphalt until it grew fainter and ceased. Throbbing gently, the boat passed a sham medieval tower at the water's edge. It was inhabited, and a young man was leaning against it and smoking a cigarette. He wore no raincoat in spite of the wetting mist, and looked at the boat as one might look at a passing cloud. If he had been an Englishman he would have been indoors or would already have gone busily off somewhere, instead of standing by himself in the cool, quiet, early morning air; but this was Ireland.

At school in England the history of this country, this producer of wits, poets, heroes, beauties, and (let us admit it) bores, had not been properly taught to us. It had either been ignored, glossed over, or given an Orange tinge. St Patrick got rid of the snakes, and after some time Cromwell arrived to 'crush the rebels' and establish 'law and order'. Shortly afterwards William III won the Battle of the Boyne. But it happened that Easter Week, the Sinn Fein ideal, and the fate of Casement had made a strong impression upon my boyish imagination. As I grew older I wondered whether the ignorance, prejudice, intolerance, injustice, folly, famine, and violence that seemed to have accompanied the English occupation of Ireland had been wholly necessary. In other parts of the world, too, the English, instead of trying to understand the feelings of other peoples, have labelled them 'rebels' or 'terrorists' and brought force to bear upon them in the name of 'law and order'. My Uncle William, who commanded the Royal Irish Fusiliers, once explained to me the military advantages of combining Irish dash with English moderation. Why, I wondered, did it have to be a *military* combination?

Often in Ireland a dwelling and a ruin stand side by side, and often the ruin stands alone—a roofless mill, full of young trees instead of machinery; or an old tower in a cloud of ivy; or a wayside or upland cabin; or a great burnt mansion of early nineteenth-century Gothic with bunches of twisted water-pipes sticking out of it like severed arteries; or a mouldering police barracks looking haunted behind overgrown hedges of flowering fuchsia, with the apple tree near it in which a sniper was once sniped. Another ruin—Bridgetown Abbey beside the Black-water, its grey stone turning a darker grey when the rain wets it. It is approached by a lane overgrown with brambles weighed

down by fat blackberries that nobody picks, the Blackwater
glides over its dark rocky bed, and trees on a cliff catch the afternoon light. Masonry has fallen, and lies where it fell; weeds have
sprung up, and a few nineteenth-century graves in a roofless
chapel keep company with old tombs. From the side of one of
these a stone slab has fallen, inside it lies flat an old thick oaken
board which was once the side of a coffin, and there is the skeleton
of its occupant; through the pelvis a nettle has thrust, and is now
in flower. Such a sight would not be lawful in England, or
orderly.

Across the meadows to what is left of the castle of Kilcolman,
where Spenser lived, wrote, empire-built, and rebel-crushed. The
bog water reflects a livid evening sky, and the haycocks cast long
lilac shadows on the grass. The place is sometimes visited by
consumptives from a sanatorium not far away. One of them has
torn up a letter and thrown the fragments on the ground, and
some phrases, in very clear writing, shape themselves on the grass
in the headstrong hopefulness of consumptives:

'... she was hoping ... said I would never ... last time darling ...
looking forward more than ever ...'

Not a ruin, but more desolate than a ruin, is a great lead-
coloured house, closed up, deserted, some of its windows
shuttered and some not, with black-shadowed ilex thickets and
overgrown lawns of a green so vivid that it hurts the eyes, with
stalactites beginning to form under the heraldic pediment, and a
solitary donkey nibbling the grass between the paving-stones in
the yard outside the coach house. These country houses, often
extravagantly built and standing in walled demesnes, were the
breeding places of that gifted race, the Anglo-Irish. 'The most
brilliant and charming people in the world,' a travelled old
Englishman had told me. 'One day last summer,' he said, 'when
I was staying over there at a perfectly delightful house, hip baths
were brought out on to the lawn and filled with cushions, and we
sat in them all the afternoon drinking port and eating gooseberries.
Such hospitality! Such conversation!'

Such conversation, yes, among all the Irish, with their seductive voices and brogue, but their enthusiastic monologues can be wonderfully fatiguing. Ireland is a heavenly country to visit, but might be less heavenly to live in. It is so melancholy, so full of the ghosts of feuds and famines, the clouds fly low, the trees sag under the incessant rain, and the very air seems charged with a sense of grievance. How could one keep out the climate, how could one keep the Pope and Ulster at a proper distance, except by settling in Rome or London, taking to drink, or cutting one's throat? I felt then that there was still scope for a Gogol to go round in a car, on some pretext that would appeal to vanity or cupidity, and visit the surviving denizens of the demesnes up and down the country. What material for a novel that will now never be written! I think Turgenev said it was the example of Miss Edgeworth that gave him the impetus to write about his own people. There were certainly parallels between pre-republican Russia and pre-republican Ireland, and a Russian reader might enjoy *The Absentee* as much as an Irish reader might enjoy *Dead Souls*. And still, in the Thirties, with the remains of a landowning class and the survival of a peasantry, Russia was brought nearer, the nineteenth and the eighteenth century too.

These impressions I owed to my brilliant friend and hostess at Bowen's Court, and among them the image of a very small lake in the hills beyond Killarney, as clear as a dewdrop, with a tumbledown pale-blue inn and a few pine trees beside it. In the pure air a spotlight of sunshine travels slowly across the scene, giving it an almost supernatural beauty. A hillock of wet grass glows in the sun like an emerald, there is no sound but the Yeatsian lapping of the lake water, a tuft of flowering heather looks like something precious, and as a background to it all the sombre mountains are slowly suffused with the colour and bloom of damsons. They seem to grow taller and gloomier and more Ossianic as their impossibly deep purple deepens still further, and the darkening clouds pass over them trailing mile-long scarves of gauzy rain. A faint seethe of sound is audible even from here. It is going to pour again. It has begun.

32

Marine Residences

Why was I drawn back to the sea? Was it simply that the whole metabolism of one 'long in city pent' needed refreshment so badly that he was driven by hunger for clean air as a man may be driven by a craving for food or drink? Or was it the return of an addict to the drug of swimming and the lulled balance of well-being that may follow swimming, especially when one lies idly in the sun? Or was it simply that to a modern, urbanised man, who had lived some of his earliest and intensest years far from anything like a town, it seemed necessary to live for a time, if in a town, at least in a town with a permanent and very large open space on one side? Not that one can love the sea. It may soothe by its calmness, impress by its radiance or majesty, its power and noise, or attract as the element over which one sails or hunts for fish. But it is oppressively elemental, and a great fidget.

It is often supposed that English seaside towns are depressing. For the greater part of the year, it is alleged, they are chilly, wet, and dark, with a deserted, out-of-season air, no 'life' either indoors or out, and no society in which a man of feeling or taste can pleasurably mix. During the short summer season they are believed to be made intolerable by moronic swarms of 'holiday-makers' or trippers ignorant of the possible graces of living, equally indifferent to nature and the arts, to good cooking, wine, conversation, music, or books, to the true pleasures of either society or solitude, wasting their time, overtiring the noisy and badly brought-up children they call 'the kiddies', spending a lot of money, and getting less for it, as a French friend of mine used to say, than they would anywhere else in the world. I see that it is possible to take such a view, but if it had been mine I should have stayed away from English seaside towns or gone elsewhere. The two seaside towns that drew me had each a character quite its own, and in each I found it possible to live an agreeable and free sort of life.

I spent one long summer in Dover, which I cannot claim to have 'discovered'. Whatever it is like now, it had then both charm and atmosphere. People elsewhere were generally astonished to learn that one had chosen to remain there for months on end. They regarded Dover as no more than part of the pipeline that took vast numbers of people back and forth between England and the rest of Europe. And yet one could live pleasantly there. A friend of mine had been in the habit of taking a flat in one of the comfortable old-fashioned houses overlooking the harbour. At the open windows on summer evenings it was pleasant to sit with a drink and stare at the calm sea. There were no trippers, there was no traffic, and the caterwauling of sea-gulls, for which the cliffs acted as a sounding-board, added a touch of melancholy to the atmosphere. Occasionally a phrase or flourish of military music from the castle far above floated down for effect, and in the evenings the streets, very quiet in the day-time, were filled with the inaudible *frou-frou* of kilts, as the young soldiers of the garrison made their ways to the pubs.

There was one good restaurant, where I sometimes dined. I used to lunch at a small commercial hotel, where the food was surprisingly good. My attendance being unexplained, I was known there (I found out by chance) as 'Mr X'. Even more enigmatic was one of my fellow-lunchers, an oldish woman. Every day she came into the dining-room at a quarter to one, looking rather pixilated under a mop of 'iron grey' hair, bobbed in the style of the Twenties. She wore slippers, and a speckled dress like the plumage of a faded guinea-fowl, and carried a large leather bag stuffed with unknown possessions; it was heavy. She invariably sat down to a breakfast of two boiled eggs, and ate them with much fussiness, daintiness, and quick, bird-like movements. As soon as she had finished she was provided with a pint-sized jug of hot water, which she carried with her out of the room, for some unknown purpose. Exactly half an hour later she returned for lunch, which always consisted of fish. Although in perfect health she had not been out of the house for a year. She used to spend all her time alone in her room, but it was known that she did not sew, or read, or write, and that she had no wireless. What did she do in there? What was in that bag? Sometimes she read *John Bull* over her fish, a paper that in those days specialised in exposing frauds and abuses. It might be, to judge by her furtive eyes and whisperings, that she saw life and the world as one vast confidence trick. Perhaps she was right; perhaps her bag contained the secret of the universe ... No concern of hers, it seemed, the rise of Hitler, the Spanish Civil War, the China Incident, the invasion of Abyssinia. Snug as a wood-louse, she would hardly have regarded them as realities.

One afternoon I walked over to Kingsdown. A strong wind patterned the sea with curly white waves. The sea was streaked with loud blues and greens, and the wind prevented the fishing-boats from making headway; with their cigar-brown sails they dipped and fluttered, like moths in glue. Everything was movement at this windswept corner of England, nothing was progress. The waves broke and whitened as far as the eye could see, the sailing-boats rocked and tilted and got no further, the grass on the cliff streamed along the ground but stuck to its roots. At Kingsdown there were villas not yet opened for the summer, and the shuttered beach-huts, their paint faded by sun and salt, had an air of secrecy, as if a crime had been committed in one of them. Between the houses and the huts was a shingle flat a hundred yards wide, where masses of pink valerian had run wild. It was all in flower, dancing against the clean buff shingle and the peacocking sea.

I came back a different way, passing one of those deserted military follies that occur in what is left of the English landscape, a town of ruined concrete huts overgrown with elder bushes and nettles, a refuge for tramps (there were still tramps in those days), courting couples, and idle boys. Further on was a deep valley where grew the fragrant, the pyramidal, the bee, and the spider orchises, and where once, in thundery weather, I picked a bouquet of mixed flowers with several sorts of butterflies firmly attached, too drowsy to fly away.

This region was a haunt of Harry Houchen, a casual acquaintance. He had been coming there ever since he was a child. Before he married he used to bring his girl there, but now she would not come because there was always so much to do at home, so he sometimes brought one of his own children to tumble about and pick dandelions or blackberries. Harry himself had a taste for sea-gulls' eggs, which he collected on the cliffs; he gathered mushrooms, snared rabbits, or lay in the sun, smoking. He owned a boat, which could be seen from the top of the cliff, moored far below, and sometimes went fishing. His clothes were ragged, and he seemed more cheerful and contented than almost anybody I knew. He had the advantage of not living in a totalitarian state, and of not being ashamed of being idle or of enjoying himself.

'I had my great chance,' he said one day, smiling at his thigh, which could be seen through a rent in his old trousers, 'and if I'd taken it I wouldn't have been like this now.'

It had happened that when he was seventeen or eighteen Harry was serving in a smallish boat engaged in coastal trade varied with occasional voyages to Holland and Belgium. In Belgium the captain had an acquaintance, a middle-aged bachelor who owned three shops, a tailor's, a barber's, and a restaurant. He was an anglophile and wished to adopt a young Englishman to help him in the conduct of the three businesses and to be a companion to him. He said that if the young man turned out well he would make him his heir: could the captain recommend anybody? The captain recommended Harry Houchen, and Harry was installed. But the boy could not manage to learn Flemish; he was looked askance at because he was a foreigner; and in spite of the kindness of his patron he found that after three months he could bear his exile no longer. So one night he crept out of the house, joined a boat, and returned to England and his old haunts.

'And it is *all* gravel?' an American visitor wistfully asked me, looking at the shingly, shelving beach. It was a windless morning for once. The sea was perfectly calm, a milky green. Smoke, blackish or yellowish, coiling from a thin and distant funnel here and there, seemed to enter the waiting air and spread like some dark substance injected into a vein. Far away to the right a fog signal in the heat-haze made a noise like a cow deprived of her calf; far away to the left a dredger was clanking and creaking in the outer harbour. In the garden not a leaf moved, the curtains hung motionless at the windows, and the girl who was sitting on the balcony put down her sewing and looked out to sea, but it was impossible to tell where the sea ended and the sky began.

Suddenly the sun came out, and all the bathing children became children of light. Three very fair and slender little girls in pale blue, pale yellow, and white bathing suits hovered at the water's edge, and people sat on the shingle and idled in boats, like figures in that great *Baignade* by Seurat. A boy with red bathing-drawers waded into the sea and stood, with the water up to his waist, gazing at the horizon. His biscuit-coloured torso, apparently severed from the rest of him, rested on the calm surface as if on a sheet of glass. Attention was attracted by a small, splashing figure in shallow water: I immediately recognised it as Elsie. Attention was something she was constituted to attract.

I had first got to know Elsie a couple of weeks earlier, when I was sunbathing one morning on the then lonely and so-called Shakespeare beach. I was approached by a young girl who asked me if I would guard her clothes while she bathed, but I could not imagine anybody wanting to steal them. She rapidly undressed beside me, talking and giggling as she did so, and then sat down, still uncovered above the waist. Finding that I took little notice of her (to one with my Afro-Asian past, naked little girls were no novelty) she made for the water, buttoning up her bathing suit as she went. Her bathing consisted of ostentatious floundering in the shallow water a few yards from my feet, and her movements were punctuated with loud cries of delight and invitation. When she came out she talked incessantly, and presently came to the point.

'Where do you live?' she asked.

'Over there,' I replied.

'Is your wife there?'

'No.'

'Why not?'

'Because I haven't got a wife.'

'Do you live with your Mum?'

'No.'

'Who looks after you?'

'Oh, various people.'

'Wouldn't you like me to look after you?'

'Thanks, but I'm very well looked after.'

'Who do you sleep with?'

'It depends.'

'Do you sleep alone?'

'Sometimes.'

'Don't you get lonely when you sleep alone?'

'Not a bit.'

'Wouldn't you like to sleep with me?'

'You'd never stop talking.'

'What would you do if I walked into the bathroom when you were having a bath, and you were standing up and facing the door?'

'I always sit down in my bath, but it's quite likely I might tell you to buzz off and not be so nosy.'

'Wouldn't you like to marry me?'

'Not today, thank you.'

'What's your name?'

'Mickey Mouse.'

'Oh ... ! You fibber! Oh, what a fib! God is listening to you. How can you tell such fibs when God can hear us?'

'I'm sure God has a great many more interesting things to listen to.'

'Oh ...'

'By the way,' I said pleasantly, 'why don't you go and drown yourself?'

'Would you rescue me?'

'Certainly not.'

'But don't you like me?'

'You talk such a lot.'

'Would you like me if I didn't talk so much?'

'I doubt it. But I can't answer any more questions today.'

The sun was nice and warm, and I lay back and closed my eyes. Elsie began to balance stones along my outstretched arm, arranged others in patterns on my chest, and then, giggling delightedly, began to build a little cairn on a more personal foundation.

'Now, now,' I said ...

Elsie undoubtedly had a future; Lady Chalkham lived in the past. The first time I went to see her she noticed that I was looking at a framed photograph.

'A tremendous beauty, isn't she? It's Princess Eudoxia. She used to stay with us before the war.'

I saw a young woman in radiant health, straight backed, with her hair in a bang, a high bust, and her satin hips so smoothly corseted that she looked like a fish. *To dear Ada*, ran the inscription, *Cordially, Eudoxia Victoria of Blundenburg-Stettin*. And what a handwriting! What energy! What confidence! Lady Chalkham herself must have looked like that. She too was a product of all kinds of lucky chances and patient cultivations, a perfect specimen of a kind of woman that would never be produced again. I imagined an early environment not without stateliness, in which convention allowed for playfulness; but it is now difficult to gauge the incredible innocence in which, like many women of her class and generation, she had married.

Somewhere there must be an early photograph of herself yearning towards the camera, her head turned over a bare shoulder thrust up from a fuzz of tulle like an egg emerging from the fluffy recesses of a hen. It might have prompted one to evoke, one by one, little scenes from her past, each with its convention of clothes and behaviour, its special setting and companions, successive phases in the long evolution of a personality. I see her as a young woman reclining in a punt, with a Japanese fan in her hand, wearing balloon sleeves of *broderie anglaise*, and a hard straw-hat tilted over bright eyes fixed on a young man in a tall hard collar and narrow white flannels; sitting at a dressing table with silver-backed brushes and a little book of *papier poudré*, lifting her soft arms so that the loose sleeves fall back from the elbows, and slowly going through that beautiful lost movement, slowly withdrawing the long, jewel-headed pins from a huge hat heaped up with white roses; gathering up her skirts in one hand as she crosses the road, and then pausing to consult a watch suspended over her left breast from a diamond brooch in the form of a bow; peppering the backs of postcards (views of Venice, Cairo, or St Petersburg) with exclamation marks; seeing poverty at a distance or Naples through a port-hole; watching the slow-motioned withdrawal of Alps, vast, useless, and dazzling, from the steamy windows of a railway carriage; settling a feather boa round a lace collar supported with stiffeners, stepping with card-case and parasol into a carriage to pay calls, and driving off between banks of ferns in a smell of horses; bathing at Biarritz in waterlogged black serge with white pipings; going motoring in an ulster, thickly veiled, perched high above the ground, and moving off with a jerk in a cloud of blue vapour among respectful but sceptical onlookers, who step back in alarm as the machine snorts by; attending weddings, funerals, garden parties, musical evenings; appearing on lawns, the decks of yachts, race-courses; playing diabolo, bezique, puss in the corner; arriving at a tango tea, wearing a small hat adorned with sweeping ospreys, carrying a flat leopard-skin muff as square as the top of a table, and hardly able to put one foot before the other because of the tightness of the skirt above the ankles, a skirt split upward from the hem for four inches, attention being called to this provocative opening by two red buttons as big as half-crowns. A little later she follows the fashions of the early war-years, going out in a plumed shako, a frogged coat, a tent-shaped skirt well off the ground, and high laced boots. It seems only the other day that she passed laughing, to the music of Suppé, under a striped awning to a sunlit lawn; and then she found herself bending graciously over wounded soldiers in beds, a little troubled by the mingled smell of men, flannel, and iodoform. The time of wounds had come.

It was easy, it was not false, to see her in these fashion-plate terms. It was not false, but it only made a type of her, not an individual. I looked out of her drawing-room, through the french windows into the rainy garden, where the fuchsia bushes were hung with coral pendants and each pendant was covered with sliding raindrops, and I thought sadly how easy it is to falsify the past with generalisations, romantic fables, with envy, ignorance, and prejudice. I did know enough about Lady Chalkham, as it happens, to see below the gracious surface; I knew there had been turmoil and suffering, and something of its nature. These were the Thirties: I knew they would seem remote in thirty years' time — falsified, romanticised, despised for their weaknesses and absurdities. The Nineties, in which Lady Chalkham had been a young woman, were cheaply referred to as 'gay' or 'naughty'. I doubt if they were any more or less gay or naughty than any other period, except that wealth and over-confidence allowed some kinds of people in some ways to be frivolous and irresponsible — but so does poverty and insecurity, if they are bent that way.

I happened to have made some investigation into life at Dover in the Nineties. Naturally there were gaieties of sorts, public or private, open or secret; naturally the over-confident note of jingo imperialism floated down in bugle calls from the castle above the off-white cliffs; but all was not beer and skittles. Religious activities played a large part in the life of the town. Meetings were continually being held by missionary societies, Bands of Hope, synods, Lord's Day Observance societies, and similar bodies; 'sacred concerts' were frequent, and much was made of 'a three-days' conference on the Second Coming'. The English love of minding other people's business was being indulged, and meetings were held 'in support of the persecuted Armenians'. The English capacity to 'feel for woes beyond the wave' may be a good thing, but in the last century, as in this, charity did not always begin at home; and Ebenezer Elliott had perhaps been right to complain, even if in bad verse, at the readiness of the pious in his day to send Bibles to the heathen and 'bacon to the Jews'.

> Their lofty souls have telescopic eyes,
> Which see the smallest speck of distant pain,
> While, at their feet, a world of agonies,
> Unseen, unheard, unheeded, writhes in vain.

I don't think there was a world of agonies in Dover in the mid-Nineties, but it was disquieting to learn of the apparent prevalence of suicide among the working class, with its suggestion of less public agonies. An engine-driver cut his throat; a baker threw himself from the western heights 'during a state of temporary insanity'; a maid-servant 'was killed by falling over the cliff', two bottles of a drug being found where she fell; a boot-maker was found dead on the downs 'with a half-full bottle of poison beside him'; an artillery-man 'shot himself and died immediately'; and a messenger boy 'died from taking carbolic acid' among those bramble thickets which were a haunt of Harry Houchen's. Two seamen were committed to prison for refusing to serve in a steamer that took the Prince of Wales to France. Why? On political or moral grounds? Social history is more complex than it is sometimes made out to be.

My attention to the social history of Dover as it was being made around me, and by me, was diverted a little by a book I was editing for publication. It was by Haruko Ichikawa, the wife of a professor at the Imperial University in Tokyo, with whom I had been acquainted. With him she had done a tour of Europe, subsidised by an American foundation. She had kept a travel diary; this had been translated into English, and it appeared here as *Japanese Lady in Europe*. 'Unsophisticated sensibility as on a photographic film unmarked with any preconceived ideas' was the state of mind Mrs Ichikawa had aimed at, and it gave her book a flavour of its own. She and her husband 'often spoke unkindly' of the English for being 'stolid' or 'too composed', but when it was time to leave she felt a slight pang. It was the only European country that had that effect upon her: she felt, so she wrote, that she had left here about a fiftieth part of her soul. 'Stolid tenacity and obtuse stubbornness' were, in the eyes of Natsume Soseki, peculiarly English qualities. That eminent Japanese writer spent three years in this country at the beginning of the century. His teeth seem to have been set on edge by English genteelness.

'Gentleman!' he wrote. 'What is a gentleman? Who is a gentleman? The most ungentlemanlike English people never tire of harping on this everlasting string.' Elsewhere he wrote:

> Go to England to see what is meant by good manners. They say this is nice, that is nice. Everything seems to them nice enough. Strange to say, however, it is those who use the word most that do not know its meaning. Go along dirty streets of London, and you may pick up any quantity of 'nice'. There is no place where 'nice' is sold at such a cheap rate and in such abundance. And what for? Merely to please others! They do not know a person may be offended by being called nice by those who do not know what 'nice' is.

Was this just the bitterness of a young man from the Far East isolated in London? If so, he was not the last to feel it.

My other, and later, marine residence was at Brighton, where I lived for the best part of two years in the later Thirties. It was right in the very middle of the town, between the two piers, not far from the sea, and what estate agents call perfectly secluded; a small house in one of those alley-ways—or 'twittens' as they are traditionally called in Sussex—known as 'the Lanes' and famous for their antique shops and junk shops. No wheeled traffic could pass my door, and in bed late at night it was often pleasant to listen to the dwindling tattoo of the belated footsteps of a passer-by. It put me in mind, for some reason, of Thomas Hardy, and so, sometimes, did other aspects of Brighton (he spent, by the way, his first honeymoon there). At the back, the house opened on to an enclosed garden, not overlooked, not large certainly, and wonderfully isolated, sheltered against the rampaging south-

J. R. Ackerley

E. M. Forster

Charles Erdman and Richard Rumbold with William Plomer

westerly gales, and open in a proper summer to the blessed sun for many hours a day. A few steps from this unexpected little hide-out one could be in the full hurly-burly of Brighton. It is only a suburb of London but was agreeable to live in, especially in the winter.

My landlord was of what used to be called humble origins. He told me he had grown prosperous by diligently writing what he called 'mush' for the twopenny weeklies for women. He had also a serious side, and assured me that he had read fourteen times a book by Middleton Murry called, quite bluntly, God. I did not urge him to enlarge upon this addiction.

I had taken the place furnished. Everything in the life of a nomad is conditional, particularly when there are men like Hitler, Mussolini, and Stalin in the ascendant. I did not know how long I intended to stay, and I had for years been careful to avoid accumulating possessions. I had not particularly noticed the furniture; it seemed serviceable and was clean and adequately comfortable. I might perhaps have foreseen the horrified reaction of Herbert Read when he stepped into one of my rooms and found himself confronted with a piece of ill-designed machine-made furniture. After one glance on first arriving, I had ignored it. I had now no inclination to defend it, but after hearing my visitor's exclamations and seeing his expression of horror, like something in a picture by Fuseli, I rapidly tried to improvise some excuse for allowing it to share my habitat. I believe, by the way, that I may be the only man living who has said to him, perhaps with more courage than mischievousness, and in, of all places, a severe London gallery hung with still more severe abstract paintings, 'But, Herbert, why can't every picture tell a story?' It is a wonder I am alive to record this: he is not such a mild man as he looks.

33

The Typewritten Word

My temperament and talent did not impel me to try and make a living by writing books; they impelled me to write books only when I wished and only of whatever kind I wished. Though startled, and naturally gratified, by the comparative success of *The Case is Altered*, I could not imagine myself turning into a novelist of regular habits, whether a popular one or an unpopular one. Literature has its battery hens; I was a wilder fowl. The history of modern literature abounded with instances of novelists of great or of more than ordinary gifts who had written too much and too often, struggling to support themselves and their families, more or less embittered by want of the recognition and income they felt they deserved, haunted by fears of a drying-up of their inventiveness, a trial to their dependants, and liable to lose their own as well as other people's esteem. It was not so much prudence that kept me from adding to their number as the lack of a sense of vocation as a wholetime storyteller. I have stuck to my intention to write fiction deliberately, not constantly, and when I published my fifth novel I noticed with mild astonishment that eighteen years had passed since the appearance of my fourth. In the intervals I had produced other books in prose and verse.

During the Thirties, when printing and publishing were much cheaper and easier than they are today, there seemed to be, as there seem still to be, many authors no better than mere book-makers. Many men and women of mediocre capacity used to manufacture an annual novel. By dint of repetition and with luck, many of them made some kind of name for themselves, obtained the notice of reviewers, and created some kind of demand, or at least a lack of resistance, among subscribers to the circulating libraries. Some made a living, some pocket-money only. Most of them gave their real or hoped-for public what they thought it wanted or found it would accept. Among them were many purveyors of various grades of what my Brighton landlord called 'mush', but they were often less honest about it than he was, and deluded themselves that their mush was something of value. If mush is to be defined, perhaps it may be called the kind of writing which titillates the least exacting kinds of reader by appealing to the cheaper and shallower emotions — easy lust, sentimentality, or excitability — and by flattering uncultivated understandings, ignorance, prejudice, self-complacency, and accepted ideas. The mush-mongers are as active as ever, and there is no shortage of the titillant reading which in Afrikaans is called *prikkel-lektuur*.

Young men who wish to write are sometimes advised to earn their livings in some way that has nothing whatever to do with writing. They are urged to go out into the world, to travel, and earn their living as they go, and learn about life in spheres unknown to them. If they have had a narrow, conventional upbringing and have not been about at all, this may be good advice. But constant changes of environment and a variety of experience in the first thirty years of my life inclined me now to the world of writers and writing. If a man's bread-winning work is akin to what he regards as the work for which he is best fitted it may keep him in training, broaden his technical knowledge, and develop his command of the medium he works in: Blake got his bread as a hack engraver. I saw no reason to shrink from reviewing, broadcasting, or editing, and having since those days had a good deal to do with these activities I regard them as a useful part of that process of education which for a writer is continuous. A devotee of the written word, and not without critical as well as creative tendencies, I was out to learn as much as I could about it, by reading as well as writing; so when Edward Garnett ceased to act as literary adviser to a conspicuous firm of publishers and I was invited to take his place, I did not immediately recoil in alarm and distaste.

I was acquainted with Edward Garnett, and I remember his showing me some photographs in which he appeared as a young man. They showed his noticeably fine hands, and I remarked on them.

'Oh yes,' he said, with perhaps a touch of natural pride in a good feature, 'those are the family hands.'

They seemed to me the reverse of grasping or ambitious; they showed refinement rather than suggestive initiative; they were shapely, not *shaping*. I think it is true to say that he was a man in whom the critical faculty quite outweighed the creative, but that he had shown himself creatively critical, notably in his friendships with writers of the calibre of Conrad, the fineness of Hudson, and the worthiness of Galsworthy, as well as in the encouragement of lesser talents. The husband of Constance Garnett, whose translations from the Russian—whatever idiosyncrasies they may show —had opened up new worlds of the imagination to readers of English, and the father of David Garnett, he had a distinction of his own.

I did not take the invitation lightly, and accepted it with some diffidence. My critical faculty, though sometimes misused through a want of charity or good sense, had not been disused; I had for some years exercised it publicly in the regular conduct of a page of fiction reviews in the *Spectator*, as well as in occasional literary criticism, private as well as public. To advise an established and eminent firm of publishers how to invest their money, especially in my ignorance of the mechanics and finance of publishing, seemed at least as great a responsibility as advising casual readers of a politico-literary weekly what not to read in their spare time. I knew I had much to learn, and set myself to learn it; and I can honestly say that from the beginning I wrote full and conscientious reports on the material submitted to my judgement. Not on all of it, naturally, nor even on most of it, because most of it was either unsuitable, trivial, or worthless. But wherever there had been a real effort by a would-be author, a real effort was made by this reader to assess it.

When it becomes known that a man is a publisher's reader, his professional services will be in demand by many others besides his employer. Near relations, distant connexions, old friends, new acquaintances, persons who have been recommended to approach him or are even quite unknown to him, and bores of every imaginable and of many a not easily imaginable kind will ask him to read what they have written and give them his advice. They do sometimes say, 'I realise how busy you are, but—' If these supplicants realise that they are picking the brain and soliciting the help of a professional man, they do not always show it, either by offering him a fee, making him a present, or even thanking him for bringing his innate and acquired expertness to bear. He cannot help addressing himself to every single new typescript at least with mild curiosity—which is only a very distant connexion of hope. It is not nothing to find out what a human creature has chosen to commit to paper as his or her response to the opportunity of living and exercising the body, the brain, the heart, and the imagination in this bizarre world. Even if the writer's motives are no stronger or more complex than vanity and a hope of gain, it must be at least of momentary interest to see what kind of utterance these motives have driven him to: it is more likely than not to be an utterance of mush.

As a pearl-diver may be presumed to prise open every dull and commonplace-looking oyster-shell in case it has anything in it of the slightest value, so the reader turns over every title page: it is never impossible that his eyes may be caught by the seed-pearl lustre of a tiny talent. But, as he sits in his study knee-deep among the empty shells of disappointed expectation, it is one of his constant exercises to convey to literary aspirants—and to practised authors as well—news that is unwanted and unpalatable. Civility requires a certain restraint. He has been taken into their confidence, and even if to enter it has proved only a backward step into the inane, he cannot decently tell them that they know what they can do with their typescript. On the contrary, with what he believes to be tact, restraint, patience, and politeness commingled, he will have to convey, ninety-nine times out of a hundred, that his correspondent is an incompetent amateur deluded by vanity and ignorance, whose dull understanding has miscarried, who has been wasting the time of more than one person, and who might be more usefully and indeed more gainfully employed with a spade or scrubbing brush than with a typewriter. His command of evasive euphemism becomes so facile that diplomatists could go to school with him. It is an acquired skill that merits greater rewards than he is ever likely to receive.

There is no great mystery about what kinds of typescripts his adviser will suggest to a publisher are ripe for refusal. They will be those which are hopelessly obscene or libellous; those which are out of keeping with his list; and those which are bad in one of the many ways in which badness is possible—insane, for example, dull, stale, thin, cheap, pretentious, dim, flashy, or mushy. The typescripts which the adviser is likely to commend to the publisher's attention will probably be in one of the following categories:

1 books with literary merit of some kind and with good and immediate commercial prospects;
2 books with literary merit and possible long-term commercial prospects;
3 books with literary merit and no prospects of sales;
4 books of topical interest or importance;
5 books that might have prospects if they were improved, reduced, or expanded.

It is not generally realised, outside publishers' offices, that a great deal has often to be done, before the typewritten word is fit to print, in the way of suggesting or making improvements, and correcting errors of fact, taste, or judgement, as well as of construction, proportion, style, syntax, grammar, or spelling.

I was once asked what I considered the main difference between male and female authors of fiction, biography, and so on. I could only reply that males tend to be too solemn and earnest, females too trivial and unselective. If women sometimes tend to regard everything that happens as of equal significance and to be unable to seize upon or evolve what is summary or symbolic, the seriousness of men can be doughy, doctrinaire, and deadly. Never impressed by undue earnestness, I have often and often been reminded of what Sydney Smith wrote to Bishop Blomfield, 'You must not think me necessarily foolish because I am facetious, nor will I consider you necessarily wise because you are grave.'

In its way, I believe, a varied experience of the typewritten word has been as valuable to me, in learning to understand human nature, as a good deal of the varied experience I have had in contact with living persons. I have certainly learnt something about the weaknesses as well as the virtues of authors and would-be authors, publishers, and publishers' advisers. If there is one conspicuous common attribute of authors it is the same one so much in evidence among human beings generally; I mean vanity. Evidently some degree of self-esteem is necessary if we are to get through life at all, but it does sometimes seem as if the act of darkening paper with rows of words also darkens the writer's ability to regard himself with detachment. The self-importance and touchiness of authors is no longer a surprise to me, nor is their capacity for envy and malice. But even graver, among would-be authors, is a general incompetence. It is disquieting to find how often people have nothing to say, and say it at length and badly.

One might think it the first business of a would-be author to try and reach some approximate assessment of what he is or is not able to do. He has before him frequent bad examples in print of the work of known authors who exhibit the same fault, and he has illustrious examples of all kinds from whom to learn; but the miseries and splendours of others are nothing to the self-absorbed; he will not try and form himself on good models, he will not perceive the dangers of bad ones; and self-doubt, like self-examination, is beyond him. Incompetence and stupidity have no bounds, and the self-absorbed would-be author often shows himself totally indifferent to the inclinations of any kind of reading public, so to whom he supposes he is addressing himself remains totally obscure. Still stranger is his bad presentation of what he is trying to sell. Every publisher knows those typescripts which are third or fourth carbon copies, sometimes done in single spacing with a worn-out typewriter ribbon; those dirty, dog-eared typescripts, fouled with cocoa stains or cigarette ash, which have evidently been hawked about in vain; those long fictions clamped in some formidable binding cover, too heavy to hold with ease, and impossible to open flat; those spring-back covers from which the contents are apt to fly out, with all the élan of a kangaroo, the sheets when recovered proving to be unnumbered; those long productions typed on something like toilet paper and fastened imperfectly with sharp, stiletto-like fangs of brass not only apt but poised to cause a nasty wound. And all this has to be faced before attempting to investigate what is almost certain to prove yet another dreary hotch-potch of cliché, cant, and commonplace.

And what are the little weaknesses of publishers? They are those of the rest of mankind, with some occupational variations. They tend to be either too literary or too commercial. If they are too ready to publish work of some literary merit or potential promise and are at the same time short of experience, capital, flair, and commercial acumen, they may be, as publishers, benefactors of mankind but without staying power. If they are too disdainful of literary merit and too greedy for profit, and have no more than the faculties of businessmen, then they are nothing more than businessmen. Like other people, publishers may be too old-fashioned or too up-to-date: if they are advanced in years, they may fail to realise, like other old men, that the swans of yesterday may be dodos today; if they are young, they may think newness, fashionableness, and topicality of an enduring nature. And it is always interesting to notice that publishers, like other people, have their blind spots and little manias; like other people they reject chances of backing a right horse, and obstinately back wrong ones.

It will not be for a moment supposed that publishers' advisers are immune from all the failings of authors and would-be authors, publishers and might-have-been publishers. Vanity easily gets a hold on them. Long practice in discrimination easily tempts them to think themselves infallible, and the sheer drudgery of a perennial inspection of many varieties of tripe makes them liable to irritability. They too have their prejudices and passions, their blind spots and little manias. They are liable to advise the rejection of typescripts that might have popular success and be money-makers, or success of esteem followed perhaps by durability and influence. Or they may advise the acceptance of typescripts that flatter or appeal to some personal quirk, interest, or enthusiasm of their own.

I have heard that Edward Garnett could not bear, let alone enjoy, the writings of Firbank. Not to perceive their technical innovation, skill, and influence seems to me a blind spot; not to be able to enjoy their wit and fantasy seems to me a sad deprivation. But then I have myself more blind spots than any leopard. I will not betray myself by displaying them in public, but I do not feel (to give a single instance) that there would be a general conscious-ness of a dreadful void in modern literature if there had never been any such writer as — but no, what is the good of flogging a dead dog? What seems to me certain is that the services of a man like Edward Garnett, or of a man like Daniel George in these later times, are so helpful that their little failings must be allowed for. That capricious and amorphous mass, the reading public, has in general little or no conception of the functions of a publisher's reader, and even literary persons are often strangely unaware of the great obligations not only of would-be authors, but of accepted and admired authors, to the careful thought, the patient coaching, and the laborious revisions that occupy much of the nights as well as the days of such men. Of what publishers owe them publishers ought to be the best judges.

The functions of a publisher's reader are far more complex than I have indicated. He has to act as a kind of barometer in relation to the literary weather. For example, any reader during the last forty years will have had something to do with war books. Whether after the first or the second world war, it was necessary to judge not only the merits and originality, but the timeliness of such books. It became sadly clear to those who saw them in an

12*

unpublished state that for many a male inhabitant of this country, service in the armed forces in time of war had provided a one and only personal experience of any significance. This may be taken as an indication of the sobriety and security of English life in general, and also of the stimulating effect upon sober souls of danger, excitement, comradeship, violence, and suffering. But for a man to be driven to some fictional or reminiscent expression of the effect upon him of these stimuli, though it might in some instances result in a noteworthy book, seldom proved that the author of it was thereby equipped to follow it up and become a professional writer. And to the hard-working reader, in the years after the second world war, it must often have seemed that almost every man who had been airborne, or at sea, or in the Eighth Army, or a prisoner of war, had felt impelled to write some sort of book about it.

Part of the publisher's adviser's task is to try and discern at what moment saturation point has been reached in regard to any form of book. And for this it is necessary for him to be *au courant* with changes in habits, taste, and education, and with the effects upon them of economic change and pressure. In the Thirties, for instance, a publisher's reader thought he could recognise pretty easily what would be considered obscene (even though he did not necessarily think it so himself), and he was able to warn the publisher accordingly. But after the second world war, partly owing to a spread of candour under American influence, he could no longer be sure what would or would not be considered obscene. Fiction, in particular, is seen by him to be peculiarly subject to changes of taste. It is said that before the war fiction made up something like 30 per cent of the total of new books published in England, and that today it is less than 20 per cent, while nearly three times as many technical books are published, and nearly twice as many on art and architecture. In the Thirties there were certainly a great many empty souls with leisure, who filled their heads and their time with more or less trivial fiction. Now leisure has diminished, tastes have changed because people have changed and ways of life and thought have changed; novels have changed because the writers of novels have changed; and, also, the high costs of book production now make it far more of a risk for the publisher to issue novels. Right up to the war there was still a considerable concocting of regional and rustic novels. Today there are only vestigial remains of regionalism and rusticity, and England has become more like one large town with standardised habits of life and thought. But to begin discussing what is called 'the novel' is to risk spreading tedium, and this is not the place to do it. My own belief is that, since the novel in the nineteenth and twentieth centuries has been evidently not only one of the highest and most elastic forms of literature, but one of the most valuable means of interpreting social and private life, and one of the most various and splendid forms of entertainment ever evolved, there is no reason to stand around lecturing, or sit around theorising, whether orally or on paper, on the real or imagined decline and supposed future of 'the novel'. So long as fiction is well written by new and resourceful authors, it is likely to find readers.

Although in the Thirties the examination of novels took up a larger part of the time of an adviser to a general publisher than perhaps it does today, it should not be thought that his attention was not given to many other forms of writing—biographies, travel books, criticism, verse, and miscellanea. Not long after I had begun to read typescripts professionally I was asked if I had 'discovered any masterpieces'. Simple, romantic souls imagined that such a process was one of the rewards of this occupation. Luckily I was soon able to tell them that I had had to do with a book that seemed to me of exceptional interest and some importance. It was not a work of fiction.

34
The Curate of Clyro

The word was not always typewritten. Short stories or experi-
mental verse by some girl or boy might arrive in manuscript, a
charwoman's memoirs, or some crazy dotard's demonstration, by
means of numerology or cryptograms, that Bacon was the Dark
Lady of the Sonnets. Also one was exposed to a desultory bom-
bardment of matter written before typewriters were invented,
and preserved by family pride. It was, and still is, a delusion
widely held by persons who ought to know better that antiquity
is in itself a virtue. Those eighteenth-century letters from a
Member of Parliament, that diary of a carriage tour kept by a
young lady who visited the field of Waterloo in the 1820s, may
serve, dear sir or madam, to inflate your over-estimate of your
own forebears, but I do assure you that wigs, flowered waistcoats,
and shoe-buckles were often inseparable from pompous mediocrity, and that bonnet and shawl were no less often the ornaments
of skittish inanity; and, further, that dullness is often hereditary.
Ancestor-worship, when examined, is sometimes found to be an
inflation of nincompoops. To receive one morning from a man
in Dorset a couple of old notebooks which he said were specimens
of his uncle's diary was not in itself therefore to feel pressure on
the trigger of expectation: it was only when I began to read them
that the pressure was perceptible.

What I saw made me send for the rest of the diary. It was
contained in twenty-two notebooks closely written, as if for
economy, in a cramped, angular hand characteristic of the period,
which was the mid-Victorian, and was the work of a country
clergyman who had died before he was forty. Like most diaries it

was largely trivial and of ephemeral significance, but unlike most diaries it was the work of a writer of character and sensibility. I believed that if it were winnowed it might be made into a book of more than ordinary interest and of some importance. I undertook to edit it myself, and the process took up much of my time for three years. *Kilvert's Diary* was published by Jonathan Cape in three volumes during the years 1938, 1939, and 1940, and soon became famous. If it had been published as it stood it would have filled nine stoutish volumes, running to well over a million words. Not one of those words went unweighed by me.

I do not think this unique manuscript could easily have fallen into more interested hands. A strong predilection for autobiography; an association in boyhood with the very part of the Welsh border country where Kilvert had flourished; an interest in the Victorian age; a particular interest in literary country clergymen of that age, men like Hawker of Morwenstow or Charles Turner, the brother of Tennyson; associations, by heredity and early environments, with the Church of England; a liking for landscape; the sense of character of which I am conscious, and the nature of my literary taste—all these things seemed to have prepared me for the task of extracting Kilvert from his diary. Kilvert speaks for himself, and I have done a little to speak for him in the introductions to the three volumes of the diary and elsewhere. Appreciations of him by Dr A. L. Rowse, V. S. Pritchett, and others have appeared in print, and he is by now a known and established minor writer with a place in the history of English literature, so to say much about him here would be to harp on an old string. Pluck it I will, however, to give some inkling of his human, period, and literary significance.

Francis Kilvert (1840–79) believed that life was 'a curious and wonderful thing' and that to be alive was 'a positive luxury': no wonder he wished to record it. The result of his recording it is a detailed picture of country life in the 1870s which is, so far as I know, unmatchable. It is a perfect piece of social history, which confirms what is known from other sources, contradicts what is falsely assumed, and is the work of a rare and graphic artist.

Kilvert had an eye for his surroundings and a command of words to record the shape and colour of what he saw. 'His great virtue,' as Humphry House wrote, 'is the power of conveying the physical quality of everything he describes.' He accepts without question the social stratification and conventions of his time, so he writes naturally of social life. And he writes with a surprising frankness at times about himself. His natural male appetites and expectancy were constrained by his priestly status and sense of responsibility; by a sense of sin; by social decorum; and by his celibate state, which seems to have been protracted by want of money. But if his appetites were repressed or sublimated, they did not disappear. He continued highly susceptible to all feminine beauty, the younger the better. As I wrote in the introduction to the second volume of the *Diary*, Kilvert in his middle thirties was in a state of almost continual bewitchment and emotional upheaval, tended to endow natural phenomena with feminine personalities, and was at least once on the brink of a major indiscretion. He does not hide any of this. Some readers have found his supercharged rhapsodisings over young girls mawkish, and his interest in flagellation morbid; others have praised his candour. At least his feelings may have helped him, as a priest, to understand and perhaps allow for the little weaknesses of others. There was something magnetic about him. An old cousin of his told me he remembered him as 'very sleek and glossy and gentle, rather like a nice Newfoundland dog'. Glossy sleekness, an envelope of well-being, might easily be attractive. Kilvert's nephew told me that he had 'a curious power of attracting', and Kilvert himself alludes to what he calls his 'strange and terrible gift' of exciting love. He eventually married, in his thirty-ninth year, and died suddenly just over a month later. His wife survived him for thirty years. It had been her hope to be buried beside him in Bredwardine churchyard, but she had delayed so long that the remains of two maiden ladies were already installed on either side of him, so she had to lie at a distance—a turn of events which seems made to have been the theme of a poem by Hardy.

While editing the *Diary* I revisited what has now come to be known as the Kilvert country, attaching myself at once to local life by staying at a farm on a hillside above Kilvert's village of Clyro in Radnorshire. As soon as I got there I went out into the fields to help with the work. Every lane and path was identifiable in the *Diary*, which was already known locally. Reviewers had compared Kilvert to Dorothy Wordsworth, to Proust, to Pepys, to Amiel, to Gerard Manley Hopkins, and even to D. H. Lawrence, but round about Clyro persons were still living who could remember him and felt no need of such comparisons. I had seen him in his full-length manuscript diary as he appeared to me; I had seen how he appeared to various readers of the published *Diary*; and now I learnt what sort of fragrance his memory had left round about Clyro. There was Mrs Amey, for instance, who wrote to me from Cusop to tell me how men had waited in her mother's cottage at Bredwardine for Kilvert's return from his honeymoon, and how they took the two black horses out of the shafts and pulled the carriage to the vicarage through the pouring rain. Seventy years later Mrs Amey still cherished a photograph of Kilvert and his wife. They were people worth remembering, she said. She told me of his discretion: 'You could tell him everything and you knew it wouldn't go any further.' And she said that whenever he had a chicken for his dinner he always cut off a good helping before he began, and took this afterwards to some sick parishioner. With such anecdotes this Christian man was remembered and his memory cherished. After seventy years he seemed to be still living. *He being dead, yet speaketh* is the fitting inscription on his grave; his magnetism and his gift of exciting love gave him a kind of immortality, driving him, year after year, to build up by candlelight, phrase by phrase, his own monument. Against his window the colossal country silence pressed — like wadding, but not too thick to shut out the cry of an occasional owl or the sighing hiss of rain. Already the last decades of silence were passing; perhaps the hush was never deeper than then, before the pandemonium set in, of motor traffic, radio, aircraft, and bombs. In that doomed hush he lived and wrote.

One blazing midday, after a bathe in an ice-cold pool under a ferny waterfall, I made my way over rough ground to a house called Whitehall. In Kilvert's day it was in ruin, and he has left a Hardyesque account of it. A house with a past, it had been the scene of rough merrymakings after hard work long ago. Since his day it had been rebuilt and lived in and had again fallen into ruin. Under the vertical sun two owls in the ivy just above my head stared at me with amazement and incredulity. If I had been Kilvert himself — or Dr Gruber — they could not have been more surprised. Not far off were places that meant much to Kilvert and had changed little since his time, Whitty's Mill and Bettws. The unpopulous landscape, which emigrants spurred by enterprise and economic pressure had long been deserting for distant counties and other countries, retained its richness and wildness. A roadman in a lonely lane told me I might not admire this countryside so much if I had to get a living out of it. His world, the world of the lonelier hill-farmers, was no softer than that visioned later in the poetry of R. S. Thomas. It was a world of old ruralities, still a Kilvertian world, where it was possible to encounter a girl carrying home-made perry over the fields to some unmechanised haymakers, to gossip with a voluble blacksmith at his forge, to visit a recluse in a half-ruined house crammed with mouldy books. You can't live on a heath and be vulgar, said Hardy, and those who lived on this heath spoke with meaning and were hospitable to a stranger.

Sweating from one of many long walks, I sat on a bank of heather in the afternoon sun, listening to the seedpods of the gorse bursting open in the heat. Between me and the climbing flowery hills lay the Rhos Goch, a sinister bog where many have been drowned; over there was Llanshifr with its dark past, and Cefyn-y-Blaen, where giants once lived; and there was the road to Newchurch, up which Kilvert, bearded and repressed and dressed in black, used to stride to see his sweet but *maladive* Emmeline; and further off was the beautifully named and remote Michaelchurch-on-Arrow, through which I had just been wandering myself. (So late as 1955 the church there had no lighting, and at the harvest-festival service each member of the congregation brought with him a candlestick with a lighted candle in it—a scene that would have delighted Kilvert.) All very well in the summer, the hinterland of Radnorshire, but a small-holder up in the hills told me he always took a spade to bed with him in the winter; he never knew when he might wake to find his house snowed up and have to dig himself out. Only a couple of winters before, a young married woman with several children, the wife of a farmer away up in the hills, went down on horse-back on Christmas Eve to Hay (just across the Wye from Clyro) to do some Christmas shopping. There was snow on the ground and in the afternoon a wild snow-storm set in. Friends tried to dissuade her from returning home, but off she went. She wanted the children to find their stockings full when they woke in the morning. In the dark blizzard she lost her way, and was found by a search party on Christmas morning, frozen to death, face down in a snowdrift, with the presents for the children clutched in her hand.

The region was still a region, not yet part of a standardised, suburbanised, industrialised England without secrets. Even after the second world war it retained something of its former charac-ter. I remember hearing then of the two old brothers who lived together at the ruined cottage on Cusop Hill, beyond Trevannoc, on the northern slopes of the Black Mountains. They were reclusive and illiterate. One or the other used to come down once a week to Hay to draw their old-age pensions. They signed with a cross. Once, when one of the brothers came down, and somebody asked how the other was, he said, 'I don't know what's the matter with him. He's been lying in bed these last two or three days and when I speak to him he won't answer me.' It was felt that the silent brother might be ill and in need of attention, so somebody went up to investigate. His silence was easily accounted for; he had been dead for some time. The place had fallen into decay when I was last there. Approached by a grass-grown avenue of stunted, wind-bent hawthorns, with rain driving across the lonely moor, it was an old-world image of desolation.

Kilvert was a frequent visitor to Hay, and especially to the

Bevan family at Hay Castle. A more recent and more notorious local figure was more vividly remembered there. Hay had, as they say, 'become news' with the discovery that one of its respected citizens, a professional man who used to read the lessons in church, was a murderer. Through the sham-Gothic machicolations of the Jubilee Clock Tower crouching detectives watched him crossing from his office to the chemist's to buy arsenic 'for dandelions'. His first 'dandelion' was his wife, neatly done away with in their neat villa with its hanging wire baskets of geraniums and its ornamental ironwork painted dead white. A local friend of mine had had a drink with him one evening after he had already attempted to get rid of the second 'dandelion'.

'The trouble is,' he said, confidentially tapping my friend on the knee, while discussing this second victim, 'the man isn't a gentleman.'

It became known later that he had invited this dandelion to tea. 'Excuse fingers!' he had said gaily, as he pressed his guest to a carefully prepared arsenical scone-and-butter.

There is always plenty of scope in such a place for a Kilvert. The trouble is that good diarists are excessively rare.

An interesting consequence of the publication of *Kilvert's Diary* was the proposal to form a Kilvert Society. It came from the late Sid Wright, a merchant of Hereford. He was a man of unmistakable benevolence with a lifelong knowledge of the Border country and a keen interest in both the human and topographical aspects of the *Diary*. I was in favour of the proposal for a number of reasons, and in a lecture at Hereford appealed for support of it. Soon after the publication of the last volume of the *Diary* I had learnt that Kilvert's grave at Bredwardine was in a state of neglect, and had corresponded with his nephew about this. Fortunately a local admirer of the *Diary* had put it in repair, but I felt that a Kilvert Society might assume the responsibility for keeping it in order. Then I had had complaints from readers of the *Diary* who had gone on pilgrimage to Clyro and had searched in vain for some sign of Kilvert's having lived and served the church there. I urged that whether there was to be a Kilvert Society or not, steps should be taken to put up a memorial tablet in the church at Clyro as soon as possible. I suggested that the best way to commemorate Kilvert was to read his *Diary*, and another way was to see that as far as possible the places he loved should be kept unspoilt by unsightly buildings or advertisements, or by invasions of trippers scattering litter. I argued in favour of promoting consciousness of local history and tradition, in both of which Kilvert could now be seen to occupy a significant place, and accordingly in favour of the collection of records and associations concerned with the diarist himself and with relevant persons and places. Naturally there were signs of a want of enthusiasm on the part of dunces, materialists, and sentimentalists. There were snobs or envious commercial rivals, who resented the leading part being played by Sid Wright. Illiterates, so far as they were capable of wonder, wondered what all the fuss was about. And the sentimentalist view had been put as early as 1939 by an amiable contributor to *Country Life*. He was like those persons who would fend off sightseers from Haworth and, if logical, from Stratford-on-Avon too. 'Some of us,' he wrote, 'shudder' to see a charabanc labelled 'The Hardy Country' and so on ...

> We feel there is something of desecration in a three-and-sixpenny tour of these districts. They are precious, almost faery regions, steeped in mystery and rich with treasure, to which, we rightly judge, the 'Open Sesame' costs rather more than three shillings and sixpence.

But even by heading his article 'The Kilvert Country' and dwelling on its 'enchantment' he was drawing attention to his precious, faery region. And why not? So far as I know, nothing but good has come of the Kilvert Society.

The inaugural meeting was held at Hereford in July 1948, and preceded by a mayoral reception. The declared object of the Society was 'to foster an interest in the Rev. Francis Kilvert, his work, his *Diary*, and the countryside he loved'. A delightful coloured film was shown, after my lecture, of scenes in the

Kilvert country, and on the next day a service of commemoration was held at Bredwardine church. The preacher was the Dean of Hereford (the Very Rev. Hedley Burrows), who had shown an early and keen interest in Kilvert, and had laid proper stress on his significance as a priest. The lessons were read by the Vicar of Clyro, the Rev. J. Lloyd, and J. P. L. Thomas, M.P. (now Lord Cilcennin), and before the service the Dean had dedicated in the churchyard a stone memorial seat with an inscription finely carved by Sid Wright, who had been unanimously elected first president of the Society. I wound up the proceedings with an oration in the village hall. In the following year a memorial plaque was duly unveiled in the church at Clyro, and every summer a service of commemoration has been held in one or other of the parishes associated with Kilvert. There have also been organised visits to various places round about, and to Kilvert's other country in Wiltshire. After Sid Wright's death, his widow succeeded him as president, and the Society is blessed with a most energetic and well-informed secretary, C. T. O. Prosser.

I give these few details to show how Kilvert's local fame has been upheld. I cannot believe that he would have been displeased to know that his homes and haunts have become places of pilgrimage, though he might have been surprised, because he seems to have been a modest man little aware of his uniqueness and of his literary power. He is, I suppose, now generally recognised as one of the half-dozen best English diarists, and I am naturally pleased to have had so much to do with him. Perhaps some day some rich foundation may subsidise the publication of the diary *in toto*; it will then be possible to judge my abridgement of it, which I am pleased to say was approved by Kilvert's nephew, the owner of the manuscript. As my selectiveness was exercised with the general reader (that mythical creature) in mind, it would be found that I was not able to do full justice to Kilvert's preoccupation with his priestly functions. But, to judge from the utterances of the late Bishop of Swansea and Brecon and other dignitaries of the Church, I do not believe his repute as a faithful parish priest could be higher than it is.

I recall with pleasure the essay on *Kilvert's Diary* by V. S. Pritchett. He notes the diarist's sincerity, sensibility, and dignity; the acuteness of his eye and ear; his power of writing straight from nature; his lack of self-importance or self-consciousness; his art in conveying the chance effects of life, and his art in rendering tenderness of feeling—'an art which we have lost'. (Perhaps we have learnt to be ashamed of it; 'toughness' has been the common ideal in this century—and look where it has led us!) V. S. Pritchett sums up in these words:

When we contrast the note and rhythm of our lives with those of Kilvert's, we see there is more than a change of fashions between the generations. We perceive with a shock that it is *we* who are unnatural, because we do not live within the walls of a long period of civilization and peace.

35

An Extra Skin

In January 1937 I happened to be living on the ground floor of a house that overlooked the route taken by the funeral procession of King George V. Extract from a letter to my parents:

I was awakened at early dawn by the buzzing of some thousands of people outside the window. It reminded me of the sound of the London crowds that Gissing heard on the Jubilee Day in 1887 – 'the low, unvarying sound that suggested some huge beast purring to itself in stupid contentment'. It certainly didn't suggest mourning, but a mood of expectation. Between nine and one it would have been next to impossible to leave the house even if one had wanted to. Without asking permission, people even stood on my windowsill, so I had to stand on the inner sill to see over the tops of their heads. They smashed a balcony on the next house, and a large slice of it is now hanging by a thread. They smashed branches of trees in the square. And sometimes they went for each other: some women on a sort of grandstand beat off with their umbrellas some late arrivals who tried to climb up to get a view – the sort of thing one might have seen, I suppose, at a public execution a hundred years ago. 'Did you ever!' said Mabel, bringing me some tea. 'They're just like a horde of wild animals.'

Ten thousand people are said to have fainted, but this is no doubt a reporter's estimate, calculated to provoke more exclamations of 'Did you ever!' No doubt a great many more caught colds. It was an unattractive crowd, ugly, dowdy, and abounding in faces that wore stupid, cold, or vacant

expressions. Apart from the people in front or those perched
up high, few can have seen much of the procession. Many of
the people at the back used cardboard periscopes, which
mostly reflected a whole forest of other periscopes. It did not
seem as if they were missing much. The procession was ill-
organized and straggling; there were unaccountable delays,
and dreary detachments of soldiers in khaki lent no splendour
to the occasion. I saw some of the representatives from other
countries chatting animatedly, shrugging their shoulders at
a long hold-up, and exchanging jokes. The crowd chattered
like monkeys the whole time, especially when they recognized personages whose faces they knew from newspapers
and news films. The personages looked like their photographs, but not so clear. When the crowd dispersed, it left
the usual vast excretion of litter.

In the afternoon I went to the Woolves, where I found
Elizabeth Bowen and Iris Origo and Ethel Smyth ... I went
on to Elizabeth's to dinner, and Eliot was there. His gravity
seemed decidedly male in comparison with those excep-
tionally quick-witted women with their shining eyes and
brilliant, rapid utterance (in Iris Origo's case extremely rapid)
outpaced by the quickness of their brains and senses.

There have been times in history when the death of a monarch
has seemed to mark the end of an epoch, but on that day I seem
to have been more impressed by the quick than the dead. I did not
feel as I had felt when I heard of the murder of the Czar, which
really did seem to mark an end. But epochs are not quite like
plays, on which a curtain rises and falls: they overlap, they are
untidy round the edges. Sometimes they are identified with
dictators—'the Napoleonic era', 'the rise of Hitler', and so on.
George V, born in 1865, was a Victorian, and the Victorian age
seemed to be petering out at about the end of 1918. The British
Empire seemed to end with the news of the fall of Singapore; the
Thirties seemed to end with the fall of France in the summer of
1940; the Asia I had known, at Pearl Harbour. Eminent persons

die; prodigious institutions begin to change or decay; cities are destroyed, countries invaded and occupied; but many individuals survive, and the relations between them and the public events of their time, infinitely variable, may be closer than they appear. As these pages are to some extent autobiographical, perhaps I had better look a little into my own relationship to the times about which I am writing. (It will be difficult, but there is the awful example of the elderly writer who said, '*Toute ma vie j'ai raturé, aussi mon œuvre est-elle nulle.*')

On the surface it seemed a distant relationship; underneath it was closer than appeared. I am not a man of action, but a man of reflection. The more developed a man is, says Chekhov, the more he reflects, the more undecided he becomes, and the less inclined to take action. The action that had been taken between 1914 and 1918, the deliberate and elaborate slaughter of man by man, was quite enough to convert a reflective child to inaction for life, even if he had not been naturally inclined that way. Like any other reflective person, I guessed that another world war could not be long delayed. The Spanish Civil War was plainly a rehearsal for it, but I had not therefore felt impelled to learn how to kill other people or how to prevent them killing me. I believed that the springs of action, as Lowes Dickinson once said, lie deep in ignorance and madness. I wished to cultivate my understanding and to be sane. The dangers of such an intention are obvious. They may make a man feel superior, smug, priggish, and fill him with that intellectual vanity which is a form of spiritual pride, with the distasteful self-sufficiency of the rationalist. And they may unfit him for action when action – at least in the judgement of others – seems vital. If, of course, he were wholly detached and wholly pessimistic, he would have no fear of death or other consequences: but who is wholly detached or wholly pessimistic? Not the cultivated, not the sane.

Looking back, I think I had something in common with Axel Heyst, Conrad's leading character in *Victory*. Heyst was nomadic. He was very little interested in worldly success. Early influences had made him aloof and non-attached. It was not weakness of character, or vice, that had made *him* resolve to drift; it was conviction. He saw, or believed he saw, that action was bound to be harmful and to cause suffering to oneself and to others. He thought that by drifting and taking no action he could avoid causing or incurring suffering. But the unarmed man is armed, although he thinks he isn't. Heyst was still armed with disgust, because he retained standards of taste in human behaviour; in other words he was armed with a conscience and a heart.

In my case, weakness and vice may have contributed to a tendency to drift, but with me too to drift had become almost a philosophy, a conviction, a way of life. If only I were Dr Gruber, and if Dr Gruber were a doctor of the psyche as well as of the body, it may be that I could now be more precise about the state in which I then found myself. Some glandular imbalance, some chemical excess or deficiency in the blood, some deep lesion in the unconscious, might be retrospectively diagnosed by him. All I can do is to impersonate him, and with amateurish tests, palpations, and analyses try and discover the workings, and perhaps the disorders, of a discarded, earlier self.

I did not for a time believe in free will. I think it probable that Far Eastern influence in early manhood had contributed to my fatalism, or determinism. I simply could not understand how human beings, who have no choice in regard to entering this world, could be so arrogant as to suppose that, having entered it, they immediately or even gradually gain the power to choose how they shall or shall not act. 'But if I come to a fork in the road,' one of them might have said, 'I can take the left turning or the right, or neither, or stay where I am, or turn back.'

To which I would have replied, 'Whatever you do will be in accordance with your character, which is predetermined by causes either inside or outside yourself.' Evidently to hold such a belief would not stop a man drifting, but it would not necessarily make him inactive: whatever happened, or failed to happen, his behaviour would be in character. A man of action would be such because it was his nature: a reflective man might be driven to action—as Heyst was—and perhaps too late.

The menace of public catastrophe seemed too great to imagine. When it came it would, I supposed, destroy much in civilisation that had not been easily won; and it would destroy human beings who had not been easily evolved and could not be replaced; and it was bound to weaken liberal and humane ideas and ways of life. Tidal waves of cant and propaganda, greater even than in the first world war, could be expected. They would swamp whole nations with self-delusion and drive them to mutual destruction. It would not have been senseless to regard the prospect with despair; it was easy to regard it with a kind of resigned disillusionment, more especially during phases of grave private trouble— as when, for example, one of the persons I have loved best, with one of the most balanced and compassionate understandings, twice, from altruistic motives, made unsuccessful attempts to commit suicide.

Nothing can be more commonplace than the process by which hopeful, youthful, or romantic sentiment gives way to resignation, scepticism, or cynicism. It is almost a physical process, like growing up. But I do not wish to give the impression of drifting along in a state of fatalistic gloom. I am a person of considerable energy and powers of enjoyment, and they had not gone into abeyance. I was not without hope, and had not lost the ability to be amused. But I found my amusement sometimes taking an unforeseen course.

In common with millions of others, I have lived through an apocalyptic half-century. It would be tedious to make a list of the happenings and inventions that have made it so, but it hardly seems an exaggeration to say that the world has changed more in the lifetime of my coevals than in any other previous historical period. Political or religious revolutions are nothing new; inventions like printing and photography altered the workings of the human mind and the manner of human life; but the revolutions and inventions of our time appear to have set loose new forces which have greater power for evil as well as good than any previously imagined. Also, though the idea of 'total' war is ancient and primitive and was the rule with savage tribes, it has been given a completely new scope by the savage tribes of the northern hemisphere (including ourselves) whom we were brought up to take pride in as the makers and spreaders of civilisation. Add to these considerations the effect of quick communications, and the instantaneous and universal dissemination of cant and propaganda, together with the mechanising and standardising of life; and the effect of the ideas of Marx, Freud, Pavlov, and others; and it must follow that human nature (which, we were once taught, 'doesn't alter') is altering.

It seems probable that in the present century the nature of Western man may have been undergoing an ever spreading and accelerating process of change. With its astonishing resilience and adaptability mankind has unconsciously been trying to adapt itself to the new strains and stresses — physical and mental — which its own activities have brought into being. And among the manifestations of this process of readaptation are the prevalence of materialistic principles and practice, whether under Marxism or capitalism; a decline in individuality; and the erection of 'toughness' (always, in some degree, a necessity) into an ideal. Perhaps we are to expect a gradual atrophy of the capacity of Western man to be touched, to be moved to sympathy or pity or happiness, or even to love, in the way that many people used to be unashamedly touched or moved in former times. If that is so, it is worth looking for signs of the process in the individual, and considering whether it should be counteracted, and if so, by what means.

An inflammable sensibility may or may not be an advantage. Apathy or callousness can only be enemies of civilisation. But between the man of feeling and the man of no feeling there is a far more numerous species — the man of middling feeling. Forced to find some defence or anaesthetic against the violent complexity and complex violence of the world in which he finds himself, he may have grown, without knowing it, an extra skin. If in fact such a change has come over mankind in the past half-century, perhaps one might try and trace it in an individual. The difficulty would be to distinguish between the usual hardening process of experience and maturity, and the hardening process of adaptation to the peculiar experience of living in the twentieth century. If I am to try and trace the distinction in myself I can attempt to do it in terms of poetry.

I am not a prolific poet, but since I began to write I have never found prose the only possible medium. To be longed for are the clarity, order, and moderation of prose; but they are not enough. Poetry seeks to attain a clarity of a different kind; it makes an order of its own, and does not make it out of moderation, but out of intensity, complexity, and seemingly indefinable sensations. They seem indefinable because they require unforeseen arrangements of words. These sensations make the poet acutely conscious both of his alienation from the rest of mankind and of his membership of mankind. Poetry is an attempt to fuse together the sense of difference and the sense of sameness. The greater the sense of difference, the less familiar and generally acceptable his mode of expression is likely to be, and the more acute his consciousness of himself as a poet. The greater the sense of sameness, the nearer will be his mode of expression to what is used or easily grasped by his actual or hoped-for readers.

I see myself, in regard to poetry, as a lone prospector, engaged in an intermittent but lifelong exploration of a particular territory, where drought prevails, vegetation is generally sparse, ghosts abound, and cataclysms occur, yet where there are paradisal places, offering more than promises of joy and peace. In the earliest stages of prospecting, my discoveries were slight and fragmentary. I found stones that resembled what others had found, or handfuls of dust and rubble in which, now and then, there was the gleam of something hopeful and unusual. Sometimes, with out-of-date equipment, I opened up a worked-out seam, believing that it was not worked out. Sometimes my gain was a handful of semi-precious stones, which came in for the admiration of others, but were not much in demand. Then there came a time, in a borderland country which had never been properly mapped, when I was able to stake out a claim to an area in which I found a particular interest. I had long had my eye on it, but now I began to work away in it, and found more than I had bargained for. There is something to be said for a mine of one's own, even if it is not very productive, and even if it does not produce quite the metal one might have expected.

I had from the first a tendency to write poetry in which a response to character, in its associations of time and place, led to occasional celebrations of it in ballad-like form, not untinged with irony. In the mid-Thirties I found this tendency becoming stronger. In a volume called *Visiting the Caves*, for example, published in 1936, there is a piece called 'Murder on the Downs'. When confronted with this, as soon as it had been completed, I felt a mingled surprise and uneasiness, as if I were being impersonated. Somebody else seemed to have written it, not the self with which I thought myself acquainted. Was I perhaps Doctor Gruber? And was Doctor Gruber perhaps a poet?

The poem is about an erotic murder committed in daylight in fine weather, on the Sussex Downs. So far as I know, the crime, its perpetrator, and its victim are wholly imaginary. The mild, familiar aspect of the country is noted in strictly and even scornfully anti-Romantic terms. There is a non-religious note as well, inserted apparently to emphasise the absolute estrangement of these two persons from the traditional beliefs and values of their environment. There is also a fatalistic note: the victim of the crime, in her last words, declares, quite unprotestingly, that it is what she expected; and there is no room for doubt that such an end is what she half invited and half desired. The whole happening is treated with a light, mocking touch as if it was quite as ridiculous as horrible or tragic.

The process by which a poem is evolved may be slow, complex, and obscure, but I think I recognise in this ballad a hardening of sensibility that had set in unconsciously. And I think it was the recognition of it that had given me a shock. Perhaps in looking back I am reading too much into it, but the mood of the murderer and his victim seems to me the prevailing mood of the period. Compulsive violence unchecked by religious scruples or humaneness was matched with compulsive, unreasoning surrender: there was no effort to avert what seemed invited, desired, and inevitable.

What I do not quite understand is the psychological signifi-cance of the mocking tone. Is it a mark of resignation and passiveness? I do not think so. I see it as a mark of defensive adaptation to a world in which too tender a sensibility would be either useless, or a handicap, or a danger—or all three. A few years earlier it would, I believe, have been impossible for me to dwell upon, or perhaps even to perceive, and certainly to be witty about, any aspect of the murder of Mrs Fernandez. And as for the subject-matter, I have no morbid interest in crimes of violence; I have no more interest in crime than anybody else whose curiosity about human behaviour is excited by newspaper reports. But it is a truism that poetry can reflect coming events—and the most momentous coming events were acts of violence.

During the next few years I published a number of ballads, or ballad-like poems which, when they appeared in book form, I described as satires. In a prefatory note I said:

> These satires are concerned with points in human experience at which the terrifying coincides with the absurd, the monstrous with the commonplace. Such points are perhaps commoner in our time than usual, for we have seen horror and absurdity on an enormous scale.

One of them, for example, describes playfully an innocent war-time gathering in a vegetarian guest-house. The party is broken up by blast from a flying bomb, which flings among them a singed fragment of a dismembered horse. The bitter humour of the incongruous is softened by playfulness. Other poems in the same batch throw details of private behaviour similarly into high relief against backgrounds of doom and actual or impending disaster. When these, together with some later and less ominous pieces, were collected into one volume for publication in America, I gave it the title *Borderline Ballads*, explaining that I was naturally drawn to a region near the indefinable frontiers between serious-ness and irony, between the tragic and the vulgar, between mockery and sympathy, and between the past and the present. I have once or twice been reproached with 'cruelty' and a choice of sordid themes. No defence seems necessary. The themes brought themselves forward. In so far as they are what used to be called 'unpleasant' they reflect an age for which unpleasant would be a very mild term. And what seemed cruelty in the treatment of these themes can only have been evidence of that hardening process to which I have alluded. Call it detachment, call it objectiveness, call it the growing of an extra skin, but do not call it cruelty. That would imply a wish to give pain, or a pleasure in giving pain, where no more is being done than to offer instances of how men and women behave, or might easily behave, in or near our own lifetime.

A sense of the past has prevented me from limiting the subject-matter of these ballads to contemporary characters. As Conrad said, today is a scramble, tomorrow may never come, and it is the precious yesterday that can never be taken from us. I have from time to time been so kindled by some episode told in an out-of-date book of memoirs, it has so exactly caught the atmosphere of a period, the uniqueness of a situation, and the quiddity of one or more persons that I have isolated it for enjoyment. And a wish to communicate and enlarge enjoyment has been part of the motive that has, soon or late, transmuted it into a ballad. The memoirs of Tom Trollope, brother of the novelist, those of Mrs Hwfa Williams, and the exceedingly dull ones of the Hon. Lionel A. Tollemache are among those which have stimulated me in this way. The ballads have been written to be declaimed or, where more than one person is made articulate, to be performed. Intended as entertainments, they have been received with every appearance of attentiveness and amusement—but not without uneasiness. They are by-products of an uneasy time.

A final instance is a ballad called 'The Self-Made Blonde'. An unaccountable mating of two main and separate emotions set going the impulse of composition. One was caused by a detailed account of the consequences to dwellings and their inhabitants of the bursting of a huge dam; the other by an oral description of a deaf and dumb prostitute, combined with a memory of personal acquaintance with a deaf-mute. The peculiar chemistry of ballad-making, working upon these conjoined elements, brought into being what seems to me a sensual and macabre fable of love, or at least of erotic satisfaction, destroyed by *force majeure*. 'The worse taste your ballads are in,' said an old friend, a woman, on hearing this one, 'the better they are.' I took that as a compliment. I have not wished, in writing poetry, to see words and images cool or rot in some petrifying or putrefying atmosphere of so-called 'good taste'.

36

Incorrigible Barbarism

Mrs Hagworthy, in Osbert Sitwell's *Miracle on Sinai* (1933), gave it as her husband's opinion that 'before a war we should do all we can, while fully prepared for it, to prevent it: and that when it becomes inevitable – which, under these circumstances, it always does in time – we should be the first to enter, and should prosecute it with the utmost violence'. But in the opinion of Father Munnion, a character in the same book, 'It isn't war: it wasn't war! It's something quite different. It shouldn't be called *war* any longer ... It's more like an earthquake ... something with which no individual or group of individuals can grapple.'

Anyone who happens to have read elsewhere of what I called my innate pacifism may wonder how – if it was innate, and if it was pacifism – this individual was preparing to grapple with an earthquake. The same question was put by a neat-looking woman in a coat and skirt who rang my front door bell in London in the autumn of 1938.

'Good morning,' she said pleasantly, raising a notebook in a kind of salute. 'I'm from the Town Hall. I want to inquire what you will be doing in the event of an emergency.'

In the event of an emergency! Could anything be more English than this memorable phrase? Did the Town Hall hold classes of instruction in the use of litotes? My first reaction (no less English) was naturally to say 'What sauce! Why don't you and the Town Hall mind your own business?' But in fact I said, 'Do you mean when the war begins?'

She winced at such bluntness.

'If this is a Gallup poll,' I said, 'you had better put down that I don't know.'

She murmured something about organising evacuation, a word which had hitherto suggested castor oil, and as this did not seem a desideratum, I politely wished her a good day.

In the event of an emergency! What had given rise to such a phrase? Refinement? Wishful thinking? Hypocrisy? War was now a certainty. Was she, or was the Town Hall, accustomed to refer to the Emergency of 1914–18, the Boer Emergency, the Hundred Years' Emergency, the Second Punic Emergency, or the Emergency of Jenkins' Ear? Cry havoc, and let loose the dogs of emergency!

How was one to 'grapple'? There was reason to suppose that the impending 'total' war would be catastrophic. There was no reason to be ashamed of feelings of disgust, disappointment, and depression. One might easily have said of the war what Gosse said to Gide about the publication of his *Corydon*, 'Is it wise? Is it useful? Is it necessary?' But if it was not to be called *war* any longer, what likelihood was there of any prospect of a later condition describable as *peace*? I had no firm belief in non-resistance as a principle, and at the same time felt no urge to fit myself for any precise part in what seemed as incalculable as an earthquake. But the possibility that the life of Europe might be dominated by an odious paranoiac like Hitler was clearly not compatible with civilisation, and against such a possibility disapproval would not by itself be much of a defence.

To disclaim any concern with the war would have been ridiculous; to renounce involvement in it would have been impossible. Not even Axel Heyst would have been able to do that, nor would he have wanted to. The war was expected to be total. Apart, therefore, from any question of defence against attack, it was plain that everybody was in danger. It is a commonplace that danger can bring people together, and although it may be only the herd instinct that arouses a sense of solidarity, I found myself, as the danger approached, looking at those who are called ordinary people with new eyes. Often in the Thirties it had been easy to feel a dislike for the vulgarity which is 'the behaviour of other people' and for their foolishness or unseemliness. But now their humanness seemed to shine even out of ugly, cramped, mean, debased urban types. It was not their unattractiveness that was conspicuous now, but their vitality, innocence, and vulnerability. It was possible to see, as if in a light of revelation, what is meant by the saying that we are all members of one another. A protective feeling arose, a wish to help spare 'ordinary people' from the consequences of their own impercipience.

It was all very well for Flaubert to complain, as he understandably did in 1870, of the incorrigible barbarism of the human race and of the mystical element in war that enraptures the mob. But in 1939 it was as difficult to feel superior to the mass of mankind as it was impossible to remain aloof from it. And it would have been a great mistake to suppose that it was only men of reflection who were disgusted by the prospect and the event: I read lately that in October 1940 Lord Alanbrooke had written in his diary, 'There are times when the madness and the fallacy of war almost choke one.' They did choke many.

This reminded me that as a child I was troubled by the paradox that professional soldiers, though trained to kill their own species, did not seem at all like murderers. Officers of the old regular pre-1914 army, whom I had encountered because they were relations, or were acquaintances of my family or their friends, had often seemed (as some survivors still seem) amiable and balanced beings. Personable, alert, athletic, and moulded by tradition and discipline, they had excellent manners, unforced kindliness, and often a sort of boyish zest. They seemed to enjoy life and to be considerate of others. Some, the most obviously modest, had proved themselves brave. They compared more than favourably with many civilian types who had enjoyed freedom without responsibility, and whose weaknesses were not hidden from a child—self-importance, for example, cockiness, pompousness, sloppiness, mean-mindedness. Conventional, yet genial, they tended to match the image of Uncle Durham. One liked and respected them, and without effort some of them might easily inspire, or had inspired, devotion. How was it, then, that their business was to slaughter their kind? Why did they seem more warm-hearted, courageous, and admirable than many civilians with, presumably, more idealistic principles? The paradox did not resolve itself. And as I grew older it was seen in relation to the paradoxical nature of Christianity.

The folly, and the economic folly, of war have never been more unanswerably commented upon than by two old countrymen in Devonshire during the first world war. What they said was recorded by Cecil Torr in his well-written *Small Talk at Wreyland*. 'What be the sense of their contendin'?' said the first. 'Why, us in Lustleigh don't wage war on they in Bovey, and wherefore should the nations fight?' The other man said, 'It be a terrible thing, this war: proper terrible it be. I never knowed bacon such a price.' One of them was offended in his reasonableness, the other in his pocket: but Flaubert's reference to the incorrigible barbarism of the human race suggests a concern with something more than folly; it is more like a willingness to admit something like the doctrine of original sin. He seems to imply the need of redemption.

Rationalists, philosophical anarchists, and other idealists sometimes argue, or seem to assume, that man is naturally good but is corrupted by his own institutions, by tyrants, governments, bureaucracies, priestcraft, vested interests, property-owners, and so on; and that he can put things right if he will only use his head and be unselfish. That man is corruptible is obvious; they imply that he is self-corrupting, and that he needs saving from himself, from the horrible conditions into which he continually gets himself and his fellow-creatures. But to expect his own good sense or goodwill to save him is fanciful. An occasional or fortuitous altruism, a well-intentioned inclination to mind other people's business, may be survivals of religion; they are not an adequate substitute for it. Where is man to look for hope except in faith in some power greater and less earthbound than himself? But if he looks to Christianity to deliver him from the madness and incorrigible barbarism of war the prospect does not seem good.

The paradox of Christianity is that while appearing to advocate peace it is militant, and often militarist as well. During the first world war it was a shock to many simple people, who had been taught that Christ was the Prince of Peace, and that we were to forgive those that trespass against us, and that peacemakers were blessed, to see, for example, priests publicly blessing instruments of destruction. Arguments are adduced to prove that Christ was not on the side of peace. The Thirty-Seventh Article laid down that it was lawful for Christian men to 'serve in the wars'. A good Christian, it is explained, cannot be a pacifist, because it is his duty to fight against evil. But men do not seem to be reliable judges of good and evil: the help of the same God is invoked by opposed nations, each believing that it has right on its side against a wicked enemy. Christians who might hesitate to join in a direct, calculated, warlike attack upon some other nation or faction than their own would still conceive that they had the right to join in the defence of their own nation or faction, and of their lives, families, and property. Not to defend oneself would be to lay oneself and one's children open to oppression, slavery, or extermination. But here paradox comes in again. If a Christian's hopes are properly fixed upon a future life beyond the grave, he ought not to shrink from suffering and martyrdom on this side of it. But such an attitude requires a degree of saintliness that would seem absurd to most men, and is far beyond their reach. Finding themselves attacked, or believing themselves in danger of attack, they naturally set about defending themselves, determined to maintain their own being or at least their property and 'way of life' for their own offspring or successors. Regardless of Lustleigh's reasons for aggression, Bovey springs to the defence: blood flows, and up goes the price of bacon. Paradox again arises in the act of defence: there is no exact division between defence and attack, and attack may be the best form of defence. Directly armed conflict begins (and often without it) the way is open for incorrigible barbarism.

There is nothing new, I repeat, in the *idea* of total warfare. Such warfare was habitual with savage tribes who did not exclude non-combatants, the weak, the helpless, the young, and the old from their ferocity. Only the *methods* of Auschwitz and Hiroshima are new. Scientific ingenuity diabolically applied, monstrous extravagance, and wastefulness have made what was always cruel and unreasonable suicidal. Some years ago, two fine stags were found drowned in the lake in Arundel Park. They had been fighting, had become inextricably locked together by the antlers, and had fallen together, exhausted and inseparable, into the water. Their mutual murder was in fact a double suicide: each probably thought it was rightly defending its way of life; both perhaps invoked the help of the same antlered god against a wicked enemy.

Religion, it might be thought, is chiefly concerned with the private soul and its relationship with God, but it has been and often is constituted as something more like a claim upon God for the predominance of a particular race or nation. This is less unreasonable than it may seem. The soul can only attempt to commune with God by maintaining its own life and character; the nation fears that without Divine help it may lose its own life and character, and this fear is kept alive both by those whose political or economic power depends on its maintenance and by those whose spiritual power is derived from faith, or professed faith, and enabled by authority to function. But as history shows that religions which claim universal validity are open to abuses that may lead to corruption, injustice, and oppression, it is hardly surprising that nationalistic religions lead to similar abuses, and attempt similar justifications.

The less admirable consequences of accompaniments of Shintoism in Japan, for example, of Greek Orthodoxy in Cyprus, or of the Dutch Reformed Church in South Africa, are plain, but it would be indecent to condemn them without inquiry whether the Church of England is above reproach. From a national tradition a Church may derive its character and its strength to continue in existence, but whenever it allows itself to defer to a narrow and exclusive racialism or nationalism, or to support violence or falsehood, or oppression, or militarism, or persecution, in the name of justice or patriotism, or of law and order, it is bound to weaken the confidence of others in its claims, or even to destroy that confidence. All human institutions are open to abuses, but one does not therefore give up one's attachment to them or belief in them. When they are constituted for the service of God, it is even more important to hold fast to what is best in them. The beauty of the Church of England is partly in its Englishness—as that of Shintoism is in its Japaneseness, or of Orthodoxy in its Greekness, or of the Reformed Church in its South African Dutchness—but the greater beauties of these and other cults are not divided from one another by racial or national barriers; they belong to that exalted sphere where local virtue is a part of universal life and truth, or contributes to them.

If in fact man needs to look to some greater power than himself to sustain him and deliver him from evil, he must not expect to be able to rely solely upon ideas that seem to him reasonable. In one of Landor's *Imaginary Conversations* the view is expressed that 'religions keep and are relished in proportion as they are salted with absurdity', and that 'all of them must have one great crystal of it for the centre'. The elements of Christian doctrine—the Incarnation, for instance, the Resurrection, and the Ascension— must seem absurd to a rationalist, and may seem so to a moralist. There is an interesting passage in a letter written by Conrad (a moralist, if ever there was one) to Edward Garnett in February 1914. He was ready to concede that Christianity was great and compassionate, and that it could be improving and softening, but he was irritated by its having arisen from what he called an 'absurd oriental fable'. It is questionable whether human beings are to be trusted as judges of what is or is not absurd. (An un- commonly strong impression was made upon me in the Thirties by a film of the documentary variety, which showed what are called ordinary people going about on an ordinary day, and had been taken without their knowing: the self-importance, purpose- fulness, lack of purpose, and incidental antics of the man or woman in the street, or the house, were absurdity's own self.) If Conrad meant the word 'oriental' to be understood in a pejorative sense, that was absurd of him. And the same is true of the word 'fable', since some of the profoundest utterances of humanity are in the form of fables. But when he went on to say that Christianity had very easily lent itself to 'cruel distortion', that it had 'impossible standards', and had brought 'an infinity of anguish to innumerable souls — on this earth', he cannot be refuted.

If Christianity is to be believed in, it cannot rely on its rationality or much of its record. Christianity is an aspiration. It can be believed as a poem can be believed, because of its language and imagery, and for what they offer, promise, and suggest. They offer hope, a view of life, and a way of life; they promise a compensation for evil and for suffering; they suggest what humanity is sometimes capable of. That it has given scope to weakness and wickedness is not the fault of Christianity but of those who have professed it. Not only is it used by evil as a pretext and a mask, but by mediocrity as a refuge. The Sacraments are effectual, says the Twenty-Sixth Article, 'although they be ministered by evil men': it might have added 'or ineffectual men'. But those who speak of 'empty churches' have seldom looked inside to see how full the churches are, and where churches are not full it is they themselves who have left places vacant.

'In my view,' wrote Canon Vidler of King's College, Cambridge, in a letter to *The Times* in May 1957, 'both the clergy and the laity of the Church of England are, with rare exceptions, monstrously conventional and depressingly docile.' Exactly: it is easier to conform to a set of rules than to transcend them creatively. It is less disturbing to fall in with accepted, current, and prevalent social and political ideas and habits and to pretend that they are not in conflict with the basic tenets of Christianity, than to point out that they are (which is usually true) and act accordingly. Initiative is always dangerous; dogma and discipline can always be made an excuse for shirking or condemning it. But dogma and discipline are not the chief glories of the Church of England.

To claim that the Church of England is the only admissible form of Christianity would be as narrow as to deny the merits of other than Christian forms of religion. But it is a cult with a peculiar appropriateness to a civilised disposition. There is wisdom and beauty in its function as a *via media* between sectarianism and authoritarian rigidity and pretension. Among its peculiar dangers are the monotonous conventionality and depressing docility singled out by Dr Vidler. It is also, by its very tradition, in danger of conforming too narrowly to nationalist, and even militarist, forms and tendencies. And with what are those impossible standards of which Conrad spoke to be identified if not with puritanical disregard of man's physical needs and appetites? It is just as much a fault of Catholicism as of Protestantism to turn the sense of joy to a sense of guilt, and unless Christianity can teach that cruelty is more obscene than sexuality, and that the idea of praise is more fruitful than the idea of sin, it will not deserve the support it ought to deserve.

A writer, an English writer, may exist snugly enough in the shelter of agnostic indifference, or drift easily along on the dirty current of materialism, preening himself from time to time on his superior wisdom. But if he has any sense of the literature which he pretends to be enlarging, or of the rich variety of literary character, genius, and talent associated with the Church of England since the Reformation, let him ask himself whether, if he were to disregard it or its influence upon himself, he might not be risking literary as well as moral bankruptcy. A Church which has been found worth the support and adherence of Donne and Eliot, of Jeremy Taylor and Sydney Smith, of Robert Herrick and John Betjeman, is not to be written off as an outmoded fantasy because today it does not command, any more than before, the support of youthful rebels, worldly wise busybodies, or fashionable entertainers.

It was the wise opinion of Jeremy Taylor that 'musick was brought into Churches, and ornaments, and perfumes, and comely garments, and solemnities, and decent ceremonies, that the busie and less discerning fancy being bribed with its proper objects may be instrumental to a more coelestial and spiritual love'. But whether services be traditionally adorned or evangelically plain, they cannot always be attended even by those who would wish to attend them. The exercise and expansion of Anglicanism in the nineteenth century may be variously accounted

13*

for; they could not have occurred unless the educated classes had had the leisure allowed by their ability to employ cheap labour in their homes. Today, when so many of their descendants look after themselves and find it a whole-time occupation, to go regularly to church, or to go at all, has become scarcely possible. To look after themselves and their habitations and their children does not easily allow them to look after their souls. The proper exercise of religion is thought to require communal worship and private prayer. It also requires faith of some kind – which is often lacking – and a degree of determination and persistence which are more likely to be attainable by the old and retired than the young and active.

In these conditions, it seems a pity that the habit of prayer is not more often and far more intelligently made acceptable to the young, so that when they are grown up they can heal and strengthen themselves and others by this exercise. Reason alone is too fallible. 'A boxe of Quicksilver,' said Jeremy Taylor. 'It looks to me otherwise than to you who doe not stand in the same light that I doe.' It is difficult to see how, unless prayer is added to meditation, an adequate power of self-criticism can be developed. Reason can always be used to try and justify selfishness, envy, self-pity, revengefulness, violence, war, and the opposites of what St Paul called 'love, joy, peace, long-suffering, gentleness, goodness, faith, meekness, temperance'. So can Christianity; but prayer can even show ways to overcome or avoid the abuses of religion and the harm done by the do-gooder as well as by the do-harmer. The only defence against the incorrigible barbarism of the human race (which lurks, is rampant, or is liable at any moment to reappear in the human heart) is to attack it. Reason is a powerful means of attack, but it did not prevent the first world war; nor was it able to prevent, even after such unthinkable horror, the second. Nor was religion. Neither was active enough, nor was there any proper liaison between them.

The road to hell may be paved with good intentions, but there are many worse pavements; and one need not be ashamed to be a product of a tradition of well-meaning. Where my own behaviour seems (though I can hardly judge it) to have been perhaps not wholly reprehensible, and where I have felt any strength to deal with difficulties, I have often felt indebted to my forebears. In the last couple of centuries they have often shown Whig, or liberal, or humane, or evangelical tendencies; the Church of England gave them form, method, and guidance; and who am I to condemn either the tendencies or the institution? What was good enough for our predecessors can never be good enough for us, because we live in different conditions and are different people. It is, or should be, part of the strength and wisdom of the English tradition, and of Anglicanism, that it can enlarge and adapt itself to changing circumstances. Otherwise the pleasure of being English would soon be only a memory.

37
His Light Still Burning

During the war I spent five-and-a-half years doing what I was thought fitted to do in that state to which it had pleased the Admiralty to call me. My situation was as characteristically anomalous as some of those earlier ones I have indicated in this book. In plain clothes among uniforms, a harmless drudge among men of action, I was politely designated as a contradiction in terms, a 'civilian officer' on the Naval Staff. As a fish out of water, I was in my element. Allergic to seafaring ever since those childhood voyages back and forth between Southampton and the Cape, I detested the confinement, the motion, and the very smell of all ships. Fortunately those departments of the Admiralty in which I was confined were not afloat; they might sometimes have been pleasanter if they had been. The early attacks from the air were noticeable enough for a naval officer to be heard saying playfully to another, 'What! Going to sea, are you? So you're showing the white feather!'

London suffered much less than a number of other European cities, and I will keep my bomb stories to myself, except to say that I made the acquaintance of more than one 'near miss' — which term I translated, for the benefit of a Free French acquaintance, as *demi-vierge*. During the war years the senseless noise at night and the senseless destruction, the tedium of suspense and the repulsiveness of the news were made up for by being often in agreeable company and making new friends and acquaintances. In the later stages of the war, and as a result of it, I was ill with a hyperthyroid condition. The symptoms were disquieting. With the fine frenzy of an exophthalmic gleam intensifying behind the spectacles, a pronounced tremor, and disordered skin, digestion, and blood pressure, I was chiefly conscious of the workings of the heart, which felt and sounded like the engine of a motor bicycle. I felt myself rapidly receding from the vale of health. I was no longer, as they say, myself. Nor was I Dr Gruber, who would have taken steps to prevent the onset of such an affliction.

Life became distorted. Reactions to small stimuli were disproportionate. A sudden noise would produce an uncontrollable fit of trembling. A cup of coffee or a few pages of Balzac shook me to the roots of my being and seemed to fill the brain with blue sparks. Acutely pleasurable excitement alternated with its opposite, and a natural irritability began to verge upon mania, as if the body itself had developed a neurosis, from which the mind was not nearly as detached as it was accustomed to be. All this was disturbing to me, and must have taxed the forbearance of those who were either near or dear to me, or both. Harley Street insisted upon rest, but a sense of obligation was against it. After all (I was still able to reason), if at such a time everybody with a disordered metabolism took to bed, it would never do. I knew other people who had not allowed graver illness to stop them from doing what they had set themselves to do. I was not wounded or mutilated, or in any but a figurative sense a prisoner of war, so who was I to abdicate? Good advice, good medicine, a good constitution, and luck united to display the team spirit, and gradually pulled me back from the troubled sphere into which I had felt myself inexorably drawn.

The atmosphere in November 1918 had been exultant; at the end of the second world war the temper of London seemed to be one of guarded relief. Furnished by naval authority with unsolicited testimonials, I found myself again living in Bayswater, a quarter on which I thought myself something of an authority. I could have pointed out the Red House, designed in 1874 by J. J. Stevenson, a friend of William Morris, and regarded by historians of architecture as a pioneer act in the revolt against the mid-Victorian conventions of house-building; or the smallest house in London, which filled an interstice next to the Tyburn

Convent, and of which the upper room measured thirty feet by
four; or Nos. 23 and 24 Leinster Terrace, houses which were
nothing more than façades masking an exposed section of the
Metropolitan Railway.

I had already lived long enough to be well aware of change.
The typical Bayswater house dated from the eighteen-fifties or
eighteen-sixties. It formed one of a row of identical houses all
joined together and designed by a speculative builder for the
occupation of well-to-do families of the commercial, professional, or leisured classes. It consisted of a basement with a
railed-in area, a ground floor, and four storeys above that. The
front door was approached by two or three steps and over-
shadowed by a portico which supported a balustraded balcony.
On the first floor there was a big double drawing-room with an
imposing chimney-piece of Italian marble, a decorated plaster
ceiling, and french windows opening on to the balcony. The top
floor consisted of attics originally intended as servants' bedrooms.
The house was heated by open coal fires and lighted by gas, and
the architects apparently took for granted the continuance, 'far as
human eye could see' (never very far), of a standard of living
immune to social, economic, and domestic changes of any
magnitude. Not many years after the quarter was at its apogee it
became necessary to adapt or convert many of the houses to
modes of living much less lavish than that of the large and well-
endowed mid-Victorian family with its abundance of cheap coal,
cheap servants, and elaborate meals.

In 1927 a topographer had written that 'the large houses of
Bayswater have gone out of fashion as the homes of the wealthy
classes and have been converted into maisonettes and private
hotels'. Long before that, many of them had been turned into
flats or boarding-houses or apartment houses, or had lapsed into
tenements or rookeries. While in 1870 Lancaster Gate was stylish
enough for Cora Pearl to be kept in, and in 1906 was still stylish
enough for Mrs Craigie to die in, the periphery of Bayswater,
never smart, soon turned shabby or slummy. Even in the eighteen-
eighties, streets and houses regarded as 'highly respectable' when

new, only twenty years earlier, were already decaying. An example was the melancholy establishment in St Luke's Road, near Westbourne Park Station, where W. H. Hudson, that rare migrant from the Argentine pampas, was for many years caged in by poverty, habit, and ill-health.

Even in some of the more pretentious streets many of those first-floor drawing-rooms had been divided up, between the wars, into bed-sitting-rooms, sometimes euphemistically called 'one-room flatlets' or, later, 'divan-lounge-dinettes'. Many a business girl found herself living in a cell of inordinate height, with only half of an ornate plaster medallion in high relief on her ceiling, and only a thin partition between her and the occupant of the adjoining cell. A cold draught nipped her ankles when she climbed a gloomy flight of stairs to a conservatory converted into a bathroom, where she risked asphyxiation from the geyser, of which the chimney seemed, like the trunk of a pushing palm tree, to have forced its way through the glass into the open air. Often the task of adapting these houses to newer purposes and habits had seemed so daunting or futile that they had been pulled down and replaced by new blocks of flats, often with modern inconveniences of their own — like want of peace, space, and privacy — but more easily kept warm and clean. Or one could see, as in Stanhope Street (where my father was born in 1870), squat, 'easily run' houses of the Thirties adjoining Victorian houses of the old type.

In the eighteen-eighties, when my father was a boy, Bayswater was facetiously known as 'Asia Minor', because, like Bath and Cheltenham, it swarmed with retired Anglo-Indian soldiers and civil servants and their families. A number of cramming establishments were kept busy preparing the offspring to follow their fathers to India, and the shops in Westbourne Grove ('the Chowringhee of Bayswater' as a local chronicler called it) had good stocks of chutney and curry powder for the veterans in retirement, and of chlorodyne and cummerbunds for the departing tyros. Sixty years had gone, and in the later Forties the provision shops of Bayswater were expected to stock paprika, matzos, Knackwurst, and Schweinsohren. Since the rise of Hitler the population, both floating and settled, had become less and less English. Bayswater had for some time been favoured by the Jews and the Greeks as a quarter to live in, and by second-class tourists as one to stay in: after the war it became steadily more cosmopolitan. In the frowstier 'guest-houses' or 'private hotels' (which were neither private nor hotels), and in new and inferior restaurants, Irish waitresses or Cypriot waiters could now be seen plonking down plates of so-called 'shepherd's pie' (which had nothing to do with shepherds and was not a pie), made of minced whale and a sloshy paste of water and potato powder, before some seedy cabal of ageing Baltic irredentists or the discarded mistress of a currency manipulator who had escaped from the débâcle on the last tram out of Bratislava. Less than most waiters and waitresses did they know whom they might be waiting upon next—swarthy students of law, medicine, or the economics of immoral earnings, from Gambia, Trinidad, or Ceylon; or perhaps some Australian remittance-girl with vain hopes of the concert platform and occasional walking-on parts in amateur documentary films, hesitating meanwhile whether to bestow her temporary and lackadaisical favours upon a ruined Polish veterinary surgeon or a Hungarian publisher's nark. Such were some of the types who had largely ousted what was left of the indigenous bloc of well-to-do or depressed persons who with more or less reason regarded themselves, or wished to be regarded, as 'gentlefolk'—senescent, church-going ex-officers of the regular or the Indian army; theosophical widows and anti-vivisectionist spinsters, towed along by overfed, sex-starved, and incontinent dogs; survivals, misfits, or just 'ordinary' families or wage-earners; so that now, if any survivors of this earlier population happened to hear the King's English spoken in the street, they looked up in amazement from their reveries, as if they were in Batum or in Bogotá.

Just as the edges of Bayswater—and not only the edges—had frayed into slums, so the population had a grubby fringe, or rather a fluid margin in which sank or swam the small-time spiv, the deserter, the failed commercial artist turned receiver, the tubercular middle-aged harlot, the lost homosexual, or the sex maniac. In the eighteen-fifties the Frith family, living at 10 Pembridge Villas, had been agitated by the real or rumoured activities of garrotters in the slums of Notting Hill; in the nineteen-forties Pembridgia itself knew crimes of passion, and one of its typically discreet-looking small hotels became a cynosure when it was reported to have sheltered the baleful energies of a quickly notorious erotomaniac murderer. I believe the gutter Press coined the term 'the Murder Mile' for the region just north of Notting Hill Gate. Occasionally I found myself passing the house which had once filled Mrs Fernandez with hope and her husband with suspicion, and I thought of old, unhappy, and already far-off things.

The five-and-a-half war years seemed like a slice cut out of my life, but what was the loss of a slice? To be alive, when so many others were dead, seemed a kind of privilege. To have survived two world wars and a good many other hazards besides those of the Murder Mile, might cause a pious man to suppose himself spared for some special purpose, as if God were to say, 'You have been granted an extension of your lease of life. See that you make the most of it.' But it is not necessary for a man in his forties to be pious to begin to notice that his own light is still burning after other lights have gone out. He may become conscious more often than before of the briefness of life and may find himself a little more concerned not to waste it by surrendering to undesired pressures and fatuous intercourse: he may (if I may borrow an image from an unaccountably popular game) know better which balls to play.

'Do give me a ring,' a smart young woman said to me in such a dulcet voice that she seemed to be saying, 'I am the honeysuckle, you are the bee.'

'Impossible,' I said, and explained that I disliked the telephone and its untimely intrusions.

'Oh, but you can't *not* have a telephone!' Her voice had turned shrill.

'Oh *can't* I!'

One need not be a Cézanne to have as great a dread as his of *grappins*: and, as Alain Fournier wrote in one of his letters, '*Surtout il faut fuir ceux qui se prétendent vos amis, c'est à dire préten-dent vous connaître et vous explorent brutalement.*' Even by not cultivating quite pleasant acquaintances one is apt to be written off as an eccentric recluse, but that is a small price to pay for a modicum of solitude. Not, I hasten to say, that I was living alone, or living aloof. A man cannot expect to reach maturity without having acquired responsibilities for the welfare of others. He may be led to assume them by love or duty, or a mixture of both. The nearness of the last twenty years or so would make it untimely or unseemly to speak of my own more private responsibilities, even if I had a mind to do so, and I do not wish now to anticipate later happenings.

With my headquarters in the familiar but changed and changing environment of Bayswater, I began to address myself to a new phase of existence. I resumed my profession as a publisher's adviser, and had now begun to do a good deal of broadcasting, under the persuasion and tuition of John Morris. He had sur-prisingly returned from Japan in the middle of the war. I had not previously met him. We were drawn together by the fact that for each of us living in Japan had been an important and delightful experience, and before long we were all but blown to glory together by the same flying bomb. A solid and unemotional-looking man, a kinsman of William Morris, he had developed an Asian look, the protective mimicry that unconsciously moulds the facial expression, and almost the bones, of some Europeans who live, in a sympathetic frame of mind, among Asians in Asia. Years in a Gurkha regiment, a sojourn among the Lepchas, travels in Himalayan solitudes, a partial ascent of Everest, and a contented participation in the confidences and amusements of the Japanese, had arched the eyebrows above the spectacles, behind which the eyes were watchful rather than expressive; and the mouth, especially in uncongenial company, could be as immobile as the beak of the reputedly wise old owl who sat in an oak.

Appointed to take charge of broadcasts to Asia, he invited me to take part in them. I had when young in Tokyo had some practice in trying to make English prose and verse, and English ideas, intelligible and interesting to Japanese ears; I now had to do the same for imaginary ears in Asia generally. I was assured that they existed, and were attentive. Improbable as this seemed, I found the writing and delivery of these talks a valuable exercise in composition and speaking; and when I spoke sometimes on the Home or the Third Programme (of which John Morris was later appointed Controller), it was no less valuable to learn to vary the content, diction, and tempo accordingly. The spoken word cannot oust the written word, but the ease with which it can now be transmitted or recorded is important for the writer. It is to be hoped that the spoken word will be raised to the level of the written word, and that the written word will gain in clarity, directness, and flexibility. I hope that poetry will be more and more written to be spoken or acted, and that it will become more and more part of the writer's function to learn to speak and read aloud, and, where necessary, to act. Even before I had done much broadcasting I found myself disinclined to write verse that was not meant to be read aloud or spoken.

It was my intention after the war to begin a novel which would commemorate a certain residuary and unstandardised way of living in a London sphere of which I had intimate knowledge before the war. Not being a tempestuous or regular novelist, I took my time over this book, with the result that I was able to shape it exactly as I wanted it. I worked within what I believed to be my proper scope, and intermittently, as the distractions of everyday life allowed. The book appeared under the title *Museum Pieces*. I have a special affection for it, and would not wish to alter a word or a comma. When I speak of distractions, I should perhaps explain that I have tended in life to give precedence to personal relationships, and there have been some which have seemed exacting, and agitating, and tedious all at the same time: but where I have had the belief, or the illusion, that my constancy was useful, pleasant, or necessary, I have not allowed it to lapse. A perhaps feminine side of my nature has in these instances taken charge. If I had lacked it, I suppose I might have more furiously and single-mindedly stuck to writing; but the pleasures and duties of human intercourse, to say nothing of the business of earning a living, have with me alternated with the lonely struggle of composing books. There has been this advantage, that I have not written against time to make money, and that everything I have written is related to everything else and to its originator. Such as it is, it is all of a piece.

38

A Friend Writes

Before the war more space was given in *The Times* to obituary notices, especially to those supplementary ones sent in by friends of the deceased, than is given now. Real emotion is likely to be either eloquent or silent. If it finds expression in flat or trite phrases it seems, though it may not be, unreal. The prevalence of cant and cliché in these notices showed an almost total want of spontaneity and inventiveness. Again and again one read of *unremitting* labour or toil, of *consummate* tact, of *indefatigable* industry, of *unabated* zest, of *selfless* devotion, of *utter* unselfishness, of *inflexible* determination, of *deep* loyalties, of *long* experience, of *varied* responsibilities, of *indomitable* courage, of a *keen* sense of humour, of *infectious* laughter, of *sterling* integrity, of *conspicuous* success, of *untiring* energy, of *unfailing* generosity. Could it be believed of any human being that 'all children and animals worshipped him'? *All*? Or of another that 'he achieved instant popularity with everyone'? Or of another that 'he was loved by all'? Or of another that 'he was quite incapable of a mean thought'? Or of another that 'no one who met him could fail to be influenced by him'? Or of another that 'he had an immense affection for all animals'? Did he cherish wart-hogs and dote on hyenas? Did he take the skunk to his bosom?

The effort to prove that the deceased was a superman often took the form of saying that 'if ever there was a born soldier' — or 'saint on earth', or 'leader of men' — 'it was he'. Or, 'one felt instinctively that here was an individual of no ordinary mould'. There were many variations on the theme that the world would be 'the poorer for his passing' (surely an ambiguous statement), that 'his death has cast gloom over a wide circle', or that 'he has left a gap which can never be filled'. This last statement is hardly worth making, because it is true of every human being that dies. It was very refreshing to read, by contrast, about one man that 'he was a zealous beagler', and about another that 'of boomerangs he had a large collection'. There at least was something to remember him by.

'Is it not strange,' asks Mr Forester in *Melincourt*, 'that even the fertility of fiction should be so circumscribed in the variety of monumental panegyric?'

'I have often thought,' replies Mr Fox, 'that these words of Rabelais would furnish an appropriate inscription for ninety-nine gravestones out of every hundred: *Sa mémoire expira avecque le son des cloches qui carrillonèrent à son enterrement.*'

Somewhere between the ostentatiously loyal friend and the painfully candid friend is the affectionate and understanding friend, and perhaps he can sometimes note down something more worth reading than banal generalities.

A number of the persons dear to me, admired by me, or well known to me, who had died during the war had not been killed by bombs or bullets, mines or torpedoes, but their deaths had evidently come sooner because of the anxiety, strain, fear, grief, gloom, and uncertainty about the future brought on by the war. As a disease of the body politic, war is felt in all its members. When more is understood about psychosomatic illnesses greater knowledge may help the doctor and the psychiatrist towards recognising them and their causes, but hardly towards the prevention or cure of international catastrophes.

Of persons mentioned in this book, my mother had died in the first few weeks of the war. Nearing her last days, she was strangely haunted and evidently tormented by dreams and delirious visions of troop movements in Asia. She described them to me, and they proved strangely prophetic. The suffering that was to come to millions after she was dead seemed part of her own while she was still alive.

Just before she took to her deathbed, I went to see her one

morning in the nursing-home where she died. She was sitting by the window in a dressing-gown, polishing her nails.

'If I'd known you were coming,' she said, 'I would have done this earlier. But I dare say you won't mind if I go on with it.' She looked up, and then said, in a lightly ironical tone of voice, 'After all, one has to do one's nails.'

Those were not her last words, but they would have done very well. They were wonderfully characteristic, mingling self-mockery, calmness, courage, and a kind of disdain for the world and for the last of the various traps in which her destiny had caught and wounded her; but, most of all, those words expressed her devotion to the order in which she believed and which her life had been a constant struggle to maintain against great and various odds.

Virginia Woolf was dead, a being not designed to withstand incorrigible barbarism, the ceaseless activity and energy of her word-shaping mind leaving behind her the trail of a comet, of which the luminosity will not be properly appreciated until the rest of what she wrote is printed. The ebullient but diabetic Hugh Walpole, whom she had so enjoyed teasing, was dead. He had served on the Russian front in the first war but was clearly neither young enough, strong enough, nor calm and balanced enough to withstand the second on the London front.

Anthony Butts's death had been doubly horrible, in its cause and in its details. To the very last he never lost his nerve. The freedom of his nature and his satirical high spirits had never diminished. He had foreseen in his twenties the disasters which a civilisation in which he had lost confidence had brought upon itself. Born in 1900, a child of this century, he had thought, rightly or wrongly, that Europe had lost its way and that the benefits it had brought to Asia and Africa had been fatally outweighed by arrogance, exploitation, want of imagination, want of foresight, and puritanical materialism.

I thought of him in January 1957, when a remarkable letter appeared in the *Spectator* from Mr J. C. Longhurst, with whose views he would have been likely to find himself in sympathy.

'Rather than glory in our past and continue to justify discrimination against those whose skins and ways of life are different from ours,' wrote Mr Longhurst, 'the present generation would be wise to try to earn their friendship; for theirs is the future, ours is the past.' Having worked among Chinese, Indians, and Negroes in various places, he had found that resentment and loathing, not liking or respect, was what Europeans most often incurred. It was not 'the Christian ethics of love and understanding' that had impressed them, but rather 'the history of killing and subjugation (interpreted in Europe as "keeping law and order" and "bringing civilisation and industrial development") practised by most European nations ... throughout Africa and Asia'. And in his view 'the nemesis threatening Western Europeans, North Americans, and all other white skins, and even exceeding the threat of Communism, is that of revenge by the formerly subject lands of Asia and Africa for the cruelties and indignities endured by them in the past'.

I would not myself go so far as to say 'theirs is the future, ours is the past', though the decline of Europe's former expansive powers and conquering rapacity, and the rise of the new expansiveness and rapacity in Asia and Africa have already altered the look of the world. But the concatenation of circumstances that fixed me when young in Asia and Africa made me acquainted with the wounds and anger of the insulted and oppressed; and my writings show, I believe, some consciousness of them. It is to me remarkable that I should have happened to live in South Africa, where the idea of white domination, raised by fanaticism to a matter of principle, is making its last, blind, unscrupulous stand; and in Japan, the first Asian nation to take over successfully the mechanical and industrial techniques of the West, the first in modern times to defeat a European Power in war, and the first to explode finally, by conquering and occupying colonial territories, any remaining illusion among Asian peoples of European invincibility. Japanese militarist imperialism proved no less odious than any other variety. Having foreseen its tendencies and probable consequences, and expressed my hatred of them, I was not surprised by them. And though I should not wish to try and excuse Japanese barbarities during the second world war, it would not be senseless to try and perceive their causes, and to recognise among them a desire to avenge contempt shown towards the Japanese people by Europeans and Americans. Directly the war was over I resumed contact with my Japanese friends. If they were responsible for the maltreatment and murder of prisoners, I was no less responsible for the fate of Hiroshima. If the ties that bind individuals together are broken, what is left? Nothing but hopes of a better world or a better future, and better than hopes are handshakes.

Anthony Butts left behind him, besides cherished memories, a few paintings, and the imperfect draft in typescript of a book he had written with my encouragement. He hoped I would edit it for publication. I did so, and it appeared in 1945, under the title *Curious Relations*. It has entertained many readers on both sides of the Atlantic. Some of them would be surprised to know how much stranger than fiction are some of its apparently far-fetched characters and incidents. The book is a kind of satirical fantasia solidly based upon fact. The genial verve of its author's disillusionment with the late-Victorian and Edwardian society which had evolved him and in which he grew up might blind a reader to its significance as the work of a man who had found out that the values of that society were false and wished to replace them with other values.

Not very long after the war died Lilian Bowes Lyon. She, too, was not satisfied with the values that her background and upbringing had seemed to require her to take for granted. But where to Anthony Butts there had seemed a lack of vision on the part of Europeans in regard to Asians and Africans, to her it seemed that there was a want of vision in England about the genius of the English people, which she believed to be partly warped or thwarted by, chiefly, the poverty of a great part of them in her time. If some of the intellectuals of the Thirties were sentimental about the working class, some were uneasy and ashamed, where a great mass of comfortable Philistines were indifferent or complacent, about unemployment and its conse-quences. I used to tease her and call her a Bolshevik, but I am not sure that she was a political being at all. She was not interested in the levelling down of the more fortunate to the condition of the less fortunate, nor in any kind of levelling at all. She was a poet with an acute response to the creative stirrings, however blind or dumb, of every human being.

Women who can no longer rely upon youth, or the resilience of health, or the natural attractiveness that goes with both, or upon a settled social or family status, or upon the accepted claims of domestic responsibility, must still maintain their own being. In the effort to do so, they easily tend to become domineering; or, if they fail in that, to become discontented; and then, at the same time as they instinctively try to hide their frustration, they un-consciously draw attention to it, and grow cranky or grotesque. This may show in their appearance, manner, belief, or way of living, or some mingling of these, which may also be a mingling of the absurd, the disagreeable, and the pathetic. Of the least tinge of such grotesqueness Lilian Bowes Lyon remained utterly free. Too large a nature to impose upon others or to be sorry for herself, she felt a personal responsibility for the suffering of others. Her own physical anguish and her compassion for others seemed to eat her away like a double fire. In such a state she had chosen to go and live in Stepney and share the exposure of its people to the hazards of poverty and war. From time to time I was able to visit her there. Her concern with the lives around her seemed so different from that of those who used to go slumming that I asked her to try and put something down on paper about it. She did so, and what she wrote appeared pseudonymously in print, in the form of a letter addressed to myself.

She had always known, she said, that England was 'two nations' and had felt it to be wrong. This conviction had been fortified by her life in Stepney. She felt that even in peacetime it had only been their 'innate brotherliness, sanity, and grit' which had enabled the poor to stand up to life. She felt that, apart from actual want, poverty can so arrest development that people can be kept at what she called 'a psychological subsistence level', a condition in which 'the person nearly everybody could be, the hatched-out butterfly or imago, remains a chrysalis'. Deeply as I respect her longing for 'the natural burgeoning of body and mind', her suspicion of the do-gooders and 'the Planners', her ability to be 'thankfully aware' of other people, and the stress she laid upon the importance of freedom and love being given to children, I could not altogether share her belief in the possibilities of beneficent change. Children, she felt rightly and strongly, must be given the chance to act their dreams. But when she suggested that 'a practical way to help the imago in the great mass of our fellow countrymen' would be to let them make manifest their dreams and aspirations, I felt a little out of my depth, and began to tease her again. They needed security, she said, to give them scope; they needed 'freedom to become'. Yes, but—scope for what? to become what? If by chance dreams and aspirations are base or cheap or noxious, is it so desirable for them to be made manifest? And what degree of 'security' is desirable? In countries with a high level of social security—Sweden, for example—has there been no increase in boredom, no weakening of 'sanity and grit', and of those fibres of character which insecurity can toughen?

Whatever the answers to those questions, the wisdom or logic of her arguments seemed to me far less important than the glow, the warmth, the generosity of her feelings. She had a rare sense of the potential creative power of 'ordinary' people, a respect for them and love for them, and a wish to share her own vision with them, to which they quickly and no less warmly responded. 'East Ends, wherever they may be,' she wrote, ' ... should be seen not primarily with the objective eye but as Blake perhaps would see them if he were alive today, in terms of pity and terror and the mighty rushing wind of inspiration.' In short, there was nothing prosaic about the inhabitants of *her* East End.

I have known and admired a good many poets. It ought not to be necessary to say that their lives are conditioned by the needs of their poetry. It may not be easy always to see the point of their

irregular lives, to agree with their unreasonable views, to sympathise with their obsessive fantasies and stupid prejudices, to regard
as seriously as they do the attitudes they assume, but these things
are part of the medium in which alone they may be able to function. A duchess whose devotion to poetry seemed wholehearted,
and who herself wrote poetry, complained to me of a poet whom
we both knew that his nails were dirty: I could not help saying
that we both knew a great many people with clean nails who
could not write poetry. Lilian Bowes Lyon did not happen to
belong to the dirty-nail school, but in her own way was as much
agitated by ideas of social change as some other poets of the
Thirties. Whatever their limitations, their tendencies were prophetic of the social revolution that has since taken place.

When friends die, part of oneself seems torn away, but really
they have added a cell to that transitory agglomeration of cells
that is oneself, enabling one to reflect life, to reflect about life,
and to live more fully than before. And if they have had some
power with the written word, that is something specially personal
to remember them by. I did not feel able to write the introduction
to Lilian Bowes Lyon's *Collected Poems*, which fortunately
appeared in time for her to see them. It was admirably done by
Cecil Day Lewis: I had introduced them to one another in
Gloucestershire about fifteen years earlier. 'More rigorously,
more devotedly, more intimately than most poets of our time,'
he wrote, 'Lilian Bowes Lyon has identified herself with suffering
humanity.' He perceived the depth and the darkness in her
writings, and the note of passion which he felt Christina Rossetti
and Emily Brontë would have recognised. And he quoted some
lines that I too have found memorable, for instance:

> So chary of breath
> Each alien burr
> Clings light to earth,
> Foredoomed to thaw.
> Sigh and they are gone,
> Like snow bees following sweetness;

> The ghostly are blown,
> Are chosen away to brightness.

And,

> Some covet life to lose it; some agree
> With Christ at last, like dew the sun draws up.

I myself am haunted besides by the following lines:

> And where, too, martyrs lie after long suffering,
> Drained all of anger's colour, blank as snow
> In the shadeless dream of their achieved self-offering,
> Ask that for these may blow
> The hot south rage of life again, up-levering,
> To stand erect, a choir of close-knit bones.

'In nature,' Chekhov once said, 'a repulsive caterpillar turns into a lovely butterfly. But with human beings it's the other way round: a lovely butterfly turns into a repulsive caterpillar.' That is a doctor's-eye view. To a doctor the physical and psychological habits, the flabby tissues and shabby complainings of the ageing must always seem a gross degeneration from the clean-eyed pliancy of the young. But often the characters of the sick and dying have seemed to me to be stepping like heroic figures out of the beggarly trappings of mortality, the sentence of death having smoothed away from their mental lineaments what was mean or trivial.

Another poet whom I knew, Demetrios Capetanakis, who died young in 1944, had the rare distinction of finding himself able to write in English although it was not his mother tongue. It is gratifying that so learned and subtle a mind should have found English 'the poetic language *par excellence*'. Dame Edith Sitwell, in an essay published after his death, spoke of the strangeness, wisdom, and profundity of his poetry, and of his mastery of

English. I was greatly interested in his feeling about England and the English, and wrote after his death:

> We of the north and the west turn towards the sun; we look to the south and the east and the past for beauty and strangeness; we have looked with curiosity and passion to the Mediterranean, our Goethes and Byrons to Italy and Greece, our Flauberts to Carthage, our Gissings to Rome; we have looked to the Arab countries and towards Asia for the unknown and the exotic, the strangely stirring. But Demetrios in the lucid aridity of Greece had dreamt of the north and the west and the present, the blond energies of the German, the Englishman dreaming and smiling in his fogs, the fantastic activity of the American.[1]

Drawn to the dampness and darkness of England and the Dickensian aspects of London, and fascinated by its febrile atmosphere in the nightly blackout of wartime, he had discovered that the English were the gentlest and the most stubborn people in the world – gentle and stubborn at the same time, because neither too gentle nor too stubborn. 'Balance', he wrote, 'is the secret of the English genius', and the English language could express the light as well as the darkness of the soul, he found, with equal power. By his discovery of England he helped me to understand my own.

---

[1] From 'A Recollection' in *Demetrios Capetanakis: A Greek Poet in England*, edited and published by John Lehmann in 1947.

39

If I were Doctor Gruber

Suppose I were in fact Dr Gruber. What kind of England might I have discovered? Let us postulate a man just turned thirty, settling in England in the early Thirties for politico-racial reasons and in the hope of pursuing his career and bringing up a family in comparative security. One of my great-grandfathers was a country doctor at Frome in Somerset in the time of William IV, and when he died, in the early eighteen-forties, the tradesmen shut up their shops and pulled down their blinds – which is more than they would do today. I like to think of Dr Gruber as living, but as a man who would be worth pulling one's blinds down for if the occasion arose; a humane and tolerant man with high standards of professional conduct, with medical and psychological curiosity and powers of observation, and a readiness for varied experience.

It is not unlikely that when Dr Gruber first came to England he had formed some general opinion about the English, or had accepted it ready-made. He would have heard that the English are cold and reserved, stolid and unemotional, mad, hypocritical, lazy, dull, either indifferent or hostile towards foreigners, class-conscious, obsessed with ball games, dog addicts, and cherishers of all sorts of archaic survivals. But being a cultivated man, he will naturally have distrusted generalisations about national character. He will have known that the English are a mixed and mongrel race, and have expected to find among them every sort of contradiction and variety. His expectation will not have been disappointed.

He will never, I daresay, have quite got over the discovery that the English are in general not merely unemotional but incapable of emotion, let alone passion. Their pudding faces are not masks, but the surfaces of puddings that are puddings all through ... But are they? The question will often have posed itself, because he will have noticed evidence of gentleness and stubbornness, and these are not attributes of the pudding. If there have been moments when he has agreed with John Stuart Mill about 'the general meanness of English life', about 'the low objects on which the faculties of all classes of the English are intent', and about the way in which their feelings and intellectual faculties remain undeveloped, so that passion is incomprehensible to them and intellectuality absurd, he will have found this picture reversible. Inclined at first to think the tameness and dullness of English life boring—its brief exchanges of formulae about the weather seeming, for example, a sad change from the copious exchange of ideas in cafés—he may have begun to perceive that it is restful. He may have learnt that it allows an unusual degree of freedom to the individual and to the workings of his mind and conscience—if any. He will have noticed that there is less likelihood here of riot, massacre, and assassination than in some other countries. The Englishman's want of excitability, his disinclination for scenes, his common inability to be easily or badly rattled are indicated by his habit of understatement, just as his distaste for boasting finds expression in self-depreciation: to Dr Gruber these will not be signs of stupidity, but signs of a reserve of strength. As a doctor he will soon have seen that the Englishman's habit of not working frantically hard saves him from the nervous and physical tension that often afflicts those who do. The Englishman's stolidity he is likely to have found inseparable from a formidable tenacity, and the Englishman's reserve sometimes only preoccupation, broodiness, or shyness, and often a mask for kindliness.

After a varied experience of English life in many aspects, and having for a time carried on his practice in urban environments, Dr Gruber will know that some of the conditions he has found, whether physical or mental, are not specifically English, but are due to the pressures of overpopulation in any industrial environment in the twentieth century. He will have noticed a progressive standardisation of behaviour, a degeneration of individuality, and a want of taste and inventiveness in everyday life, in food, clothes, and furniture—but not in mechanical and applied science. He will inevitably have found the English in many ways a dirty people. He well remembers having read in the report for 1955 of the chief medical officer of the Ministry of Education that a quarter of a million children were found with verminous heads. He will have noticed uncleanness for which poverty is not accountable. He will have visited patients in dirty habitations, and patients will have exposed dirty bodies to him in his own consulting-rooms. The goatish armpits of a waitress, the scarlet-painted but filthy nails of a bus conductress, the expectorations of some oafish pipe-smoker, dirty feet, the grime and litter of railways, streets, parks, beaches, and other public resorts will have obtruded themselves upon his senses. And, knowing that it is a human failing to accuse others of our own failings, he will hardly have been surprised to hear, for example, contemptuous allusions to 'dirty Wogs' or 'Gyppoes'. Not easily shocked, he will have been shocked by instances of cruelty to children, of a kind seldom or never heard of among races regarded as inferior. The Teutonic love of uniforms, and of leagues, and of patriotic or military rituals and routines will have saddened him; and as a doctor, dedicated to the preservation of life, he must particularly have noticed the daily massacre on the roads and the callousness of many of its perpetrators: but this, like dishonesty, or meanness, or insolence, he will certainly not have considered peculiar to this island.

Reading (again in Mill) about 'the error always prevalent in England ... of judging universal questions by a merely English standard', he will have marked this phrase (methodically trained and methodically minded man that he is) with a line in the margin. And it will have led him to reflect (not for the first time, and so far as his professional duties have allowed) on the whole question of the English attitude to the non-English—a question with which he

14

has inevitably been a good deal concerned. Though not politically minded, his residence in England will have caused him to reflect a little upon the rise and decline of the British Empire. He will remember one of his compatriots, who had been at school in England, recalling how the expression 'law and order' seemed like one word—*lawnorder*—and was at first believed by him to show some connexion between the *Pax Britannica* and the well-kept patch of grass in the Englishman's garden. Sometimes, noticing the expression 'law and order' in some newspaper or radio report, Dr Gruber may have meditated over Europe's expansive past. Where other nations have sometimes been far more oppressive and unjust, and have not always provided anything like the same framework of roads, schools, hospitals, law courts, and cricket fields, the English, to him, may seem to have been—and still at times to be—too heavy-handed in their determination to impose *lawnorder* upon peoples of quite different temper and aspirations to their own. A phrase like 'judging it necessary to impose (or maintain) *lawnorder*', issuing from administrative lips or rattled out on pedagogic typewriters, may have seemed to him to have meant to those upon whom *lawnorder* was imposed a cold and arrogant disregard of what they passionately believed to be their rights and knew to be their ethnic or religious traditions, an indifference towards their familiar habits of mind, and a disdain for their customary ebullitions of temperament. It may have seemed to him that when these supposed rights, accepted ways, and usual vagaries did not conform with those of the English, *lawnorder* might prove to mean not tidiness and decency but force, punishment, and war, where a little more imagination might conceivably have led to compromise, partnership, and mutual loyalty. Ireland and South Africa may have seemed to him examples where a long persistence of rapacity, shortsightedness, and military extravagance ended in retreat and moral defeat as well.

Like others of English domicile but not of English origin, Dr Gruber can hardly have ignored the existence of xenophobia among the English. He may have heard the word 'foreigner' used as disparagingly as the words 'nigger', 'Kaffir', or 'Jew' are used in various parts of the world. He may at times have longed to point out that to most of the human race an Englishman is a foreigner. I myself learnt this fact in many different ways when young. Once in my early twenties, for instance, I was walking through a village in the Japanese Alps. 'A foreigner, a foreigner!' I heard the people calling out to one another, and the whole village, dogs included, turned out and ran after me in great excitement. I was told they had never seen a European before and that I was probably the first who had ever set foot in the place. Those villagers belonged to one of the many nations who have held the belief that they were of divine origin, a chosen race with a special destiny and a civilisation that set them above all others. My presence may have seemed like a vague threat to their security, and the fear that somebody from outside is endangering the inside may be ancient and primitive but is often well founded. It is closely linked with the notion that an outsider must be inferior.

I once knew a military man who had a violent prejudice, of personal and childish origin, against the French. As he was certainly part of the backbone of this country I will call him Major Vertebra. His prejudice had cut him off from one of the great sources of our civilisation; he professed to believe that the French were good for nothing—politically, militarily, collectively, and individually. But even in his own country his peace of mind was threatened by outsiders. The poor man was once heard to say, not humorously, not in a moment of exasperation, but in deadly earnest, 'I must say *I can't stand civilians!* I can't make them out at all!'

If that was what he felt about the greater number of his fellow-countrymen, including his wife (if not uniformed) and his mother (if he ever had one), no wonder he was contemptuous about all those lesser breeds who, in his view, so obviously began at Calais and extended all over the globe—dirty, excitable, unreliable, and equally contemptible whether civilians or aspiring to military ascendancy. He was the kind of man who is provoked

by some item of news into exclaiming, 'I can't stand the Baby-
lonians!' or 'The only good Visigoth is a dead Visigoth!' He was
as much a disseminator of nonsense as those foreigners who assert
that all the English are cold, arrogant, and perfidious; or as some
Arab who believes that all Westerners are rich; or some knowing
Asian who explains that all Europeans are hairy, and that intimate
physical contact with them (except for money) is best avoided
because they smell like camels or like corpses.

The distaste with which Major Vertebra would regard Dr
Gruber is easily imaginable. He would resent him as a Jew, as an
intellectual, and as an outsider. It would not have occurred to him
that there are particular reasons why in this island we should be
careful what we say about outsiders—chiefly that a variety of
them went to the making of us. We are, thank goodness, a mixed
race. The idea of pure breeding has its place on the farm, in the
kennel, or in the sty, but since Hitler the thought of it among
human beings is not easily acceptable. A few years ago a physicist,
Dr Furth, addressing the British Association at Edinburgh, gave it
as his view that the formation of what might be called 'pure
communities' of people belonging to the same race—whatever
that meant—was dangerous for the maintenance of democracy.
He felt that to establish a stable human society it was necessary to
allow a certain amount of mixing of populations. He recalled
some of the things that have been done with a view to strengthening social or national communities—things like segregating
different races within a community, or expelling minorities—and
he pointed out how these things had produced an exactly opposite
effect to what was intended.

The English tradition of admitting foreign refugees from
political, racial, or religious persecutions is sound and sensible.
When they choose to stay here, to learn our difficult language
and acclimatise themselves to our complex and, to them, foreign
ways, they will not be pleased to hear themselves spoken of a
'bloody foreigners': by their lives and work they are contributing
to our lives and our work, and their temperaments, like their
special skills, must diversify and enrich the texture of English

life. Dr Gruber (as I imagine him) and I have more in common than our appearance. I conceive of him as having settled in this country, and I have done the same myself. Where he must regard himself, though naturalised, as an exile, I find myself fortunately conscious of roots and background and affinities, and at home. But our reasons for staying here may be to some extent the same. English gentleness, English stubbornness, English well-meaningness, English balance and tolerance, the English disinclination to panic or boasting, English stoicism, many graces, something in the atmosphere—these we find worth living with and worth living for. Affection and habit deepen into love and loyalty, and occasions of agreement are made fruitful by the still inalienable right to differ.

I wonder if Dr Gruber sometimes thinks, as I do, of the deformity of the England we have lived in, and of the France we have visited. It has been at best a mutilated civilisation we have known, a makeshift, because it has had to do without those who were killed between 1914 and 1918. The enormity of that loss, the destruction of such an inestimable treasure of heart and head, is not to be imagined. By me, at least, it is never long forgotten. I tend to think of the boyish Euseby Beecher, a young assistant master at my preparatory school near Sevenoaks. I remember rides on the back of his motor bicycle and his supple waist between my hands. I remember his talent for drawing, and his enigmatic smile. Nature expends much to save little, but I am no more reconciled to his death, or persuaded that it was necessary, than I am to the death of Wilfred Owen and all those slaughtered contemporaries of many nations. Perhaps after all the greatest thing said in those days was that 'Patriotism is not enough'. It took a woman to say that.

I have felt no compulsion to return to Asia or Africa. More than once I have declined invitations to take up positions in Japan. I know that I have left more than a fiftieth part of myself there, I know that part of me is part of Japan, but I do not yet feel that this cross-grafting process must be repeated. As for South Africa, since the Twenties I have had no relations there except dead ones—

my infant brother John, buried at Louis Trichardt half a century ago, and 'poor Uncle Durham who was killed in the war'. I had neither friends, nor ambitions, nor purpose, nor property, to draw me back there. I remembered Africa as a complex and violent revelation made to me when young. From all that I knew, its complexity and violence had increased: I could not imagine living there in a state of tension that I should only find endurable if bent upon martyrdom or at least victimisation.

Twelve years after the second world war I did revisit South Africa, in response to an invitation from the University of the Witwatersrand, than which I am older. I had not seen Africa for thirty years, and so learnt what it must be like to return as a ghost to scenes of former life. The account of my haunting of those scenes does not belong here. I will allude instead to a ghost that haunts me – the ghost of an African woman. In the summer of 1862 a Mrs Price, the wife of a missionary, arrived one evening with her husband at Mashuwe in Bechuanaland. Under a tree they saw a creature lying. It was a human being. It was female. At the approach of the white strangers she rose and gazed wonderingly at them. If she had not risen to her feet, she might have been presumed dead. She was a living skeleton – and yet parts of her body were 'bloated and swollen with virulent smallpox'. One of her hands was huge and shapeless, and blood was oozing from a wound in her face. Her breasts were full, like those of a nursing mother. In her diseased condition and a very advanced state of pregnancy she had been driven from home by her mother and husband. She had taken refuge under this tree alone, and the day before the Prices arrived had given birth, unaided, to her child. In the night she was attacked by a hyena, which dragged her baby from her arms and devoured it. After a time the hyena came back and attacked her, causing the wound that Mrs Price saw, but she had somehow managed to defend herself from being killed by it.

This hellish happening[1] has fixed itself in my mind as an image

[1] Described in the entry for 21 November 1862, in *The Journals of Elizabeth Lees Price*, edited by Una Long (Edward Arnold, London, 1956).

of Africa, almost as clearly as if it were a memory. It is easy enough to remember the wrongs of Europe's incursions into Africa – the slave trade, commercial exploitation, racial contempt, and social injustice: but it is as well to remember that the wrongs done by Africans to Africans, out of greed, cruelty, callousness, superstition, and ignorance, are beyond computing. What seems to me now far more worth remembering is all that has made less likely the solitude of that woman under the tree – compassion, charity, disinfectants, education, art, literature, even a measure of *lawn-order*; the idea of personal responsibility; the lives given to understanding, to forgiveness, to moral and material betterment; the scope given to pleasure and playfulness; the grounds given for hope.

In my early writings about South Africa and Japan it was plainly stated or implied that both were heading for trouble. In one country racialism was undermining the hope of unity, in the other militarist nationalism was preparing national disaster in a more impetuous way. But I was not a preacher or a political agitator, merely a youthful sensibility exposed to conditions of growing violence and falsehood and driven by a myth-making, image-making, character-drawing faculty to put these things in words, to try and shape them in prose and verse. The current doctrine that a writer has to be engaged with the problems of his time does not seem to have much novelty if one has had to live from an early age among the tensions created by 'problems'. But if I have since felt myself more widely and deeply engaged – with human nature, with the past, with the arts, with the battle against the cheapening and levelling of what is rare and diverse, and of life itself – this has been chiefly made possible for me by England, by English civilisation, and by English men, women, and children.

Postscript by Simon Nowell-Smith

William Plomer's two volumes of autobiography took the story of his life hardly beyond 1939 when he was rising thirty-six. He was engaged in revising those volumes when he died, and he had only the vaguest plan for a further volume. He left a scrap-book of press cuttings, sandwiched among which were a few undeveloped reminiscences; and he left a folder titled 'Notes & papers of possible autobiographical interest', which contained memoranda of his movements transcribed from diaries which he then discarded, a wartime national identity card (with terrible photograph), a chit from the Director of Naval Intelligence ('the valuable services which you have rendered in the war against the Axis Powers ... good wishes for your future welfare'), and little else. Out of these and other oddments he, and he alone, memory

aiding, could have woven a third instalment of autobiography.
Memory and irony. Remember 'Miss Robinson's Funeral'. Friends
at William's cremation, or at the memorial service at St Martin-
in-the-Fields, may have recalled how mourning motors mourning
motors follow, and undertakers are not volatile or sad or merry —
('Neither are waxworks going by machinery') —

> But the ghost of the late Miss Robinson is floating
> Backside upwards in the air with a smile across her jaw:
> She was tickled to death, and is carefully noting
> Phenomena she never thought of noticing before.

Indulgent irony, not cynicism, was always William's note. And
few phenomena escaped him.

The lines quoted at the head of this Postscript were sent to
William by a friendly critic as a commentary on *At Home*: they
were titled, 'Ah! did none e'er see Plomer plain?' (The page-
numbers have been adapted to the present book.) His response:
'I grant you authority for all but the last line, for which you
quote no page-reference.' Several reviewers made much the same
point: William's autobiographies did not reveal the whole man;
he was holding back. This, William wrote, puzzled him:

> It suggests a kind of affectation I don't feel addicted to. But
> to complain of being misunderstood would in itself perhaps
> be to pretend to complexity or inscrutability, so I *sha'n't*
> complain ...
>   I fear that writing autobiography is just goose-stepping on
> thin ice, but I sha'n't stop until I have written the last word
> of *Mors Plumigera*, or at least of *Dusty Anser*.[1]

---

[1] These characteristically complex quips arose from some critic having compared William, to his mild indignation, to Ruskin, author of *Fors Clavigera*,
and from William's having lately been re-reading Meredith's *Modern Love* in
Cecil Day-Lewis's edition. He perverts Meredith's 'dusty answer' to *'anser'*
which is Latin for 'goose'.

This holding back in autobiography had its parallel in social relationships. Stephen Spender in his own autobiography, *World Within World*, wrote that William, on their first acquaintance in the 'thirties, had spoken to him of the need to present a mask to the world: Paul Bailey, writing in the commemorative issue of the *London Magazine* (Dec./Jan., 1973/74), is one of several contributors who stress William's 'mysteriousness', and he says that William repudiated Spender's portrait of himself. William was most generous and outgoing in his friendships but, as obituary tributes make clear, he did not expect, or help, his acquaintances in one circle to mingle with those in another. Thus John Morris, in a broadcast: 'More, very much more, than anyone I have ever come across he tended to keep his numerous friendships in different compartments: some of his most intimate friends were unknown, even by name, to one another.' I emphasise this aspect of William's character simply to suggest that it must present a stumbling-block, not only to the writer of a Postscript, but to any future biographer. It is perhaps best to leave the last word to William. He had been asked, a year or more before he died, what he would wish an obituarist in *The Times* to write of him. In the train between Victoria and his Sussex home he made a few jottings, including:

> P. was by nature both sociable and reclusive. He greatly valued his wide range of friends and acquaintances, but needed domestic insulation. This was fortified by his taste for simple living. He would not drive a car or watch television, preferring to walk or read, and on buying a house in Sussex he had the telephone pulled out, as he said, 'like a tooth'. [1]

[1] He was in fact required by the Admiralty to have a telephone installed in his London flat during the war. He divulged the (ex-directory) number to very few friends, and had the offending mechanism removed as soon as the war was over.

In the summer of 1959 he broadcast on the B.B.C. General Overseas Service 'On Not Answering the Telephone'. This sprightly piece has been kept in print in Kokyo's English Reading Series, Tokyo, ever since.

Poor eyesight was enough to preclude William from a combatant role in the Second World War. Ian Fleming, whom he then only slightly knew, was personal assistant to the Director of Naval Intelligence, and on his recommendation William joined me in the Admiralty where I was editing a secret *Weekly Intelligence Report* in the summer of 1940. It meant giving up his job as chief literary adviser at Cape's. For more than five years we sat opposite each other at the same table, or rather series of tables. He wrote this account of what we and our colleagues were up to.[1] I endorse it all, except what he says about patience and amiability, good temper and good manners: William was a model of all these; not all of us were.

A civilian officer on the Naval Staff recruitment had a phantasmal unreality, like a horse-marine, but the ambiguity of his position had its advantages. Wearing no uniform he was able to maintain a degree of independence, and perhaps more tolerance than a certain major of Marines who had been heard under the Admiralty roof to declare that he couldn't stand civilians or understand them either. (One much hoped that his mother, for instance, had avoided the stigma of being civil rather than military).[2]

We civilians in the Information Section had been taken on, I suppose, because we were thought fairly responsible and articulate. It would be pleasant to believe that the supposition made up a little for our inevitable ignorance of naval technicalities. Whatever our failings, we were almost priggishly conscientious, perhaps at times even more conscientious, about security for example, than some persons in uniform. In conversation one or other of our naval superiors would occasionally give us a quizzical look, as if wondering whether the N.I.D. could be kept afloat with such a crew;

[1] Contributed to *Room 39, Naval Intelligence in Action 1939-45*, by Donald McLachlan (1968).

[2] This character figures in Chapter 39 above as Major Vertebra.

but, for better or worse, we were all in the same boat together, and they never treated us with the least asperity or
discourtesy.

I spent most of the War in a series of small enclosed spaces,
more suitable for submariners than claustrophobes, with
Marjorie Napier, a still youthful veteran of the previous
World War, with Simon Nowell-Smith and later Dudley
Massey. I seize this chance of saying what a pleasure and
privilege it was to be with them and to learn the extent of
their patience and amiability, qualities conspicuous elsewhere in N.I.D. As everybody knows, living and working
in London, especially with some inside knowledge from day
to day or from hour to hour of the War and its more menac-
ing possibilities, was no picnic, but good temper and good
manners in the N.I.D. made it much more like one than it
would otherwise have been ...

The function of our Section was to learn all we could,
from all available sources, about political and economic
developments throughout the world; to condense it; then,
with the help of persons with special knowledge and qualifications, to estimate its truth, value and implications; and
finally to get the information we had collected into print,
in a form and style useful to naval officers. What we hoped
was that, by doing something to dispel fogs of ignorance and
uncertainty, we should be helping them to know better
what the enemy was up to and his good and bad fortunes, as
well as those of our allies and of neutral nations, and in
general to improve visibility.

I learned anew, every day, that in the processing of official
information several heads are as a rule better than one. And
in looking back over the five-and-a-half years I spent in
N.I.D. I feel it was no loss to me as a writer to have a great
deal of practice not only in composing plain English but in
extracting from masses of various papers their gist, drift or
main points—an exercise with which, before and since those
days, my life has been much occupied.

In his lighter moments William would draw on the back of teleprinter messages illustrations for absurdities in official reports or the daily press. I recall a drawing of a Harley Street specialist who, according to his obituary in *The Times*, had 'died literally in harness'. (William collected 'literallys'.) Among other topical rhymes he celebrated H.M.'s diplomatic representatives whose cables — 'signals' in naval parlance — epitomised the comparative quiet, at that time, of Spanish Morocco and Spanish America:

> Stonehewer-Bird and Millington-Drake
> Didn't know what reports to make.
> So Millington-Drake and Stonehewer-Bird
> Only reported the things they had heard.

Once only was I able to slip an epigram of William's into our otherwise solemn printed report. Moscow radio had announced that in the Red Aviation Day celebrations the Parachute Band would descend playing the Red Aviation march.

MARTIAL MOUJIK

> Angels? Or hairy-wristed nuns? Neither we understand,
> But Stalin's Rhythm Boys playing to beat the band.
> The Heavens ope: more loud the harps and trumpets play.
> 'Tis not the Judgment, but Red Aviation Day.

We always worked on Sundays, days of least interruption. Besides 'literallys' William collected restaurants (the less said about wartime feeding the better[1]) and statues and the names of

---

[1] Ah, that ingenious Ministry of Food!
It may be clever, but it is not good
To turn potatoes into jam, and dine
On offal, oats and home-made cabbage wine.
What do I do when I am told to try
A groundsel salad, or a toadstool pie?
I fast for victory. It is not nice
To take the Ministry of Food's advice.
                                        W.P. 1942.

houses. In Sunday lunch-hours we sought these out. It was the oddities of statues, designed or accidental, that appealed to the schoolboyish side of William. In Westminster Palace Gardens Emmeline Pankhurst's bronze pince-nez were twisted and awry; on the Victoria Embankment was Samuel Plimsoll whose jer-seyed torso ended in a 'line' of dropped stitches; facing St James's Park from King Charles Street was Clive of India, known to William, because of an aberration of the stone-cutter on the plinth, as 'OLIVE'; in Waterloo Place Lord Lawrence (also of Indian fame) had a neat shrapnel hole where an essential button ought to have been concealed; on the Albert Memorial a lady on an elephant had suffered Amazonian amputation in an air-raid ... For some weeks of high blitz we were exiled to distant Cricklewood, and at lunchtimes relieved what William called the *taedium belli* by wandering past suburban cots named 'Nestle-down', 'Hersamine' or 'Ecnamor' (read backwards, reader), or — saved up for later use in ballads — 'Nellibert' and 'Ye Kumfi Nooklet'. It struck him as aptly ironical that when, years after the war, he moved into his first real house-of-his-own, it should have been a bungaloid residence yclept, after the same manner, 'Rossida'.

The war atmosphere was perhaps congenial to ballad-making. With a single exception William wrote no novel after 1934, and few short stories. With few exceptions — one, it is true, dating from his Japanese period — he had not taken seriously to the ballad form before the mid- or late 'thirties. He once explained why he had moved away from prose fiction:

> You ask why I stopped. Not, I'm sure, because of any lessen-ing of intense interest in human character and in the way people behave in a particular time or place. Perhaps from various causes rather than for various reasons. I think such talent as I may have had for fiction would have worked more effectively, and perhaps gone on working, in a society bound

much more by convention than the world we have lived in since, say, 1930 ...

I don't myself think that I had a strong, compulsive, inventive kind of 'novelistic', or 'story-telling', talent. I think I've been more interested in defining observed behaviour, rather than imagining or inventing behaviour. As I got older I felt happier working on a smaller scale, as in poetry, or in *libretti*.

To the war years, then, belongs the beginning of William's reputation as a ballad-monger, with 'Night Thoughts in the Tottenham Court Road, 1942', 'The Flying Bum, 1944', and other 'satires intended to be read aloud *con brio*'. (His reputation as a public reciter of his own verses *con espressione* came later.) The most moving of his poems of the early war years was 'In a Bombed House' (privately printed in 1942), an elegy on the death of Anthony Butts. Nothing need be added here to what William wrote in his autobiography about Butts except that his death spelled the end of the deepest friendship in William's life since he had settled in England. It was an intellectual and emotional relationship never to be repeated.

With his capacity for compartmentalising, William outside Admiralty hours lived several social and literary lives, the two kinds merging when he entertained, or was entertained by, friends with feet in more than one of his worlds. To Hugh Walpole in 1940:

My dear Hugh, – Oh, oh, what a slanderous letter! ... I don't 'pass from circle to circle': I haven't got a circle, and if I neglect old friends it's because I'm not in a position to entertain them ...

William must have been surprised, if nothing more, to be told by Walpole after a party, when he was rising forty, 'I stood and stared at you: you looked like a very young bull in a field of asphodels – asphodels by Duncan Grant.' When John Lehmann started *Penguin New Writing* early in the war, William was always available to supply, when not a ballad over his own name, a light topical article over his *nom-de-plume* 'Robert Pagan'. Pagan had a character of his own: the son, according to the list of contributors, of a Scots father and a Greek mother from Zante, he was educated in England, was in Barcelona before the Spanish Civil War, had published a novel in French, and in New York an account of a social experiment in Bolivia. In this description Plumiger had indeed taken wing.

He continued to read books occasionally for Cape's, and his reports passed through the hands of his former colleague Veronica Wedgwood. These reports, she has written of this period, were a liberal education to a beginner, clear, penetrating, careful, 'though often elegantly brief'.

> One was aware that he never skimped his reading through haste or fatigue, that he was always alert and eager to detect a potential talent ... He had both integrity and generosity in his judgment and a breadth of interest that enabled him to cover a wide range of subjects. In publishing history there have been readers who were his equal; I am sure there has never been one who was better.

William's publications in the war years were a volume of *Selected Poems* and the final volume of *Kilvert's Diary* in 1940; a reprint of the book of short stories of Japan, *Paper Houses*, originally of 1929 and now (1943) a sixpenny Penguin with an introduction modestly justifying his estimate, pro and con, of a nation since at war with Britain; and in 1943 *Double Lives*, the original version of Chapters 1–21 of the present book. *The Dorking Thigh*, a slim collection of 'satires', and *Curious Relations* by 'William d'Arfey', some account of which he gives on page 409 above, followed in 1945. It was these two books, together with *Kilvert's Diary*, of which a single-volume selection had come out the year before, that set William on the path to a wider fame than he had so far known. It was his occasional talks on B.B.C. programmes aimed at 'Ormuz and Ind, the shores of Araby the blest, and various other continents and islands and great vacuums beyond the seas', his experience and success as a wartime broadcaster to the Far East, that led to his even greater success as a home broadcaster in the years of peace.

The war over, William turned down offers from the British Council of a job in Athens and, from the Foreign Office, that of cultural attaché and educational adviser to the U.K. liaison mission in Tokyo. He returned to Cape's in Bedford Square ('one of the handsomest squares in London') a little disappointed perhaps that the post of chief literary adviser, which he supposed he had inherited from Edward Garnett, was now filled by 'Daniel George', the anthologist. One of the first manuscripts to be put into his hands was Malcolm Lowry's ultimately celebrated novel *Under the Volcano*. Already a dozen publishers in the United States had rejected the book. Many modifications had been proposed, some of which the author had accepted before approaching Cape's in the late summer of 1945. It was now read first by Daniel George, who was generally in favour of it, then by William who, generally, was not. Jonathan Cape, who also read it, agreed to publish it provided certain changes proposed by William were made, and with his letter to Lowry he enclosed a copy of William's detailed report. Lowry's reply to Cape, running to some 16,000 words, was a brilliant exposition of his aims and technique in writing *Under the Volcano*, and in the event Cape's published the book, without modifications, in 1947.[1]

The sequel came twenty years later when proofs of an American book were submitted to Cape's and given to William to read. He found his original report set up in full in an appendix. He wrote to Cape's:

[1] William's report is summarised in *Malcolm Lowry, a biography*, by Douglas Day, 1973; Lowry's letter to Cape is printed in full in *Selected Letters of Malcolm Lowry*, edited by H. Breit and M. Bonner Lowry, 1967; and William's comments on Lowry's letter are printed in *Jonathan Cape, Publisher*, by Michael S. Howard 1971.

I suppose somebody gave permission for this printing. But nobody asked me if I minded. *I do mind.* I regard readers' reports as *confidential.* I have twice incurred odium ... by the sending on of copies of reports by me, or parts of reports, to authors. Also, a good many people know that I have been a reader for Cape's for thirty years or so. I don't see why *everybody* should be in a position to know what I have written *confidentially* at any time about a particular book or author.

It was a rare outburst. Besides the question of confidentiality, there was the other question of copyright. William even consulted the Society of Authors. The problem was new to the society, but their lawyer's opinion was that the copyright in a reader's report probably belongs not to the reader who writes it, but to the publisher who pays for it.

It was in this context that William committed to paper his *credo* as a reader:

The functions of a publisher's reader are not universally understood. He regularly reads a good many offerings and does not write his reports about them as a critic, in the grander sense of the word, but as a taster and adviser. It is his business to tell the publisher what sort of book he had been reading, and not merely to sum up its literary merits or faults, but to give an opinion about its prospects as a published book, either in its offered form or a revised one.

He has to take into consideration not only its matter and manner, but the author's reputation (if any), previous books, and future prospects; the readability and probable saleability of the book; its topicality or absence of topicality; its potential appeal to the supposed general reader or the specialist; the literary fashions or tendencies of the moment; the present conditions of publishing; the particular status, tastes, list, prestige, and solvency of the firm whose head or heads he is advising, and various other matters.

His report is as a rule likely to be written concisely and promptly, and to be more like a snap judgment than an analytical essay. Whether the report is favourable or not, the publisher, if interested enough, may like to try it out upon one or more other readers, and perhaps to read it himself, before coming to a decision.

William did not object to allowing literary researchers to see his reports provided he had been consulted in advance and his name was not divulged. Nor did he regard confidentiality as necessarily persisting beyond the grave – he read with appreciation George Meredith's posthumously published reports to Chapman & Hall. In the character of the late Miss Robinson he would, I think, look down amusedly on a few excerpted illustrations of his style as a reader:

... a real writer of evident talent. It is the fashion among reviewers now to sneer at *New Yorker* contributors: I see nothing to sneer at, and something to respect, in this one.

The author, whose address is in Bedford Court Mansions, is a lively spark to find in such a dreary dump.

It is, I suppose, possible that this author might be chosen to succeed the present Poet Laureate, and the same idea may have occurred to him.

I don't think one could go far wrong in backing this chap.

I don't think this book would suffer from a lack of attention.

I don't think it would be a bad idea to tell her that we feel it would be a good idea to put it by for the present.

Possibly he may be thought a bit pro-Boer: this should stimulate the sale, which ought to be considerable, in South Africa.

I have taken trouble with this offering because the author has no doubt taken a lot of trouble over it. I feel that in both cases the trouble was wasted.

One can easily imagine the busy little hatchet of some conceited prig on the T.L.S. when he discovers a patch of imitation A. E. Housman.

Solemn twaddle, I fear, and Irish solemn twaddle at that.

Incompetent would-be thriller. Confused chronology; non-topical theme and time; no thrills.

And again and again, whether recommending or 'disrecommending' a manuscript, the reader proposed that the firm should encourage authors with possible futures:

He deserves a civil note of regret, saying that, interesting as it is, the book seems to be unlikely to appeal at all widely — or some such stuff.

It might be a good thing, and cheering to the author, if somebody could write him an encouraging word about the book.

No reader expects all his recommendations to be adopted, but it saddened William when authors he thought had futures – the irreverent Betjeman before, and the indecorous Nabokov after, the war – were for old-fashioned reasons turned away from Bedford Square. (There came a time, he once said, when the veteran Jonathan Cape could have been called 'one of the handsomest squares in English publishing'.) Meanwhile he regularly attended the Wednesday editorial conferences at Cape's, saying little – but that little with good humour and wit – and leaving always with another half-dozen manuscripts to taste before next Wednesday.

Thrillers, with or without thrills, were as much grist to William's mill as straight fiction, plays, verse, South African history, United

States policies abroad, Far Eastern travel, what-have-you. In the thriller field he secured for Cape's the creator of James Bond – his most profitable capture for the firm.

As a teenage schoolboy at Eton Ian Fleming had read *Turbott Wolfe* in 1926 and written a fan-letter to its 22-year-old author, then in Japan. They did not meet for several years, and even after Fleming had introduced William into the Admiralty their friendship was slow to mature. But there was a real respect for each other's very different qualities. Something of the 'fan' element led Fleming, one day in 1951, to reveal to William, and at first only to William, that he had written a thriller, and the same element persisted to the point when he long afterwards told a director of Cape's that he was 'slavishly' accepting William's instructions to do a 'hatchet-job' on one of his manuscripts. William from the first was a convinced and determined advocate of *Casino Royale*. He pressed it on Jonathan Cape in person. Cape was no reader of thrillers, had hardly published any, disliked this one, and, though he grew to like Fleming personally, probably never even opened any others of the Bond books. These followed annually, regular as clockwork, till the year after the author's death in 1964. By then the Bond baker's dozen had sold more than twenty million copies in eighteen languages: and of course there were the films. William had done well by Cape's (and indeed by Fleming, who left him £500 in his will with which to commit 'some extravagance'). William's final comment, as an observer less of literature than of publishing, was:

> The name of James Bond was to become not only a household word, it became world-famous. There was something about Fleming's books which appealed directly and almost universally to a prevalent mood of their time. There has generally been hardly more than one such author in a generation, and such an author is what a publisher needs – and needs, incidentally, if he is to allow himself to publish, for pleasure, prestige, or prospects, books on which he won't make, and may lose, money.

Talent-spotting involved a literary adviser in 'literary circles', and these William despised, or affected to despise:

> that endless, clamorous succession, during the later 1940s and the 1950s of publishers' parties ... It is not in such circles that new talents or trends, changes of taste, or nascent literary fashions are always best discernible.

But many parties, and social life generally, he did enjoy. His memoranda of movements record what seems an endless, though not necessarily clamorous round of what he used to call 'jamborees'—lunches or cocktail parties or dinners given by or for Rose Macaulay, Iris Origo, Edith Sitwell, John Lehmann, Rupert Hart-Davis, Robert Frost, Jonathan Cape ... (Other memoranda record a cuckoo in Richmond Park, elderberries on Clapham Common, tea with Princess Mary, coffee alfresco in an English December ...) Two events are recurrent. For several years William never missed a celebration of E. M. Forster's birthday on January 1st, or the Aldeburgh music festivals.

He was invited to lecture on Edward FitzGerald at the first Aldeburgh festival in 1948, and made subsequent appearances as, in his own phrase, a performing poet. So began a new interest in his life, music at close quarters, more especially the operatic music of Benjamin Britten. Later, when Britten persuaded Forster into a collaboration, it was William who suggested Herman Melville's *Billy Budd*[1] on which Forster, aided by Eric Crozier, based the libretto of one of Britten's most successful operas. For his next full-scale work the composer chose William as librettist. This, an opera on the theme of Elizabeth I and Essex, was to be dedicated with royal approval to Elizabeth II in celebration of her coronation.

A new interest? A new challenge, demanding new techniques:

---

[1] William wrote introductions to Melville's *Redburn* (1937), *Selected Poems* (1943), *Billy Budd* (1946), and *White Jacket* (1952).

The problems of language, of the English language in particular, when it has to be sung are not light. The great thing is to avoid phrases like 'To thee as guerdon proffer I this baldrick'.

Those problems were overcome: no poet who had successfully taught English to the Japanese could fail to appreciate the demands of clear enunciation. It was not the libretto but the whole opera in its conception and execution that came under attack after the gala performance in the Royal Opera House, Covent Garden, on June 8th, 1953. The audience, William wrote privately, were hostile. At the final curtain composer and librettist in their box heard 'no more than a mere cold sprinkle of applause'. Britten leaned over above the stalls muttering 'Clap, damn you, clap!' William was, for a man normally equable, profoundly upset, though more for Britten than for himself.[1] It was thirteen years before the opera was revived, this time before enthusiastic audiences at Sadler's Wells. 'Towed' on to the stage by Britten for curtain calls William forgot to smile. 'I was thinking of the long delay in the recognition of *Gloriana*, and kept a grave face.'

He had, he wrote soon after the first performance, never envisaged himself as an operatic librettist, still less as bowing from the Covent Garden stage before a Queen Elizabeth II:

The Royal Family turned up in force and in state — the men hadn't worn their Garters in public since 1939 — and were affability itself ... Britten and I had had a long evening in private beforehand with the Queen and Prince Philip to tell them what they were in for. They couldn't have been more amiable, and although neither is musical, both paid close attention. Prince Philip is quite as Germanically thorough as

[1] For an account of the mixed reception of early performances of *Gloriana* the reader may go to an uncharacteristically bitter article, 'Let's Crab an Opera', which William contributed ten years later to the special Benjamin Britten number of the *London Magazine* (October 1963).

the Prince Consort, but has a more practical and varied experience of life, is versatile, and has a much lighter touch and a
sense of fun. He struck me as uncommonly capable, sensible
and likeable.

In the same letter, with reference to the same august personages,
William recalled the street-scene in *Gloriana* when a slattern
empties a chamber-pot over a rabble-rouser. The Lord Chamberlain's office blue-pencilled this and a basin was substituted. 'This
caused a good deal of amusement *in a certain quarter*, where homely
fun is always appreciated.' The Lord Chamberlain, it seems, did
not object on grounds of prudishness or *lèse-majesté*: 'there just
happens to be a rule of long standing,' William was told, 'and
the Lord Chamberlain has had *to set his face against chamber-pots.*'
	The next stage in what was to prove a growingly fruitful colla-
boration started when Britten, planning a visit to Japan in 1955,
asked William what in particular he should look out for. The
theatre, was the reply: see a Nō play. When Britten returned he
said, 'in a quiet voice but with what I recognised as a disturbing
firmness', that he wished to produce an English equivalent of
Sumidagawa (Sumide River) with his own music and William's
words. William found the prospect alarming, judged the project
impossible. Medieval Nō was the most traditional, stylised, rarefied form of theatre in the world. How could one transmute a
remote Buddhist legend into a Western, Christian ideology, at
the same time retaining a formalised, hieratic structure? – how
adapt it to the modern English stage, and the operatic stage at
that? Where could one present it? – in the Nō theatre there is no
applause ('Clap, damn you, clap'?) and the audience sits in dedicated silence. Britten was not at a loss for the answers: in simple
terms, for medieval Buddhist read medieval English, and for a
theatre … a church. Hence *Curlew River, a parable for church performance*, first staged in the parish church of St Bartholomew,
Orford, near Aldeburgh, in June 1964 and performed in the
following month in Southwark Cathedral. Hence also the collaborators' two other church operas ('choperas' to William), based

on Bible stories but retaining the Nō conventions, *The Burning Fiery Furnace* (1966) and *The Prodigal Son* (1968).

Throughout these collaborative years William was also of course 'doing his own thing'—a 'sixtyish expression that amused him. This included a good deal of book-reviewing and criticism; and he sat on the editorial board of the *London Magazine*. In 1949 he brought out *Four Countries*, a collection of short stories, those set in Africa, Japan and Greece being reprinted from pre-war volumes, together with four English stories of more recent vintage. Of all his books of fiction this was the one that least pleased his critics. By contrast *Museum Pieces* (1952), his only post-war novel and a high-spirited sequel to *Curious Relations*, put him back immediately into public favour. In 1955 came *A Shot in the Park*, a second slim volume of satires. In that year a larger collection, *Borderline Ballads*, introduced the American public for the first time to his whole range of balladry, old and new. (He had had some ill-success with American publishers, including the Oxford University Press in New York, because his particular brand of humour was judged 'too English' for transatlantic taste.) *At Home* —Chapters 22–39 of the present book—was published in 1958; *Collected Poems* in 1960; the first reprint of *Turbott Wolfe*, with a long introduction by Laurens van der Post (William was needlessly apprehensive lest 'my *storiette* is going to be a miniature in a big baroque frame'), in 1965; and two final volumes of poetry, *Taste and Remember* and *Celebrations*, respectively in 1966 and 1972. Besides these books of his own, William edited in 1964 *A Message in Code*, the diary of Richard Rumbold, a younger cousin to whom he was much attached and who had recently committed suicide.

In the summer of 1953 William decided to leave London. He had lived too long in the shadier purlieus of Earls Court, Maida Vale and Notting Hill, environments appropriate to the shady characters in *The Case is Altered* and *The Invaders*. His flat since early in the war had been in Linden Gardens ('by courtesy, Bayswater'), a quarter known to the gutter press, according to him, as 'The Murder Mile', and one so densely packed with private tragedies that 'one can hardly see the cake for the slices of life, so to speak'. Here he had been joined in mid-war by Charles Erdman. If William used sometimes half humorously to describe himself, born in South Africa, as a 'displaced person', Charles was a displaced person in very truth, being of German extraction and destitute in London. He came as a general factotum, with domestic responsibilities, and remained as a devoted friend. Together they now moved into 'a bungaloid sort of little house' named Rossida in a region of market-gardens a short walk from the sea (and close to William's octogenarian father[1]) at Rustington in Sussex. After a quarter of a century in London it was a luxury for William to breathe good clean air and indulge his old passion for swimming. Here, living the life of a hermit – 'or of a fairly firmly rooted carrot' (market-garden analogy?) – and with Charles suffering from a virulent neuritis, he settled down to house-management and cooking. Recipes, some pretty exotic, began to appear among his press-cuttings. He travelled weekly on Wednesdays to Cape's editorial conferences, tasting manuscripts in the train on the journey home. And it was the same after the late summer of 1966 when he and Charles moved inland from the 'cigarbox' that was Rossida to a 'matchbox', his last home, in Adastra Avenue, Hassocks.

The picture of William as a firmly rooted carrot accords oddly with Hugh Walpole's fancy of a bull among Duncan Grant asphodels, or with other friends' vision of an amiable Siberian bear. (A cross between a doctor and an army chaplain, wrote James Stern. For some quirky reason William saw himself, in one of Janet Stone's photographs, as a dentist.) His memoranda of movements show him to have been, in the 'fifties and 'sixties, remarkably mobile for a carrot. Hardly a month passed but he was lecturing or reading poetry, live or on the wireless (he pre-

---

[1] Eighteen months later William's father was 'condemned to life-imprisonment in a nursing home'. Sentence was mercifully commuted to death within a few weeks.

ferred 'wireless' to 'radio'), or opening an exhibition. His visits to the Kilvert country in the Welsh marches were only less frequent than those to the Crabbe/FitzGerald/Britten country in East Anglia. Torquay, Stratford, Leicester, Newcastle, even Edinburgh knew him. (He seldom visited the Continent, America never, South Africa only once.) 'A-Kilverting' one year, he spoke from the pulpit in Hereford Cathedral, and he preached a sermon in a church in St John's Wood. Westminster Abbey held no terrors for him: he there delivered an oration on the bicentenary of Wordsworth's birth and unveiled the memorial, long overdue, to Byron. He became much in demand as a writer and speaker of obituary tributes, so much so that he had to refuse ... but no: perhaps he had other reasons for refusing some requests. It will be a trouble to his eventual biographer that William lived to put on record, in print or from the pulpit, tributes to many friends who, *ex hypothesi*, did not live to record their memories of him, among them Leonard and Virginia Woolf, Rose Macaulay, E. M. Forster, Ian Fleming, Lilian Bowes Lyon, Jonathan Cape.

Of a fundamentally modest nature, reserved in youth to an almost pathological degree, William none the less enjoyed recognition and limelight in his later years. He was of the generation of—indeed slightly older than—the Oxford trio that made their reputations on either side of 1930: Auden, Spender, Day-Lewis. His own university, he used to say, was farming and trading in South Africa, teaching what he had not learnt and learning what the West could not have taught him in Japan. Between the lines of some of his public and private writings there may be detected an awareness that rival poets had known advantages he himself had missed. The honours that eventually came his way were the more rewarding—an honorary doctorate from Durham University in 1959, the Queen's gold medal for poetry in 1963, and the C.B.E. ('Clearly Bought by the Establishment') in 1968.[1] But he

[1] In Day-Lewis's last illness, before the press began to canvass the future of the poet laureateship, William told a friend, 'If he doesn't last it is possible that I may be asked to succeed him. I wouldn't wish to do so, but should find it awkward to refuse.'

was hardly less gratified when asked to become president of the Poetry Society and of the Kilvert Society.

He had a perfect reading-voice alike for pulpit, lecture hall and radio, warm, clear, deliberate, orotund without preciousness or pomposity – once indeed described as 'plummy', but that he thought was an unconscious echo of his name: for strangers who had heard that he did not pronounce 'Plomer' as spelt would as likely call him 'Plummer' (incorrect) as 'Ploomer' (correct). It was an article of faith that poetry should be written, as traditionally it always had been written, to be read aloud: no clean white pages spattered with disjointed words, or English interrupted by Chinese ideographs.

Of his own view of his own poetry two statements may be of interest. Formally, in the third person, as for an obituary, he wrote:

P.'s *Collected Poems*, 1960, often bring into focus his view of life as a mixture of the terrible and the absurd, his sense of character in relation to place and period, his tendency to satire, and his gentler feelings.

Off the cuff in an interview about that time he said that as he got older he became less inclined to write sardonic and satirical ballads and was a little more melancholy – 'or at least sober' – in his verse. This claim is certainly borne out by his two later volumes, though in these there is certainly no lack of humour, and the gentler feelings are in abeyance in one or two of the poems relating to South Africa.

William was not 'a South African', although he liked to remind people that he was a 'native' of South Africa. ('I once had a cat that had kittens in an oven, but nobody mistook them for cakes.') Just as he accepted that publishers – though this had been doubted – were human, so in more sober vein he maintained that 'all the inhabitants of South Africa without exception are demonstrably human beings, in spite of protestations by some of them to the contrary'. It was with this belief, and with a determination to hold to it, that he allowed himself to be persuaded to revisit the country exactly thirty years after he had left it, as described in Chapter 17 of this book. The occasion was a conference on English literature at the University of the Witwatersrand, the date some four months before the opening of the notorious Johannesburg treason trial in the winter of 1956–7, and he took the opportunity of returning to various places he had known in his childhood. He told John Betjeman on his return that his hands were clenched the whole time he was there because the atmosphere was so tense.

Politics aside – and he gave a courageously outspoken interview to journalists on the day he left – he was mainly interested to meet writers of all generations and pigmentations. He saw at first hand, what indeed he knew in advance, that the 'non-white majority', for all the beauty of the Zulu language, were the least articulate because of palpable disadvantages in education, leisure and opportunity, and he regretted that the Afrikaner poets and novelists had so far not made the same impact outside their own country as what he called, for short, the Anglikaners. ('I really can't go on saying, "English-speaking South Africans".') But he was considerably impressed by young liberal Afrikaner writers and returned to England with a number of manuscripts which he hoped, not altogether hopefully, to place with British publishers.

William's personal contribution to the South African debate, however, is not to be found in his talks in that country or in the all-too-well-balanced report that he contributed to the *London Magazine* after his return. His contribution must be sought in his own later poetry, especially in the elegy he wrote on two poets who committed suicide in the same month in 1965, the Afrikaner Ingrid Jonker in Cape Town, and the Xhosa Nat Nakasa in the United States. In 1968 he collaborated with Jack Cope in translating a selection of Ingrid Jonker's poems. When his own last verse volume was in the press he wrote to his publishers, 'I *think* the censorship in South Africa have not yet learnt that poetry can be dangerous. Otherwise they may boggle at a poem in *Celebrations* called "White Gloves".'

In 1962 William broadcast on the B.B.C. Third Programme *Conversation with My Younger Self.* The two selves ran over the course of his (their) life up to his (their) return to England from Japan.

> WILLIAM PLOMER: I understand all that. But surely there is also the question of love and sex. You aren't young for nothing ... You talk so solemnly about exchanging ideas and so on, but unless your inclinations are purely exotic, I imagine you might want to exchange kisses as well as ideas in your own country.
>
> YOUNGER SELF: You have reached a point where I think you ought to mind your own business.

Some thirty years earlier Harold Nicolson, reviewing William's Japanese novel *Sado*, had written: 'If I started to write a book on inversion, I think I should be more plucky about it from the start.' William replied:

> If my book is, as you say, 'pretty feeble' as a novel, I can only hope to do better in future; but is it altogether fair to accuse me of a want of courage, and of having failed to 'grasp the nettles'? What nettles? You admit that I have made the homosexual theme 'abundantly plain', and at the same time reprove me for reticence. But am I to blame because it is not possible to be so frank in this country as in France or Germany or China?

Homosexuality was a theme on which, except no doubt privately among close friends, William always maintained reticence. If he had written a third volume of autobiography he would almost certainly have said as little about it as in his two published volumes. He regarded the autobiography of his close friend Joe Ackerley, *My Father and Myself*, as 'a book that should never have been written, let alone published'. E. M. Forster at one time wished William to become his official posthumous biographer, and enjoined candour about all aspects of his life; but William, reluctant—other reasons apart—to embark upon the homosexual theme, let the opportunity slip. There was some ambivalence in his attitude. Having read *Maurice* in 1932—the novel that remained unpublished until after Forster's death in 1970—he wrote that if only he had read it when he was seventeen 'it would have been something to steer by'; but when *The Life to Come and Other Stories* appeared in 1972 he told a friend that he had felt 'a strong incuriosity' about the stories while the author was alive and still felt 'no keenness' to read them. Of himself he wrote:

> You're quite right to suggest that homosexual overtones or undertones are present in my writings, and I hasten to say that any general view of my writings—and my life—should take notice of them. Although, as we know, it is now possible and customary to be much more candid than it was when I was young, I never feel that candour is a constant necessity, if only because people who keep telling one all about themselves, in print or *viva voce*, are apt to be unduly self-centred, to assume that what is important to them will seem so to others, and therefore to be extremely boring. I think blatant homosexuality, like other forms of blatancy, can be tiresome and uncivilised.

In 1973 William was in his seventieth year. His birthday would fall on December 10th, and plans were afoot to celebrate it. Cape's proposed 'a modified jamboree' at the Café Royal. ('These anniversaries, silver and golden wedding celebrations, memorial services, &c., are the children's parties of one's second childhood.') They planned also an enlarged edition of the *Collected Poems* with a preface in which William would record his objectives and development as a poet: this duly appeared on the appointed day.

Meanwhile he had been working on a task quite alien from any-thing he had attempted before, a task 'a little taxing and more than a little enjoyable', writing verses to illustrate Alan Aldridge's colour drawings for a children's book, *The Butterfly Ball*. Of the quality of the verses it need only be said that William, while pleased with them, characterised them as doggerel; the repro-duction of the drawings was masterly; the book, published in September of that year, achieved greater publicity than any previous book of William's had done. He lived to give advance copies to his friends, but not long enough to enjoy the venture's success. Many months earlier his doctor had told him 'to slow down, go easy, say No oftener than Yes, and take little white pills—none of these activities, or inactivities, is congenial to me.' He suffered a slight heart-attack early in September, and died of another on the 21st.

Index

15

449